The Korean Economy

From a Miraculous Past to a Sustainable Future

This volume is part of the multivolume study
Rising to the Challenges of Democratization and Globalization in Korea

Harvard East Asian Monographs 375

The Korean Economy

From a Miraculous Past
to a Sustainable Future

Barry Eichengreen,
Wonhyuk Lim,
Yung Chul Park,
and
Dwight H. Perkins

Published by the Harvard University Asia Center
Distributed by Harvard University Press
Cambridge (Massachusetts) and London, 2015

Printed in the United States of America

The Harvard University Asia Center publishes a monograph series and, in coordination with the Fairbank Center for Chinese Studies, the Korea Institute, the Reischauer Institute of Japanese Studies, and other facilities and institutes, administers research projects designed to further scholarly understanding of China, Japan, Vietnam, Korea, and other Asian countries. The Center also sponsors projects addressing multidisciplinary and regional issues in Asia.

Library of Congress Cataloging-in-Publication Data

Eichengreen, Barry J.
   The Korean economy : from a miraculous past to a sustainable future / Barry Eichengreen, Wonhyuk Lim, Yung Chul Park, and Dwight Perkins.
      pages cm. — (Harvard East Asian monographs ; 375)
   Includes bibliographical references and index.
      ISBN 978-0-674-41718-2 (hardcover : alk. paper)   1. Economic development—Korea (South)   2. Korea (South)—Economic conditions.   3. Korea (South)—Economic policy. I. Title.
   HC467.756.E43 2015

   330.95195—dc23   2014011100

   Index by Amron Gravett

   ∞ Printed on acid-free paper

Last figure below indicates year of this printing

25   24   23   22   21   20   19   18   17   16   15

Contents

Tables and Figures

Tables

Figures

Foreword

Economic development and political development go hand in hand. Either the egg comes first or the chicken: economic development has often been preceded by political development and often followed by it. Many have taken a similar path to development, where economic prosperity fueled citizens' demand for enhanced protection of their political rights and wealth, which eventually led to a promotion of democracy. Korea is no exception in this regard, with economic development leading to political development, furthering the maturation of its economy.

A little less than 40 years ago, when the Korea Development Institute (KDI), in collaboration with the Harvard Institute for International Development (HIID), published a ten-volume monograph series on Korea's economic and social transformation from 1945 to 1975, Korea's economy was highly intervened in, if not absolutely controlled, by its government. A second KDI series of three books, also published by Harvard, highlighted the Heavy and Chemical Industry Drive from 1973 to 1979, macroeconomic adjustment in the late 1970s and early 1980s, and labor-management relations during the 1980s. This third series focuses on Korea's economic and political development during the era of globalization and democratization.

During the course of Korea's development the global perception of the Korean economy has drastically changed. When it joined the Organization for Economic Cooperation and Development (OECD) in 1996, Korea substantiated that it was no longer one of the poorest nations that relied heavily on foreign aid. Despite a severe hit by the Asian financial crisis of 1997, the Korean economy quickly rebounded and learned to respond wisely when swept up in the global financial crisis of 2008. Not only does Korea stand as the world's fifteenth largest economy, but it also plays a pivotal role as a middle power, working as a bridge and an honest broker between the developed and developing countries, as evidenced by its successful hosting of the G20 Summit in Seoul in 2010. We therefore saw the need to share with the world, through analysis from multifaceted perspectives, how Korea achieved such a transformation in a period of less than half a century.

Throughout the new KDI series, consisting of seven titles, we look at the challenges faced during the course of Korea's democratization and globalization since the 1980s. In addition to this overview volume, the individual studies provide insights from different perspectives: growth, political economy, finance, industrial organization and corporate governance, human resource development, and income inequality and social welfare. This series calls for urgency in finding a new development path for the Korean economy, one with a major focus on human resources, capital, and technology. The government-driven growth strategy is no longer efficient or effective. Both external and internal factors that influence the Korean economy today are much different from the factors that shaped Korea decades ago. It is high time that Korea embraces the ever-changing dynamics of the world's economy and politics, and quickly seeks new ways to ensure future growth.

Joon-Kyung Kim
President
Korea Development Institute

Acknowledgments

Projects like this, not unlike the emergence of mature economies such as South Korea's, have long gestation periods. During the years of this volume's development we have accumulated a correspondingly lengthy list of debts. Our most important debt is to the Korea Development Institute (KDI) and its current and past presidents: Joon-Kyung Kim, Oh-Seok Hyun, and Jung Taik Hyun. Without their commitment, leadership, and continuous support, and that of KDI generally, the series of which this volume is a part never would have been initiated, much less seen the light of day. We would also like to thank an additional past president of KDI, Yung Chul Park, who would not allow our enthusiasm to wane or our energy to diminish when the project encountered difficulties, as long and complicated endeavors do.

Others at KDI too numerous to mention provided intellectual input, logistical support, and financial assistance along the way. They answered our questions, pointed us to sources, helped us organize our analysis, and critiqued our conclusions, for all of which we are thankful. In particular, we are especially grateful to Sookyeong Hwang, Hisam Kim, Kiwan Kim, and Gyeongjoon Yoo.

We also gratefully acknowledge the input and advice of our academic collaborators in the KDI project, most importantly the authors of the six published and forthcoming companion volumes in this series, Rising to the Challenges of Democratization and Globalization in Korea, 1987–2007: Chong-Bum An, Barry Bosworth, Kyungsoo Choi, Richard Freeman, Joon-Kyung Kim, Sunwoong Kim, Jongryn Mo, Randall Morck, Jungsoo

Park, Kwanho Shin, and Barry R. Weingast. We draw on their analysis and findings in this volume, as will be clearly evident. (Listing their names here is also our way of encouraging those who have not yet submitted their final manuscripts to do so sooner rather than later.)

In the course of designing and completing this set of studies, we held organizational and review workshops in Seoul, Palo Alto, and Cambridge, Massachusetts. At each of these meetings, colleagues from academia, international organizations, think tanks, and government agencies provided feedback on our work in progress. For their input, we thank: Woo-Hyun Cho, Kwang Choi, Nicholas Crafts, Paul Gruenwald, Chin Hee Hahn, In June Kim, Kihwan Kim, Mahn-Je Kim, Jisoon Lee, and Jin-Hyun Paik (Seoul); Marianne Bertrand, Stephen Haber, Stephan Haggard, Takeo Hoshi, Jun Il Kim, Michael A. McFaul, Ramon H. Myers, and Henry Rowen (Palo Alto); and Alice H. Amsden, Effi Benmelech, Stijn Claessens, Robert Dekle, Jeffrey Frankel, Swati R. Ghosh, Ricardo Hausmann, Paul D. Hutchcroft, Dale Jorgenson, Anil Kashyap, Jun Il Kim, John Lie, David L. Lindauer, Katharine Moon, George G. Pennacchi, Danny Quah, Gustav Ranis, James A. Robinson, Dani Rodrik, Steven B. Webb, and Jeffrey G. Williamson (Cambridge).

We are grateful also to the Harvard University Asia Center, which has supported this volume, other books in the series, and the larger project on the Korean economy. The center's involvement reflects the long association between Harvard University and KDI, extending through several earlier projects. We thank two successive managing editors of the Harvard East Asian Monograph series, William Hammell and Robert Graham; the members of the Publication Committee, who were exceptionally patient with their authors; and five demanding if exceptionally careful referees.

At the University of California, Berkeley, Barry Eichengreen thanks Cheryl Applewood for help in organizing the front matter and the volume in general. In Cambridge, Dwight Perkins thanks Gretchen O'Connor for editorial support. In Seoul, Wonhyuk Lim and Yung Chul Park thank Eunwon Yang and Sohyoung Park for research assistance.

It has been a long haul. We dedicate this volume to our spouses, who have remained beside us (better than "beside themselves") through it all.

Berkeley, Cambridge, and Seoul
March 2014

CHAPTER I

Introduction

The Republic of Korea, or South Korea, has a prominence in the academic and policy literatures all out of proportion to its weight in the world economy. From a starting point in the 1950s, when it was one of the poorest countries on the planet, more than four decades of rapid growth elevated South Korea to high-income status and membership in the Organization for Economic Cooperation and Development (OECD), the club of advanced industrial democracies. Despite being poor in natural resources and only midsize in terms of population, Korea has become an industrial powerhouse and the world's seventh largest exporter. Its economic rise persisted through the transition from authoritarianism to democracy and in the face of chronic tensions with the Democratic People's Republic of Korea, the country's difficult neighbor to the north. For all these reasons, South Korea's progression from agriculture to industry and its graduation from developing- to advanced-nation status have fascinated generations of scholars and policymakers.

At the same time, close observers of the Korean economy have always understood that its story is not one of unmitigated success. Korea has a history of financial crises interrupting the growth process. The disproportionate power of a handful of large family-controlled business groups, or chaebol, has created problems of political influence and hindered entry and competition for small firms and start-ups. Questions are increasingly raised about whether its education system, which rewards rote learning more than originality and favors the graduates of a handful of elite universities, can adequately serve the needs of the economy and society. Korea has an unusually large male-female earnings gap and a high poverty rate among the elderly. Productivity in the service sector, where the majority of future employment growth will necessarily be located, is disappointing. Now that economy-wide growth appears to have slowed, some observers are asking whether the Korean miracle is over.

The earlier phases in the Korean growth story have been thoroughly studied. In the 1970s the Korea Development Institute (KDI), the country's leading government-supported economic think tank, commissioned a series of book-length studies of the initial decades of high growth; the findings of this research project were summarized in an overview volume by the project organizers (Mason et al. 1980). In the wake of the Heavy and Chemical Industry Drive of the late 1970s and the transition to democracy in 1987, KDI commissioned an additional three studies designed to update the story (Haggard et al. 1994; Lindauer et al. 1997; Stern et al. 1995). This volume follows in that tradition. It synthesizes the findings of a KDI-supported research project culminating in a series of monographs that bring the story of Korean economic growth and development up to date.[1] While any adequate analysis of Korean economic development must situate recent events in their historical context, our focus here is on the period subsequent to that covered in the earlier KDI projects.

Political Democratization and Economic Liberalization

A theme of this volume and the series as a whole is that the dual processes of democratization and economic transformation that have shaped the development of Korean economy and society over the past quarter century are profoundly linked.[2] Democratization led initially to the election of governments that displayed considerable political and policy continuity with their predecessors. It is not surprising that voters did not immediately repudiate politicians tied to the prior authoritarian regime, given the success with which earlier governments had delivered the goods, and the priority attached by the electorate to continued economic growth.[3]

---

1. The notes in this chapter reference the companion volumes in the series Rising to the Challenges of Democratization and Globalization in Korea, 1987–2007.

2. This is also the theme of the volume in this series by Mo and Weingast (2013). See also Mo and Moon (1998) and Kihl (2004). We elaborate on this further in Chapter 2.

3. While the Kim Young-sam government sought to distance itself from previous policies, in practice there was considerable personal and policy continuity with the earlier regime. For discussion, see Chapter 2.

And the first postdemocratization governments of Roh Tae-woo and Kim Young-sam succeeded in delivering high growth in the manner of their predecessors. But after the 1997–1998 Asian financial crisis disrupted the economic status quo, causing output to fall by nearly 10 percent, voters elected a series of left-of-center governments that promised to administer fundamental reforms to cure the ills bequeathed by the crisis and to root out the structural problems that had rendered the economy vulnerable to destabilization.

Again, this response is not surprising, given the social dislocations of the crisis and the urgency it engendered for pursuing structural reforms. What was surprising was that the subsequent governments of Kim Dae-jung and Roh Moon-hyun, while adopting populist rhetoric, pursued distinctly unpopulist policies. They offered carefully calibrated social welfare initiatives designed to level the distribution of income and provide support for the poor and unemployed, not radical reform with the goal of creating a European-style welfare state. Rather than opting for renationalization and re-regulation, they pushed through the most far-reaching economic liberalization in Korea's history (although they may not have gone as far as some of their conservative rivals had hoped). They deregulated product and factor markets. They eased barriers to entry into legal and accounting services. They restructured the financial system. They stripped away barriers to foreign investment in the corporate sector. They introduced special economic zones and tax incentives for foreign investors. And while they cared deeply about basic welfare and balanced regional development, they relied not just on state intervention in the economy but also on market-friendly reforms, on the assumption that faster economic growth would ameliorate social problems in due course.

A first question addressed in this volume is thus why South Korea's post-crisis populist governments pursued such unpopulist policies. The answer, in a nutshell, is that the post-crisis governments, no matter how radical their inclinations, had to contend with the objections of a conservative opposition and the conservative media. Korea, for reasons described further in Chapter 2, did not emerge from the period of authoritarian rule with a single charismatic leader or dominant political party. From the start, its political system was characterized by checks and balances—what political scientists refer to as "multiple veto points"—that worked to prevent sharp changes in the direction of policy, whether warranted or not.

An additional factor was a binding external constraint. Foreign exchange reserves having been exhausted at the end of 1997, Korea was forced to appeal to the International Monetary Fund (IMF) for emergency assistance, requiring it to accept IMF-style policies of liberalization and limited redistribution. Of course, this observation only raises additional questions. Why did subsequent Korean governments not abandon those policies once the country was no longer dependent on the IMF? Korea paid off the last of its debt to the IMF in August 2001. Why did the government not advance a more populist agenda at that point?

It could be that the binding constraint was internal rather than external: that the government's limited fiscal resources constrained its social-policy ambitions. The problem with this explanation is that countries poorer than South Korea have pursued more ambitious policies of redistribution. And even if tight fiscal constraints help to explain the limited extent of redistribution, they cannot explain the continuing commitment to deregulation and market liberalization.

A final possibility is that the rapid pace of economic and financial globalization convinced Korean politicians and their constituents that there was no choice but to restructure and liberalize, if the country was to compete in a globalized world. This hypothesis points, in turn, to the still more interesting question of how Korea, unlike many other crisis-stricken countries, managed to take advantage of the financial crisis to carry out structural reforms.

Recent Economic Growth

A second surprise was that these far-reaching post-crisis reforms did not more fully resuscitate economic growth. After having an average growth rate of 7 percent per annum in 1990–1997, growth in 2001–2008 decelerated to 4.6 percent per annum, less than two-thirds the previous pace.[4] Following the global financial crisis of 2008–2010 it decelerated further, to 3.6 percent in 2011, 2.0 percent in 2012, and 2.6 percent in 2013.

Why did post-crisis reform fail to restore growth to pre-crisis levels? It may be that there still has not been enough time for firms to adapt to the

---

4. We omit the crisis and the immediate post-crisis recovery, since growth was exceptionally volatile in both periods.

new market and policy environment.[5] Liberalization and deregulation that expose firms to entry and competition also squeeze profitability, production, and investment in the short run. In the long run, however, producers will either adapt or be forced to exit the market. After such adaptations—once Korean firms restructure their operations in ways better suited to a deregulated business environment—efficiency, production, and investment should recover. One can think of this as survival of the fittest: efficiency rises because the least efficient domestic competitors vanish from the scene. In this way reform eventually produces the hoped-for results. But patience is required—given the disruptions through which the world economy suffered in 2008–2009, unusual amounts of patience.

A different interpretation is that additional reforms will be needed in order to achieve faster growth. Korea, in this view, is stuck between the two banks of the river.[6] There has been sufficient deregulation and market liberalization to disrupt old ways, but not enough for firms to restructure decisively. The most difficult reforms—deregulating the service sector, removing barriers to foreign acquisition of financial firms, relaxing restrictive labor market regulations—tend to be left for last, and because of this, uncertainty lingers about whether the commitment exists to follow through. In the absence of these remaining elements, reforms already in place may fail to produce the desired results, thus creating pressure to roll them back. And in the face of such uncertainty, firms are reluctant to restructure and invest. The implication is that pushing ahead with reform will help restore economic growth to earlier levels. But the political will must be there.

Yet a third interpretation, with entirely different implications, is that the presumption that the Korean economy is underperforming and that liberalization and restructuring have failed to deliver positive results is simply wrong. The fact that the rapid growth of the pre-1997 period culminated in a crisis may indicate that the period's rapid growth was not, in fact, sustainable. Korea, in other words, is now doing as well as its circumstances can allow. A country far from the technological frontier can

---

5. These interpretations are elaborated in Chapter 3, drawing on the companion volume by Eichengreen, Perkins, and Shin (2012).

6. The phrase, along with the notion that partial reform may not deliver results or may even make things worse before it makes them better, is from Bertola and Ichino (1995).

achieve rapid growth by importing foreign technology, shifting labor from agriculture to industry, and otherwise making up lost ground. Eventually, however, easy gains will be exhausted and growth will slow to rates more typical of a country approaching the technological frontier. Rather than simply shifting workers from agriculture to manufacturing and services, Korea now has to raise productivity in those self-same manufacturing and service activities. Rather than simply licensing technology from abroad, Korea now must generate it. The country had already begun to experience this transition at the end of the 1980s, although this reality was disguised by a debt-financed boom during which large business groups engaged in breakneck capacity expansion.[7] But the debt-financed investment boom was unsustainable, something that became clear in the crisis of 1997–1998.

As a result of these circumstances, growth downshifted abruptly rather than slowing gradually to lower levels as predicted by textbook models of catch-up and convergence.[8] But while the shift may have been striking for its suddenness, Korea's slower growth rate is not a sign of economic or political failure. It is simply the normal condition for what is now a relatively mature economy.

Finally, the slower growth of the Korean economy may be a corollary of a more difficult external environment.[9] In 2008–2010 the world experienced the most serious global financial crisis in 80 years. The advanced countries dug themselves into a deep hole from which they now find it difficult to recover. Burdened with heavy public debts, they are growing more slowly than before. Deleveraging by foreign households promises to subdue the demand for consumer goods for an extended period, including the consumer goods produced and exported by Korean corporations. The continuing financial problems of the advanced economies, and the policies adopted in response, accentuate the volatility of international capital flows, making monetary and financial management more difficult for what remains a small open economy.

---

7. Eichengreen, Perkins, and Shin (2012) pinpoint two break points when Korean economic growth decelerated, in 1989 and 1998.

8. The textbook model, with evidence, is laid out in Barro and Sala-i-Martin (1995).

9. We analyze this further in Chapter 7. The role of international transactions and the external environment in Korean economic growth feature in the volumes by Eichengreen, Perkins, and Shin (2012), which focuses on trade and foreign direct investment, and Park, Kim, and Park (forthcoming), which focuses on international finance.

Emerging markets, for their part, have driven up energy and raw material prices, creating an especially burdensome situation for an economy like Korea's that is poor in natural resources. That said, it should be emphasized that emerging markets also create new opportunities for Korean producers: the non-OECD world now purchases 70 percent of South Korea's exports.

But gaining and maintaining market share in the non-OECD world, as elsewhere, requires meeting the competition, most notably, China. China's emergence has arguably been the single most important development reshaping the world economy at the outset of the twenty-first century. While there is a tendency in some circles to blame Chinese competition for whatever ails, Korea has special reason to ask how China's rise has affected its economic performance. China and Korea are neighbors. They share many of the same natural markets, including each other's. They have similar resource endowments in that both are more labor than land abundant and both rely heavily on imported energy and raw materials. China seems to be ascending the same industrial ladder that Korea climbed from the 1960s to the 1980s, moving from the production of labor-intensive exports like textiles and footwear to the assembly of consumer electronics and now the production of capital goods. This creates the impression that it is not just South Korea's low-wage, labor-intensive industrial sector that is being squeezed by Chinese competition but the country's manufacturing as a whole.

Still, is the rise of China really having a negative impact on Korean growth prospects and performance?[10] Chinese competition has clearly accelerated the decline of South Korea's labor-intensive industries. At the same time, however, capital- and skilled-labor-intensive industries, both those producing capital equipment and those producing relatively sophisticated parts and components going into Chinese assembly operations, have benefited from China's emergence as the assembly platform for the Asian-Pacific region.

What is true of foreign trade is similarly true of foreign direct investment, or FDI. China's emergence as a rival in the competition for FDI may have diverted some foreign investment away from Korea, but China also offers an attractive and profitable destination for Korea's

---

10. Again, we draw here on the analysis of Eichengreen, Perkins, and Shin (2012), especially ch. 4.

own outward foreign investment. Korea is the fourth most important source of FDI in China.[11] Setting up assembly plants and other operations is an important way in which Korean firms can maintain and enhance their international competitiveness.

The shift to more capital-intensive industrial production and the substitution of foreign for domestic investment is cold comfort for Korea's unskilled workers, who must accept lower earnings in self-employment or small family-run businesses. To limit the impact on them, Korea will have to upgrade its institutions of skill formation and knowledge creation. To avoid being caught in China's headlights, Korea also needs to continue graduating from assembly to product design. It needs to complement its success in manufacturing with more productive banking, insurance, communications, and health and business services.

Successive governments have offered initiatives to reform the national education system and transform Korea into a knowledge economy. South Korea has world-class researchers (in bioengineering, for instance) and technologically innovative firms (like Samsung, which is renowned for its leading-edge electronics). Korea is the most wired country in the world in terms of Internet connections per capita. Some progress has been made toward becoming a knowledge economy, in other words. But competition from China remains intense. Exports no longer create the same GDP and employment growth as before because of the growing imported-input component of Korean manufacturing. Productivity is also disappointing in the service sector, which already accounts for a majority of employment and, as in all mature economies, will account for an even larger share in the future.

Business, Government, and Finance

Why do commentators pay so much attention to the supposed "hollowing out" of Korean industry? The obvious answer is that the Korean growth story is fundamentally the story of industry. From a starting point where

---

11. In its share of FDI in China, Korea follows only Hong Kong, Japan, and the Virgin Islands—and the figures for the Virgin Islands presumably reflect money originating in Hong Kong and perhaps the People's Republic of China (PRC) itself. Attributing that money to Hong Kong and domestic investors raises Korea to number three on the list of source countries. At the same time, it is also possible that official PRC figures significantly understate Taiwan's FDI in China.

industry produced little and exported less, manufacturing grew rapidly for four decades. The reallocation of labor from low-productivity agriculture to high-productivity manufacturing explains a substantial portion of the rise of labor productivity in Korea in the second half of the twentieth century and especially at the beginning of the high-growth period.[12]

Initiating and sustaining industrial development, recent scholarship has emphasized, required Korean industrialists and their collaborators in government to solve a number of specific problems.[13] Growing Korea's industry required mobilizing finance for investment, given that manufacturing is more capital intensive than agriculture and services. In addition to using a relatively high ratio of capital to labor, industrial firms use large absolute amounts of capital. Capital requirements thus exceeded what any one individual or family could provide. Relatively high minimum efficient scale also meant that growth would be constrained by the size of the market unless firms succeeded in exporting. Finally, manufacturing requires specialized inputs that either the firm or its suppliers must provide. Here, too, the capital intensity of production comes into play, for a disruption of the reliable provision of those inputs can have debilitating costs if a capital stock is forced to sit idle.

These are not problems that arms-length markets—with transactions between otherwise unrelated agents—can necessarily be relied on to solve. Entrepreneurs, lacking reputation and collateral, may find it hard to obtain funding on the requisite scale. Outside investors, worried that their funds will be diverted by those in control, may hesitate to commit. Industrialists requiring specialized inputs may hesitate to rely on third parties, fearing that their own production will be held up. Producers lacking commercial contacts may find it hard to break into export markets. Not surprisingly, these problems are particularly pervasive in economies still on the cusp of modern economic growth.

A number of solutions suggest themselves. Government can directly mobilize the capital. It can substitute its own reputation and collateral, in the form of its power to tax, for the reputation and collateral of private

---

12. It makes sense that the Korean economy should have become a net exporter of manufactured goods, since the country is necessarily a net importer of agricultural goods and raw materials, reflecting its limited endowments of fertile land and resources.

13. Here we again draw on Mo and Weingast (2013).

borrowers, providing firms with external financing and insurance against risk. It can coordinate investments in complementary industries, all of which must get up and running in order for any of them to succeed. Bureaucrats can supplement other sources of managerial expertise. And government can provide consular and commercial services to help producers break into international markets. The Korean government took all these steps in the export push of the 1960s and the Heavy and Chemical Industry Drive of the 1970s.

Business groups offer another conceivable solution. As we describe in Chapter 5, business groups form through repeated contact or out of the simple fact that a controlling share of the ownership of each of the constituent firms is in the hands of the same economic or familial coalition. With family ties serving as a guarantee of good faith, cash-rich firms can provide finance for not-yet-profitable but potentially viable affiliates. The risks of doing business in sectors where capital requirements are high but finance is uncertain can be managed by within-group transfers. And when the firms in question are members of the same business group, they can outsource the production of specialized inputs without fear of being held up by suppliers. In Korea, these functions were carried out by the chaebol, which evolved out of the country's family-owned trading companies.

Financial institutions offer a third possible response. Banks mobilize the capital of small savers. They also invest in specialized monitoring technologies to determine which loan applicants are reputable and possess attractive investment projects. Venture capital firms can combine specialized knowledge of technology with financial expertise to fund start-ups attempting to commercialize innovative products. Banks, as large investors, occupy seats and cast blocks of votes on corporate boards, enabling them to advocate on behalf of outside investors. Representatives of the same bank can sit on the boards of different companies in up- and downstream industries, easing coordination and hold-up problems. Korea was for many years the prototypical example of a late-developing country with a bank-based financial system engaged in these functions.

None of these solutions is perfect. Government bureaucrats lack the high-powered incentives of owner-managers, who stand to reap enormous returns from correct decisions. They do not obviously possess the specialized knowledge and talents of those who have risen to the top through the process of natural selection known as market competition. Those whose businesses they support may operate as if facing soft budget constraints, expecting to be bailed out in the event of losses. They may make decisions on the basis of noneconomic objectives at odds with the pursuit of efficiency, be they social goals or outcomes in the interest of their political supporters and campaign contributors.

Business groups whose members interact mainly with other group members may similarly be insulated from the chill winds of competition. Groups with captive banks may be freed of having to compete for funds. In addition, business groups organized as pyramids, with the firm at the top owning a controlling interest in the next tier of firms, each of which owns a controlling interest in a next tier of firms, may have a wide gap between ownership and control, which can aggravate agency problems. The firms at the top of the pyramid, having become too big and politically well-connected to fail, may take excessive risks.

Financial institutions, too, are susceptible to agency and moral hazard problems. Outside investors can find it difficult to determine whether a bank's managers are acting to advance their personal interest or that of the shareholders. Portfolio managers and loan officers will take excessive risks if they expect to be bailed out by the authorities. And if management feels pressure from government to lend, it will develop just such an expectation in the event that things go wrong.

Standard logic suggests that the benefits of these extramarket arrangements dominate their costs in the early stages of economic growth, when there is a need to jump-start industry and market mechanisms remain underdeveloped, as was the case in Korea in the 1960s and 1970s. But with growth and modernization come an improved information environment and stronger contract enforcement, at which point it is possible to rely more heavily on arms-length transactions. With the development of multiple suppliers of inputs, both domestic and foreign, hold-up problems become less severe. And with growth of the domestic market and penetration of foreign markets, adequate demand is assured. At this point the advantages of extramarket arrangements diminish and come to be outweighed by the costs.

The problem is that institutional substitutes for missing markets do not slip quietly into the night. While the phenomenon of "institutional overhang" is a concern everywhere, it has been especially serious in Korea because of the exceptional dependence of Korean businesses' early growth on extramarket mechanisms and the telescoped nature of the country's economic and market development. The challenge for the authorities overseeing the chaebol, for regulators responsible for supervision of the banking system, and for policymakers who determine the contours of Korea's public-private risk-sharing partnership is to update this inherited dependence to better meet the needs of the twenty-first century. It is for them to do so in the face of resistance from entrenched stakeholders.

Labor and Social Development

In the early stages of the high-growth era, South Korea was a model of success in reconciling growth with low levels of inequality. One might expect this pattern to have been maintained with democratization and the end of government repression of unions, but a growing body of evidence points in the other direction.[14] It suggests that Korea's dualistic labor markets, in which a core of permanent workers receiving extensive training on the job coexists with an unstable fringe of temporary workers who provide employers with flexibility, give rise to undesirably high levels of wage and income inequality. While temporary workers have lower incomes in all economies, in Korea they account for twice as much of the labor force as the average share for OECD countries.[15]

In addition there is growing evidence of persistent income inequality transmitted across generations. These differential outcomes can be traced, in turn, to differential access to early childhood education and, more generally, to the fact that children from disadvantaged families have inferior access to education in their formative years. The more limited access of such children to Korea's distinctive system of after-school tutoring and instruction, known as *hagwon*, reinforces the problem. Tuition fees for tertiary education are also a burden for children of low-income families, something that may limit intergenerational mobility. Government could address this problem by more closely keying tuition payments to family

---

14. This section draws on the companion volume in this series by Freeman, Choi, and Kim (forthcoming). We will elaborate on these points in Chapter 6.

15. Moreover, the prospect that one's first job may be temporary and that this may make moving into permanent employment more difficult is one explanation for Korea's unusually low rate of youth employment. Many employers offer a one- or two-year entry contract and then have a vetting process for permanent employment at the end of that time, based on job performance. Some observers point to the country's unusually high rate of university enrollment as another explanation for youth unemployment, but the two stories are compatible—some young people avoid entering the labor market by extending their years of formal education.

income. It could address the limited availability of high-quality university education and the superior employment prospects for graduates of the country's elite universities by upgrading other institutions of higher education. It could strive for a better balance between investing in university education and developing vocational training for students for whom attending university is not appropriate.

Korea has the highest gender-based wage gap in the OECD. A corollary of the relatively low wages received by women is an unusually low female labor-force participation rate of around 60 percent. The participation rate of women with a tertiary education is especially low by international standards, reflecting the fact that the gender pay gap for university graduates is exceptionally high. These problems could be addressed by expanding public support for day care and education expenses, moving to full-day programs for school-age children, and legislating additional parental leave and more family-friendly workplace practices.

Recent data also point to a disturbingly high poverty rate among the elderly. As we describe in more detail in Chapter 6, 45 percent of Koreans of retirement age live in relative poverty, far in excess of the OECD average of 13 percent. Not only is this problem exceptional for an OECD economy, it is also likely to grow more serious as the Korean population continues to age. This highlights the importance of further developing the country's National Pension Service. It also suggests rethinking the convention that workers should retire from their main job at the age of 60 (according to legislation passed by the National Assembly on 30 April 2013 that raised the minimum legal retirement age from 55), at which point many move into informal employment, often at a significantly reduced income.

Poverty rates are also high among households with no active worker. This demonstrates the urgency of expanding redistribution through the tax and transfer system with the goal of alleviating poverty. It highlights the underdevelopment of the National Basic Livelihood Security System, the country's principal social welfare program, and the fact that social benefits more generally remain inadequately targeted at the needy.[16]

Identifying problems is easy; solving them is harder. Although weakening the generous job-security protections enjoyed by permanent workers

---

16. For more on the National Pension Service and the National Basic Livelihood Security System, see Chapter 6.

might help to reduce labor-market dualism by reducing the incentive for employers to rely on a rotating cast of temporary employees, such reforms will be resisted by the incumbent workers and those bargaining on their behalf. While it would be nice to boost spending on vocational training, this is likely to be resisted by the higher-education establishment. It would be desirable to provide greater access to the social safety net for temporary workers in order to provide for basic needs when they are between jobs, but doing so would be expensive; this reform will therefore have to compete with other priorities. Similarly, expanding the National Pension Service and Basic Livelihood Security System so they provide the same levels of support as services in other OECD economies, extending blanket reductions in tuition to university students, increasing state support for day care, and mandating paid parental leave would strain the resources of what is still a middle-income economy.

A Roadmap to What Follows

These are the issues around which we organize this volume. Chapter 2 begins with a review of the political economy of economic policymaking, focusing on the post-democratization period and the years following the financial crisis of 1997–1998. Chapter 3 then develops the natural-slowdown hypothesis, the idea that the observed deceleration is a predictable concomitant of the country's increasing economic maturity. It contrasts that concept with the policy-failure hypothesis: that with a more concerted and coherent agenda, Korea could achieve faster rates of growth.

Financial liberalization and reform have been touted as promising a more efficient allocation of resources, better risk diversification, and faster economic growth. But as we show in Chapter 4, the evidence on the effects of financial liberalization is ambiguous. What is clear from Korea's own history and from the experience of other countries is that financial deregulation does not guarantee improvements in economic efficiency and stability. An inadequately regulated financial system can be dangerously procyclical—that is, it can amplify business-cycle fluctuations. Korea has stumbled from crisis to crisis, from the investment and commercial bank crisis of 1997–1998 to the credit card crisis of 2003 and the savings bank crisis of 2010. For much of its history, financial stability has remained elusive. How to best secure it remains a prominent item on Korea's public-policy agenda.

Another perennial issue is the role of the chaebol, which remain the leaders of the country's industrial sector. Chapter 5 analyzes both the causes and consequences of this state of affairs. Among the consequences is a growing bifurcation of economic prospects for large versus small firms. More generally, there is concern in Korea and also in organizations like the OECD about issues of distribution and social cohesion and about the chaebol as a locus of concentrated power. There are questions about the labor market and the education system and whether they are well suited to the needs of an increasingly globalized Korean economy. There are questions about whether the social welfare system can be extended and redesigned to better reconcile the imperatives of efficiency and equity. We address these concerns in Chapter 6.[17]

Then there is Korea's place in the world economy. This issue is of special concern to outside observers, given the prominent role of the external sector in the country's economic growth and development. In Chapter 7 we review the importance of the external sector in the past and pose questions about its future. Prominent among those questions: What are the implications of Chinese competition, and should Korea continue to specialize in the cluster of heavy industries that have been the traditional basis for its industrial success, move up market into the production of high-tech products, or attempt develop a comparative advantage in tradable services?

An important future challenge and source of uncertainty is North Korea, in terms of the prospects for the North Korean economy and the possibility of reunification. Chapter 8 provides an overview of the state of the North Korean economy. It analyzes the different approaches taken by successive South Korean governments in managing relations with its difficult neighbor and embeds them in the larger geopolitical context, in which the United States, China, and Japan also play consequential roles.

In the concluding chapter we sketch a way forward for the Korean economy, drawing on our own analysis and the work of other contributors to the volumes in this series.

---

17. In doing so, we draw on the companion volumes by An and Bosworth (2013) and Freeman, Choi, and Kim (forthcoming).

CHAPTER 2

The Political Context

Before it was divided into northern and southern halves in 1945, Korea had existed within what were generally its current borders for more than a thousand years.[1] The people living within those borders speak a common language and share a unique phonetic writing system, which facilitates mass literacy.[2] Unlike many developing countries, the Korean nation and its borders were not the artificial creation of a colonial regime. Koreans have long had and continue to possess a strong sense of their common culture and nationality.

Until 1910 Korea was ruled by a king who was aided by bureaucrats selected on the basis of their formal education in the Confucian classics, performance on meritocratic state examinations, and family status. This political structure can be characterized as a "centralized oligarchy" rather than absolutist rule.[3] Under ideal circumstances, a benevolent monarch supported by competent scholar-officials can mobilize resources for

1. Allied with the Chinese Tang dynasty, the Korean kingdom of Shilla defeated Baekje and Goguryeo (or Koguryo) in 660 and 668, respectively, but its territorial reach fell short of Pyongyang. Instead, Goguryeo's former general worked with the Manchus to establish Balhae in the northern region. It was not until 936 that a unified nation more or less within the Korean Peninsula was established, under the name Goryeo (or Koryo).

2. Hangul, the Korean alphabet, is a scientific writing system. Until the 1970s, hangul supplemented Chinese characters in official documents and reports, but since the 1980s hangul has increasingly supplanted Chinese characters, and now texts are written entirely in hangul with a few exceptions, such as homonyms. Because hangul is easy to learn, it has contributed to widespread literacy in Korea.

3. See Henderson (1968) and Palais (1975).

economic and cultural development. But with few competing sources of power, such a centralized oligarchy can just as easily engage in factional, rent-seeking competition. In fact, after the reformist monarch who had led Korea's revival died in 1800, a series of weak kings and corrupt officials dominated the political scene. Their exploitation of the peasants and failure to modernize the nation set the stage for Japanese colonial occupation, which lasted from 1910 through 1945.

Japan's defeat in World War II brought an end to the Japanese empire and its Korean colony, but agreements at the end of the war divided Korea between the Soviet Union and the United States. The Soviets established a Communist regime in the north, while a regime supported by the United States was set up in the south. Although a provisional government in exile in China, led by Kim Koo, returned to Korea, the United States chose to support Rhee Syng-man (or Syngman Rhee), a Princeton PhD and longtime exile in the United States who had pro-independence and anti-Communist credentials but little to no domestic power base.

The newly divided Korea then became the battleground for an internationalized civil war from 1950 to 1953, pitting South Korea and the United States against North Korea and China, with the Soviet Union in the background. The war devastated the country. It ended with an armistice but no peace treaty, with both sides maintaining large armed forces facing each other across a demilitarized zone at the border.

South Korea was then faced with the task of building a political and institutional structure on the foundation of a long Confucian tradition, aborted modernization, a bitter colonial legacy, a divided nation, and a physically devastated country, all within the context of the Cold War.[4] At the end of the Korean War, the United States reassessed South Korea's geostrategic importance and provided generous assistance. Foreign aid

---

4. In the area of higher education, for example, Sungkyunkwan University had been founded in 1398 as the highest national institution to produce Confucian scholars. Around the turn of the twentieth century, Western missionaries and Korean modernizers had played a key role in establishing Yonsei, Ewha, and Korea Universities. In 1924, the Japanese colonial government established the Keijo Imperial University in Seoul, in part to respond to Korean independence leaders' plan to set up a citizens' university. Around two-thirds of the students were Japanese at Keijo Imperial University during the colonial period, when Japanese residents in Korea accounted for only 3 percent of the population in Korea.

amounted to nearly 8 percent of South Korea's gross national product (GNP) from 1953 to 1962 (Mason et al. 1980, 185).

By the second half of the 1950s, Korea had a government not unlike those in many dysfunctional developing countries today. Political support from the National Assembly was more often obtained with cash payments than through discussions of policy. Although the president was chosen by election, checks and balances on the executive were ineffective. Economic policy was focused on maximizing foreign aid, which would be spent in Korean currency but settled in U.S. dollars. The key policy for achieving this goal was an overvalued exchange rate that had the additional effect of discouraging exports. Complicated multiple exchange rates and export-import linkages (favoring established primary exports) made it difficult to promote promising new exports. President Rhee used the multiple exchange rates; the discretionary allocation of foreign exchange, aid goods, and import licenses; and government contracts as instruments to consolidate his power. The economic development that occurred was largely the result of the massive rebuilding effort after the war, much of it funded by U.S. aid.

At the end of the 1950s, Korea was an aid-dependent economy with one of the lowest per capita incomes in the world. The division of the peninsula in 1945 and the destruction wrought by the Korean War, together with rampant corruption and crony capitalism, cast a shadow over development prospects. The government derived more than half of its revenue from U.S. aid. Manufacturing constituted barely 10 percent of GNP. Exports amounted to only 3 percent of GNP when the average for other countries of comparable size and per capita income was about 15 percent (Perkins 1997).

At the same time, a closer examination of Korea's situation revealed strengths that would become integral to the economy's subsequent development. First, despite the existence of crony capitalism, Korea had a vibrant private sector in which entrepreneurs seeking profit opportunities were expanding their businesses. Many of the country's family-based business groups, the chaebol, were established during this early period.

Second, Korea had a cohesive egalitarian society characterized by cultural and ethnic homogeneity, basic administrative capacity, and high social mobility. The collapse of the traditional hierarchy, combined with the leveling effects of land reform and war, placed everyone at the same starting line, leading Koreans to believe that they could better their situation if they dedicated themselves to education and hard work. Land reform was important for this perception; it was initiated by the United States and expanded by the Rhee government in 1949, partly in response to a previous land-reform effort in North Korea. Much of the reform resulted from the war, when landlords and tenants made private deals that were favorable to both, more than from the Rhee policy, which also tried to use the process to increase government revenue.

Third, Korea had primary and secondary school enrollment rates similar to those in countries with two or three times its per capita income, thanks to its extraordinary investment in education. In 1945, when Korea was liberated from Japanese colonial rule, its primary school enrollment rate was around just 45 percent, and illiteracy was at 78 percent. But by 1960 the primary enrollment rate had increased to 86 percent and illiteracy had dropped to 28 percent as a result of the institution of universal primary education in 1950 (McGinn et al. 1980).

Student demonstrations brought the Rhee government to an end in 1960. Democratic elections produced a new government under Prime Minister Chang Myon and President Yun Bo-seon that began to institute reforms such as the adoption of meritocratic examinations for recruiting government officials. The Chang government also drafted a rudimentary economic development plan and a blueprint for what would eventually become the Economic Planning Board (EPB).The Chang government proved short-lived, however, and was overthrown in 1961 by a military coup led by Park Chung Hee (Table 2.1).

By the early 1960s, then, Korea had one well-organized institution, the army, which had been restructured and trained under heavy combat conditions. It had a weak bureaucracy and the beginnings of a militant student movement. It had universities that would form the basis for educating the elites (the private Yonsei and Korea Universities and Seoul National University). It had the experience of a decade of universal primary education. Protestant churches were relatively strong, owing to their opposition to Japanese colonialism. But recent political experience was confined to a decade of Rhee's authoritarian rule and one free election that was immediately overturned by the army.

This chapter focuses on how politics played a central role in determining economic and social policy, and how economic and social issues in turn influenced politics and political development. It does not cover the full range of issues that influenced politics or were influenced by the

Table 2.1. Presidents of the Republic of Korea, 1948–Present

Name	Terms	Party affiliation
Rhee Syng-man (Syngman Rhee)	1948–1952 1952–1956 1956–1960	National Alliance for the Rapid Realization of Korean Independence (1948–1951) Liberal Party (1951–1960)
Yun Bo-seon	1960–1962	Democratic Party (1960–1962) New Democratic Party (1962)
Park Chung-hee (Park Chung Hee)	1963–1967 1967–1971 1971–1972 1972–1978 1978–1979	Democratic Republican Party
Choi Kyu-hah	1979–1980	Independent
Chun Doo-hwan (Chun Doo Hwan)	1980–1981 1981–1988	Democratic Justice Party
Roh Tae-woo	1988–1993	Democratic Justice Party (1988–1990) Democratic Liberal Party (1990–1993)
Kim Young-sam	1993–1998	Democratic Liberal Party (1993–1996) New Korea Party (1996–1997) Grand National Party (1997–1998)
Kim Dae-jung	1998–2003	National Congress for New Politics (1998–2000) New Millennium Democratic Party (2000–2003)
Roh Moo-hyun	2003–2004 2004–2008	New Millennium Democratic Party (2003) Open Uri Party [Our Open Party] (2003–2007) United New Democratic Party (2007–2008) United Democratic Party (2008)
Lee Myung-bak	2008–2013	Grand National Party (2008–2012) Saenuri Party [New Frontier Party] (2012–2013)
Park Geun-hye	2013–present	Saenuri Party [New Frontier Party] (2012–present)

Source: Republic of Korea National Election Commission.

Note: The presidents' names are given in the standard Romanized spelling, followed by the pre-ferred spelling in parenthesis.

political system, such as international relations and policies toward North Korea (issues that are covered in Chapter 8).

The Years of Authoritarian Rule

The world has seen numerous military governments that have done little to foster economic development. In contrast, the government of Park Chung Hee introduced an effective economic development plan and stuck with it for eighteen years. The success of that plan led the succeeding military government to build on the effort and thereby to sustain Korea's high rate of growth.[5]

Although the political system under President Park Chung Hee in the period between the restoration of elections in 1963 and the adoption of the Yushin constitution in 1972 had some of the trappings of democracy, it was less open than it appeared (Table 2.2). There was a National Assembly with some seats held by opposition parties, but those parties were systematically harassed. Although Park recruited competent technocrats, he had a tight circle of former military officers in positions of power over political and security matters. The Korean Central Intelligence Agency ran a vigilant domestic surveillance system that suppressed dissent; anyone challenging the system was jailed, or worse (although this was more common after 1972).

Partly in response to U.S. pressure, Park Chung Hee held direct presidential elections. In 1963 he was elected by a narrow margin of 150,000 out of 10 million votes cast (1.5 percentage points), and the opposition candidate, former president Yun Bo-seon, contested the result and claimed a moral victory. Invalid ballots accounted for 9 percent of total votes cast (Table 2.3). In 1967 Park won by a comfortable margin of 10 percentage points against the same opposition, on the strength of the stability and progress delivered by his government. In 1971 Park defeated Kim Dae-jung by a margin of 1 million votes (8 percentage points) out of more than 12 million votes cast. (Prior to this election, the constitution had been

---

5. It is important to note that Korea's economic performance did not suffer much after democratization. In terms of purchasing power parity (PPP) exchange rates, Korea's per capita income in 1970 was 12 percent of the U.S. level. When Korea achieved democratization in 1987, its per capita income was 27 percent of the U.S. level. After suffering a setback during the Asian economic crisis of 1997–1998, Korea's per capita income reached 64 percent of the U.S. level in 2010.

Table 2.2. Comparative Political Development, Korea and Other Countries

	1972			1980			1990			2000			2010		
	PR	CL	S	PR	CL	S	PR	CL	S	PR	CL	S	PR	CL	S
Korea	5	6	NF	4	5	PF	2	3	PF	2	2	F	1	2	F
Italy	1	2	F	1	2	F	1	1	F	1	2	F	1	2	F
Japan	2	1	F	1	1	F	1	1	F	1	2	F	1	2	F
Iran	5	6	NF	5	5	PF	6	5	NF	6	6	NF	6	6	NF
Ethiopia	5	6	NF	7	7	NF	7	7	NF	5	5	PF	6	6	NF
Zimbabwe	6	5	NF	3	4	PF	6	4	PF	6	5	PF	6	6	NF

Source: Freedom House, *Freedom in the World: Comparative and Historical Data*, January 2011; www.freedomhouse.org.

Note: Political rights (PR) and civil liberties (CL) are measured on a scale from 1 to 7, with 1 representing the highest level of rights and liberties. Status (S) indicates political freedom; countries are categorized as not free (NF), partly free (PF), and free (F).

amended to allow the president a third term.) The election was hotly contested, and during the campaign Kim Dae-jung famously warned that it would be the last chance to prevent Park Chung Hee from imposing a lifetime dictatorship. Park, for his part, said it would be the last time he would run in an election.

In the early 1970s President Park increasingly relied on police-enforced repression, together with a new constitution, to consolidate and hold on to power. The Yushin constitution, adopted in 1972, suspended habeas corpus, abolished direct presidential elections and term limits, and gave the president the authority to nominate one-third of the National Assembly and to appoint and remove judges. Subsequently, a series of emergency decrees banned all discussion of the constitution. Dissenting politicians, students, intellectuals, and religious leaders were arrested and imprisoned. Under growing pressure from popular demonstrations, the Yushin regime came to an end when the director of Korea's Central Intelligence Agency assassinated President Park in October 1979.

In the early 1960s Korea was still heavily dependent on the United States for military security and economic stability. The United States was not shy about putting pressure on the government to pursue the reforms it wanted. President Park understood that he could not resist this pressure so long as Korea depended on U.S. foreign aid. The first priority of the Park government, therefore, was to encourage the development of Korean exports as an alternative means of obtaining foreign exchange. In response to export support policies ranging from currency devaluation to monthly presidential meetings with industry groups, the Korean business class was greatly expanded and strengthened. At first anyone who was successful at exporting received government support, but in the 1970s support came to be focused on building up particular industries, namely the heavy and chemical industries associated in the minds of policymakers with both industrial upgrading and national security.

Government support led over time to the expansion of a number of family-based businesses into large business groups, or chaebol, which increasingly dominated exports and the economy generally. Initially the chaebol were not such a powerful political force, however. There was no doubt that the success of the chaebol depended on President Park more than he depended on them. Industrial policy was run out of the Blue House, and the chaebol for the most part did what was asked of them. In the 1960s, incentives were broadly uniform and applied to all who had success with exports. If a chaebol failed to respond adequately, those incentives (for example, access to credit under especially favorable terms, or favorable treatment by the tax authorities) were withdrawn. But, importantly, what the government asked for was export performance and industrial upgrading, not some arbitrary favor. Although the state was certainly powerful, it was the application of an impersonal and performance-based reward mechanism that served as a motor for economic growth. By the end of the 1970s, the chaebol had become richer, larger, and less dependent on the government, which was attempting to reduce its role in the economy in favor of relying more on market forces.[6] The bureaucracy, for its part, became more professional as it was called on to carry out a widening range of functions. The civilian bureaucracy was charged with designing and implementing most of the Park government's industrial and trade policies. At the same time, oversight by powerful security organizations helped to keep that bureaucracy focused on its task, and limited rent-seeking.[7]

Rapid economic growth produced large numbers of jobs requiring higher levels of skill, and Korea's education system expanded to meet this need. Despite the role that government played in directing the economy,

---

6. Chapter 5 develops these points more fully.
7. This is not to imply that rent-seeking was necessarily eliminated, as we will show.

Table 2.3. Presidential Election Results by Region, 1963–1971

		Total votes	Seoul	Gyeonggi	Gangwon	Chungbuk
1963	Park Chung Hee	43%	29%	30%	36%	35%
	Yun Bo-seon	41%	62%	52%	44%	44%
	Other candidates	8%	4%	9%	10%	10%
	Invalid ballots	9%	5%	9%	10%	11%
	Total votes cast	*10,081,198*	*1,231,578*	*1,163,847*	*749,823*	*509,767*
	Regional share	—	*12%*	*12%*	*7%*	*5%*
1967	Park Chung Hee	49%	44%	39%	49%	44%
	Yun Bo-seon	39%	50%	50%	40%	41%
	Other candidates	7%	3%	6%	7%	9%
	Invalid ballots	5%	3%	5%	5%	5%
	Total votes cast	*11,058,721*	*1,317,695*	*1,282,606*	*838,074*	*579,342*
	Regional share	—	*12%*	*12%*	*8%*	*5%*
1971	Park Chung Hee	51%	39%	47%	57%	54%
	Kim Dae-jung	43%	58%	48%	37%	39%
	Other candidates	1%	1%	2%	1%	2%
	Invalid ballots	4%	2%	3%	4%	5%
	Total votes cast	*11,923,218*	*2,016,908*	*1,407,879*	*839,979*	*545,655*
	Regional share	—	*17%*	*12%*	*7%*	*5%*

Source: Republic of Korea National Election Commission, www.nec.go.kr. *(contin.*

Note: Italicized figures show total votes cast in absolute-value terms and regional shares of total votes cast. The Korean regions are also known by the following alternate names and/or spellings: Gyeonggi (or Kyonggi), Gangwon (Kangwon), Chungbuk (North Chungcheong), Chungnam (South Chungcheong), Jeonbuk (North Jeolla or North Cholla), Jeonnam (South Jeolla or South Cholla), Gyeongbuk (North Gyeongsang or North Kyungsang), Gyeongnam (South Gyeongsang or South Kyongsang), Jeju (Cheju), and Busan (Pusan).

private demand and private money increasingly supplemented the efforts of the public sector in this area. Growth plus education produced a large, relatively prosperous middle class of skilled workers and managers. Before they became skilled workers and managers, however, they were students. As university students, they built on the tradition of early 1960s student activists and on the active role that student movements have played in East Asia more generally, and became shock troops for political change. By the mid-1980s Korean students were involved in regular

Table 2.3. (Continued)

Chungnam	Jeonbuk	Jeonnam	Gyeongbuk	Gyeongnam	Jeju	Busan
36%	44%	53%	51%	57%	63%	46%
44%	37%	33%	33%	28%	20%	45%
9%	8%	6%	7%	8%	7%	4%
11%	11%	8%	9%	8%	9%	5%
993,102	826,473	1,338,142	1,504,330	1,144,032	116,503	503,601
10%	8%	13%	15%	11%	1%	5%
43%	40%	42%	61%	66%	54%	62%
44%	46%	44%	25%	22%	31%	30%
7%	8%	8%	9%	8%	11%	4%
6%	6%	6%	5%	4%	5%	3%
1,078,918	926,388	1,464,369	1,693,362	1,221,996	129,387	526,584
10%	8%	13%	15%	11%	1%	5%
51%	34%	32%	73%	71%	53%	54%
42%	59%	58%	22%	25%	39%	43%
2%	3%	3%	1%	1%	2%	1%
4%	4%	7%	4%	4%	6%	2%
1,040,628	870,344	1,393,181	1,762,817	1,214,721	137,580	693,526
9%	7%	12%	15%	10%	1%	6%

confrontations with the police and enjoyed the support of large sectors of the middle class.

Unions and factory workers, in contrast, were not yet a major political force. Government action was particularly severe in response to any political activity on the part of workers. Unions were accused of Communist sympathies and, with the exception of those controlled by the government, were effectively banned. In essence, the government of Park Chung Hee adopted the Bismarckian strategy of suppressing unions and limiting their popular appeal by delivering broad-based growth and social security in the form of health care and other social services.

After a brief period of instability following the 1979 assassination of President Park and the coup that followed in 1980, a new government led by another former army general, Chun Doo Hwan, successfully implemented macroeconomic stabilization and liberalization measures. The Chun government adjusted the exchange rate, reduced monetary growth, and evaluated budget expenditure items from a zero base to restore macroeconomic stability. The technocrats enlisted by Chun felt that excessive state intervention had produced serious imbalances and advocated a transition to a more market-oriented economy.[8] They introduced the Monopoly Regulation and Fair Trade Act (MRFTA), reduced tariffs and import restrictions, and reoriented industrial policy from sectoral targeting to functional support (for R&D, for example). They phased out preferential policy loans and took steps to liberalize the financial sector.

These stabilization and liberalization measures, combined with global recovery, permitted the economy to resume its rapid growth. Korea soon enjoyed the so-called "three-low" boom, driven by low oil prices, low interest rates, and the low value of the Korean won relative to the Japanese yen. The country had consistently run a current account deficit, except in 1977, but starting in 1986 it began recording sizable surpluses, thus attracting scrutiny and criticism from its trade partners. This was another factor prompting policymakers, encouraged by the three-low boom and faced with greater external pressure to open the Korean market through trade and economic liberalization.

Mass demonstrations against the 1980 coup had been suppressed with much bloodshed, but by the middle of the subsequent decade opposition to authoritarian government found renewed mass support. In early 1987, civil disobedience and public rallies demanding political democratization intensified. Unable to control the swelling popular

---

8. For instance, in the preface to their book on business-government relations in Korea, Jones and SaKong (1980, xxxv) argued: "Decentralization of decision-making, reduced reliance on command, increased use of field manipulation and the market, and reduced discretion of civil servants all become increasingly desirable in a more complicated environment where the information available to a small number of civil servants is a decreasing share of the total needed to run the economy." SaKong went on to serve as senior economic secretary to Chun Doo Hwan in the 1980s.

sentiment, the government announced a constitutional change mandating a single five-year presidential term and a free presidential election in December of the same year.

Development of the economy and the creation of economic opportunity that was not entirely dependent on government thus created an imbalance in which the economy was open and relatively free but politics was closed and tightly controlled. As described in the volume in this series by Mo and Weingast (2013), this created pressure on the regime to open up the political system as well as the economy. However, additional elements were also at work. Democratization was more movement-based in Korea than in other countries undergoing similar transitions. The imbalance between economic liberalization and political control was not the motivating force for political movements. It was not as if prodemocracy activists looked at the market liberalization going on around them and found in the "imbalance" the inspiration to fight the authoritarian regime. Popular anger at the Chun government had more to do with the bloody suppression of prodemocracy demonstrations and the perceived illegitimacy of the regime.

At the same time, rapid and broad-based growth created a large middle class whose members increasingly came to support prodemocracy activists, demanding political freedom commensurate with their economic prosperity. In addition to the broadening of the democratic base, what changed between 1980 and 1987 was the U.S. decision to support prodemocracy forces, in part to prevent anti-American sentiment (based on the perceived American acquiescence to the policies of the Chun government) from becoming widespread.

President Park's main sources of support had been the army and a rural population that benefited from land reform in the 1940s, the write-off of rural debt in the 1960s, and rural development under the Saemaul Undong (New Village Movement). Over time, the chaebol also became a force that could provide significant support, including financial support, to political forces allied with the military regime. The importance of rural support diminished with urbanization, and increasingly in the 1970s, support for the Park government came from the Gyeongsang (or Kyongsang) provinces that benefited disproportionately from the government's development strategy. Although the Jeolla (or Cholla) provinces had supported Park in 1963, they increasingly felt left out and shifted their support to his rivals in 1967 and 1971, but not as disproportionately as the Gyeongsang provinces shifted their support toward Park.[9] In 1980 the bloody suppression of the Gwangju democracy movement left an indelible legacy and led the Jeolla provinces to vote overwhelmingly against Park's military successors. These were the origins of the regional political division that continues to play a major role in Korean politics today.

These changes in political structure took place in the context of continuing hostility from the north. It is important to recall that North Korea in this period was far from the failed state that it would become. There was still a nightly curfew in Seoul, and air raid sirens were tested regularly. However, as the threat from the north began to recede or, more accurately, as the south became more confident about its economic and military power and security relative to the north, it became more acceptable to challenge the government without fearing that bringing down the current government might bring down the South Korean political system. The threat from the north also played a role in keeping an activist industrial policy from turning into a rent-seeking exercise that enriched the politically powerful and paid off the president's allies. A failed economy would have threatened the existence of South Korea as much as the North Korean army.

The First Phase of Democratization

Roh Tae-woo, the ruling party candidate and another former military general turned politician, narrowly won the first freely contested presidential election in December 1987. One might have thought that Roh's role as the second most influential figure in the authoritarian regime would have augured poorly for his chances, but voters feared political instability if an inexperienced opposition-party candidate triumphed. There were also regional factors at work, given that there were four major candidates from four different regions. Roh was from North Gyeongsang province.

---

9. The Jeolla provinces (Jeonbuk and Jeonnam) supported Park over Yun (49.3 percent versus 34.6 percent) in 1963, and gave a slight edge to Yun over Park (44.6 percent versus 41.1 percent) in 1967. In 1971, they gave majority support to Kim Dae-jung over Park Chung Hee (58.6 percent to 32.8 percent). But this was nothing compared with the support the Gyeongsang provinces (Gyeongbuk and Gyeongnam) gave Park over Kim (73.6 percent versus 21.9 percent). Even in 1967, the Gyeongsang provinces had voted overwhelmingly for Park (62.6 percent to 24.7 percent). See Table 2.3.

Kim Young-sam, a prominent prodemocracy politician, was from South Gyeongsang province. Kim Dae-jung, who had challenged Park Chung Hee in 1971, was from South Jeolla province. Kim Jong Pil, a former military officer who had supported Park in the 1961 coup, was from South Chungcheong province. While it was expected that Roh and Kim Young-sam would win North and South Gyeongsang, respectively, the winning margin in those two provinces was anybody's guess. Kim Dae-jung was projected to receive overwhelming support from the Jeolla provinces, but they were not as populous as the Gyeongsang provinces. Although Kim Jong Pil was the weakest of the four candidates, he could play the spoiler's role, given the tight competition among the other three candidates and the absence of runoff elections in the Korean system. In the end, while Kim Young-sam prevailed in Busan (or Pusan) and South Gyeongsang province and came in second in most other regions, and Kim Dae-jung came in first in Seoul and received overwhelming support in the Jeolla provinces, Kim Young-sam and Kim Dae-jung effectively split the prodemocracy vote and handed the presidency to Roh. Of more than 23 million votes cast, Roh received 37 percent. Kim Young-sam and Kim Dae-jung came in second and third, each with around 27 percent, and Kim Jong Pil finished a distant fourth with 8 percent (Table 2.4).

Thanks to a divided opposition and a first-past-the-post voting system without runoff elections, Roh was elected president with only a plurality of votes. But the same first-past-the-post system in National Assembly elections ensured a combined majority for the opposition parties in April 1988. Having suffered the wrath of prodemocracy voters for handing the presidency to a former general, Kim Dae-jung and Kim Young-sam launched a proactive reformist agenda in the National Assembly. They worked together to lead legislative efforts covering a wide range of issues, from labor unions to national medical insurance. The number of bills submitted to the National Assembly in 1988 surpassed the total number of bills in the previous four years combined.

Although there were substantive legislative accomplishments in 1988–1989, Roh found it frustrating to lead a minority government. This perception formed the background to his proposal to join forces with two of the three opposition parties to create a supermajority party in January 1990, based on an unexpected alliance among a former general (Roh Tae-woo), a prodemocracy politician (Kim Young-sam), and a Park Chung Hee loyalist (Kim Jong Pil). According to his own account, Kim

Table 2.4. Presidential Election Results by Region, 1987–1997

		Total	Seoul	Gyeonggi	Gangwon	Chungbuk	Chungnam	Jeonbu.
1987	Roh Tae-woo	36%	29%	41%	58%	46%	25%	14ᶜ
	Kim Young-sam	27%	29%	27%	26%	27%	16%	1ᶜ
	Kim Dae-jung	27%	32%	22%	9%	11%	12%	81ᶜ
	Kim Jong-Pil	8%	8%	8%	5%	13%	44%	1ᶜ
	Other candidates	0%	0%	0%	0%	0%	0%	0ᶜ
	Invalid ballots	2%	2%	2%	2%	3%	3%	3ᶜ
	Total votes cast	*22,603,411*	*5,618,729*	*2,905,323*	*921,214*	*757,457*	*1,534,906*	*1,136,97*
	Regional share		*25%*	*13%*	*4%*	*3%*	*7%*	*5ᶜ*
1992	Kim Young-sam	41%	36%	36%	42%	38%	37%	6ᶜ
	Kim Dae-jung	33%	38%	32%	16%	26%	29%	89ᶜ
	Chung Ju-yung	16%	18%	23%	34%	24%	25%	3ᶜ
	Park Chan-jong	6%	6%	7%	7%	9%	7%	1ᶜ
	Other candidates	1%	1%	2%	2%	2%	2%	1ᶜ
	Invalid ballots	1%	1%	1%	2%	2%	2%	1ᶜ
	Total votes cast	*23,775,409*	*5,951,777*	*3,451,395*	*820,255*	*736,171*	*952,454*	*1,112,35*
	Regional share		*25%*	*15%*	*3%*	*3%*	*4%*	*5ᶜ*
1997	Kim Dae-jung	40%	44%	39%	23%	37%	47%	91ᶜ
	Lee Hoi-chang	38%	40%	35%	42%	30%	23%	4ᶜ
	Rhee In-je	19%	13%	23%	30%	29%	26%	2ᶜ
	Other candidates	2%	1%	2%	2%	2%	2%	1ᶜ
	Invalid ballots	2%	1%	1%	2%	2%	2%	2ᶜ
	Total votes cast	*25,642,438*	*5,854,773*	*4,535,524*	*830,943*	*789,816*	*1,001,198*	*1,169,18*
	Regional share		*23%*	*18%*	*3%*	*3%*	*4%*	*5ᶜ*

Source: Republic of Korea National Election Commission. (continu▪

Note: Italicized figures show total votes cast in absolute-value terms and regional shares of total votes cast. Korean re▪ gions are also known by their alternate names and/or spellings: Gyeonggi (Kyonggi), Gangwon (Kangwon), Chungbu▪ (North Chungcheong), Chungnam (South Chungcheong), Jeonbuk (North Jeolla or North Cholla), Jeonnam (Sout▪ Jeolla or South Cholla), Gyeongbuk (North Gyeongsang or North Kyongsang), Gyeongnam (South Gyeongsang ▪ South Kyongsang), Jeju (Cheju), Busan (Pusan), Daegu (Taegu), Incheon (Inchon), Gwangju (Kwangju), and Daejeo▪ (Taejon).

Table 2.4. (Continued)

Jeonnam	Gyeongbuk	Gyeongnam	Jeju	Busan	Daegu	Incheon	Gwangju	Daejeon	Ulsan
8%	65%	40%	48%	32%	70%	39%	5%		
1%	28%	50%	26%	55%	24%	30%	1%		
88%	2%	4%	18%	9%	3%	21%	93%		
0%	3%	3%	4%	3%	2%	9%	0%		
0%	0%	0%	0%	0%	0%	0%	0%		
3%	2%	2%	3%	1%	1%	2%	1%		
1,459,870	1,669,019	1,925,412	242,098	1,995,317	1,132,078	828,860	476,153		
6%	7%	9%	1%	9%	5%	4%	2%		
4%	65%	72%	40%	73%	60%	37%	2%	35%	
92%	10%	9%	33%	13%	8%	32%	96%	29%	
2%	16%	12%	16%	6%	19%	21%	1%	23%	
1%	8%	5%	9%	7%	12%	8%	0%	11%	
1%	2%	1%	2%	1%	1%	2%	0%	2%	
1%	2%	1%	2%	1%	1%	1%	1%	1%	
1,270,023	1,531,637	2,093,590	260,884	2,115,389	1,158,193	1,066,288	680,600	574,403	
5%	6%	9%	1%	9%	5%	4%	3%	2%	
93%	13%	11%	40%	15%	12%	38%	96%	44%	15%
3%	61%	54%	36%	53%	72%	36%	2%	29%	51%
1%	21%	31%	20%	29%	13%	23%	1%	24%	26%
1%	3%	2%	2%	2%	2%	2%	0%	2%	6%
2%	2%	2%	2%	1%	1%	1%	1%	1%	1%
1,301,836	1,539,608	1,648,014	273,577	2,094,406	1,329,088	1,292,611	775,199	682,893	523,763
5%	6%	6%	1%	8%	5%	5%	3%	3%	2%

Young-sam was concerned that a divided opposition would again hand the presidency to a former military general; to catch a tiger, he felt, he had to go into the tiger's den.

With the demise of the authoritarian regime, new actors vied to play a greater role in policymaking. Freed from a long period of suppression, labor sought higher wages and better working conditions. It attempted to block policy changes deemed to be against its interest, sometimes resorting to violent tactics. Civic-movement organizations headed by former dissidents developed into a political force intent on advancing an agenda for social policy reform and approaching North Korea for a more extensive and constructive dialogue. Over the next decade they would help bring about significant changes in the political system, including a real-name financial-transaction system, the disclosure of assets held by high-ranking officials, campaign finance reforms, and other anticorruption measures.[10]

Although the Roh government was essentially conservative, it supported some of the reform measures championed by these progressive groups. To fight the rise in property prices, it introduced regulations designed to prevent land speculation. In foreign policy it pursued *nordpolitik,* seeking to improve relations with the Soviet Union and China as well as North Korea, in emulation of West Germany's *ostpolitik* under Willy Brandt. The end of the Cold War in the late 1980s would fundamentally transform the international context of Korea's political and economic evolution.

To be sure, Korea was by no means immune to the political instability and disorder that characterize new democracies lacking the precedents and established procedures that lend order to decision making. As in any polity (young or mature, authoritarian or democratic), given calls for reform, on the one hand, and rearguard action by vested interests, on the other, it was difficult to formulate and execute a coherent economic policy agenda. Yet despite those obstacles, the Roh government and the National Assembly did introduce a number of important market-oriented reforms, ranging from increased competition, price liberalization, and central bank independence, to horizontal (that is, R&D-supporting) rather than vertical (sector-targeting) industrial policy.

---

10. The real-name financial transaction system was a transparent system that prohibited the use of fictitious or borrowed names.

Those concerned about excessive state intervention hoped that the Roh government would dismantle or at least loosen the collusive arrangement in which the government worked out incentive schemes in cooperation with large business groups and banking institutions—the system that had been used to govern the export-led developmental state in the 1970s and 1980s. Indeed there was good reason to think that the earlier collusive system had outlived its usefulness. Even where it still had utility, the change in political balance prevented the continued use of earlier methods: the scrutiny of opposition parties, the media, and civic organizations did not allow the government to support the chaebol as openly as before. At the same time, the government was reluctant to dissolve its ties to big business, partly because the latter was its major source of political contributions. As a result, the relationship between the chaebol and ruling elites became more covert. The upshot was a hotbed of corruption, at least until civil society became strong enough to effect campaign-finance and other political reforms in the 1990s. Roh himself took enormous bribes and political donations from the chaebol, for which he was later prosecuted and jailed.

Thus despite the rise of interest groups opposed to the ruling coalition of the army and the chaebol, the influence of the chaebol increased at first, if anything. Earlier authoritarian regimes had the power to prevent the chaebol from abusing their favorable access to credit and the corridors of policymaking. Now, however, removal of the old governance mechanism, coupled with market deregulation gave the chaebol greater freedom. Politicians who depended on the chaebol for campaign funds were unwilling or unable to control or sanction them. And those politicians had a ready justification for their inaction: the opening and deregulation of the market.

The Roh government was a provisional regime in a country undergoing a transition to democracy. Yet economic performance under Roh was quite good, despite the lack of consistent government leadership in matters of the economy, perhaps implying that government leadership was not as important as before. In spite of its unpopularity, the Roh government muddled through, introducing scattered trade and financial liberalization measures and a national pension system.

In the December 1992 presidential election, Kim Young-sam, a prominent opposition leader who joined forces with conservative elements, defeated the leading prodemocracy candidate, Kim Dae-jung. With this change in leadership, civilian rule took hold. President Kim Young-sam set to work to weaken the political influence of the military. In 1993 he broke up an army faction (Hanahoi) that had backed the earlier authoritarian regime and adopted the real-name financial transaction system to improve transparency and make it more difficult for others to set aside both corporate and political slush funds. In late 1995, Kim Young-sam arrested two former presidents—the former military generals Chun Doo Hwan and Roh Tae-woo—on charges of corruption and treason, thus removing all remaining traces of the military's presence in national politics.

Having dispensed with military intervention, the Kim government embraced economic liberalization and globalization as the cornerstones of its economic policy. The government set its sights on Korea's becoming a member of the OECD, a symbolic move toward joining the ranks of the industrial democracies and a tactic for fostering broader domestic support for globalization. In the first two years of the Kim government, numerous regulations were lifted, consistent with OECD codes. Building on earlier liberalization efforts, industrial policy and export promotion largely disappeared from the government's vocabulary, notwithstanding the reluctance of the bureaucracy to part with its customary instruments of control. A substantial relaxation of capital account restrictions was also carried out as a precondition for Korea's entry into the OECD.[11]

In the process of liberalization, the apparatus of financial control was dismantled but without putting in place an adequate system of prudential supervision. The distinction between old-fashioned regulation and modern prudential supervision was not fully appreciated, much less implemented, and Kim feared a new system of prudential supervision might be seen as a step back toward financial repression. At the same time that the Kim government was relaxing capital account restrictions, the policy community—not only in Korea but also in Washington, D.C., from which Korean policymakers took their cues—was minimizing the pitfalls of financial opening. There was little appreciation for how the economy could be destabilized if the preconditions for safe capital account liberalization were not met.

Similarly, despite the professed need for chaebol reform, little was done to control the financial behavior of big business groups. Corporate

---

11. See Chapter 4 for details.

governance was not strengthened (as we describe in more detail in Chapter 5). Meanwhile, the easing of restrictions on capital account transactions allowed the chaebol freer access to global financial markets. Taking advantage of this, the large business groups went on a borrowing and investment binge. Interest rates in global financial markets were low, the prices of oil and other raw materials came down, and the yen continued to appreciate, all of which helped to enhance Korean competitiveness for a time. Banking on these favorable circumstances, the large industrial groups took on more risk and larger amounts of leverage.

Regulation proved singularly inadequate for checking this unsustainable appetite for expansion. While the chaebol could not expect the same preferential treatment as before, neither were they compelled to abandon past practices. They colluded with politicians and parties out of inertia, but mostly in pursuit of guarantees of their own survival, in return for political payoffs. Members of the ruling elite, such as the second son of Kim Young-sam, were flagrantly abusive in peddling their influence. Some were charged, prosecuted, and sent to jail, tarnishing the clean-government image that Kim had sought to cultivate.

Three years into Kim's five-year term, his government became afflicted with lame-duck syndrome. In June 1995 Kim Young-sam's party suffered a humiliating defeat in local elections (including the Seoul mayoral election). However, after President Kim arrested Roh and Chun on corruption and treason charges in late 1995, his popularity rating soared, at some points exceeding 70 percent. It was not long, though, before corruption scandals in 1996 involving his associates dented his popularity again. Despite the setback, Kim pushed ahead in late 1996 with a major amendment of the labor law designed to enhance labor market flexibility by making layoffs easier. When the ruling party tried to push the labor law through the National Assembly, however, it triggered demonstrations by white-collar workers and blue-collar unions, forcing Kim to withdraw the bill. Hanbo, the fourteenth largest chaebol, then went bankrupt in January 1997 and surrounding events implicated the president's second son in a corruption scandal. The Kim government had neglected to take measures to rein in the chaebol's borrowing and to more tightly regulate the banking system that was the intermediary for their borrowing. Chickens were now coming home to roost.[12]

---

12. These developments and problems are discussed further in Chapter 4.

With the surge in chaebol spending, the current account swung into a deficit approaching 5 percent of GDP in 1996. The government meanwhile maintained its rigid exchange rate policy, closing off one potential avenue for current account adjustment. The investment boom also created a real estate bubble. Foreign investors noticed these trends and grew increasingly restive. Unease then gave way to panic when a financial crisis broke out in Thailand in the summer of 1997 and spread from there to Indonesia and Malaysia. Investors exited Korean financial markets just as the lame-duck Kim government was drawing to the end of its term.

Democratization alone, therefore, did not guarantee a stable balance between the political and economic systems. The chaebol used the leverage they gained through economic openness to pursue the relaxation of regulatory constraints, notably on borrowing, and to prevent the implementation of other significant reforms. So long as the economy continued to expand, their strategy of heavy borrowing, extensive investment, and high leverage was profitable. But if growth slowed, it rendered the chaebol, and the economy as a whole, highly vulnerable.

The first ten years of democratization thus consolidated the shift to civilian democratic rule and furthered the economic liberalization begun in the 1980s. It brought to the fore new political organizations, actors, attitudes, and ideologies that had been suppressed in the past. These factors reduced the power of key elements—notably the army and the bureaucracy—that had dominated the authoritarian period. But the consequence was an even more politically powerful large-business sector and even weaker political and bureaucratic oversight.

Kim Dae-jung and the Shift in Power

In the fourth quarter of 1997, the Korean economy experienced a financial crisis and economic collapse: GDP contracted by 6.9 percent in 1998, a nearly 12-percentage-point swing from the 4.7 percent growth of a year earlier. Prices jumped by 7.5 percent owing to depreciation of the won, which fell by 27 percent against the dollar. Unemployment reached 8 percent, the highest since the beginning of the economic miracle. All this was a rude shock to a country accustomed to robust growth, stable prices, and full employment.

Given the shock of the crisis, one might imagine that almost any opposition candidate could have won the 1997 presidential election. But the election was close. To win, Kim Dae-jung, the prodemocracy candidate from the Southwest Jeolla region, had to form a coalition with Kim Jong Pil, a Park Chung Hee loyalist with a power base in the Chungcheong region, traditionally a swing state. Kim Dae-jung also received unexpected help from Rhee In-je, a maverick who bolted from the ruling party and split the conservative vote. As in 1987, regional rivalry was important in the outcome. More than 90 percent of voters in the Jeolla provinces cast their ballot for Kim Dae-jung, compared with fewer than 15 percent of those in the Gyeongsang provinces.[13]

Toward the end of 1997 the newly elected Kim government accepted IMF policy conditions that laid out an array of financial, corporate, and public-sector reforms. Labor-market reform was geared to facilitating interindustry mobility and smoothing industrial relations; the device chosen to achieve these ends was a tripartite committee of unions, government, and business. Financial institutions were required to overhaul their risk management systems, adopt global accounting standards, and meet internationally recognized capital requirements. The chaebol were instructed to reduce their debt/equity ratio to less than 200 percent, abolish cross-ownership among their affiliates, and consolidate their operations. Korea embraced the Anglo-American approach of competition, free enterprise, strong property rights, and limited government intervention. But in contrast to previous liberalization efforts, deregulation this time was combined with an expanded social safety net, strengthened prudential regulation, and meaningful corporate governance reform.

The Kim Dae-jung government was widely known for favoring a progressive approach to managing the economy. However, the financial crisis of 1997–1998 erupted while the presidential campaign was still under way, forcing the outgoing Kim Young-sam government to turn to the IMF for help. The Kim Dae-jung campaign could have opposed calling in the IMF but instead chose to reassure investors even before the election that a Kim Dae-jung government would faithfully implement the IMF agreement.

---

13. As already noted, this division was and is the legacy of military rule that favored the southeast of the country and brutally suppressed Gwangju demonstrations in the southwest in 1980. Seoul was more evenly divided, with Kim Dae-jung receiving a modest 4 percent majority. But then Seoul was mainly made up of migrants from various other parts of the country. See Table 2.4.

Kim Dae-jung, unlike his predecessors, had a long history of opposition to the chaebol. This dated from the 1970s when he offered his vision of a "mass participatory economy" as an alternative to Park Chung Hee's economic model (Rhyu and Kim 2013). His government now sought to carry out structural reform in the financial, corporate, labor, and public sectors. While this reform effort preoccupied the government for the first few years, Kim did not neglect the other progressive issues on which he had campaigned—an agenda known as workfare and, alternatively, as productive welfare. The National Basic Livelihood Security Act was enacted in September 1999 and became effective in October 2000, less than three years after the presidential election. The Kim government also made massive investments in information technology and promoted the development of venture firms in an effort to accelerate Korea's transition to a knowledge-based economy.

By the end of third quarter of 1998, the worst of the crisis had passed. The current account moved into surplus and stability returned to financial markets. The rebound was as dramatic as the earlier collapse: GDP grew by 9 percent in 1999 and 8 percent in 2000.

The Kim Dae-jung government had an opportunity to create an extensive economic-policy legacy thanks to the crisis and the response it required. Kim's government altered the makeup of the ruling elite, which had long been dominated by the Gyeongsang provinces, by appointing to senior posts individuals from the Jeolla provinces.[14] It adopted structural-reform and knowledge-economy agendas to make Korea a much more efficient, resilient, and innovative economy. And it established the foundation for productive welfare (workfare).

In addition, the Kim Dae-jung government introduced a corporatist approach to managing industrial relations by establishing a tripartite commission intended to foster industrial peace and mobilize societal support for economic reform.[15] When the commission was inaugurated in early

---

14. Park Chung Hee and Chun Doo Hwan did not completely ignore the Jeolla provinces. They appointed a number of technocrats from the region to top posts. With only a few exceptions, however, they did not make available real positions of power (military, police, intelligence, legal prosecution, and finance) to people from the Jeolla region.

15. The demand for labor participation has led to the institutionalization of a large number of tripartite initiatives involving labor, management, and government in East Asia, and the crisis appears to have given these initiatives a new impetus. Campbell

1998, hopes were high that it would provide a basis for agreement between labor and management on how to share the burden of restructuring. In its first year, the commission was successful in eliciting labor support for a restructuring program that entailed layoffs in exchange for improved workers' rights and social security. But a year later, when the economy began to recover, the two labor federations represented on the commission grew restless and opposed further initiatives along these lines. When their demands for wage hikes were not met, one of them withdrew from the commission.[16]

Although the tripartite commission continues to meet, there is little sign that it will evolve into a mechanism for achieving consensus on economic and social policy issues in the manner of similar bodies in Europe. Whereas European countries have long histories of tripartite cooperation, often tracing to the 1930s and earlier, Korea has no such tradition. Workers' organizations in Korea are young and have had little opportunity to contribute to the formulation of economic and social policies at the national level. Government and management representatives, unaccustomed to dealing with unions as equals, find it difficult to conduct productive discussions at commission meetings.

Finally there is the fact that the two union federations participating on the commission represent only a small segment of the labor force. That so many workers are left out robs the process of legitimacy. The formation of economy- and industry-wide unions, which might have addressed this problem, was discouraged for many years. Industry-wide labor unions existed but did not obtain legal status until 1997. Even now labor laws do not allow industry-wide unions to engage in collective bargaining or to stage strikes (only firm-level unions are authorized to negotiate wages, benefits, and working conditions). These restrictions reflect concern that industry-wide unions would become too powerful politically if they were allowed to engage in collective bargaining. As a result, only loosely structured federations of enterprise unions have represented labor on the tripartite commission. These federations are unable to control the members

---

(1999) argues that the Korean experience with its tripartite approach, which has been most extensive and influential in East Asia, is evidence that better social dialogue leads to better economic performance.

16. Although that labor federation subsequently returned, the work of the commission continued to be stalled by one dispute after another.

of company unions, owing to the absence of consultation mechanisms at the industry and regional levels. This, in turn, limits their ability to enforce policy decisions made by the commission, further eroding the body's effectiveness.

That members of the tripartite commission were nonetheless able to reach a consensus at first reflected the special circumstances of the time. Korea was experiencing an unprecedented crisis; commission members had to hang together or they would hang separately. But once a semblance of normalcy was restored, the commission became just another outlet for airing long-standing grievances.[17] A further development during the Kim presidency was the declining influence of the chaebol, at least for the time being. Having been burned by the crisis, many chaebol now hesitated to take risks. They reduced their debt/equity ratios and accumulated cash reserves, which meant they were no longer forced to rely on government support to the same extent as before. Some established footholds in China, transforming themselves into multinationals. Still and all, the chaebol remained influential and deeply interested in national politics. This would continue to have important implications as Korean politics and policy evolved.

The outcry over corruption that had tarnished the image and tainted the credibility of the Kim Young-sam government should have been a warning that the public would no longer tolerate such practices. If so, it fell on deaf ears in the Kim Dae-jung years. Although Kim affirmed his determination to root out corruption, he could not keep his political partners out of trouble. Many of his political associates, including his sons, were implicated in cases of influence peddling and bribery. Some were prosecuted and sentenced to prison. This suggests that it was not the progressive orientation of the new regime but political democratization and economic globalization, with the associated pressures to improve management and financing practices, that were mainly responsible for rendering the chaebol more transparent and accountable and for freeing up space for other interest groups to shape public policy. In particular, nongovernmental organizations such as People's Solidarity

---

17. The tripartite approach revealed itself to be ineffective during the subsequent Roh Moo-hyun administration and did little to reduce labor-management strife, even though that administration came to office as a champion of labor rights. See Y. C. Park (2006).

for Participatory Democracy (PSPD) and Citizens' Coalition for Economic Justice (CCEJ) became increasingly influential in setting the reform agenda.

Roh Moo-hyun: Continuity or Change?

The Kim Dae-jung government, even as it was preoccupied with recovery and corporate restructuring, succeeded in strengthening the social safety net and introducing productive welfare. The election of Roh Moo-hyun as president in 2002 meant that the progressive orientation in economic policy would continue.

Roh was born into a poor family in the South Gyeongsang region. Although he did not receive a formal university education, he passed the prestigious national bar examination and became a human rights lawyer in Busan in the early 1980s. He initially supported Kim Young-sam, a prodemocracy politician also from the South Gyeongsang region, and became a rising star in the National Assembly after the parliamentary election in 1988. But when Kim agreed to the three-party merger with former military generals in January 1990, Roh criticized him for betraying his supporters and tried to chart an independent course with other progressive politicians from the same region. Voters in Busan turned their back on Roh, however, and elected a conservative candidate endorsed by Kim Young-sam in the next parliamentary election. Roh spent several years in the political wilderness and then joined forces with Kim Dae-jung, who was from the Jeolla region and had competed with Kim Young-sam for leadership in the prodemocracy camp since the 1970s. The bitter rivalry between the two Kims split the prodemocracy vote in 1987 and, at least for Kim Young-sam, provided a justification for the three-party merger in 1990. Kim Young-sam's victory in the 1992 presidential election seemed to validate his decision, but it also had the effect of aggravating regionalism in Korean politics.

In 2002 Roh successfully campaigned as the presidential candidate of the Millennium Democratic Party (MDP), which had been created by Kim Dae-jung and was dominated by politicians from the Jeolla region. He ran as a progressive candidate who could resolve the problem of regionalism. He won the election by securing the support of the voters of Jeolla and Chungcheong and of the progressive camp, as well as a sizable fraction of voters in the Gyeongsang region. Although the vote difference between the two major candidates was only 2.3 percent, regional disparities differed significantly from those in the 1997 elections. In 1997 Kim Dae-jung had received only 13.2 percent of the votes in the Gyeongsang region. In 2002 Roh almost doubled the vote share and received 25.5 percent in the Gyeongsang region. He won in every province except for Gyeongsang and Gangwon, a sparsely populated, traditionally conservative province bordering North Korea. Unlike the two Kims in 1992 and 1997, Roh won the election without having to form a coalition with conservatives (Table 2.5).[18]

Although Roh won the election as the candidate of the MDP, as a progressive politician from the Gyeongsang region he did not have a strong power base within the party. After the election, he distanced himself from the ruling party, which he felt was dominated by politicians from the Jeolla region. He wanted to set up his own political party and establish a power base in his home region of Gyeongsang, which had a relatively large share of conservative voters. Instead of remaking the MDP to strengthen his position within the party, Roh decided to support a new progressive faction, the Uri Party.[19] The Uri Party had been formed by Roh's close political associates from the Gyeongsang region who believed that it would be impossible to win National Assembly seats in the region under the banner of the MDP and by junior members of the MDP who were impatient with traditionally minded politicians within the party. Although some senior members of the MDP who had actively supported Roh during the 2002 election requested a meeting, the president refused to see them and left the party instead. His defection turned some of his most fervent supporters into his strongest critics.

Roh embroiled himself in further controversy by endorsing candidates of the Uri Party in the National Assembly elections in April 2004. This

---

18. There were only two major candidates in the 2002 election and three in the 1997 election, so the results are not strictly comparable. In 1997 Rhee In-je, who had bolted from the conservative ruling party, received 4.9 million votes out of 26.0 million. The winning margin for Kim Dae-jung over Lee Hoi Chang in that election was 1.0 million votes. In 2002 Roh Moo-hyun defeated Lee by a margin of 0.7 million out of 24.8 million votes cast. In other words, although Kim had a larger margin in 1997 than Roh in 2002, Kim could have lost the election had it not been for his coalition with Kim Jong Pil and Rhee's decision to run as an independent candidate.

19. Yeolin Uri Party, the full name of the Uri Party, literally means Our Open Party, reflecting the party's emphasis on participatory democracy.

violated a constitutional provision barring a sitting president from campaigning for candidates for national or regional office and made him a target of the conservative Grand National Party and the remaining MDP, which together had more than two-thirds of the seats in the National Assembly.

Roh was impeached by the assembly in March 2004. The impeachment motion provoked widespread public anger against the Grand National and Millennium Democratic Parties, which were perceived as using a minor infraction, Roh's endorsement of assembly candidates, in an effort to unseat the elected government. The backlash led to a landslide win for the Uri Party in the National Assembly. A month after the election, the constitutional court reversed the assembly's impeachment motion, reinstating President Roh, who promptly joined the Uri Party.[20]

The MDP, bitter in defeat, hardened its opposition to Roh. Although progressive voters in Jeolla and other regions supported the Uri Party in the National Assembly elections, they were soon alienated by Roh's repeated attempts to build his power base by appealing to the conservative Gyeongsang region. Ironically, the presidential candidate who had pledged to resolve the problem of regionalism and won in almost every province put his regional identification ahead of political orientation. His actions generated resentment and divided the progressive camp. The conservative Grand National Party, for its part, felt that it had to appeal to its own base in order to consolidate its position, and fought tooth and nail to block Roh's legislative agenda.

During the presidential campaign, Roh pledged that he would relocate the capital to what would be called the city of Sejong, 150 kilometers south of Seoul, with the goal of achieving more regionally balanced development while also appealing to voters in the Chungcheong region. In December 2003, four months before parliamentary elections, the National Assembly passed a special law to establish the new administrative capital in Sejong. Some opinion leaders opposed this plan because of its high cost and inefficiencies and issued a constitutional challenge. In October 2004 the constitutional court ruled that Seoul is the capital of Korea by unwritten, "conventional constitution," and that relocating it would require

---

20. For the causes and constitutional implications of the impeachment, see Y. Lee (2005).

Table 2.5. Presidential Election Results by Region, 2002–2012

		Total	Seoul	Gyeonggi	Gangwon	Chungbuk	Chungnam	Jeonbu
2002	Roh Moo-hyun	48%	51%	50%	41%	50%	51%	91
	Lee Hoi-chang	46%	45%	44%	52%	42%	41%	6
	Kwon Young-gil	4%	3%	4%	5%	6%	5%	1
	Other candidates	1%	0%	1%	1%	1%	1%	1
	Invalid ballots	1%	1%	1%	1%	1%	1%	1
	Total votes cast	*24,561,916*	*5,443,990*	*4,798,006*	*762,937*	*725,162*	*909,818*	*1,054,8(*
	Regional share		*22%*	*20%*	*3%*	*3%*	*4%*	*4*
2007	Lee Myung-bak	48%	53%	52%	52%	41%	34%	9
	Chung Dong-young	26%	24%	23%	19%	24%	21%	81
	Lee Hoi-chang	15%	12%	13%	17%	23%	33%	4
	Moon Kook-hyun	6%	7%	7%	6%	6%	5%	3
	Other candidates	4%	3%	4%	6%	5%	7%	3
	Invalid ballots	1%	0%	0%	1%	1%	1%	1
	Total votes cast	*23,612,880*	*5,051,369*	*5,017,407*	*723,503*	*696,096*	*915,505*	*952,4*
	Regional share		*21%*	*21%*	*3%*	*3%*	*4%*	*4*
2012	Park Geun-hye	51%	48%	50%	62%	56%	56%	13
	Moon Jae-in	48%	51%	49%	37%	43%	43%	86
	Other candidates	0%	0%	0%	0%	1%	1%	1
	Invalid ballots	0%	0%	0%	0%	0%	0%	0
	Total votes cast	*30,594,621*	*6,276,699*	*6,996,723*	*908,254*	*922,053*	*1,162,936*	*1,136,5.*
	Regional share		*21%*	*23%*	*3%*	*3%*	*4%*	*4*

Source: Republic of Korea National Election Commission. *(contin*
Note: Italicized figures show total votes cast in absolute-value terms and regional shares of total votes cast. Korean r gions are also known by their alternate names and/or spellings: Gyeonggi (Kyonggi), Gangwon (Kangwon), Chungb (North Chungcheong), Chungnam (South Chungcheong), Jeonbuk (North Jeolla or North Cholla), Jeonnam (Sou Jeolla or South Cholla), Gyeongbuk (North Gyeongsang or North Kyongsang), Gyeongnam (South Gyeongsang South Kyongsang), Jeju (Cheju), Busan (Pusan), Daegu (Taegu), Incheon (Inchon), Gwangju (Kwangju), and Daeje (Taejon).

a constitutional amendment, not merely a special law. As a result, a compromise was reached to relocate only some government ministries and public institutions. But, compromise notwithstanding, the decision by the constitutional court weakened the reform capacity of the Roh government. The opposition parties were encouraged by the ruling to block Roh and the Uri Party's other controversial agenda items, which included amending

Table 2.5. (Continued)

eonnam	Gyeongbuk	Gyeongnam	Jeju	Busan	Daegu	Incheon	Gwangju	Daejeon	Ulsan	Sejong
92%	21%	27%	55%	30%	19%	49%	95%	55%	35%	
5%	72%	67%	39%	66%	77%	44%	4%	40%	52%	
1%	4%	5%	3%	3%	3%	5%	1%	4%	11%	
1%	1%	0%	1%	0%	0%	1%	0%	1%	0%	
1%	2%	1%	1%	1%	1%	1%	1%	1%	1%	
146,320	1,437,938	1,604,744	264,799	1,969,093	1,288,909	1,227,816	751,416	669,846	506,322	
5%	6%	7%	1%	8%	5%	5%	3%	3%	2%	
9%	72%	54%	38%	58%	69%	49%	9%	36%	54%	
78%	7%	12%	32%	13%	6%	24%	80%	23%	14%	
4%	14%	21%	15%	20%	18%	15%	3%	29%	17%	
3%	3%	5%	8%	5%	4%	7%	5%	7%	5%	
5%	4%	6%	6%	4%	3%	5%	3%	4%	9%	
1%	1%	1%	1%	0%	0%	0%	0%	0%	1%	
962,851	1,424,472	1,533,330	249,522	1,759,252	1,263,678	1,205,357	661,552	677,948	518,586	
4%	6%	6%	1%	7%	5%	5%	3%	3%	2%	
10%	80%	63%	50%	60%	80%	51%	8%	50%	60%	52%
89%	19%	36%	49%	40%	19%	48%	92%	50%	40%	47%
1%	1%	1%	1%	0%	0%	0%	0%	0%	0%	0%
1%	1%	1%	0%	0%	0%	0%	0%	0%	0%	0%
162,959	1,701,511	1,994,771	329,335	2,213,405	1,581,840	1,652,966	895,586	901,878	692,433	64,697
4%	6%	7%	1%	7%	5%	5%	3%	3%	2%	0%

the national security law and reforming the country's private universities and media relations.

Faced with sliding popularity, in the summer of 2005 Roh proposed to form a coalition with the Grand National Party, which had a strong base in the Gyeongsang region. This was widely seen as a betrayal of his progressive supporters, especially those in the Jeolla region who had supported him in 2002 during the presidential election and through the impeachment crisis in 2004. Roh suffered a further setback when the party rebuffed his proposal.

In his fourth year, Roh attempted to reverse his decline in popularity by negotiating a free-trade agreement (FTA) with the United States. He did so in response to guidance from advisors, many of them former officials in economic ministries, who convinced him of the agreement's strategic importance as a device for repairing the falling out with the United States that had occurred earlier in his term. The FTA was pursued over protests from the same progressive constituency on which Roh depended for support. He nonetheless succeeded in pushing negotiations forward, although it was not until 2011 that the pact was finally ratified by the U.S. Congress and the Korean National Assembly.

During his presidential campaign, Roh had accused the opposition of graft and excessively close ties with the chaebol. He vowed to root out illegal contributions to politicians and political parties. According to Transparency International, a nongovernmental organization (NGO) that monitors corruption in areas of international development, the Roh government achieved some improvement in the situation (Figure 2.1). Although chaebol were periodically accused of making illegal campaign contributions, they at least grew more discreet. While certain of Roh's family members were implicated in taking illegal donations from business supporters, there is no evidence that the president or his political associates took illegal contributions themselves. The Roh government was clean by Korean standards. It succeeded in keeping the large business groups at arm's length and further weakening the collusive relationship between the government and the chaebol.

The other change resulting from the elections that brought Roh Moo-hyun and the progressive party to power was generational. The first fifteen years of democratic rule had been dominated by a generation of leaders (among others, the three Kims and Roh Tae-woo) who had lived through the Korean War. Political parties had often been little more than the personal vehicles of these individuals. The election of Roh Moo-hyun marked the political coming of age of a population among whom fewer than 20 percent had any experience of war.[21] It was also a population that

---

21. As of 2010, the share of the population that was over eight years old at the end of the Korean War had fallen further, to 12 percent.

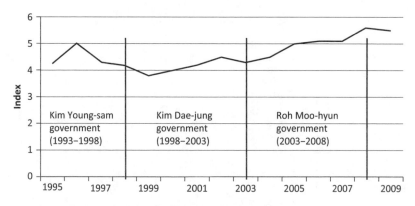

Figure 2.1. Corruption Perceptions Index for South Korea

The Corruption Perceptions Index measures perceived public-sector corruption on a scale from 0 (perceived as highly corrupt) to 10 (perceived to have low levels of corruption).
Source: Transparency International (2009).

appeared, at least initially, to have a less negative view of North Korea. Born in the 1960s and coming of age in the 1980s, the generation that benefited from Korea's industrialization and led its democratization was the driving force for Roh's election. Voters in their thirties overwhelmingly supported Roh Moo-hyun (59.3 percent) over his conservative rival, Lee Hoi-chang (34.2 percent). Voters aged 19 to 29 supported Roh over Lee by 59.0 percent to 34.9 percent (Table 2.6). Although Lee received strong support from voters aged 50 and above, he could not overcome the younger voters' support for Roh. Whether this generation will continue to hold the views of its youth in coming years remains to be seen, but the election marked a shift in emphasis from leaders' personalities to parties and politics based more on ideology and interests.

The Return of Conservative Government and Response to the Global Crisis

Dissatisfaction with the nation's economic performance mounted toward the end of Roh's five-year term. The government appeared incapable of restoring the pre-crisis growth and investment rates to which Koreans had grown accustomed. Even though the pre-crisis growth rate had been higher than justified by underlying fundamentals and had set the stage for the 1997 crisis, voters still yearned for a return of rapid growth. The Roh government had raised taxes on real estate ownership, transfers, and

Table 2.6. Presidential Election Results by Age Group, Based on Exit Polls, 2012 versus 2002

	2012 election (voters: 40,507,842)					2002 election (voters: 34,991,529)					2012 v. 2002
Age group	Voter share (%)	Voting rate (%)	Park support (%) (conservative)	Moon support (%) (progressive)	Share gap[a]	Voter share (%)	Voting rate (%)	Lee support (%) (conservative)	Roh support (%) (progressive)	Share gap[a]	
19–29	18.1	65.2	33.7	65.8	−3.8	23.2	56.5	34.9	59.0	−3.2	−0.6
30–39	20.1	72.5	33.1	66.5	−4.9	25.1	67.4	34.2	59.3	−4.3	−0.6
40–49	21.8	78.7	44.1	55.6	−2.0	22.4	76.3	47.9	48.1	0.0	−1.9
50–59	19.2	89.9	62.5	37.4	4.3	12.9	83.7	57.9	40.1	1.9	2.4
60 and older	20.8	78.8	72.3	27.5	7.3	16.4	78.7	63.5	34.9	3.7	3.7
Total	100.0	75.8	50.1	48.9	1.0	100.0	70.8	46.6	49.2	−1.8	2.9

Source: Korea Broadcasting System (KBS) exit polls (2002) and KBS–Munhwa Broadcasting Corporation (MBC)–Seoul Broadcasting System (SBS) joint exit polls (2012).

[a] Share gap = voter share × voting rate × (conservative support − progressive support).

transactions to squelch asset market speculation, alienating property owners. Although these tax measures, together with debt-to-income and loan-to-value regulations, had helped to cool an overheated property market and spared Korea another crisis, the rich and not-so-rich who believed they would benefit from a real estate boom voiced objections. Many of the progressive political reforms promised by the Roh government were put off or cast aside, with the National Assembly and the administration unable to agree even on limited measures. The economy's perceived disappointing performance was blamed on the government's incoherent policies.

Against this backdrop, the conservative party candidate Lee Myung-bak handily won the election in 2007. Lee received 48 percent of the vote, while a former candidate of the conservatives now running as an independent, Lee Hoi-chang, received another 15 percent. The progressive parties together received 36 percent, or a little more than a third of the votes cast. Lee Myung-bak won in every region except for the Jeolla provinces and Gwangju (see Table 2.5). The conservative parties also won 185 of 299 seats in the National Assembly elections of April 2008, giving the new ruling party, the Grand National Party, a slight majority on its own (153 seats).

Whatever mandate the presidential and National Assembly elections might have produced was then overwhelmed by other events. In May 2008 President Lee made a mistake by deciding, without adequately preparing public opinion, to open the Korean market to U.S. beef, raising great public concern over exposure to mad cow disease. This led to protests by civic organizations aligned with the earlier Roh government, the largest anti-government protests in twenty years.[22] Protesters complained that the beef-import deal had been rushed through to meet the schedule for Lee's visit to the United States, and that political calculations had been allowed to overshadow concern for the health and well-being of the citizenry. Public anger ran even higher when the government was found to have made technical errors in its negotiations with the United States. To appease the protesters and minimize political fallout, Lee fired the aides responsible for mismanaging the beef-import issue.

---

22. No case of mad cow disease in humans has been linked to consumption of U.S. beef, but U.S. beef imports had been a contentious issue in South Korea–United States relations since the closure of the South Korean market to U.S. imports after the discovery of a U.S. case of bovine spongiform encephalopathy in 2003.

The protest organizers had a point, but they also had a broader agenda. In mobilizing mass opposition to the government, they were trying to block other policies, such as privatization of state-owned enterprises, the Korea-U.S. FTA, the Grand Korean Waterway (also known as the Grand Canal Project), educational reform, and a variety of other probusiness policies they felt would aggravate economic and social disparities. The "beef over beef" weakened the government's hand. Although the Lee government eventually recovered from the nationwide outcry against beef imports, the protest indicated that the progressives had created a large power base during previous administrations. Despite the fact that the political swing to the right had also given a majority of seats in the National Assembly to Lee's conservative party, the new government was incapable of capitalizing on its majority. Opposition parties were not disposed to support the new government's policy agenda, and Lee's own party was divided between two factions, one led by the president, the other by a former party head, Park Geun-hye, Park Chung Hee's eldest daughter.

The first thing to go was the "747" pledge (a pledge to achieve 7 percent growth and a per capita income of $40,000, and to become the seventh largest economy in the world), Lee's campaign promise to restore the high growth of the pre-crisis years. The 747 pledge was abandoned not simply because Korea was politically polarized and fractured but also because even members of the ruling party thought it was unrealistic. Then, faced with opposition from environmental and religious groups, the Grand Korean Waterway had to be repackaged into the more modest Four River Restoration project.[23]

In 2007, with the economy expanding at an annual rate of 5 percent, it had looked as if Korea were set for robust growth. The current account was in surplus. The won was strong. The central bank had accumulated $260 billion in foreign exchange reserves. So, contrary to popular sentiment, the Roh government's economic policy might not have been a failure. Its earlier

---

23. According to an investigation by the Board of Audit and Inspection in 2013, the Lee government carried out the Four River Restoration project in such a way that the Grand Korean Waterway could be readily revived if political conditions turn favorable again. Riverbeds were dug up at a depth of 6 meters (approximately 20 feet) to allow the passage of large ships, even though this could distort water flows between main rivers and tributaries. The Lee government also championed low-carbon green growth as a new development paradigm and justified the Four River Restoration project as a part of that effort.

efforts to invest in information technology now seemed to be paying off, as Korean firms moved increasingly into the production and export of information technology–related goods. The chaebol had become leaner and savvier about marketing their products to foreign consumers. The strong growth of China, an important trading partner and source of demand for Korean exports of capital goods, also worked in the economy's favor.

Then, however, the roof fell in. Following the failure of the international investment banking firm Lehman Brothers in September 2008 and the subsequent global flight from financial risk, foreign investors liquidated their positions in Korean markets. The Bank of Korea saw its foreign reserves fall by $60 billion as it intervened to support the Korean won and provide emergency liquidity to Korean banks and markets. Not only financial markets but also exports plummeted. To the disappointment of policymakers, the financial deregulation and more flexible exchange rate nurtured for more than a decade did not prevent financial instability and a disruptive recession.

This time a solution was found not through the IMF, as in 1997–1998, but through the U.S. Federal Reserve, which extended a $30 billion currency swap to the Bank of Korea. The swap was perceived by the market as a commitment by the United States to prevent the collapse of Korea's financial system. The Lee government also took steps to stabilize the economy by enacting a fiscal stimulus in concert with other Group of Twenty (G20) countries. Through this combination of policies, a full-scale crisis was averted. Not that a slowdown was avoided: Korean growth slumped to 2 percent in 2008 and then to 0.3 percent in 2009.

But even before the eruption of the crisis, market orientation and opening had failed to live up to expectations in the eyes of the reforms' detractors. Growth had hovered at just 4 to 5 percent, significantly below President Lee's initial pledge of 7 percent and far lower than in the miracle years. Whether this slower growth was the new norm for what was now a more mature economy or a sign of economic underperformance is disputed; we take this up in Chapter 3. But either way, it was a political problem.

The Rise of Populist Politics

The global recession contributed to a shift toward populism with major impacts on both the opposition Democratic Party and the ruling conservative Grand National Party.[24] As the *JoongAng Daily* put it, "The whole country is irrevocably mired in an unprecedented typhoon of populism amid the deepening polarization of the general population."[25]

Behind the populist surge was widespread discontent with the unequal distribution of income and wealth.[26] During the 2007 presidential campaign, Grand National Party candidate Lee Myung-bak had pledged that his administration would bring the economy back onto to a path of 7 percent growth and create three million new jobs, and also achieve more equality of income distribution through economic growth.[27] Not only did the Lee government fail to keep those promises, but its tenure also saw stagnant real wages in manufacturing that resulted in a further decline in distributive equity. Growing dissatisfaction with perceived poor economic performance and with the government's ideological vacillation alienated conservative voters, to say nothing of progressives; together they dealt a severe blow to the Grand National Party in local elections held in June 2010.

The Democratic Party, in part because of the reception of its more populist agenda—advocacy of free lunches for all students at elementary, middle, and high schools, for example—was the winner in local elections. In response, the Lee government moved to the center-left of the policy spectrum, announcing a "fair society initiative" emphasizing shared growth between large industrial groups and their small and medium-size subcontractors. It created a Presidential Commission on Shared Growth,

---

24. While populism generally connotes a political philosophy and ideas that are intended to represent the needs and wishes of ordinary people—a definition that is not necessarily negative and can be understood as the opposite of elitism—in Korean politics the word "populism" carries a strong negative connotation of catering to popular demands with little concern for fiscal sustainability.

25. This was on 27 June 2011.

26. The Gini coefficient for urban households rose from 0.260 in 1997 to 0.325 in 2008, and the proportion of the middle-income class shrank to 66.7 percent in 2009 from almost 70 percent in the early 1990s. For more on distribution see Chapter 6.

27. As it turned out, the pledge was no more than a device for distancing Lee from the Roh Moo-hyun government, which was perceived as favoring a populist ideology with more emphasis on distribution than growth. Interestingly, during the election campaign of 2002, Roh had also given voters assurances that he would raise the annual growth rate to 7 percent and create 2.5 million new jobs during his presidency. Both Lee and Roh apparently felt that they had to accommodate popular expectations for high growth, which in turn were based on Korea's earlier exceptional performance as an "economic miracle."

whose chairman proposed profit sharing as a means of leveling the income distribution. (His proposal was dismissed by the business community as an unrealistic populist scheme.)

In December 2010 the Seoul metropolitan city council, dominated by Democratic Party members, passed an ordinance and budget bill for a free school-lunch program for all students at elementary schools regardless of financial status, over the objection of the city's mayor and the Grand National Party. This was followed in early 2011 by a Democratic Party proposal, as part of its campaign for the National Assembly, for far-reaching welfare reforms offering free medical care, free child care, free school meals, and cuts in college tuition.[28] The ruling party had apparently come to the conclusion that the Democratic Party's welfare initiatives for low-income families played a critical role in the opposition's overwhelming victory in the local elections. Therefore, in May 2011 the newly elected Grand National Party floor leader proposed to cut college tuition by half.[29] In addition, the party created expectations that it would support a plan to cover preschool expenses for five-year-olds by 2016.

With the mounting discontent caused by the perceived hollowing out of the middle class, and distributive conditions continuing to deteriorate, the Lee Myung-bak government moved further toward the center-left of the ideological spectrum. Claiming that Korea could no longer blindly follow the model of Western capitalism, Lee offered "ecosystemic development" as a new approach "that creates jobs, reduces income gaps and preserves the environment."[30] "What is now being demanded," the president

---

28. The party's own estimates put the annual cost of the new program at about 17 trillion won, but the Health Ministry forecast was that free medical care alone would require an additional 30 trillion won per year.

29. At the end of 2010 more than 3.6 million students were enrolled at 411 universities and colleges across the country. Since 2004 more than 80 percent of high school graduates entered various colleges and universities, compared with an average of 30 percent for the European members of the OECD. Tuition fees increased steeply after the Roh Tae-woo government lifted the regulation on tuition fees at private universities and colleges in 1989. College tuition rose by double digits each year from 1990 to 1996, until the Asian economic crisis of 1997–1998 moderated the increases. Between 2001 and 2010 college tuition rose by 82 percent, while the consumer price index (CPI) climbed by 31 percent. Interestingly, Lee Myung-bak and the Grand National Party had also called for a 50 percent reduction in college tuition during the presidential election campaign of 2007.

30. See President Lee Myung-bak's Liberation Day national address in August 2011.

argued, "is a new model of the market economy that evolves from greedy management to ethical management; from the freedom of capital to the responsibility of capital; and from the vicious circle of the rich getting richer and the poor getting poorer to mutual prosperity." This new model, such as it was, was premised on the notion that the Anglo-American paradigm was no longer an appropriate framework for economic governance. It implied that the ills of the Korean economy could be cured if government, reversing the thrust of Grand National Party policy in previous years, was again allowed to play a larger role in resource allocation.[31]

This reversal did not satisfy an increasingly hostile electorate. In the by-election for mayor of Seoul in October 2011, the Grand National Party candidate lost by a large margin to the civic activist Park Won-soon, former leader of People's Solidarity for Participatory Democracy and an independent candidate without previous electoral experience, who had joined the Democratic Party just before the mayoral election.[32] Analysts concluded that the public was repudiating the policies of the Lee administration, which had failed to deal with the high rate of joblessness among younger voters, and those voters were understandably venting their anger against establishment parties and politicians.

The establishment parties scrambled to win back the confidence of voters and to hold on to their political power base. In November 2011 the main opposition, the Democratic Party, merged with the Citizen Integration Party and the Korean Federation of Trade Unions to broaden its constituency. The conservative Grand National Party was reorganized under the leadership of Park Geun-hye and given a new name, the New

---

31. This assessment is also reflected in the popularity of a recent book on capitalism by Chang (2010), which argues that there is no such thing as a free market—that individuals are not smart enough to leave things to the market—and that governments can pick winners, sometimes spectacularly well. The popularity of this book, especially among young voters, may reflect the distrust of the Lee government's conservative market-oriented policies more than agreement about its content.

32. During the election campaign, Ahn Cheol-Soo, a medical doctor by training and a successful maker of antivirus software who had no political background or experience in public administration, burst onto the national political stage, capturing the imagination of many voters. Ahn threw his support behind Park Won-soon, and it is widely believed that his backing was critical to Park's electoral success. Ahn emerged as a role model for many young Koreans, making him a potential presidential candidate. The popularity of Ahn, many analysts pointed out, rested on the voters' negative views of existing political parties and establishment politicians.

Frontier Party. Adopting the "economic democratization" agenda as her own, Park led the transformation of the party, changing its logo color from blue to red, a taboo color that had long been associated with communism. She spoke out against the chaebol's intrusion into bakeries and other small businesses and supported strengthening social welfare and education programs. Her efforts paid off in parliamentary elections in April 2012, as the New Frontier Party won 152 out of 300 seats, less than six months after its devastating defeat in the Seoul mayoral election.

For the presidential election in December 2012, Park Geun-hye further distanced herself from Lee Myung-bak and redoubled her effort to address popular concerns about socioeconomic disparities and insecurities. She pledged to reduce household expenses for education by transforming primary schools into all-day schools, offering universal high school education, and halving college tuition by 2014 (with differentiated support based on income level). She even went so far as to pledge a basic pension "demo-grant" of 200,000 won (around US$180) per month for anyone aged 65 and above, regardless of income. She thereby managed to outmaneuver the opposition candidate, Moon Jae-in, who had served as chief of staff to President Roh Moo-hyun.

In a closely contested election, Park defeated Moon by 51 percent to 48 percent. She won in every region except for Seoul, Gwangju, and the Jeolla provinces (see Table 2.5). As in 2002 and 2007, the winning candidate thus prevailed in almost every region. This hinted that traditional regional cleavages were giving way to demographically structured policy preferences.[33] Compared with 2002, generational disparities in voting patterns were greater. Voters age 39 and under strongly voted for Moon, whereas voters aged 50 and above overwhelmingly voted for Park. At the same time, voters in their fifties in 2012, who had been split in 2002, strongly supported the conservative candidate, while voters in their thirties in 2012, who had voted progressive as twenty-somethings in 2002, became even more progressive in 2012 (see Table 2.6).

---

33. The share of voters age 50 and older increased from 27.3 percent in 2002 to 40.0 percent in 2012. Older voters were much more enthusiastic about voting than younger voters in 2012, who themselves had a higher voting rate than their counterparts in 2002. While the voting rate for those in their thirties rose from 67.4 percent in 2002 to 72.5 percent in 2012, the voting rate for those in their fifties increased from 83.7 percent to 89.9 percent.

Future governments, regardless of their complexion, will undoubtedly seek to promote job creation, expand welfare programs, tinker with industrial policy, and pursue chaebol reform. But in an economy with a large open financial sector, a populist approach could easily backfire if it is perceived as causing slower growth and larger fiscal and current account deficits. A significant deterioration in macroeconomic indicators could unsettle foreign lenders and investors, thereby pushing up the cost of external borrowing, depressing domestic equity valuations, and placing growth and financial stability at risk. Given Korea's history of financial crises, this is likely to restrain the ambitions of even the most left-leaning government.[34]

The State of Play

The decision to hold free elections in 1987 set in motion a fundamental shift in the balance of political power among major groups in Korean society. It inaugurated a process that is still playing out.

Some aspects of this process have proceeded more quickly than others. The influence of the military in politics disappeared as soon as civilian candidates began winning presidential elections (although the courage required for Kim Young-sam to disband the army's Hanahoi faction in 1993 and arrest Roh Tae-woo and Chun Doo Hwan in 1995 should not be minimized). In contrast, the power of the chaebol has waxed and waned. The considerable expense of campaigning for the presidency and National Assembly enhanced chaebol influence, since the business groups were able to mobilize the largest sums to support favored candidates. But insofar as those methods of funding were illegitimate, if not actually illegal, the voting public demanded accountability. This led ultimately to the weakening of money politics and chaebol influence in a setting of growing media and civil-society activism.

The formation of a progressive coalition providing an organized alternative to the conservative politicians and elites that had long dominated Korean politics was a development of considerable significance. This coalition contributed to the election of Kim Dae-jung but achieved its greatest

---

34. In addition, any new government will inherit the current government's plans to negotiate free-trade agreements with China, Japan, and other important trading partners. Given Korean producers' dependence on exports, these commitments to further market liberalization will not be easily abandoned.

strength with the election of Roh Moo-hyun in 2002.[35] While the inability of the Roh government to achieve many of its goals and its tendency to alienate its own supporters brought the conservatives back into power in 2007, the coalition of progressive forces continued to exert substantial influence over the direction of the country. Park Geun-hye had to adopt much of the progressive agenda as her own in order to win the election in 2012.

This shift in the balance of power among major social groups played out against an international background dominated for much of the period by what has been referred to as the Washington Consensus. While deregulation of overregulated markets was helpful, efforts to increase reliance on market forces too often ignored the need for a minimal regulatory framework to establish rules, prevent abuses of market power, and contain threats to financial stability. The major financial crises of 1997–1998 and 2008–2009 came about as a result. The 1997–1998 crisis played an important role in the development of a consensus around policies that began to rein in the power of the chaebol. Time will tell what lessons Korean policymakers and society draw from the 2008–2009 crisis.

Korea's political transition has been exemplary compared with the experience of many other young democracies. Five years after the collapse of the military, civilian rule was firmly established, bringing a professional military into existence. The power of the executive branch was increasingly shared by the legislature, and the judiciary consolidated its independence. The constitutional court's decision on the new administrative capital (the city of Sejong) in 2004 is the most prominent recent evidence that the judiciary has come a long way since the Yushin days, when it was subservient to the executive branch. The media today include both progressive and conservative dailies and broadcast networks, all of which enjoy press freedom and exert political influence. Civic organizations work to shape national priorities and participate in policymaking. The influence of the chaebol has diminished as a result of economic liberalization, the phasing out of industrial policy, scrutiny by public and private watchdog agencies, and public disapproval of collusive relations between government and political parties.

---

35. This was particularly the case after the reaction of the public to the impeachment effort of the National Assembly in 2004.

The resulting changes have moved Korea a substantial distance from the interventionist economic policies of the past. They have done less to build the stable institutional framework required for a well-functioning political and economic system. Although the electoral process has taken root and there have been no attempts to rig elections of the sort witnessed in other countries during their early experience with democracy, the party system remains weak. The legal system has been strengthened and judicial independence has been reinforced, but because the starting point was an unusually weak system, the country has some distance still to go. Whereas NGOs and churches have become more influential, labor unions are better known for their militancy than for their broad-based support or policy leadership. And, as noted earlier, the effort to create a tripartite commission to mediate disputes between labor and management has not worked out as intended.

When a system functions well, the interests constituting a democratic polity are harmonized through the operation of institutions for conflict and risk management. In Korea, reflecting its relatively short history of democratization, institutions for managing social risk remain relatively underdeveloped. The country often lacks the capacity to resolve tensions between those with and without valuable economic skills and mobility, between employers and employees, and between urban and rural interests. While the government has introduced programs for conflict management, their effectiveness remains in doubt. The country's past experience suggests that one of the best remedies for conflict is an effective and consistent macroeconomic policy that ensures a high level of employment, maintains price and financial stability, and creates job opportunities. But this is difficult to guarantee in a globalized world where macroeconomic outcomes are influenced by more than just what happens in Korea itself.

Prior to democratization, opposition parties and dissident groups refused to comply with laws and regulations promulgated by an authoritarian regime that sought to suppress democratic movements. This tradition has persisted. In the National Assembly, dissident members regularly seek to frustrate the will of the majority. If the opposition cannot muster enough votes to block a bill, its members resort to physical means to obstruct the voting process, and if they fail to block legislation, they go to the streets to stage protests. All of this weakens trust in the political system, leading to deeper political divisions and making it harder for politicians to resolve their differences. The situation is symptomatic of the fact that Korea is still a young democracy, even though supposedly mature democracies have problems as well. At the same time, there are important indications that change is under way. Violations of prevailing laws and norms are increasingly reported through websites, blogs, and other Internet-based media. This makes a difference in what has become the most wired country in the world.

Then there is the problem of building stable political parties. Parties have come and gone in South Korea. New parties are established to influence presidential and National Assembly elections and then dissolved or absorbed into other parties once a campaign is over. Most are organized around strong political leaders rather than by individuals with a common ideology or political platform.

An important factor continuing to undermine the formation of a stable polity and political parties dominated by conservatives or progressives, respectively, has been the role of regional divisions, as noted. This reflects the favoritism extended to the Gyeongsang region in the authoritarian period and, insofar as this is the case, it is something that will dissipate only with time. Even today, a quarter of a century after the transition to democracy, the major political parties are still strongly influenced by regional rather than national interests. Although ideological differences are often small, parties have not been able to mediate remaining differences or to offer real public policy alternatives. Instead, advocacy-oriented civic NGOs have had to take on quasi-party functions in representing public interests and dictating policy (S.-J. Lee 2005). This weak party system, together with the routine violation of rules and laws by its members, has undermined the credibility and effectiveness of the National Assembly as an institution for managing social conflict.

A further weakness limiting the effectiveness of the political system is the single-term, five-year presidency, with no vice presidency nor any other mechanism for carrying on the legacy of a government. Governments cannot implement long-term policies because they become lame ducks three years after they are inaugurated, when the next electoral cycle commences. This system also tends to produce ruling-party presidential candidates who try to differentiate themselves from the current president, dividing the ruling party even when it has a parliamentary majority. Every government since 1988, on taking office, has offered its vision of an affluent, stable, and equitable Korean society. This vision is often accompanied by a detailed long-term projection for macroeconomic growth and social development. But to be implemented, these visions have to be shared by future administrations. In practice, new governments regularly disregard the policies of their predecessors, in particular their long-term development strategies, in favor of their own agendas. Since 1988 governments have regularly introduced their own 5-, 10-, and 20-year policy blueprints, but none of these has been implemented, much less completed. As a result, Korea has not been able to adopt consistent long-term plans for regional and rural development, nationwide infrastructure construction, and investment in new industries. Advocates of reforming the electoral system have argued for a two-term presidency with two four-year terms, as in the United States, whereas others favor a parliamentary system like those in Europe. But all such proposals would have to overcome the opposition of the leading political parties and candidates of the moment, which would not be easy.

While there is still much to be done to build more effective political and economic institutions, it is also clear that a great deal has been accomplished. Compared with other countries that have similar initial political conditions, Korea has not done badly in building a stable and democratic society and transforming the way in which it manages internal disputes and conflicts. The priority now should be removing the remaining obstacles to developing institutions that foster continued economic growth, allow for improvements in the social safety net, and encourage healthy democratic political processes.

CHAPTER 3

Perspectives on Growth

Korean economic growth is a study in contrasts. The rate of growth of real GDP was high in the 1987–1996 period, averaging 9 percent, despite the political turbulence accompanying the transition to democracy. The 1997–1998 financial crisis then led to a sharp fall in GDP but was followed by an equally sharp recovery in 1999–2000, when the growth rate returned briefly to 9 percent. From 2001 to 2012, however, growth decelerated to 3.9 percent, less than half the prior pace.[1] In only two years during that time did growth exceed 5 percent.

The evidence shows clearly that Korea's economic growth has slowed; the question is, how to interpret the slowdown? We believe that this slower rate of growth is precisely what one would expect of an increasingly mature economy. As GDP per capita rises and an economy approaches the technological frontier, the era when it is possible to grow rapidly by shifting labor from agriculture to industry, importing technology from abroad, and raising the capital-to-labor ratio from early low levels draws to a close. As a late-developing economy catches up to the technological leaders, in other words, the attainable growth rate falls.[2] Korea's experience since 1987, and specifically the growth slowdown that the country has experienced since the turn of the century, are consistent with this view. The

---

1. As in Chapter 1, we omit the 1997–1998 financial crisis and its immediate aftermath, when growth was volatile and outcomes were unrepresentative of longer-term trends.

2. This is known in the economics literature as the convergence hypothesis. See, e.g., Barro and Sala-i-Martin (1995).

only distinctive aspect of the Korean case is that the slowdown was delayed by an artificial investment boom in the first half of the 1990s and then came on suddenly when the consequences of that unsustainably high investment came home to roost in 1997–1998.

But a second interpretation could be that growth slowed more sharply than necessary because the country experienced an avoidable slump in investment in plant and equipment, research and development, and other determinants of productivity growth, and then the negative effects of that investment slowdown were reinforced by the intensification of foreign competition.[3] Since the crisis, Korean policymakers have sought to keep the current account of the balance of payments in surplus. By definition, this has meant domestic investment rates have been lower than domestic savings; the critics of Korean policy complain that this has worked to unnecessarily slow the rate of growth. In addition, Korea has been subject to increasingly intense competitive pressure from China, Japan, and other regional and extraregional economies. By this interpretation, the reforms of labor and product markets necessary for Korea to compete and for firms to engage in customary levels of investment were pursued with inadequate conviction. The chaebol responded to rising labor costs and opportunities in emerging markets by investing abroad rather than at home. Small and medium-size enterprises, feeling the brunt of Chinese competition, were unable to finance investments in capacity.

Relatively few observers are still of the view that correcting these remaining weaknesses in Korean policies and institutions will allow Korea to enjoy another golden age of near double-digit growth like that experienced in the decades prior to 1997–1998. But with appropriate policy and institutional reforms, it is possible that Korea could do better.

An Overview of Korean Economic Growth

Prior to the recent slowdown, many Koreans had come to regard the third of a century from 1962 through 1996, when the growth rate averaged 9 percent and reached double digits in nine separate years, as the South Korean norm. Only in 1980, owing to the "perfect storm" of the assassination of President Park late the preceding year, a failed harvest, a jump in oil prices, and a global recession, did the economy actually contract.

---

3. See, for instance, Song (2001).

Table 3.1. Comparative Growth Experience: Gross National Income (GNI) Per Capita, 1962–2007

Income classification	Mean growth per year (%)	Volatility (standard deviation) per year (%)	Share of years with positive growth (%)	Average positive growth per year (%)	Average negative growth per year (%)
Countries grouped according to 2008 GNI per capita					
Low income	0.2	6.0	60	3.6	−4.7
Middle income	2.3	5.0	78	4.1	−4.4
High income	3.1	3.6	89	3.9	−3.1
Countries grouped according to 1962 GNI per capita					
Low income	2.0	5.5	72	4.6	−4.3
Middle income	2.1	4.7	79	3.8	−4.5
High income	2.0	2.0	89	2.6	−2.0
Republic of Korea	5.7	3.8	94	6.4	−4.5

Source: Winters, Lim, Hanmer, and Augustin (2010).

Although growth had occasionally fallen as low as 5 or 6 percent, slowdowns of that sort were exceptional and had rarely lasted more than a year. To be sure, Koreans older than 70 could remember the war years, when the country's physical infrastructure was destroyed and incomes barely exceeded subsistence levels, while individuals still older might recall the pre–World War II era when Japan was the main beneficiary of whatever growth occurred.[4] But the post-1961 experience is the norm in the minds of 85 percent or more of the Korean population.[5]

Between 2001 and 2012, in contrast, growth averaged just 3.9 percent, a rate that is entirely respectable for an OECD country but less than half the 9 percent that many Korean observers had come to see as customary. As a way of comparing Korea with the global norm, Table 3.1 summarizes

---

4. According to Suh (1978, 170–171), agriculture, forestry, and fishery production grew annually by 2.1 percent from 1910 to 1940, whereas the mining and manufacturing sector grew at 9.5 percent over the same period. The two sectors taken together (that is, excluding construction, utilities, trade, and services) grew at a rate of 3.2 percent. Overall, per capita commodity production grew annually by 1.6 percent from 1910 to 1940.

5. In 2012 only 12 percent of Korea's population was over the age of 65.

Table 3.2. Savings and Investment in Korea, 1962–1981

	1962–1966	1967–1971	1972–1976	1977–1981	1962–1981
Annual GNP growth	7.9%	9.7%	10.2%	5.7%	8.4%
Investment / GNP	16.3%	25.4%	29.0%	31.0%	25.4%
Domestic savings / GNP	8.0%	15.1%	20.4%	25.5%	17.3%
Foreign savings / GNP	8.6%	10.0%	6.7%	5.6%	7.7%
Foreign savings / investment	52.8%	39.4%	23.1%	18.1%	30.4%

Source: Economic Planning Board (1980, 1988).

the growth experience of low-, middle-, and high-income countries, in 1962 through 2007.

Understanding this slowdown in growth requires, first, an understanding of the high-growth period itself. An initial observation about Korea's economic miracle is that it was not fueled by high levels of saving and investment at the outset. Domestic savings rates remained in the single digits in the first half of the 1960s, the takeoff period. Investment fluctuated in the range of 13 to 15 percent through 1965, and half or more of that investment was financed by foreigners, mainly through foreign aid (Tables 3.2 and 3.3).[6] South Korea had been on the receiving end of foreign capital for a decade and more. Evidently, then, neither savings nor investment was what changed in 1964.[7]

The most dramatic change was, in fact, the rapid growth of exports. Exports at constant prices grew by 35 percent per annum from the end of 1963 to the end of 1969.[8] They fueled faster growth of output and employment. In part the extraordinary growth of exports reflected the fact

---

6. In the first years of the 1960s the savings rate was very low (around 10 percent of GDP) and investment was higher (around 15 percent of GDP in 1962–1965), although that was still far below levels achieved in later years. The gap was filled by foreign capital inflows, mainly but not exclusively in the form of foreign aid. U.S. and United Nations grants accounted for 84 percent of foreign capital flows into Korea in 1962–1965.

7. It was around this period that the United States, in particular, began making noises about winding down its aid to Korea. The predominant form of foreign capital inflow into Korea subsequently shifted from grants to loans, even as Korea's dependence on foreign capital did not change.

8. Economic Planning Board (1980), 15.

Table 3.3. Composition of Foreign Capital Flows into Korea, 1945–1992 (current US$ millions)

	1945–1961	1962–1965	1966–1972	1973–1978	1979–1985	1986–1992
Public loans	5	62	1,130	3,431	10,105	4,688
	(0.1%)	(7.1%)	(26.4%)	(30.6%)	(28.9%)	(15.4%)
Commercial loans		71	1,950	5,858	7,937	5,206
		(8.0%)	(45.6%)	(52.2%)	(22.7%)	(17.1%)
Foreign direct investment		13	227	704	1,157	5,684
		(1.5%)	(5.3%)	(6.3%)	(3.3%)	(18.7%)
Bank loans			205	1,007	11,892	4,318
			(4.8%)	(9.0%)	(34.1%)	(14.2%)
Bonds				219	2,989	5,978
				(1.9%)	(8.6%)	(19.7%)
Bonds (firms)				—	834	4,515
					(2.4%)	(14.9%)
U.S. and United Nations grants	3,117	739	552	—	—	—
	(99.9%)	(83.4%)	(13.0%)			
Reparation grants			211	—	—	—
			(4.8%)			
Total	3,121	886	4,275	11,219	34,914	30,389

Source: Ministry of Finance and Korea Development Bank (1993), 616, 618, 621.

Note: Public loans include concessional loans, but this source does not provide a detailed breakdown. Nor does it separate the grant element in concessional loans that meet the definition of official development assistance (i.e., loans with a grant element of 25 percent or more).

that the starting point was low.[9] But it was also supported by a series of devaluations from January 1961 through May 1964 that allowed Korean products to compete successfully in global markets. The growth of exports was also fostered by tax concessions, import-duty drawbacks, investment subsidies, and preferential access to credit.[10] In the 1960s the government supported any firm that met its export-performance targets. In the 1970s, during the Heavy and Chemical Industry Drive, officials

---

9. Exports in 1962 were valued at only US$54.8 million, or 3 percent of GDP, whereas imports, financed mostly by foreign aid, totaled US$421.8 million.

10. That said, the role of export subsidies should not be exaggerated. According to Frank, Kim, and Westphal (1975), the average effective rate of subsidy on total exports in the second half of the 1960s was basically offset by the degree of currency overvaluation.

still emphasized export performance, now targeted support at particular industries and firms, and also sought to more fully exploit economies of scale.[11]

Economists have criticized these targeted industrial policies as interfering with the market-determined allocation of resources, but there is no question that they delivered results. Gross national product proceeded to grow at 9.5 percent per annum beginning in 1970, before falling in the 1980 recession. Exports, in current U.S. dollars, grew by an astounding 37 percent annually, even faster than in the immediately preceding period. Gross investment as a share of GDP climbed from 17 percent in 1970 to 24 percent in 1976 to 29 percent in 1979.[12]

The 1980s saw changes in economic policy but more of the same in terms of growth, which averaged 8.1 percent from 1981 through 1989.[13] The Chun Doo Hwan government, which took power in a 1980 coup, had two economic goals. One was bringing down inflation, which had run in the 10 to 20 percent range in the 1960s and 1970s and at even higher rates in the aftermath of the two oil shocks. Inflation was successfully reduced from 21 percent in 1981 to 7 percent in 1982 and 3 percent in 1983. The other goal, moving away from policies of industrial targeting and chaebol support toward a market-based system, proved elusive. The implicit guarantees that had been extended to the chaebol in the period of the Heavy and Chemical Industry Drive now proved difficult to revoke. In virtually every case in which major firms experienced difficulties in the 1980s, the government stepped in. "Too big to fail" is not a new problem in Korea, in other words. Leaders also emphasized the need to support new high-tech industries, such as electronics, opening up additional avenues for government involvement. Moving toward a market-based system free of preferences, subsidies, and implicit guarantees proved more easily said than done.

In part, these difficulties reflected the fact that President Chun and his successors found the close relationship between business and government to be an easy path to political fund-raising. South Korea held its

---

11. The importance of economies of scale in period of the Heavy and Chemical Industry Drive is emphasized by Park and Kwon (1995).

12. Economic Planning Board (1988), 53. I. Hwang (1998) emphasizes the role of investment in the Korean growth process.

13. The comparable figure is 9.3 percent if one uses 1980 as the base.

first honestly contested direct election for president in 1987. The run-up to the decision to allow that election saw demonstrations by university students that were also strongly supported by the middle class. Tear gas perfumed the air of Seoul. But even against this volatile political backdrop the economy maintained its rapid pace of expansion.[14] Nor was there a fall in gross domestic investment as a share of GDP, notwithstanding the political uncertainty.[15]

In the late 1980s and even more in the 1990s, the investment share scaled new heights. Gross investment averaged 36 percent of gross national income from 1990 through 1996. The decade prior to the financial crisis is now seen as when the chaebol indulged in all manner of investments, whether economically viable or not. At the same time, signs pointed to the fact that the economy was facing headwinds. Export growth in U.S. dollar terms declined from the heady rates of the 1970s to 15 percent a year in the 1980s and 11 percent in 1990–1996. Slower growth of incomes and profits, combined with high rates of investment, by large firms in particular, meant that the corporate sector became heavily indebted. Whenever something went wrong, highly leveraged corporations were at risk of bankruptcy, an outcome that occurred with growing frequency even prior to the financial crisis.

In retrospect, the main implication of the problems brought to the fore by the financial crisis was that the investment boom of the early 1990s had in fact disguised a secular slowdown to the modest rates of growth typical of a more mature economy. Slower growth, as we shall see, was the new normal. There was no reason to expect a return to the exceptional growth rates of the past.

Understanding the Slowdown

To understand why growth slowed, it is helpful to examine more closely the proximate sources of the earlier rapid growth. For this purpose we rely on the standard growth accounting methodology that separates the sources of growth into the contributions of capital, labor, education, and human capital, and the increase in the productivity of these factors of

---

14. Growth in 1987 actually accelerated further, to 12 percent.

15. As had been the case from the mid-1970s, that investment was now overwhelmingly financed by domestic savings.

Table 3.4. Growth Accounting Decomposition of Aggregate GDP, Excluding Agriculture and Mining, 1971–2005

Year	Aggregate GDP growth rate	Contribution to aggregate GDP					Labor income share
		Capital	Human capital	Employment	Labor hours	TFP	
1971–1979	8.47%	3.54%	0.42%	4.88%	−0.55%	0.17%	0.66
(1971–1982)	(7.44%)	(3.71%)	(0.29%)	(4.02%)	(0.00%)	(−0.58%)	(0.66)
1982–1989	9.48%	3.98%	0.44%	3.85%	−0.84%	2.05%	0.69
1989–1997	7.32%	3.22%	0.41%	2.76%	−0.47%	1.40%	0.74
(1989–1998)	(5.86%)	(3.02%)	(0.54%)	(1.82%)	(−0.58%)	(1.06%)	(0.74)
1998–2005	5.75%	1.61%	0.37%	1.91%	−0.20%	2.06%	0.74
(1999–2005)	(5.29%)	(1.60%)	(0.42%)	(1.91%)	(−0.68%)	(2.04%)	(0.74)
Total period	7.10%	3.15%	0.40%	2.97%	−0.37%	0.94%	0.70

Source: Eichengreen, Perkins, and Shin (2012), 11.

Note: TFP=total factor productivity. The sample period, 1971–2005, is divided into four subsample periods, excluding the crisis years. The results for subsample periods that include the crisis years are also reported, in parentheses. Value added at 2000 year constant prices is obtained from National Accounts, Bank of Korea. Employment is the number of employees, and labor hours are average weekly hours. Data on the number of employees and the weekly hours are taken from Korea's *Annual Report on the Economic Active Population Survey* and the *Yearbook of Labor Statistics* (Geneva: International Labour Organization), respectively. The construction of human capital follows the lifetime-labor-income method of Jorgenson and Fraumeni (1989, 1992a, 1992b). Physical capital stock is net fixed capital stock constructed by Pyo, Chung, and Cho (2007). To construct the income share of the total labor force (i.e., labor income share), we add compensation for self-employed and family workers to that for employees on payroll.

production (total factor productivity, or TFP).[16] Table 3.4 presents this accounting for the period 1971–2005, for the economy minus agricultural and mining—what can be thought of as the modern sector. Table 3.5 presents the same calculations but includes agriculture and mining, thus enabling us to consider a longer period.

Prior to 1998 the growth of the modern sector was driven by the rapid growth of employment, rapid increases in capital, and total factor productivity growth that was sometimes high and at other times more sluggish.[17] The TFP growth came first. Economic reforms, with a special

16. A more detailed discussion of growth accounting and its limitations can be found in the series volume on growth, Eichengreen, Perkins, and Shin (2012).

17. This same emphasis similarly comes through in Piazolo (1995). When we consider the entire economy, including agriculture and mining, the rate of growth of the labor force is somewhat slower (by construction). For the whole economy, the growth of

Table 3.5. Growth Accounting Decomposition of Aggregate GDP, Including Agriculture and Mining, 1964–1979

Year	Aggregate GDP growth rate	Contribution to aggregate GDP				Labor income share
		Capital	Human capital	Employment	TFP	
1964–1966	9.20%	3.87%	0.59%	1.89%	2.84%	0.59
1967–1971	9.54%	7.35%	0.27%	2.10%	−0.18%	0.59
1972–1979	7.93%	3.81%	0.38%	2.41%	1.34%	0.63
Total period	8.67%	4.93%	0.38%	2.22%	1.15%	0.61

Source: Eichengreen, Perkins, and Shin (2012), 11.
Note: TFP = total factor productivity.

emphasis on promoting exports of manufactures and transforming the financial system, caused a jump in productivity. This in turn raised the rate of return to capital, inducing a rise in the rate of investment.

This acceleration in Korea's GDP and productivity growth resulted from the decision of the Park Chung Hee government in the early 1960s to make imported inputs available to domestic producers at international prices (through duty clawbacks) and to promote exports of manufactures. A second set of reforms then ended the financial repression that had hampered the development of banks and the financial system more generally. Banks received additional deposits as a result of their ability to offer higher interest rates, permitting them to provide additional support for investment in industry and foreign trade. That said, saving rose mainly as a result of the rapid rise in household and corporate incomes and the declining dependency ratio, although higher interest rates may have also played a role.

Figure 3.1 shows the savings and investment rates in question. Table 3.6 then reports some estimates of their proximate determinants. It suggests that the savings rate was driven substantially by the high growth of the economy and low old-age and youth-dependency ratios. The same is

---

the labor force is driven mainly by the birth and death rates of the entire population plus the increasing numbers of people who remain in school when they reach the age at which, in the past, they would have entered the labor force. The labor force growth rate for the modern sector alone adds to this increase in the overall growth of the working-age population the shift in labor out of agriculture and into manufacturing and other mainly urban occupations.

Figure 3.1. Gross Investment and Savings, 1982–2010
Source: Bank of Korea, Economic Statistics System (ECOS).

broadly true of investment, which is not surprising given the limited scope for financing current-account deficits and therefore the high correlation of domestic savings and investment.[18] Investment rates rose rapidly, reaching 30 percent of GDP in the late 1970s before falling back as a result of the recession induced by the assassination of President Park, the poor harvest, and the global economic slowdown (the perfect storm already alluded to). The period was dominated by the Heavy and Chemical Industry Drive, which was led by the president's office and financed by government-controlled banks.

Following the 1980 recession, the economy then returned to the 9 percent growth rate of the two preceding decades. The priority became reining in inflation, a goal that was rapidly achieved. The Chun Doo Hwan government then attempted to move away from the highly interventionist

---

18. Since the growth rate has come down and the old-age dependency ratio will continue to rise, Korea's savings rate is likely to come down still further. Much the same will be true of investment.

Table 3.6. Saving and Investment Regressions, Time Fixed Effects

	Saving			Investment		
GDP growth	0.868** [0.104]	0.842** [0.103]	0.846** [0.104]	0.678** [0.077]	0.653** [0.077]	0.655** [0.076]
Lagged GDP growth	0.826** [0.101]	0.799** [0.101]	0.804** [0.102]	0.509** [0.068]	0.492** [0.068]	0.467** [0.068]
Income	0.005 [0.050]	−0.009 [0.049]	−0.009 [0.050]	0.107** [0.034]	0.102** [0.034]	0.092** [0.034]
Income squared	0.002 [0.003]	0.003 [0.003]	0.003 [0.003]	−0.005** [0.002]	−0.005* [0.002]	−0.004* [0.002]
Life expectancy	0.045 [0.028]	0.039 [0.027]	0.041 [0.028]	0.027 [0.022]	0.023 [0.022]	0.028 [0.022]
Old-age dependency	−0.673** [0.086]	−0.622** [0.086]	−0.609** [0.087]	−0.236** [0.058]	−0.197** [0.059]	−0.178** [0.059]
Youth dependency	−0.120** [0.025]	−0.109** [0.025]	−0.105** [0.025]	−0.027 [0.019]	−0.019 [0.019]	−0.011 [0.020]
Emerging countries dummy		0.060** [0.013]			0.034** [0.010]	
Korea dummy		−0.061* [0.027]			−0.013 [0.022]	
Asian crisis countries 1960s			0.046 [0.048]			−0.022 [0.022]
Asian crisis countries 1970s			0.056* [0.028]			0.025 [0.020]
Asian crisis countries 1980s			0.039 [0.024]			0.046* [0.021]
Asian crisis countries 1990s			0.073** [0.024]			0.093** [0.021]
Asian crisis countries 2000s			0.093** [0.034]			0.013 [0.029]
Korea 1960s			−0.057 [0.081]			0.012 [0.060]
Korea 1970s			−0.097 [0.054]			−0.019 [0.045]
Korea 1980s			−0.029 [0.052]			−0.030 [0.045]
Korea 1990s			−0.047 [0.052]			−0.032 [0.045]

(continued)

Table 3.6. (Continued)

	Saving			Investment		
Korea 2000s		−0.076 [0.074]			0.020 [0.063]	
Observations	698	698	698	827	827	827
R-squared	0.54	0.55	0.55	0.35	0.36	0.38

Source: This table is from Eichengreen, Perkins, and Shin (2012) with data from Bosworth and Chodorow-Reich (2007) supplemented by World Bank, World Development Indicators. We are grateful to Bosworth for sharing the data.

Note: The regression specifications follow Bosworth and Chodorow-Reich (2007) except that we have added Asia-crisis countries and Korea dummies. The sample covers the period 1960–2004 and the data are converted to five-year averages before regression. The Asia-crisis countries dummy is a dummy variable that takes a value of 1 if the observation corresponds to five crisis countries (Indonesia, Korea, Malaysia, Philippines, and Thailand) and 0 otherwise. We have also added Asia-crisis-countries decade dummies that are defined similarly for each decade. The Korea dummy is defined in a similar manner.

** and * indicate statistical significance at the 1 and 5 percent levels, respectively.

approach to industrial policy that had characterized the 1970s.[19] It initiated a process of economic liberalization that progressively relaxed the tight import restrictions that had accompanied export promotion efforts.

The steady rise in the investment rate in the 1980s to a level that surpassed 35 percent of GDP at the end of the decade translated into rapid growth of the capital stock. Liberalization and lower inflation kept the rate of return on capital high, and hence also the level of investment. But the largest change was in productivity growth. Having fallen to near zero in the 1970s, TFP rose at a very respectable 2 percent per annum in the 1980s. The long gestation period for investment in the heavy and chemical industries may account, in part, for both the initial fall and subsequent recovery, although there may also have been a contemporaneous effect of economic liberalization and inflation stabilization in the early 1980s. Be that as it may, the high rate of return on capital stimulated a large increase in investment in new products and equipment that in turn prompted a sharp rise in total factor productivity.[20]

The most surprising aspect of the growth experience of the 1980s, as noted, is that the economy still grew at more than 9 percent a year despite

---

19. The Heavy and Chemical Industry Drive and an industrial policy that targeted specific industries and firms, however, had come to an end even prior to President Park's assassination. For details, see Chapter 5.

20. For related discussion, see also I. Hwang (1998).

the tension and tear gas that culminated in 1987 with the first truly democratic election of a Korean president.[21] The election itself went smoothly, and a split in opposition forces that put up two candidates for president led to the election of Roh Tae-woo, another former military general who carried on the economic policies of the previous government.[22]

Rapid growth was maintained through the first half of the 1990s. Total factor productivity growth decelerated to 1.4 percent per year between 1989 and 1997, down from 2.1 percent in the previous period. Investment, in contrast, remained more than 35 percent of GDP. This was when the chaebol went on their spending spree. The government's involvement in industrial policy, still substantial despite the reforms of the 1980s, was driven more by politics and rent-seeking under Roh than it had been under President Park. Increasingly, the question was whether high growth characterized by brute-force investment but tepid TFP growth could be sustained.

The financial crisis was a decisive break. After falling by 6.9 percent in 1998, GDP bounced back rapidly in 1999–2000, with growth averaging 9 percent per annum. Then, however, growth slowed markedly, to 3.9 percent a year from 2001 through 20012.

Given that this slowdown centered on the Roh Moo-hyun presidency (2003–2008), seen by many as when the government sought to introduce fundamental changes in economic and social policies, there was a tendency to attribute the slowdown to those policies. But past changes in economic policy had not led to significant slower rates of growth, even temporarily. And as we discuss in Chapter 6, changes made in the social welfare system under Roh Moo-hyun were far from radical. This leads one to wonder: were the policy changes or failures experienced in 2001 to 2012 really so different from what had come before?

Answering this question requires viewing the country's experience in an international context. Growth in GDP slows in all countries when they reach high-income status. No high-income economy grows at 6 percent a year on a sustained basis, let alone 9 or 10 percent. Virtually all economies slow down well before their per capita incomes fully catch up with those of the leading economies.

Figure 3.2 shows the timing, in terms of per capita income, of these slowdowns, where a slowdown is defined as a sustained (seven-year)

---

21. See Chapter 2.
22. Again, see Chapter 2 for additional detail.

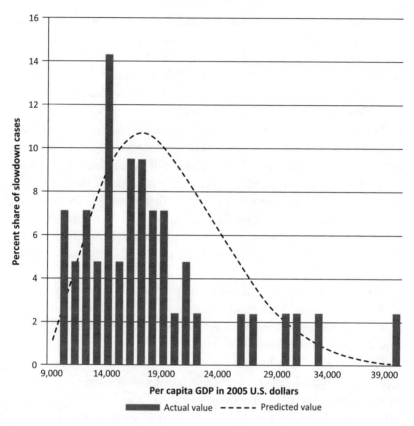

Figure 3.2. Frequency Distribution of Growth Slowdowns (Oil Exporters Excluded)

Source: The data and methodology used in constructing this figure were derived from work for the volume by Eichengreen, Perkins, and Shin (2012).

deceleration in the rate of growth of per capita income of at least two percentage points. With only two exceptions, sustained declines in the growth rates of today's high-income countries occurred within a narrow range of purchasing-power-parity (PPP) per capita incomes, from $10,000 to $16,000 per year (in 2005 U.S. PPP prices). There appears to be a natural tendency for growth to slow when per capita income reaches this level.[23]

----

23. The sample excludes oil-rich countries such as Saudi Arabia and Kuwait. Countries that still have low per capita incomes are also excluded from the analysis.

To understand the forces at work, we can begin with efforts to explain growth using multivariate regression. The one explanatory variable that registers significantly in all these equations is the current per capita income of the country in question, whose coefficient is consistently negative.[24] Put simply, the higher the per capita income, the lower the growth rate.

In Korea, in contrast to many other countries, the deceleration in growth was not driven by a decline in TFP growth. Instead, TFP growth returned to the levels of the 1980s (see Tables 3.4 and 3.5). While investment also declined to just under 30 percent a year (29.3 percent) in the years 2001–2012, this is still comparable to most years in the previous high-growth period, other than the first part of the 1990s. But with a now larger capital stock and a higher capital-to-output ratio, Korea needed a higher investment rate to maintain the same rate of growth of the capital stock and make good on depreciation. The rate of capital formation therefore slowed. This was another reason why growth had a tendency to decelerate.

The rate of growth of the labor force in the modern sector also slowed in the 1990s and following the turn of the century. This reflected the demographic transition that had brought down birth and population-growth rates more than a decade earlier. Working in the same direction was the end of labor's migration from low-productivity agriculture to the modern sector, now that there were few workers left in the countryside. These demographic changes are evident in Table 3.7, where the demographic transition shows up as a change in the dependency ratio that follows a logistic curve with growth, first rising as the dependency ratio falls and then leveling off as the ratio stops falling.

Finally, high growth appears to be associated with a rising share of manufacturing in GDP. But the manufacturing share of output and employment does not rise forever. As output and employment come to be increasingly dominated by services, growth again shows a tendency to slow.

Note also that the rate of return to capital fell sharply prior to the slowdown in GDP growth (Figure 3.3). The return to capital had already started falling in the late 1980s, plumbing low levels even before the 1997–1998

---

24. This is the well-known convergence phenomenon found in most econometric explanations for why some countries grow faster than others. This robustness analysis is carried out in Sala-i-Martin (1997).

Table 3.7. Determinants of Growth Slowdowns (multiple episodes allowed for one country)

			Deceleration		
Per capita GDP	78.062** [25.759]		101.867** [38.648]	142.396** [39.291]	146.528** [41.121]
Per capita GDP squared	−4.113** [1.349]		−3.343* [1.415]	−7.440** [2.046]	−7.651** [2.142]
Ratio		17.998* [7.223]	−109.535 [91.881]		
Ratio squared		−14.872** [5.708]	36.905 [34.966]		
Dependency				−60.008* [23.514]	−62.432* [25.750]
Dependency squared				46.988* [21.363]	50.648* [23.186]
Fertility				0.962* [0.483]	0.465 [0.544]
Manufacturing employment share					85.107* [39.976]
Manufacturing employment share squared					−192.426* [83.380]
Pseudo R-square	0.21	0.20	0.24	0.28	0.33
Observations			265		
Countries			20		

Source: Eichengreen, Perkins, and Shin (2012), 36.

Note: GDP data are obtained from Alan Heston, Robert Summers, and Bettina Aten, Penn World Table Version 6.2, Center for International Comparisons of Production, Income and Prices at the University of Pennsylvania, September 2006. Ratio is defined as the ratio of each country's per capita GDP to that of the frontier country, which is considered the United States. Dependency is defined as dependents to working-age population. Dependency and fertility data are collected from the World Bank, World Development Indicators. Manufacturing employment share is collected from the EUKLEMS Dataset, which covers mostly the European Union countries and other major countries.

** and * indicate statistical significance at the 1 and 5 percent levels, respectively.

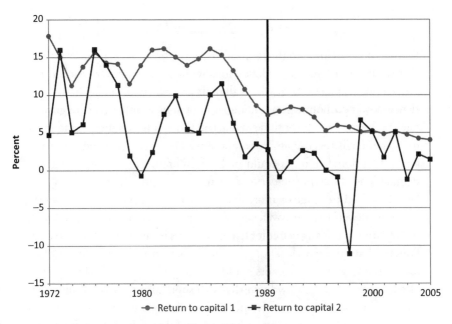

Figure 3.3. Return to Capital in Korea
Source: Eichengreen, Perkins, and Shin (2012), 17.

crisis.[25] It then recovered, but to levels still well below those of the 1970s and 1980s.[26] All this preceded by many years the Kim Dae-jung and Roh Moo-hyun governments, indicating that there was more going on than the post-crisis changes in economic policy.

---

25. Using statistical methods, Eichengreen, Perkins, and Shin (2012) place the slow-down in Korean growth at the end of the 1980s, coincident with this decline in the rate of return on capital.

26. A lower rate of return is not the same as a lower rate of TFP growth, although the two are related. The rate of return to capital is typically calculated by dividing the profits of the economy by the capital stock (for an individual firm, it is the profits of that firm divided by the firm's assets). Total factor productivity, in contrast, is the in-crease in output that cannot be explained by increases in inputs of labor and capital. Higher TFP will usually produce higher profits, but the increase in productivity can also show up in increased wages of workers. A lower rate of return probably also has some relationship to a decline in the growth of investment and hence of the capital stock. High rates of return certainly attract investors, so presumably the opposite is the case.

The Design of Progrowth Policies

While the previous analysis explains why the rate of growth of the Korean economy had a tendency to slow once the country reached the range of per capita GDP at which all high-growth countries begin to experience slower economic growth, it does not tell us whether Korean growth rates in the future will continue to outstrip those of the country's emerging-market and advanced-country competitors. Policy changes and structural and institutional reforms could make a difference in a variety of areas. Female labor-force participation in Korea, at approximately 50 percent, lags the OECD average by more than ten percentage points.[27] Male workers in their twenties, moreover, comprise almost half of all the unemployed; the situation is not any better for female workers in the 20 to 40 age bracket. Policies that raise female labor force participation and reduce unemployment among younger workers could partially offset the slowing growth of the labor force—a slowdown that will soon turn into an absolute decline if the total fertility rate among Korean women remains below replacement level, as it is today. Although female workforce participation is partly determined by slowly changing cultural norms, it also depends on policies that reduce the burden on women who wish to work outside the home after having children (by improving access to affordable day care, for example).

Although rates of return to capital have fallen in industries that have been the backbone of the economy, such as electronics, automobiles, shipbuilding, and iron and steel, they remain relatively high in high-technology and knowledge-intensive industries. It is not clear why there has not been a greater shift in investment to those industries; one interpretation is that the chaebol are comfortable concentrating on the sectors they dominate, while the high cost and limited availability of venture capital prevents small and medium-size enterprises (SMEs) from filling the gap. Much R&D has been directed toward fabricated metals, general machinery, automobiles, and electrical and electronics industries, which have been the mainstays of manufacturing, but relatively little has gone to sophisticated technology-intensive industries.

Between 2004 and 2011 Korea succeeded in raising R&D spending from 2.7 to 4.0 percent of GDP. Ratios, of course, are not the same as levels, and the absolute level of research and development spending is also

---

27. This issue is analyzed in more detail in Chapter 6.

important where there are economies of scale in R&D. In 2011 the total Korean expenditure on research and development ranked sixth in the world, but it was still less than one-fourth of the amount expended by Japan, half of that spent by Germany, and one-ninth of the total expenditure in the United States. There are limits, in other words, to the extent to which Korea can diversify its R&D investment among many industries.

Korea's success in further developing its high-tech and knowledge-intensive industries will depend in part on the availability of scientists, engineers, and other specialists with the relevant skills. The country has made a considerable investment in this area, but the rate of return remains to be seen. The goal of transforming the country into a knowledge-based economy has led to the near universalization of tertiary education. Scores of new universities and colleges are now attended by more than 80 percent of high school graduates. But despite the increase in the quantity of new schools, the quality of the education received by many of their graduates is low. If the expansion in the quantity of tertiary education is to meet the needs of a knowledge-based economy, the quality of the education received by the lower three-fourths of the university students will have to improve significantly. More universities below the top tier will have to raise the caliber of their faculty in order to contribute to research as well as teaching. Reforming universities tends to be a slow process, but a concerted effort to accelerate it would enhance the possibility that GDP growth could be higher than it is at present, or at least that the growth rate would not fall further.[28]

The Elements of a Progrowth Agenda

Gross investment and capital formation averaged around 30 percent of GDP through much of the 1980s and 35 percent in the 1990s before they plunged during the 1997–1998 financial crisis. Following the crisis, investment returned to 30 percent but then declined again with the global crisis of 2009.

It is a widely held view, as we have pointed out, that the unusually high rates of capital formation in the 1990s reflected the chaebol investment binge that helped to create the conditions that led to the financial crisis. Accordingly, it was healthy and desirable that the investment rate

---

28. Once again, for a more detailed analysis see Chapter 6.

subsequently came down.[29] The alternative view, while acknowledging that much investment in the 1990s was misdirected by the chaebol, argues that similar levels of better-directed investment could sustain a higher growth rate.[30] The fact that the gross savings rate has remained higher than the investment rate is seen as allowing a higher rate of investment, provided that the return on investment can again be boosted to the levels reached prior to the 1990s.

In fact, the decline in investment since the crisis has been most dramatic in SME-dominated sectors. Investment by firms with 300 or fewer workers has fallen in absolute terms. This contraction is attributed to a combination of two factors. One is the rapid growth of China as an exporter of a wide range of labor-intensive manufactures, a development that has disproportionately affected small and medium-size Korean firms exporting similar products. Some of these firms have responded by moving their production facilities to China and other East Asian countries, which has translated into a lower rate of investment in Korea itself.

Second, nearly two-thirds of Korean SMEs belong to the subcontracting networks of the large business groups to which they supply parts and components. More than 80 percent of their revenues come from sales to those groups. Joo-Hoon Kim (2005) has shown that these industrial groups use their monopsony power to shift cost increases to their subcontractors. The more intense the international competition, the stronger is their incentive to shift costs onto suppliers. When they experience increases in labor costs as a result of labor disputes, for example, they demand lower part and component prices from their subcontractors. In most cases the subcontractors do not have bargaining power when setting prices for their products; they have lost whatever leverage they once had because the

---

29. Analyzing data for the periods before and after the 1997 economic crisis, Lim and Lim (2007) find support for the moral-hazard hypothesis: that chaebol investment before the crisis was higher than nonchaebol investment because of implicit state guarantees enjoyed by the chaebol; the chaebol dummy in their investment equations is no longer statistically significant in the post-crisis period, when large-scale chaebol bankruptcies occurred. Their results also undermine the claim that investment was lowered by the "anti-chaebol environment" created by the Roh Moo-hyun government (facility investment by large firms actually increased by a great deal in 2003 and 2004, whereas aggregate investment in the national account showed anemic growth owing to SMEs' weak investment.

30. Again, see Song (2001) and the references cited therein.

chaebol now have alternative sources from foreign suppliers. These controversial cost-shifting practices became an issue in the 2012 presidential campaign, when the market power of the chaebol over their SME suppliers was much discussed under the rubric of "economic democracy." The issue was then flagged by newly elected President Park Geun-hye in her February 2013 inauguration speech.[31]

Policymakers understand that revitalizing the SMEs is important for boosting their investment and thus for maintaining a high investment rate overall. To this end, in addition to committing to rigorously enforcing the country's competition policies, they have put in place a range of policy measures involving tax concessions, preferential financing, and deregulation to assist the small- and medium-size enterprise sector. As shown in Table 3.8, 203 central government programs providing SMEs a total of 10.1 trillion won (US$8.7 billion) were in place in 2012. Local governments have provided an additional budget of 2.2 trillion won (US$1.9 billion) through 920 separate programs. But it is important to note that these policies, even if successful, might return SME investment only to earlier levels, rather than to higher levels than in the past. In any case, thus far gains in this area have been relatively modest.

Ultimately, revitalization will require technological upgrading and the migration of SME-based employment from manufacturing to the service sector, where firms are better sheltered from foreign competition and domestic demand is likely to be strong. But this process has been slowed by entry barriers to many service-sector activities, by the cost of retraining workers (together with the limited provision of adjustment assistance and stipends for retraining), and by the difficulties of moving from a service sector dominated by cigarette stands and corner stores and manned by the self-employed, to one where services are provided by SMEs.

In addition, there is scope for expanding the profile of large enterprises in the service sector, including the retail arms of large business groups, which have been restrained by regulatory policy from competing with mom-and-pop stores. There is further scope for developing the finance, insurance, and business service sector, which was expanding rapidly before the global financial crisis.[32] The transition to a larger and more

---

31. See Korea Economic Daily (2013).

32. Fuller treatments of the prospects for this sector can be found in Chapters 4 and 7.

Table 3.8. Central Government Programs to Support SMEs in 2012

	Outlays (billion won)	Average rate of increase, 2010–2012 (%)	Number of programs	Selected programs
Small and Medium Business Administration	6,155	1.5	86	Restructuring and start-up support Stable operation support Regional SME support Technology development support Venture company support
Ministry of Knowledge Economy	1,670	4.7	45	Industrial technology development ICT equipment investment support Software development support Activation of industrial complexes Energy-saving support
Ministry of Labor	925	2.3	23	Workplace accident prevention Workplace environment improvement Vocational training support Employment of interns Social enterprise support
Ministry of Agriculture and Food	856	8.5	9	Rice processing factory support Agricultural product processing Agricultural machine product support
Ministry of Culture, Sports, and Tourism	253	6.6	16	Film promotion fund support Sporting goods development support

Ministry of Environment	137	5.0	8	Antipollution facility support Environmental technology development support Recycling development support
Intellectual Property Office	38	24.0	4	Technology evaluation support
Ministry of Strategy and Finance	32	30.2	2	Lottery fund for SME support Start-up incubation for the low-income handicapped
Ministry of Land and Maritime Affairs	7	4.6	3	Construction technology innovation support
Ministry of Education, Science, and Technology	7	-15.7	2	Technology development support
Food and Drug Safety Administration	4	123.6	1	Hazard Analysis and Critical Control Point program support
Korea Customs Service	2	24.4	2	Authorized Economic Operator certification Certificate of origin support
Defense Acquisition Program Administration	2	2.3	2	Defense industry R&D support
Total	10,087	2.2	203	

Source: Small and Medium Business Administration and Korea Small Business Institute (2012), 5.

Note: SMEs = small and medium sized enterprises; ICT = information and communications technology.

productive service sector is under way, in other words, but completing the shift will take time.

An additional development that may have prevented a return to earlier high levels of investment was the end of the traditional chaebol-government risk-sharing partnership that supported both the Heavy and Chemical Industry Drive of the 1970s and the growth of the electronics industry in the 1980s. Whatever the merits of the shift to a less interventionist economic policy, it has left the chaebol more reluctant to undertake large investments in novel projects. Restructuring, together with pressure for the chaebol to divest affiliates outside their core competencies, has reduced their capacity to diversify risk by investing in different industries. Although a number of big industrial groups own insurance companies and securities firms, these entities are no longer allowed to serve as the groups' financial arms to the same extent as before.

Together these changes have narrowed the scope for risk diversification by the industrial groups. Investment in new industries is characterized by long gestation periods and uncertain payoffs. The chaebol cannot expect to receive subsidies before those investments begin to pay off or to be offered a risk-sharing arrangement by the government, as in the pre-crisis period. The largest Korean corporations, such as Samsung and Hyundai, may have the deep pockets and risk-bearing capacity to invest in uncertain, long-gestation projects, but this is not so for many others. To be sure, with the development of financial markets, shareholders can diversify firm- and industry-specific risk by buying and holding shares in companies in other sectors where returns follow a different pattern (where they are negatively correlated). But Korean financial markets are a work in progress. And in any case, management, which has a concentrated stake in firm-specific outcomes, is not able to effectively diversify its stake in this way.

A related factor is financial constraints (described more fully in Chapter 4). Financial reform and restructuring destroyed many of the old ties between firms and banks, and much of the dedicated information capital of the latter. Although deregulation and market opening have diversified and deepened money and capital markets, the bond market has yet to develop fully. The public segment remains small because budget deficits have been small, except in isolated years. The absence of a deep and liquid market in short-term government debt securities has made it difficult to develop a benchmark yield curve, which in turn hinders the development of the corporate bond market.[33] Weaknesses in corporate governance (weak regulatory requirements for transparency, the docility of outside directors) discourage investment in corporate bonds. The fact that only a limited number of companies have investment-grade ratings has discouraged the participation of foreign institutional investors. The equity market, for its part, is volatile, venture capital is underdeveloped, and markets for financial derivatives are in their infancy. Capital markets have thus provided only limited financing to SMEs and limited scope for diversifying the risks of investment by the large industrial groups.

A further deterrent to capital investment, it is argued, are adversarial labor relations. Among OECD members, Korea consistently loses the largest number of workdays due to strikes and work stoppages (although the number of days lost has declined a great deal since the late 1980s). In many surveys, poor industrial relations and the militancy of trade unions are cited as the two most serious problems discouraging domestic as well as foreign direct investment. The reasons for this continuing high level of labor strife are discussed in Chapter 6.

Related to the problems that labor strife causes for growth are complaints about labor market rigidities. Labor market reform after the 1997–1998 crisis led to the enactment of legislation allowing firms to shed redundant workers to facilitate corporate restructuring, and to the creation of a tripartite committee in the corporatist tradition to manage better industrial relations. But the tripartite commission has not been an effective venue for mediating labor-management disputes, for the reasons we describe in Chapter 2. And the new labor law has not been of much benefit to firms; even now, layoffs are permissible only when firms are faced with insolvency or a comparable crisis.

Summing Up

There are many areas where Korea could take steps to improve economic performance. But the question to be answered is, improve it relative to what? Countries close to the technological frontier, as emphasized, seldom grow much faster than 3 percent per capita. Most in fact grow at a considerably slower rate. Korea is not yet at the frontier in a variety of sectors.

---

33. Until 2005, a proliferation of different instruments with different yields, maturities, and other provisions limited market liquidity and forced many issues to be traded over the counter.

It can draw closer by raising R&D spending and upgrading the universities that supply quality research personnel, especially in high-technology sectors, as we will describe at more length in Chapter 9. Policy can also help to positively shape the demographic conditions that influence the growth rate. In contrast, policy is unlikely to have much influence on the rapid aging of the Korean population, since pronatalist measures have to push against deep-seated cultural factors; in any case it would take a generation for the effects of policy initiatives in this area to be felt. As we have pointed out, participation in the labor force by Korean women is unusually low, something that is now likely to change as a result of higher incomes and the changes in social norms that come with modernization. Still, policy can play a facilitating role through, inter alia, the establishment of better day care facilities. Reforming education, meanwhile, can improve Korea's stock of human capital. But educational reform is slow, given the existence of entrenched stakeholders, and even then it may take a decade or more for reforms to have an impact on economic performance.

While there is every reason to attempt to speed up these reforms, many other high-income countries are also trying to make reforms that will enhance their growth prospects. A plausible hypothesis is that those making the most effort at reform are also the ones most likely to increase their GDP growth rate to 3 percent per capita. As Japan has demonstrated for two decades, major policy mistakes, such as those that led to bubbles in the financial and real estate markets in the 1980s, followed by a reluctance to change those policies, can have the opposite effect; there, a healthy per capita GDP growth rate from 1974 to 1990 of 3.0 percent per year was replaced by near stagnation, with a per capita annual growth rate of 0.8 percent through 2010. In a similar vein, European Union policies and institutions have, as of this writing, produced nearly five years of slow or no growth. Korea has had a record of being prepared to undertake major reforms when the situation so required. Continuing in that tradition will be necessary to maintain what for high income countries is a rapid GDP per capita growth rate.

Although the days of near double-digit economic growth are over, if Korea can overcome the barriers to innovation and higher levels of investment, it will still be able to raise its growth rate relative to the past. Chapters 4 through 8 examine those barriers and the options for surmounting them. What the likely responses imply for realized growth rates will be considered in our concluding chapter.

CHAPTER 4

Financial Development and Liberalization

Since the early 1980s, financial development in Korea has been a tale of liberalization and opening.[1] After the 1997–1998 crisis, Korea made a great deal of progress in building a market-oriented financial system through sweeping reforms for the deregulation and opening of financial markets and intermediaries. But the new system did not prevent the country from experiencing a credit card boom and bust in 2003, a liquidity crisis in 2008, and a run on its savings banks in 2011. Financial liberalization, clearly, is no panacea.

There is disagreement among scholars about the causal connections between financial liberalization and financial stability, on the one hand, and savings and investment, consumption smoothing, and distributive equity, on the other. While some say that financial liberalization spurs growth by increasing saving and investment and improving the efficiency of the latter, the evidence from country studies does not always support this proposition.[2] The effect of financial liberalization on real-sector variables is an empirical question. This study attempts to answer it, at least in part, by assessing its impact in South Korea. Our conclusions, based on the companion volume in this series by Park, Kim, and Park (forthcoming), are broadly negative. In the Korean case, it would appear, financial liberalization and opening have delivered less than promised.

---

1. Some of the institutional details and developments concerning Korea's financial system are drawn from Yung Chul Park (2013).
2. Bekaert, Harvey, and Lundblad (2006); Galindo, Schiantarelli, and Weiss (2007); and Levine (2005) provide positive assessments of the impact of financial liberalization on real variables.

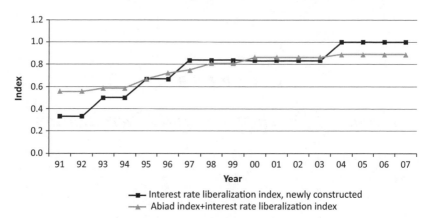

Figure 4.1. Additional Financial Liberalization Indices, 1991–2007
The interest rate liberalization index (in black) is based on the chronology of financial liberalization measures in Park, Kim, and Park (forthcoming). The second index (gray) is an unweighted average of the first index plus five indices of the extent of financial restrictions (credit controls, entry barriers, bank supervision, international capital, and securities markets) from the IMF financial market database; see Abiad, Detragiache, and Tressel (2008). Each of the six subindices can range from 0 to 3; the index shown here is computed by adding their values and normalizing by 18.
Source: Authors' estimates.

Alternative measures of financial liberalization are shown in Figure 4.1. While the alternative measures do not all move in lockstep, they are consistent with the story of progressive waves of financial liberalization set off in 1993, 1998, and 2004.

Financial liberalization matters insofar as it affects other things we care about, such as financial stability. This makes it important to attempt to measure not just policies but also outcomes. To this end, the Bank of Korea (2012) has developed a financial stability index; it is estimated by standardizing and weighting 20 different subindices, as shown in Figure 4.2.[3] This index shows a substantial decline in financial stress—and, analogously,

---

3. The 20 subindices include covered interest-rate differentials between corporate (three-year) and government (three-year) bonds; covered interest-rate differentials between government bonds (three-year) and monetary stabilization bonds; volatility of the nominal exchange rate; a stress index for the foreign exchange market (changes in the exchange rate adjusted for changes in foreign exchange reserves); volatility of KOSPI (the Korean stock price index); the rate of decline in KOSPI; CDS (credit default swap) spreads for major commercial banks; and volatility of stock prices of financial firms, adjusted for changes in the KOSPI. See Bank of Korea (2012).

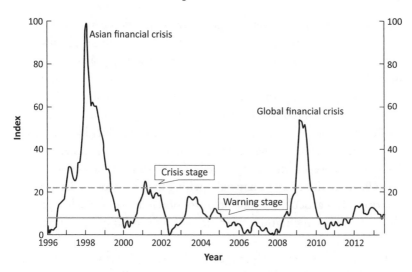

Figure 4.2. Financial Stability Index
The financial stability index is measured based on values from 0 (minimum) to 100 (maximum). The closer it gets to 100, the higher the level of instability. (In January 1998, during the Asian financial crisis, the index was equal to 100.)
Source: Bank of Korea (2013), *Financial Stability Report* (April).

greater financial stability—from 1998 to 2007, a period that witnessed a considerable advance in financial liberalization. But this inverse association does not necessarily support the idea that an open financial system is better for adjusting to internal and external shocks, since there were also significant financial disturbances in the post-1997 period.

The sections that follow examine the causes and consequences of those disturbances in order to gain insight into the causal connections between financial liberalization and financial stability. We also attempt to throw light on the question of whether a well-functioning financial system must be complemented by an efficient system of financial regulation to safeguard against financial instability—and if so, exactly what kind of system.

The Evolution of a Market-Oriented Financial System

Through the late 1970s Korea's financial system was highly repressive. Asset-liability management practices, market interest rates, and capital account transactions were strictly controlled by the government. But by the early 1980s the collusive arrangement among the government, the chaebol, and banks, the main players in the country's developmental state, came under growing strain as a result of inefficiencies in resource allocation and internal and external imbalances.[4] In response, policymakers embraced economic and financial liberalization, starting with domestic market deregulation in the 1980s. But this first wave of reform—involving partial privatization of the banks, deregulation of nonbank financial intermediaries, and phased interest-rate liberalization—made only limited progress in removing the repressive features of the earlier regime. The Kim Young-sam government, inaugurated in 1993, launched a second wave of liberalization and placed financial opening at the top of its list of policy priorities. In particular, it took steps to loosen and ultimately eliminate the panoply of regulations traditionally controlling capital account transactions.

Given the existence of interest rate differentials between foreign and domestic financial markets, and Korea's managed floating exchange rate regime, lifting restrictions on capital flows—on inflows, specifically—encouraged foreign borrowing. Much of what was borrowed was obtained on the international wholesale market and re-lent to the chaebol and other large corporations to finance long-term investment. The resulting increase in short-term foreign liabilities rendered Korea vulnerable to a sudden reversal of capital inflows. In 1997 that reversal precipitated a crisis that brought the country to the brink of insolvency. To stave off disaster, the government approached the International Monetary Fund for an emergency rescue package.

The 1997 crisis was a watershed. It led the government, consistent with IMF wishes, to launch a third wave of liberalization. The new measures were intended to render Korea's financial system as free and open as that of any advanced economy. The three years following the crisis thus saw the removal of virtually all remaining controls on interest rates and foreign exchange transactions. Most remaining regulatory restrictions on asset and liability management at banks and other financial institutions and on capital account transactions were phased out.

In addition, to encourage shareholders and internal auditors to assume the role of monitoring management, the conditions required for exercising minority shareholders' rights were significantly eased. Starting in 1999, financial institutions had to fill 50 percent of the seats on their board with

---

4. See the related discussion of the Heavy and Chemical Industry Drive in Chapter 5.

outside directors. The Financial Services Commission (FSC) established a sanction system in which civil and criminal liabilities could be imposed on directors, external auditors, and examiners of supervisory authorities. The required financial disclosure schedule for banks and securities and insurance companies was changed from semi-annual to quarterly.

Banks, meanwhile, were also required to engage in prompt corrective action when the FSC deemed it necessary because capital adequacy ratios were below stipulated levels. The prompt corrective action requirement was applied to banks, merchant bank corporations, and securities companies in April 1998 and was subsequently extended to insurance companies and mutual savings banks (June 1998) and credit unions (December 1999). The FSC also expanded disclosure requirements to the level dictated by the International Accounting Standards, while loan classification standards and provisioning requirements were strengthened in accordance with international practice.

Forward-looking asset quality classification standards were introduced for commercial banks at the end of 1999. These standards are based on the ability of debtors to generate future cash flow, rather than on their payment records. Similar standards were introduced for merchant banks (June 2000) and insurance companies (in September 2000). Asset categories subject to loan-loss provisions were widened to include commercial paper, guaranteed bills, and privately placed bonds in trust accounts, while the evaluation standard for marketable and investment securities held by banks was changed from the "lower-of-cost-or-market" method to the "mark-to-market" method. Finally, the FSC strengthened regulations with respect to the exposure limits of commercial banks, merchant banks, and other financial intermediaries.[5]

---

5. The FSC proceeded on a number of margins. First, the definition of exposure to a single borrower was broadened to include not only loans and payment guarantees in the conventional sense but also all direct and indirect transactions that carry credit risks, such as corporate bond and commercial paper holdings. Second, since May 1999 the combined exposure to firms affiliated with the same chaebol was tightened to 25 percent of the bank capital, from 45 percent. Third, the total sum of large exposures of more than 10 percent of a bank's capital to a single borrower or a group of firms affiliated with same chaebol was limited to five times the bank's capital. Fourth, the exposure to shareholders who hold 10 percent or more of shares in a bank was limited to the equity shares of the large shareholders in question, with a maximum of 25 percent of bank capital.

Following the 1997 crisis, Korea ran large surpluses on current account, reflecting weak domestic demand and exports powered by the depreciation of the won. By the end of 2004, foreign exchange reserves had risen to more than 25 percent of GDP. Despite the sterilization of current and capital account surpluses, there was strong pressure for the won to appreciate against the major foreign currencies. These developments were taken as indications that Korea was ready for further financial market opening. In the early years of the Roh Moo-hyun government, a fourth wave of financial liberalization was duly initiated with the goal of transforming Seoul into an international financial center.

Something still had to be done, however, to vent the pressure for currency appreciation. Policymakers thus stepped up deregulation of capital outflows. Meanwhile, measures relaxing residual controls on portfolio capital flows induced a large increase in short-term foreign liabilities, as institutional and private entities set out to invest in foreign securities with funds borrowed mostly from wholesale funding markets, much as they had in the run-up to the 1997–1998 crisis. This sowed the seeds of the liquidity crisis to which Korea succumbed following the collapse of the U.S. investment bank Lehman Brothers in September 2008. As it had ten years earlier, Korea again required external assistance to contain its crisis, although it obtained aid this time through a bilateral swap arrangement with the U.S. Federal Reserve System, rather than from the IMF.

In the wake of the global financial crisis, there were two new developments on the regulatory front. One was the consolidation of regulatory laws.[6] Until 2009, capital market institutions and financial investment companies—stock brokerages, asset management firms, futures companies, and trust companies—were regulated by fourteen different laws, despite the fact that the different entities offered similar services and products. There was a long debate on streamlining the fourteen laws so as to foster competition and consolidation. Proponents claimed that consolidation would facilitate the emergence of large global investment banks and better protect consumers of financial services, although there was also

---

6. The consolidation of regulatory laws (the Capital Market Consolidation Act) was in fact proposed before the global financial crisis as part of the "megabanks" initiative to merge and consolidate smaller banks into a few large, internationally competitive banks, and the move to make Seoul a financial hub, although the new law became effective only after the outbreak of the global financial crisis. The act was promulgated in August 2007 and took effect in February 2009.

a concern that it would aggravate the problem of "shadow banking," enabling entities outside the system of regulated depository institutions to perform traditional banking functions. The debate culminated in the Capital Market Consolidation Act (CMCA), which integrated the existing fourteen financial laws into one.

The CMCA legislation, however, has not been effective in providing better protection for consumers of financial services. In recognition of this deficiency, which is attributed to the inability of the Financial Supervisory Service (FSS) to reorient itself to assume more responsibility in its expanded role, the government that came to power in 2013 decided to set up a new agency independent of the FSS, to increase the scope as well as the efficiency of consumer protection.

Under the new act, investment companies were no longer limited to one type of financial business; they were allowed to market all financial services and products for which they obtained a license. Thus far, however, the new legislation has not succeeded in creating a set of world-class investment banks. In the wake of the 2008 global financial crisis, which precipitated stagnation and financial instability throughout advanced and emerging economies, Korea's policymakers had little incentive to enact another big-bang financial reform to complement the CMCA. Instead, they moved to institute tighter control of capital inflows.

The other regulatory development was a reorientation of policy toward capital flows and foreign currency exposures. The 2008 crisis was a reminder that the regulatory and policy authorities lacked adequate tools for coping with the volatility of capital flows, in particular for preventing panicked foreign investors from heading for the exits and foreign banks from refusing to roll over their short-term loans. At the same time, the IMF came around to supporting some types of capital control for emerging economies.[7] Encouraged in part by this change of heart, in June 2010 the FSS set limits on the forward foreign exchange positions of banks. Forward positions were limited to half of the banks' capital base, whereas foreign bank branches were limited to a ceiling of 250 percent of their capital. This was followed in November 2010 by the reimposition of withholding taxes on foreign purchases of local government bonds, which had been withdrawn during the 2008 financial crisis.

---

7. See the discussions by IMF staff in Ostry et al. (2010) and Habermeier, Kokenyne, and Baba (2011).

Growth and Structural Change in Korea's Financial System

The 1997 financial crisis and subsequent reforms deregulating and opening financial markets and intermediation have brought about fundamental changes in structures and institutions. They have transformed Korea's financial system into one of the most liberalized, open regimes in the emerging world. This section highlights some of the significant changes since 2000.

For seven years after the 1997 crisis, the ratio of total financial assets and liabilities to GDP—the financial interrelation ratio (FIR)—remained unchanged. Having gone through a series of far-reaching financial reforms that closed down a great number of financial institutions and removed large amounts of nonperforming loans from bank balance sheets, financial growth was bound to slow down. With financial recovery back on track, the FIR began rapid climbing again in 2005 and reached more than 900 percent by the end of 2012—twice as high as its level in 1995 (see Figure 4.3).

The share of the financial sector in GDP grew to 6.7 percent in 2002 from 5.2 percent in 2000, before tapering off to an average of 6.2 percent in recent years. Since the early 2000s the sector's share in total employment has declined to about 4 percent from more than 5 percent in the 1990s. Given the difficulty of defining and quantifying an optimum size for the financial system, Park, Kim, and Park (forthcoming) have left unanswered the question as to whether—in terms of these figures together with the FIR—Korea's financial sector is overgrown or is still too small for an adequate provision of financial services.[8]

Before the 1997 crisis, Korea's financial system was bank based. In the wake of the crisis, financial deregulation powered a marked increase in the share of direct finance—funding extended through money and capital markets—from about 46 percent in the early 1990s to 60 percent in 2012, moving the financial system in a more market-oriented direction. Between 2000 and 2012, direct finance, measured by market value, grew by 350 percent: the stock market increased 540 percent; the bond market, 290 percent; and the money market registered almost a twofold increase.

---

8. Cecchetti and Kharroubi (2012) find that when the financial sector represents more than 3.5 percent of total employment or 8.4 percent of total value added, further increases in financial-sector size tend to be detrimental to growth.

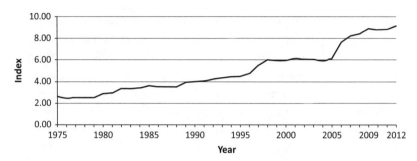

Figure 4.3. Financial Interrelation Ratio (FIR)
Ratio of total financial assets, including those of financial institutions, to GDP.
Source: Bank of Korea, Economic Statistics System (ECOS).

In the 1990s, money market instruments—commercial paper, monetary stabilization bonds, and certificates of deposit—were the most widely used forms of short-term financing, making up a combined share of 80 percent of total money market funding. Since the 1997 crisis, the majority of monetary stabilization bonds have been repurchase agreements.

In the early 1990s, corporate bonds with a three-year maturity had a commanding share of Korea's bond market. Their share then fell from more than 60 percent before the crisis to less than 17 percent in 1999, largely because of the increase in government bonds issued to pay for financial restructuring, budget deficits, and foreign exchange sterilization. The corporate bond market crashed again during the 2008 crisis, but since then it has been on the rise, in recent years capturing more than 30 percent of the market value of total bonds outstanding. In 2005 the government launched a plan for fostering long-term bonds with maturities longer than five years. A number of long-term government bonds have been issued, but their amounts have been relatively small.

In the 1990s, nonfinancial firms relied heavily on bank loans for working capital and fixed investment. Although corporations were able to raise more funds on the rising stock market, the share of equity financing was less than 20 percent throughout the decade. After the crisis that share began to soar, rising to a period high of 47 percent in 2007 before dropping to 44 percent in 2012. The expansion of direct finance was spurred by the migration of households to money and capital markets in search of higher yields, and by foreign investment in local bonds and stocks. Corporate restructuring after the 1997 crisis obliged large firms and chaebol to reduce their debt/equity ratio to no more than 200 percent (from more than 500 percent before the crisis). This provided a powerful incentive to rely more on equity and internal financing, which is the sum of net saving, net capital transfer, and capital consumption allowances. The share of internal financing, which had been less than 30 percent on average in the 1990s, began to surge after the 1997 crisis, moving up to 78 percent in 2011. The expansion of equity markets was also fueled by foreign equity investment. Stock prices, as measured by the KOSPI index, trebled between 1997 and 2012.

Financial reform also stimulated markets in new financial instruments designed to facilitate the diversification of funding and improve risk management at financial and nonfinancial firms. These new instruments include asset-backed securities (ABSs) and derivatives.[9] During the first phase of financial and corporate restructuring, which ended in 2003, ABSs were issued as a means of disposing of nonperforming loans of financial institutions. Subsequently, however, the credit card crisis, the 2008 liquidity crisis, and the stagnation of housing markets all led to some contraction of ABS markets.

In this liberalized environment, where asset prices fluctuate widely, banks and other financial institutions are more concerned about the market risk they face. The growing demand for risk reduction has led to a proliferation of derivative products. Most of these products—currency, interest-rate, stock, and credit futures, as well as options and swaps—were introduced following the 1997 crisis. Between 2001 and 2012, currency-related derivatives transactions grew tenfold. In the case of interest-rate derivative products, the transactions volume was almost 40 times higher in 2012 than in 2001; for equity derivatives, it was 12 times higher.

The global trend toward consolidation and conglomeration in finance took hold in Korea as well. Following the 1997 crisis, policymakers made concerted efforts to enhance the competitiveness of the financial sector by exploiting economies of scale and scope through the consolidation and conglomeration of financial institutions. By the end of 2012 the number of deposit money banks (DMBs) had fallen to 56: 7 nationwide commercial banks, 5 specialized banks, 6 regional banks, and 38 branches of foreign banks. The share of total assets of DMBs held by the big

---

9. Asset-backed securities include collateralized bond obligations, collateralized loan obligations, mortgage backed securities, and asset-backed commercial paper.

4—Kookmin (KB), Woori, Shinhan, and Hana—rose from less than 40 percent in 1999 to 46 percent in 2006 before falling back to about 43 percent in 2012.[10]

Financial reform has torn down the wall separating banking from securities and insurance. Together with the enactment of the Financial Holding Company Act (FHCA) in 2000, this led to a conglomeration process in which a growing number of financial groups were engaged in business activities, including groups of banks, nonbank financial institutions (NBFIs), and securities firms.[11] Before 2007 there were only four bank holding companies (Woori, Shinhan, Korea Investment, and Hana Financial). Since then nine more have been established. At the end of 2012, financial holding companies owned, altogether, a total of 248 financial subsidiaries.[12]

The practices of consolidating banks and other financial institutions, breaking down the wall separating banks from other financial service providers, and creating financial holding companies spawned a large body of empirical literature examining whether such structural changes have improved efficiency and increased economies of scale and scope at financial firms, and whether they have contributed to enhancing competition in financial markets. A majority of the studies find that most banks gained significant scale economies after the 1997 crisis; data problems have limited the number of studies on scope economies, with conflicting results.[13] Other studies estimating production functions for multiple bank products

---

10. At the end of 2012 there were 23 life insurance firms, but the 3 largest companies—Samsung, Daehan, and Kyobo—had a combined market share of nearly 70 percent. In contrast, out of the 62 securities firms in 2012, the 5 biggest controlled 40 percent of the securities business. Not surprisingly the Herfindahl-Hirschman Index, at 464, was the lowest for the securities business, compared with an index of almost 1,000 for banking and 2,045 for insurance.

11. A financial holding company's primary role is to control companies engaged in financial transactions or other companies related closely to the operations of financial businesses. A financial holding company is able to offer an extensive menu of financial services through a large number of subsidiaries engaged in different financial activities. In 2007, the act was amended to permit foreign financial institutions to establish financial holding companies in Korea.

12. Their return on assets had risen to 1.2 percent and the return on equity to 19 percent in 2005, but after the 2008 liquidity crisis they fell to 0.3 and 4.8 percent in 2009, respectively.

13. See Hall and Simper (2012), and Sufin (2011).

also find evidence of improvements in both technical and scale efficiency among Korean banks after the 1997 crisis.[14]

Looking at the high concentration ratios and the Herfindahl-Hirschman Index (HHI) for the largest five firms in banking, insurance, and securities, one might come to the conclusion that, contrary to theory, financial liberalization after the crisis did little in the way of promoting competition in financial industries (see Figure 4.4). However, more rigorous studies do not support such an observation. Most studies measure the level of competition by the H-statistic of the Panzar-Rosse model.[15]

Depending on the time periods covered and the bank cost and revenue functions chosen, research provides conflicting results on changes in the degree of competition in financial industries. This is true for studies investigating the data before as well as after the crisis.[16] Although the empirical results are not conclusive, Park, Kim, and Park (forthcoming) ar-

---

14. These studies specify production functions in terms of the distance from the production frontier. If a bank functions at a level below the frontier, then the bank's operation is inefficient. This inefficiency is then divided into technical and scale inefficiency. The distance from the frontier is a measure of technical inefficiency resulting from an inefficent use of inputs. The deviation from an optimal scale corresponding to constant returns to scale is a measure of diseconomies or economies of scale. See Banker, Chang, and Lee (2010); Park and Weber (2006); and Shin and Kim (2011).

15. In the Panzar-Rosse (1987) model, if total revenue and input prices of a firm change in the same direction this indicates a competitive market, whereas changes in the opposite direction tend to reflect some degree of market power. The H-statistic is the sum of elasticities of total revenue with respect to the input prices. A value equal to or smaller than zero indicates monopoly; a value equal to one represents perfect competition, and an H-statistic between zero and one indicates monopolistic competition.

16. Park and Weber (2006) find that the Korean banking industry was monopolistically competitive during the pre-crisis period (1992–1996) and the post-crisis period (2001–2004). This is confirmed by Shin and Kim (2013), who show that the banking industry was characterized by monopolistic competition throughout the 1992–2007 period, when the crisis years from 1997 to 2010 are excluded. They also show intensification of competition over time. In contrast, however, Lee and Nagano (2008) show that the banking industry, which had been monopolistically competitive before the crisis, became perfectly competitive thereafter. Hall and Simper (2012) examine the data from the second quarter of 2007 to the second quarter of 2011 and find that perfect competition prevailed during that period. Against those results, a study by the research department of Chun, B. K. and H. S. Kwan (2008) Assessment of the Degree of Competition in the Banking Industry (in Korean)," *Monthly Bulletin*, August, the Bank of Korea suggests that the banking industry has an oligopolic market structure dominated by a few strategically interdependent banks.

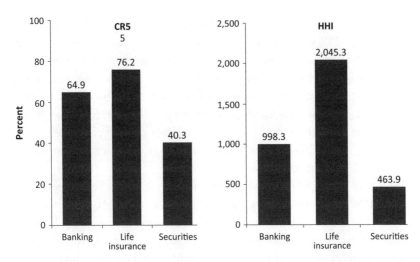

Figure 4.4. Concentration Ratios
The graph on the left (CR5) shows the concentration ratios for the largest five companies. The graph on the right (HHI) shows the Herfindahl-Hirschman Index for those companies.
Source: Korea Financial Investment Association (2012).

gue that the results of studies on competition in the banking market are rather misleading because they do not take into account the fact that banks have had to compete not only among themselves but also against insurance firms, securities dealers and brokers, and foreign financial institutions. If this feature of competition against other financial industries is properly calibrated, they argue, it is likely that the banking industry has become more competitive, despite the decline in the number of banks.

Financial liberalization also encouraged households to increase their holdings of bonds and equities at the expense of bank deposits and real property. Before the crisis, the shares of bonds and equities in household asset portfolios were less than 10 and 5 percent, respectively. Since 2005, those shares have on average almost doubled. Following the relaxation of restrictions on consumer loans, lending to households took off as banks and NBFIs set out to fill the space vacated by traditional business borrowers. Consumers borrowed heavily from banks and other nonbank financial institutions to finance purchases of housing and other types of real estate. From 1999 onward, consumer and mortgage loans to households comprised just over 50 percent of total loans extended by banks and NBFIs.

Beginning in 2001, the volume of household debt, which is the sum of consumer loans and the debt of self-employed individuals and nonprofit institutions, began ballooning rapidly. It rose to 1,152.8 trillion won (91 percent of GDP, or 164 percent of household disposable income) by the end of 2012—a level feared to endanger the soundness and stability of the financial system. It had been less than 60 percent in 1990 and about 70 percent in 2000. This rapid expansion set off and subsequently fueled the boom in the housing market. As shown in Table 4.4, consumer loans grew more than 28 percent per annum in 2001–2002, before the end of the boom in 2003. The annual average rate of growth for mortgage loans was even higher, at 56 percent.

Despite the imposition of loan-to-value regulation in September 2002 and further tightening thereafter, mortgage loans at DMBs continued to grow by 10 to 16 percent annually until 2006—except for a brief letup in 2004. Only when the debt-to-income ratio (principle and interest payments on total loans over income) was lowered and other tax and regulatory measures were implemented in 2006 and 2007 did the mortgage growth drop to 2.1 percent in 2007, bursting the housing-market bubble. Since then, however, mortgage loans have been growing by an average of about 7 percent annually despite continuing deceleration of housing prices, raising the specter of mounting loan losses at financial institutions that could again pose a systemic risk for the entire financial system.

The International Dimension

OPENING OF CAPITAL MARKETS

In December 1997 all restrictions on foreign investment in listed bonds were abolished. Ceilings on foreign investment in equities, with the exception of investment in public corporations, were then lifted in May 1998. Foreign investments in Korean bonds remained small compared with foreign investment in Korean equities: between 2000 and 2008 the foreign investor share was, on average, less than 8 percent of listed bonds. Limited maturities, a paucity of investment-grade bonds, and withholding taxes all discouraged foreign investment. In contrast, foreign ownership of stocks climbed to more than 40 percent of Korea's total market capitalization in 2004, from a little more than 10 percent in 1996.[17]

Reflecting the openness and liquidity of the market, trading in Korean stocks is sensitive to developments in the United States. A striking

---

17. It then fell to about 30 percent after the 2008 liquidity crisis.

Table 4.1. Consumer Loans by Financial Institutions in Korea

	Outstanding volume at end of year (trillion won and %)													
	1995	2000	2001	2002	2003	2004	2005	2006	2007	2008	2009	2010	2011	2012
Depository corporations	87.9 (61.6)[a]	157.6 (59.1)	206.0 (60.3)	277.0 (63.1)	322.0 (72.0)	355.5 (74.9)	393.2 (75.4)	443.3 (73.2)	474.1 (75.2)	516.0 (75.0)	549.8 (70.9)	593.5 (70.4)	639.6 (70.1)	659.9 (68.8)
Deposit money banks[b]	37.4	107.2	156.7	222.0	253.8	276.3	305.5	346.2	363.7	388.6	409.5	431.5	455.9	467.3
(Mortgage loans)		54.2	86.5	132.0	152.5	169.2	190.2	217.1	221.6	239.7	264.2	284.5	306.1	316.9
Nonbank depository institutions[c]		50.4	49.3	54.9	68.3	79.2	87.7	97.1	110.4	127.4	141.2	164.4	183.7	195.6
(Mortgage loans)									46.6	56.0	64.6	73.1	83.1	85.9
Other financial institutions	34.2 (24.0)[a]	83.4 (31.3)	97.5 (28.5)	114.1 (26.0)	98.9 (22.1)	93.9 (19.8)	100.2 (19.2)	131.1 (21.6)	121.3 (19.2)	132.4 (19.2)	184.5 (23.8)	200.2 (23.7)	217.5 (23.9)	240.7 (25.1)
Insurance companies[d]	18.5	27.1	32.6	38.7	42.9	45.3	48.2	51.6	55.9	61.7	66.1	68.0	74.7	79.6
Pension funds[e]								9.4			8.6	8.9	9.2	9.8
Specialized credit financial companies[f]	6.4	33.6	43.7	57.1	37.3	26.5	23.8	25.2	30.7	31.3	31.5	36.3	38.8	39.6
Public financial institutions[g]								25.0			31.5	30.7	30.5	31.4
Other financial intermediaries[h]								19.0			45.0	51.5	57.0	71.7
Others[i]	9.3	22.8	21.2	18.3	18.7	22.1	28.3	0.7	34.7	39.3	1.8	4.9	7.2	8.7

(continued)

Table 4.1. (Continued)

	Outstanding volume at end of year (trillion won and %)													
	1995	2000	2001	2002	2003	2004	2005	2006	2007	2008	2009	2010	2011	2012
Merchandise credit	20.5	25.8	38.2	47.9	26.6	25.3	28.0	31.5	35.3	39.9	41.7	49.4	54.8	58.8
	(14.4)[a]	(9.7)	(11.2)	(10.9)	(5.9)	(5.3)	(5.4)	(5.2)	(5.6)	(5.8)	(5.4)	(5.9)	(6.0)	(6.1)
Specialized credit financial companies[j]	7.6	21.6	35.1	45.3	25.8	24.7	27.3	30.5	34.4	39.2	40.9	48.4	53.7	57.7
Total	142.7	266.9	341.7	439.1	447.6	474.7	521.5	605.9	630.7	688.2	776.0	843.1	911.9	959.4

Source: Bank of Korea, Economic Statistics System (ECOS).

[a] Percent of total.

[b] Commercial banks and specialized banks.

[c] Mutual savings banks, credit cooperatives, postal savings, and merchant banks.

[d] Life insurance companies, non-life insurance companies, and postal insurance.

[e] Government employee pensions, military pensions, pensions for private school teachers, etc.

[f] Credit card companies, finance companies, etc.

[g] National housing fund, Korea housing finance corporation, etc.

[h] Securities companies, companies specializing in liquidizing, loan companies, etc.

[i] Korea Student Aid Foundation, for example.

[j] Credit card companies and installment financing companies.

illustration of this was the sharp increase in the correlation between changes in the Standard and Poor's (S&P) 500 and the KOSPI, and a substantial increase in the negative correlation between changes in the KOSPI and the won–U.S. dollar exchange rate following the outbreak of the U.S. subprime crisis in August 2007.[18] Whenever the S&P 500 fell, so did the KOSPI, reflecting the tendency for foreign investors to withdraw from Korea's stock market in order to rebalance their portfolios and increase liquidity—and the tendency for local investors to follow suit.

The high correlation between the S&P 500 and the KOSPI has burdened Korea's policymakers with the task of stabilizing financial markets, as it has weakened the ability of Korea's floating exchange rate regime to serve as a buffer against external shocks. As the KOSPI rises in response to a surge in the S&P 500, the won-dollar exchange rate appreciates simultaneously. Contrary to theory, the increase in the value of the won has little effect on curbing equity capital inflows and thus fails to prevent a rise in the KOSPI (Y. C. Park and H. Park 2014). Whether it moderates a rise is undetermined.

Most foreign investors do not hedge the currency exposure of their stock portfolios, certainly not as much as they do with investments in fixed-income securities.[19] Equities dominate foreign holdings of won-denominated assets. Foreigners held more than 30 percent of equities and a bit less than 7 percent of bonds by market capitalization in recent years. As a result, an external shock such as a change in U.S. monetary policy is transmitted largely through Korea's stock market, and floating rates have not been able to shield the economy from such disturbances.

---

18. Correlations were less tight but also positive and high before the crisis.

19. There are no reliable data, but market sources in Korea estimate that between 70 and 80 percent of foreigners trading in Korea's stock markets do not hedge against currency risk. There are several reasons given for this. It is difficult to forecast exchange-rate changes, given the volatility of the won-dollar exchange rate. Further, higher interest rates in Korea than in the United States mean hedging costs have been high. Finally, to some investors the currency exposure is another form of diversification. The absence of hedging is believed to have contributed to a rise in the turnover rate of foreign equity holdings. A large number of studies show that over longer periods—say, ten to fifteen years—the returns on hedged and unhedged equity portfolios are similar, although they tend to vary in the short run (Credit Suisse AG 2012).

OPENING OF FINANCIAL
INTERMEDIATION INDUSTRIES

One of the most significant financial reforms was the liberalization of foreign entry into the financial sector. This transformed Korea's financial system into one of the most open in the emerging world. The Foreign Investment Promotion Act of 1998 opened the door for foreign investment in financial institutions, and the 1997 crisis was followed by a large increase in foreign acquisitions of domestic bank stocks. At the same time, Korean policymakers were actively seeking foreign buyers of ailing bank and nonbank financial institutions. With Korean share prices still depressed in the aftermath of the crisis, and with the won expected to appreciate, restructured banks were attractive choices for foreign investors.

The total value of stock held by foreign investors in Korea's financial industries grew to more than $30 billion in 2011 from less than $5 billion in 2001. At the end of 2012 foreigners owned 62 percent of the three largest nongovernment financial holding companies (Shinhan, Kookmin, and Hana), as well as 73 percent of Taegu and 57 percent of Pusan, the two largest local financial holding companies. Among nonbank financial institutions, at the end of 2012 foreign-held shares made up more than 10 percent of the outstanding capitalization for 10 of 16 insurance firms and more than 20 percent for 9 of 30 securities firms.

Despite their large ownership shares, foreign shareholders at the three largest nongovernment holding companies do not control management decisions. In contrast, the three largest second-tier banks are or have been owned and managed by foreign financial institutions: KEB (Lone Star), SC First (Standard Chartered), and Citibank Korea (Citicorp).[20] In addition, there were 39 foreign bank branches operating in Korea at the end of 2012.

The three largest banks accounted for about 33 percent of total assets and 37 percent of loans and discounts of all DMBs at the end of 2012. While foreign investors do not control or manage the three largest domestic banks, they do exert influence by monitoring performance and pressuring bank mangers to maximize shareholder value. Moreover, depending on changes in earning prospects, foreign investors can and will

---

20. Lone Star sold its stake in KEB to Hana Bank in 2010.

adjust their holdings, which is another way of putting pressure on bank management to keep watch on changes in bank stock prices.[21]

The three foreign-managed banks have not done particularly well in enlarging their market share in terms of bank deposits and loans.[22] For instance, they lost three percentage points in 2011, dropping down from their period-high share of deposits, 17 percent, attained in 2005. During the same period, they lost more than four percentage points in loan market share, dropping to about 9.7 percent in 2011. A possible explanation for the decline is that the banks may place a higher value on earnings and profits than on enlarging their client base.[23]

The return indicators—return on assets (ROA) and return on equity (ROE)—for the four largest and the three second-tier banks have varied a great deal since 2001, with ROA in the range of −0.1 to 1.36 percent and ROE between 1.9 and almost 30 percent. From 2004 to 2012 the individual average ROAs of the seven banks were much the same; differences among the banks were statistically insignificant.[24] As for the variance, Woori displays a higher degree of volatility than other banks. In general, differences in the variance among the seven banks are statistically significant, implying that the profitability of Woori is relatively less stable than that of other banks.[25]

Lacking retail banking networks, foreign bank branches specialize in wholesale banking, foreign currency transactions, and derivatives trading. Like the three foreign-controlled commercial banks, the foreign branches have added a variety of local securities to their asset portfolios. Whereas in 2001 their share in total securities holdings of the banking

---

21. Park, Kim, and Park (forthcoming) examine the effect of changes in the stock prices on the number of shares held by foreign investors at the three majority-foreign-owned banks during the post-1997 crisis period. They find no strong association in practice. So far as asset-liability management, efficiency, and soundness are concerned, there appears to be little difference between the foreign-owned and controlled banks and other financial institutions.

22. Park, Lee, and Lee (2011) reach a similar conclusion.

23. Since building a customer base is costly and time-consuming in a market grounded on relationship banking, the three foreign-controlled banks have opted to emphasize asset management and, as a result, have drawn the bulk of their income and profits from investments in bonds, equities, and other marketable instruments.

24. The period is chosen for the relative stability of the ROAs and ROEs.

25. For an equality test for the average, the Anova and Welch F-tests were used, and for the variance Bartlett's and Levene's tests were used.

sector was just 7 percent, it shot up to more than 30 percent during the 2007–2009 crisis period, as foreign bank branches served as a conduit for capital from abroad.

On the liability side, deposits in local and foreign currencies at foreign branches have been less than 4 percent since 2000; the bulk of their funding has come from borrowing from wholesale funding markets abroad and from their own headquarters. As most of these liabilities are short-term, their assets consist mostly of short-term foreign currency loans and securities such as Bank of Korea monetary stabilization bonds.

Foreign branches obtain a relatively large share of their income and profits from trading in derivative products and fee-based services, such as making currency trades on behalf of customers, providing backup lines of credit, and guaranteeing debt securities. Between 2000 and 2004, noninterest income comprised about 30 percent of their total earnings, but from 2006 to 2008 it was almost 60 percent.

Most foreign banks with branches in Korea are large global banks active in international finance. Foreign currency lending at these branches is by and large dictated by management of global asset portfolios at their headquarters, often in disregard of local market conditions or the need for foreign currency liquidity. This was the case in 2008 when the foreign bank branches withdrew much of their foreign currency lending and liquidated their investments in local securities.

It is estimated that much of the loss of $60 billion in foreign exchange reserves in 2008 was the result of the withdrawal of foreign currency funds by foreign bank branches. Since foreign currency funds account for 30 to 40 percent of the volume of daily foreign currency transactions in Korea, the foreign bank branches were singled out as contributing to the volatility of capital flows, an assessment that prompted the adoption of regulations limiting foreign currency forward exposure to 250 percent of a bank's capital.[26]

---

26. Korean exporters—in particular, shipbuilders—and asset management firms sold their future export proceeds or their foreign-currency-denominated assets in the forward foreign currency market to hedge their values. Unlike exporters, however, importers obtain most of their foreign currency in the spot market rather than the forward market, thereby creating a shortage of forward buying. Foreign bank branches bought forward currency and also lent foreign currency through cross currency swaps with foreign currency funds they borrowed from their headquarters to domestic banks, which sought to square their positions by borrowing foreign currency. These foreign currency transactions led to a large accumulation of external debt at Korean banks.

In summary, despite the massive increase in foreign equity holdings in banks and other nonbank financial institutions, entry liberalization has not delivered what policymakers expected from innovating and modernizing Korea's financial intermediation industries. There is in fact no evidence that foreign investors at major Korean banks or foreign-managed banks have served as a catalyst for either upgrading financial technology—including risk management—or improving corporate governance and transparency. Foreign investors, whether they seek only yields or management control as well, come to Korea primarily in search of higher returns, not as crusaders for financial reform and development.

The 1997 Financial Crisis

The story of Korean financial development can also be told through the lens of the country's successive financial crises, starting with the most dramatic one, which broke out in 1997. Between October and December 1997, Korea went from being the world's eleventh largest economy to being desperate for overnight loans from the international money markets and then surviving on emergency assistance from the International Monetary Fund.

Growth from 1994 through early 1997 had been fueled by high levels of investment, which rose to 31 percent of GDP in the fourth quarter of 1996 from 26.5 percent two years earlier.[27] This rise in investment relative to savings resulted in a current account deficit in excess of 4 percent of GDP in 1996. One of the developments boosting investment was the partial deregulation of capital inflows, which, as noted, gave banks, nonbank financial institutions, and large corporations access to low-cost foreign credit. These measures brought in a torrent of capital, which rose to 47 percent of GDP in 1994–1996 from less than 30 percent in the preceding three-year period. Short-term external liabilities climbed to more than three times the foreign exchange reserves at the start of the fourth quarter of 1997 (Figure 4.5).

These inflows were channeled into financing long-term investment by the chaebol. Banks and other financial institutions borrowed short and lent long in foreign currency, causing a large increase in the currency mismatch.

Foreign bank branches' forward exposure included currency forwards and cross-currency swaps, as well as nondeliverable currency forwards.

27. Another contributing factor was the strengthening of the yen, which brought about a sharp increase in the export earnings that stimulated capital investment in 1994–1996.

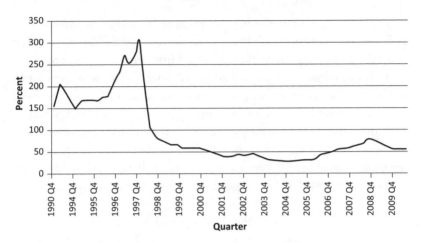

Figure 4.5. Ratio of Short-term Foreign Liabilities to Foreign Exchange Reserves, 1990–2010
Source: Bank of Korea, Economic Statistics System (ECOS), http://ecos.bok.or.kr/.

According to the aggregate effective mismatch measure estimated by Goldstein and Turner (2004, 50), Korea's mismatch had plunged to −12.4 in 1997 from about −1.6 two years earlier, and then moved into positive territory in 1999. Compared with the other crisis countries of East Asia, Korea was second only to Indonesia in terms of the extent of currency mismatch.[28]

When a slowdown in export growth and weakening terms of trade burst the investment bubble in 1996, the number of corporate bankruptcies soared, and with them, the number of nonperforming loans.[29] From December 1996 to June 1997, nonperforming loans as a proportion of total bank loans doubled (Park 1998). By September 1997 the economic slowdown had already been under way for nearly two years. Foreign banks'

---

28. Goldstein and Turner (2004) define an aggregate effective currency mismatch (AECM) as follows: AECM = NFCA/XGS (FC/TD), where NFCA = net foreign currency assets (+) or liabilities (−); XGS = exports of goods and services (national income account), when NFCA is negative; MGS = imports of goods and services (national income account), when NFCA is positive; and FC/TD = foreign currency share of total debt.

29. Korea's exports suffered partly as a result of the depreciation of the yen beginning in the third quarter of 1995, and the terms of trade continued to deteriorate for the next two years.

Table 4.2. Foreign Reserves of the Bank of Korea (US$ billions)

		1997						1998
	1996	March	June	Sept.	Oct.	Nov.	Dec.	Jan.
Official foreign reserves (A)	33.2	29.2	33.3	30.4	30.5	24.4	20.4	23.5
Deposits at overseas branches (B)	3.8	8.0	8.0	8.0	8.0	16.9	11.3	11.0
Other (C)	—	—	—	—	0.2	0.2	0.2	0.2
Usable reserves (A–B–C)	29.4	21.1	25.3	22.4	22.3	7.3	8.9	12.4

Source: Bank of Korea, ECOS.

Note: Official foreign reserve holdings are based on the International Monetary Fund definition. Deposits at overseas branches are those deposits made by the Bank of Korea at overseas branches of domestic commercial banks. In November 1997, when the domestic commercial banks were unable to repay their loans from foreign banks, the Bank of Korea supported them by making foreign currency deposits at their overseas branches.

rollover rates for short-term loans to Korean financial institutions and foreign exchange reserves had both fallen to alarming levels.

Having resisted pressure for depreciation since the early months of 1997, the government made a goal-line stand at 1,000 won per dollar, intervening heavily in the foreign exchange market. Between July and November, the central bank sold $12.2 billion in the spot market and $7 billion in the forward market. The Bank of Korea's reserves fell by $10 billion (Table 4.2). The government further strained investors' confidence by failing to divulge the Bank of Korea's actual foreign reserves and forward-market commitments. It asserted that the central bank held about $30 billion in reserves, when in fact usable reserves had already dropped below $22 billion at the end of March. By the end of November they had fallen to $7 billion.

The situation was then compounded by the downgrading of Korea's sovereign credit rating. In January 1997, Moody's Corporation had already lowered Korea's rating to A1 and Standard and Poor's (S&P) had dropped it to AA–. On 24 October, S&P lowered the country's credit rating to A+, and then on 28 November Moody's cut it further, to A3. Moody's readjusted its rating downward twice more and S&P did so three more times before the end of the year. Whenever the sovereign rating was lowered, the premium on Korean securities denominated in dollars rose. In response to each further deterioration in market confidence, the rating agencies then lowered their sovereign ratings again, generating a vicious cycle of declining ratings and deteriorating market sentiment. Foreign investors abandoned the Korean stock market in droves, and Korean banks found themselves unable to roll over their short-term foreign loans. The government had no choice but to announce on 19 November that it was approaching the IMF for assistance.

On 3 December the IMF announced that its rescue package would amount to $58 billion: $21 billion from its own resources and the remainder pledged by the World Bank, the Asian Development Bank, and the Group of Seven (G7) countries, excluding Canada. The IMF would provide the disbursement of funds, and the pledges would be used as backup financing, to be available as necessary. Initially the IMF disbursed $9.1 billion, but that amount was not enough to calm the market. On 24 December $10 billion from the backup financing was added to the IMF disbursement.

The IMF rescue financing was conditioned on policy reforms that included 73 structural policy commitments—many of which were in areas not relevant to crisis management. These commitments set in motion a wide range of financial and corporate reforms. Six months after Korea agreed to the IMF loan and its policy conditions, market sentiment began to turn in Korea's favor. The return of foreign investors and a large increase in exports supported by a massive depreciation of the won paved the way for a V-shaped recovery with a burgeoning current account surplus. Korea used $30.2 billion, including $19.5 billion from the IMF. It first paid back all loans drawn from the World Bank and other international financial organizations. In August 2001 Korea closed out the $19.5 billion loan from the IMF, two years and ten months ahead of schedule.

Financial Restructuring and Its Macroeconomic Consequences

Even before the 1997 crisis, Korean commercial banks had massive increases in nonperforming loans (NPLs). They had already lost much of their capital and were on the brink of insolvency. After accepting the conditions associated with IMF rescue financing, the government embarked on a drastic restructuring of the financial sector, the first phase of which lasted until June 2001. To establish a legal basis for financial reform, it amended the Act on the Structural Improvement of the Financial Industry (ASIFI) in January 1998.

The newly established financial regulatory authority, the Financial Services Commission, determined that 12 of 33 commercial banks had capital ratios below 8 percent (as mandated by the Basel rules on capital adequacy) at the end of 1997. In June 1998 the FSC revoked the licenses of 5 banks that were deemed insolvent, and their good assets were transferred through purchase and assumption to healthier partners. Six more banks were acquired by or merged with other stronger banks, reducing the number of banks to 22 at the end of June 2001. Since then there have been four more bank mergers and acquisitions (Table 4.3).[30] In the case of nonbank financial intermediaries, restructuring was even more dramatic. The vast majority of merchant banks had their licenses revoked. More than half of all mutual savings and finance companies and 10 out of 25 leasing firms disappeared.

In restructuring the financial system, the government created two state-owned corporations, the Korea Asset Management Corporation (KAMCO) and the Korea Deposit Insurance Corporation (KDIC), to buy up nonperforming loans from financial institutions that failed or were likely to fail, and to collect those loans. KDIC insured deposits, including those at nonbank financial institutions, paid off depositors at the liquidated institutions, helped healthy banks acquire failed financial institutions, and served as the conduit for recapitalization of banks using public funds.

This restructuring was costly, as shown in Table 4.4. By the end of June 2001, when the critical phase was completed, the Korean government had spent 137.5 trillion won altogether, or 16 percent of GDP, mostly to recapitalize ailing banks, repay depositors at liquidated institutions, and purchase nonperforming loans. Of this total, 63.5 trillion won was spent on recapitalization, 38.5 trillion went to the purchase of nonperforming loans, and 30.3 trillion was used for the repayment of deposit insurance.

The 2003 Credit Boom and Bust

In the years following the 1997–1998 crisis, Korea suffered two minor financial crises. The first was when the credit card lending bubble burst in

---

30. Table 4.3 shows 22 merchant banks as having had their licenses revoked and 5 as having been merged or acquired. The difference from the discussion here reflects the fact that 1 of the 5 banks merged with another that closed voluntarily subsequent to the merger.

Table 4.3. Restructuring of Financial Institutions, November 1997–2001

	Total no. institutions at end of 1997 (a)	Type of restructuring				Ratio (b/a)	New entries	Total no. institutions at end of June 2001
		License revoked	Merger and acquisition	Dissolution, bankruptcy, or suspension	Subtotal (b)			
Banks (A)	33	5	6 (11)	—	11 (16)	33.3% (44.9%)	— (1)	22 (18)
Nonbank financial institutions (B)	2,068	116 (169)	142 (196)	321 (564)	579 (929)	28.0% (42.4%)	50 (147)	1,539 (1,287)
Merchant banks	30	22	5 (7)	—	27 (29)	90.0% (96.7%)	1 (0)	4 (2)
Securities firms	36	5	1 (8)	1 (3)	7 (16)	19.4% (44.4%)	16 (27)	45 (47)
Insurance companies	50	5 (10)	6	4 (6)	15 (22)	30.0% (44.0%)	3 (25)	38 (53)
Investment trust funds	30	6	1 (8)	—	7 (14)	23.3% (45.3%)	6 (50)	29 (67)
Mutual savings and finance companies	231	67 (113)	26 (28)	25 (1)	118 (142)	51.1% (61.5%)	12 (17)	125 (106)
Credit unions	1,666	2	102 (137)	291 (553)	395 (692)	23.7% (41.5%)	9 (14)	1,280 (988)
Leasing firms	25	9 (11)	1 (2)	— (1)	10 (14)	40.0% (56.0%)	3 (13)	18 (24)
A + B	2,101	121 (174)	148 (207)	321 (564)	590 (945)	28.1% (45.0%)	50 (148)	1,561 (1,305)

Source: Public Fund Management Committee (2004, 2009).

Note: Figures in parentheses are for the end of 2009.

Table 4.4. Public Funds Injected for Purposes of Financial Restructuring, November 1997–June 2001 (trillion won)

	Recapitalization	Capital contributions	Deposit repayment	Asset acquisition	Acquisition of nonperforming loans	Total
Bonds issued	35.5	11.2	15.3	4.2	20.5	86.7
Funds recovered	3.3	1.0	4.2	3.6	15.7	27.8
Public funds	14.2	—	0.5	6.3	2.0	23.0
Total	53.0	12.2	20.0	14.1	38.2	137.5
	(63.5)	(18.6)	(30.3)	(17.7)	(38.5)	(168.6)

Source: Public Fund Management Committee (2004, 2009).

Note: Figures in parentheses are for the end of 2009.

2003, and the second crisis was a run on the country's mutual savings banks in 2011. The former offers a classic illustration of the vulnerability of a market-oriented financial system subject to adverse selection and moral hazard in the absence of adequate prudential regulation. The latter highlights how incentives for regulatory forbearance and moral hazard create a breeding ground for collusive behavior.

The 2003 crisis had a significant impact on Korea's financial system, but unlike the 1997–1998 crisis it did not jeopardize the stability of the system overall. Credit card firms accounted for only a small share of the consumer credit market, and they were not allowed to borrow abroad. Because of this, the government was able to contain the crisis by injecting liquidity into the banking system and through other regulatory interventions.

In 1997 the government had amended the Specialized Credit Financial Business Act to allow credit card companies to make loans or cash advances. This had the effect of making it easier for business groups to enter the financial sector. Then, to revive the sagging economy in the wake of the 1997 crisis, policymakers injected liquidity into financial markets. In May 1999 they lifted the restriction on the maximum monthly cash advances on credit cards.[31] In August of the same year they gave a tax deduction for purchases made using credit cards.[32] At the height of the credit card lending boom in 2002, the number of cards outstanding per member of the economically active population was as high as 4.6, up from fewer than 2 in 1999 (Table 4.5). Between 1999 and 2002, the volume of credit card loans plus cash services grew nearly fourfold. Between 1999 and 2002 the amount of credit card billings almost tripled, to 46 percent of private consumption.

When the dot-com bubble burst in 2001 in the developed world and brought on a mild recession in Korea, investment demand, already weakened by the 1997–1998 crisis, fell further. The slowdown in investment dampened the business demand for bank loans at a time when banks were

---

31. The prime minister's office, not the Ministry of Finance and Economy, led the initiative to abolish the ceiling on monthly cash advances as part its regulatory reform program. The monthly ceiling at the time was 700,000 won, or approximately $600.

32. The objective of the new credit card policy was to curtail the use of cash transactions for tax evasion and other illegal payments, as well as to stimulate consumption (Yun 2004).

Table 4.5. Credit Card Market in Korea

	1999	2000	2001	2002	2003	2004	2005	2007	2010
Number of credit cards issued, total in millions	39.0 (1.8)[a]	57.7 (2.6)	89.3 (4.0)	104.8 (4.6)	95.5 (4.1)	83.5 (3.6)	82.9 (3.5)	88.8 (3.7)	116.6 (4.7)
Credit card loans and cash services[b]	13,761.53 (55.1%)[c]	29,516.62 (69.2%)	36,896.51 (51.4%)	50,890.36 (44.3%)	27,295.53 (17.5%)	15,415.80 (18.5%)	15,677.22 (25.8%)	18,425.60 (38.8%)	37,605.66 (34.8%)
Credit card purchases as % of private consumption	15.5%[d]	24.9%	39.1%	45.7%	43.9%	41.7%	44.8%	—	—
Total credit card assets as % of household credit	6.4%	11.1%	10.8%	11.6%	6.1%	3.2%	3.0%	2.9%	4.7%
Cash payment fees and revenues on credit card loans as % of credit card revenues	79.9%	62.5%	53.8%	44.3%	57.5%	32.1%	28.0%	19.9%	18.9%

Source: Monthly Financial Statistics Bulletin (various issues), Financial Statistics Information System (FISIS), (http://efsis.fss.or.kr/), Financial Supervisory Service (FSS).

[a] Number of credit cards issued per person.

[b] Billion won.

[c] Percent of card companies' total assets.

[d] Kang and Ma (2007).

awash with liquidity. To make up for the decline in the demand for corporate loans, banks began diversifying into mortgage and consumer loans and into lending working capital to self-owned and other small businesses.

Commercial banks were able to cater to the credit needs only of households with collateral and proper credit records. The segment of the population with limited access to bank financing therefore turned to a large and growing number of semiregulated moneylenders. Responding to the competition, commercial banks, together with their business groups (chaebol), chose the credit card business as their entrée to the retail credit market. They were attracted to the new business because card issuers were subject to relatively loose regulation, and they earned high returns on their assets, as they were allowed to charge interest rates of 20 percent or more on their cash-advance services and loans.

By 2000, most commercial banks were offering credit card services either directly or through affiliated credit card subsidiaries. The chaebol had also moved into the credit card business by establishing monoline credit card companies. The four largest credit card issuers—Samsung, LG, Koomin, and Bank and Credit—together held 90 percent of the market.[33]

The credit card business is subject to economies of scale. The infrastructure for data processing, credit analyses, and account payment and settlements requires a large initial investment (Yun 2004). Card issuers also need to build a cardholder base to induce retailers to accept their cards. As a consequence, the credit card issuers engaged in intense competition for market share from the start. They paid ten dollars to anyone who signed up for a card, neglecting even to scrutinize his or her credit record.

Supervisors were slow to respond to these excesses. As Kang and Ma (2007) observe, the competition for market share contributed to lowering the industry-wide credit screening and underwriting standards. More important, competition led card issuers to lend a disproportionate share of their loanable funds to the least creditworthy borrowers; borrowers with good credit were able obtain cheaper loans elsewhere.

Meanwhile, credit card firms funded themselves by borrowing from banks and issuing debentures, commercial paper, and asset-backed securities. Compared with other financial products (corporate bonds, for

---

33. The chaebol succeeded in capturing as much as 76 percent of domestic credit card transactions by 2002.

example), debentures, commercial paper, and ABSs carried higher interest rates. Although the high yields reflected premiums for the default risk to which credit card firms were exposed, institutional investors largely ignored the riskiness of their investments. They acted as if their holdings were guaranteed by the commercial banks and business groups that owned the credit card issuers.

A sharp increase in the volume of credit card loans and delinquent accounts in early 2003 signaled the imminent end of the boom. Card issuers began applying tighter standards for new card and loan applicants as well when renewing existing loans. This tightening created a liquidity crunch that in turn sent more accounts into arrears. Concerned by these financial difficulties, institutional investors holding debt securities issued by credit card firms prepared to unload their investments.

At this point, an accounting scandal at a subsidiary of the chaebol SK Group, the downgrading of Korea's sovereign rating by Moody's, and growing concern about North Korea's nuclear weapons program combined to disturb money and capital markets, catalyzing a response. Investors began cashing in their shares of investment trust companies (ITCs). Unable to borrow, the ITCs were forced to liquidate assets to meet demands for redemption. And with the ITCs now unable to invest to the same extent as before in debentures and ABSs issued by the credit card companies, they withdrew from the market, creating serious problems for the card industry. By the early months of 2003, many of the credit card companies were pushed to the edge of insolvency.

In response, the Bank of Korea injected 4 trillion won, or roughly $4 billion, into the banking system, and the state-owned Korea Development Bank bailed out LG Card Company by lending it 1.5 trillion won, an amount equal to more than a quarter of its creditor claims. The government pressed Samsung, LG, and Hyundai to recapitalize their credit card subsidiaries and lent to Kookmin Bank, Woori Bank, and Shinhan Bank to enable them to inject funds into their credit card arms.

Under the emergency package announced on 3 April 2003, banks and chaebol with card businesses were required to put up an additional $3.8 billion (0.6 percent of GDP) to boost the capital of their credit card affiliates. The plan mandated that banks, brokerage firms, and insurance companies arrange $4.2 billion in bridge loans to rescue the troubled ITCs. Institutional investors holding credit card debt were required to roll it over so as to give the debt issuers more time to pay.

Regulatory failure played a key role in the crisis. Until 2011, when regulatory rules on their operations were tightened, companies had not been subject to restrictions on the number of new cards they could issue or the limits on leverage, the expansion of assets, and the amounts of borrowing from the corporate bond and ABS markets. As Kang and Ma (2007) observe, there is little doubt that failure to upgrade regulatory rules and guidelines amplified the credit card boom-bust cycle. In sum, regulatory failure was the core of the problem that caused and deepened the credit card crisis—it was the root cause.

The 2008 Liquidity Crisis

In the second half of 2008, Korea succumbed to yet another crisis. Why it was so vulnerable at this point is, on initial reflection, not obvious. This time the country was not the epicenter of the crisis. It had a stock of foreign reserves eight times as large as in 1997. It was in surplus on the current account, the exchange rate was flexible, and banks held only tiny amounts of problematic U.S.-originated derivative securities. The corporate sector was in much better shape than it was in 1997.

Still, Korea was not spared during the international financial crisis. Although it held $260 billion in reserves, the equivalent of 60 percent of 2008 imports, it had to secure rescue financing to stop the run on its central bank. But it was unthinkable to approach the IMF this time, as it had in 1997. Instead, the authorities requested and received a dollar-won currency swap line from the U.S. Federal Reserve System.

Following the collapse of Lehman Brothers in September 2008, Korean banks found it increasingly difficult to roll over their short-term foreign currency loans. At its lowest point, in November, the renewal rate fell to below 40 percent, causing a sharp drop in capital inflows and a 20 percent ($60 billion) loss of foreign exchange reserves. As dollar liquidity evaporated, the nominal exchange rate depreciated to 1,509 won per U.S. dollar on 24 November, down from about 1,000 won in April 2008. The won fell by almost 18 percent in October alone. The sovereign spread jumped to 751 basis points and the CDS premium to 700 basis points at the height of the crisis on 27 October.[34] At the end of 2008 Korea's

---

34. During the crisis period, the foreign exchange market experienced a high degree of instability. The won-U.S. dollar market is small in size, and shallow, as the number of market participants is limited. On average the volume of daily foreign exchange

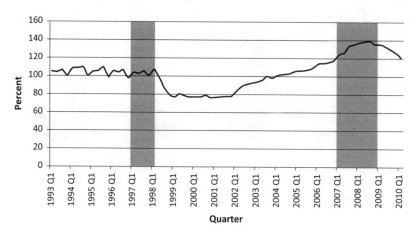

Figure 4.6. Loan-Deposit Ratio of the Korean Banking Sector
Shaded areas represent the periods from first quarter of 1997 to the first quarter of 1998, and the first quarter of 2007 to the fourth quarter of 2008.
Source: Bank of Korea, ECOS.

short-term foreign liabilities as a proportion of foreign exchange reserves rose to 97 percent, close to the so-called Greenspan-Guidotti 100 percent limit for reserve adequacy. The loan-deposit ratio had also risen steadily since 2001, as shown in Figure 4.6. Together with an emerging current account deficit, these changes signaled the existence of a sharp increase in maturity and currency mismatches in banks' balance sheets.

The question is, how did Korea get to this point? Exchange rate trends are part of the answer. The won, which had started strengthening against the dollar in late 2005, had continued to appreciate, falling below 920 won to the dollar toward the end of 2006. Faced with the erosion of export competitiveness and rising costs of sterilization, policymakers took steps to liberalize investment in foreign securities by Korean institutional and private investors. The deregulation touched off massive outflows in 2006.

By 2005 Korea's total portfolio investments abroad had risen to US$16.7 billion, the equivalent of 2 percent of GDP. They then doubled in 2006, and again in 2007. The market value of stocks, bonds, and Korean paper denominated in foreign currency held by Korean banks, insurance

---

trading has been less than 6.5 percent of GDP. The market's small size and illiquidity left it exposed to external shocks after the collapse of Lehman Brothers.

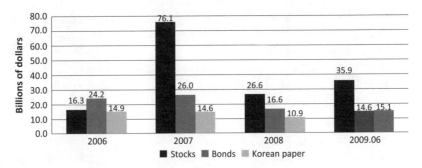

Figure 4.7. Korea's Portfolio Investments in Foreign Securities
Source: Bank of Korea, ECOS.

companies, asset management companies, and securities firms similarly more than doubled, between 2006 and 2007, to $116.6 billion in 2007 (Figure 4.7).

In 2007 the banks also purchased $60 billion of long-term forward dollar contracts from Korean shipbuilders (equivalent to 21 percent of bank investments in securities or 58 percent of bank capital). Since it takes time to build a ship, a typical shipbuilding order stipulates that the contract price will be paid in installments over the building period, in the form of advances to the builder. To limit exchange risk on future payments, shipbuilders usually take a short position, which is matched by a long position held by banks as counterparties in the forward market. Banks, for their part, are required to square their holdings of foreign currency assets and liabilities to minimize foreign exchange rate risk.[35] Because the banks held relatively small amounts of foreign currency for day-to-day retail transactions, they had to borrow the same amount of U.S. dollars of the same maturity to cover their long positions.[36]

These developments added to the demand for dollars at a time when the domestic supply was shrinking. This squeeze on the availability of dollar liquidity in the local foreign exchange market was met by a large

---

35. This arrangement can trigger a liquidity crunch if some shipbuilding orders are not fulfilled because the buyers are unable to pay.

36. At the end of 2005, the banking sector held $83 billion in foreign currency liabilities, or 44 percent of Korea's total foreign debt. Two years later the amount more than doubled to $194 billion, or 50 percent of the total foreign debt. Nonbank financial institutions and private and public enterprises were equally active in borrowing from abroad. Their external debt jumped from $89 billion at the end of 2005 to $135 billion two years later.

increase in capital inflows as banks and other financial institutions were forced to finance from abroad a growing share of their portfolio investments in foreign securities.

The total amount of external funds raised by banks by borrowing abroad came to $76 billion at the end of 2006 (equivalent to 6.2 percent of total bank liabilities). From there it shot up by 37 percent to $104 billion in 2007. Banks and other financial institutions borrowed so much in 2007 that despite a substantial increase in capital outflows, the financial account registered a $6.2 billion surplus (0.6 percent of nominal GDP). The growth of short-term foreign liabilities also exacerbated balance sheet mismatches at banks and other financial institutions. At this point, a little more than 60 percent of foreign currency assets held by banks consisted of foreign currency loans to domestic borrowers.

The risks associated with the increase in short-term foreign liabilities were further heightened by the heavy losses borne by Korean investors in foreign securities in 2007 and early 2008. Fully half of the value of their investments, which had totaled $116.6 billion at the end of 2007 (11 percent of nominal dollar GDP), evaporated in the course of 2008 as the global financial crisis worsened. More than 80 percent of the investments were not hedged against currency risk. Since they had bet against depreciation of the won, private investors ran up large foreign exchange losses when the won subsequently weakened.

The problem now was that many of these assets had been purchased with short-term loans that could not be rolled over. It became evident that some of the assets would have to be sold at deeply discounted prices. The prospect of capital losses implied a large potential increase in Korea's foreign debt burden and a drain of foreign exchange reserves. In addition, a number of ship buyers announced that, owing to the crisis, they would be unable to honor their contracts. As a result, on the delivery date shipbuilding companies were forced to purchase dollars in the spot market to clear their short positions.

How had these excesses and risks, and currency mismatches in particular, had been allowed to build up? Having seen the consequences of mismatches in the 1997 crisis, preventing them was supposedly at the top of the regulatory reform agenda. The authorities had introduced precautionary measures against their reemergence. They had adopted a regulation requiring banks to re-lend in domestic currency to local borrowers a maximum of 15 percent of foreign currency funds maturing within three months

(85 percent for foreign currency loans). Other regulations required the maturity of the local foreign currency loans to be less than three months.

But these measures were ineffective in preventing or even limiting mismatches. Their ineffectiveness stems from the role of banks as asset transformers. Banks are in the business of debt-maturity transformation, borrowing short and lending long. The maturity mismatch on their balance sheets "reflects the underlying structure of the economy in which individuals have a preference for liquidity, but the most profitable investment opportunities take a long time to pay off" (Allen and Gale 2007, 59). When banks are engaged in international financial intermediation, they are bound to incur currency mismatches, in other words.

If the global crisis of 2008–2009 was the first stiff test of the Korean authorities' new regulatory strategy, many will argue that it failed. Korea was hit harder than other Asian countries by the turmoil surrounding the Lehman Brothers collapse. In the four months ending in November 2008, the won-dollar exchange rate fell from 1,000 to nearly 1,600 (Figure 4.8). At that point there were fears that the exchange rate might spiral out of control, as first foreign and then domestic investors liquidated their positions. To support the currency, the Bank of Korea exhausted more than a fifth of its foreign exchange reserves. The KOSPI composite, meanwhile, fell from 1,850 in May to barely 1,000 in November. Clearly,

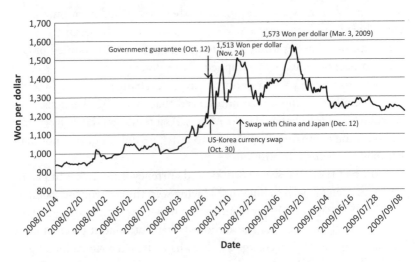

Figure 4.8. Changes in the Nominal Exchange Rate
Source: Bank of Korea, ECOS.

reforms that were supposed to deliver a more resilient financial system had not performed as expected.

Faced with a collapsing exchange rate and the rapid depletion of reserves, the government issued sovereign guarantees on new foreign loans so as to shore up foreign investors' confidence in the economy. Similar guarantees had failed to allay fears of financial meltdown at the beginning of the Asian crisis in 1997, however, and they failed again. This kind of sovereign guarantee is not credible unless the sovereign can secure hard currency. Only when Korea secured a $30 billion swap line from the U.S. Federal Reserve on 30 October did the foreign exchange market settle down. This and the subsequent renewal of the currency swap was in the U.S. interest because a massive sale of U.S. treasury bonds by Korean authorities desperate to raise dollar liquidity would have created further problems. Even so, the respite was only temporary. The exchange rate shot up to 1,509 won per dollar three weeks after the swap was announced. Apparently the swap was not enough to remove uncertainties surrounding Korea's ability to service its foreign debt, in view of large amounts of maturing bonds held by foreign investors and foreign loans to be renewed at banks in the first quarter of 2009.

Korea also succeeded in arranging swaps with the central banks of both China and Japan, each equivalent to $30 billion.[37] These additional swaps, together with the renewal of the Federal Reserve swap and a stronger current account, calmed the market. But the exchange rate remained on a roller coaster, shooting up to 1,573 won per dollar on 3 March 2009 before falling back down below 1,300 at the end of June 2009. Only gradually did liquidity and stability return.

Predictably, economic activity suffered. Growth slowed from between 5 and 6 percent to a 3 percent annual rate in the third quarter of 2008 and then to −3.4 percent in the fourth quarter and −4.3 percent in the first quarter of 2009. Industrial production fell by 12 percent year-on-year in the fourth quarter of 2008 and 16 percent year-on-year in the first quarter of 2009. The cumulative decline in manufacturing production was 25 percent. Korea had managed to grow by 0.3 percent in 2009 before rebounding to 6.2 percent in 2010. But for a country that prioritized economic growth and for a presidential administration that had prom-

---

37. Japan was reported to have been reluctant to offer a yen-won swap line. It asked Korea to approach the IMF as a condition for the swap.

ised a 7 percent growth rate, this slump was unacceptable. It was an indication that the economic and financial reforms of preceding years were not delivering the expected results.

Another interpretation is that Korea suffered such a serious shock not because of fundamental weaknesses in its economic and financial system but because it was deeply linked to a global economic and financial system that malfunctioned disastrously. Given the country's limited natural resources and energy reserves, it was natural that it should rely heavily on imports of these essential items and that it should therefore specialize in exports of manufactures. In turn this meant that the economy was disproportionately affected by the collapse of global export markets in 2008–2009. Similarly, given its relatively well-developed financial markets it was natural that Korea should have been heavily involved in markets for short-term external debt.[38] When short-term external funding dried up, it followed that the Korean financial system was placed at risk.

Comparing the 1997 and 2008 Crises

Korea fell victim to major financial crises in 1997–1998 and 2008, although neither persisted for long. The genesis and pattern of recovery was different in each case. In the run-up to the 1997 crisis, Korea continued to intervene in the foreign exchange market to keep the won-dollar exchange rate overvalued. After accepting the IMF program late in 1997, it adopted free floating. In 2008–2009 the country returned to a managed floating regime. Despite these differences, after the initial depreciation the won-dollar exchange rate ultimately depreciated by roughly the same amount in the two episodes, inclusive of crash and recovery. Bringing the exchange rate under control required intervening in the foreign exchange market, as shown in Figures 4.9 and 4.10.[39]

---

38. Rodrik and Velasco (2000), among others, have shown that countries with relatively well developed financial sectors can and do access relatively large amounts of short-term external debt. However, even during the most difficult period following the collapse of the Lehman Brothers, the volume of short-term foreign liabilities was smaller than the Bank of Korea's foreign exchange reserves. We will return to this point.

39. In Figures 4.9–4.12, period 0 corresponds to the last pre-crisis month, June 1997 (1997.6) or June 2008 (2008.6). Foreign exchange reserves and gross domestic product are computed as indices equaling 100 in each period 0.

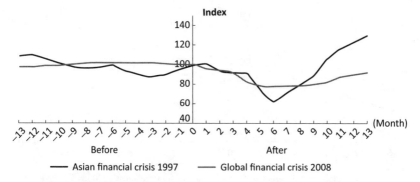

Figure 4.9. Foreign Exchange Reserves

Periods covered are May 1996 to July 1998 for the Asian financial crisis; May 2007 to July 2009 for the global financial crisis. Period 0 corresponds to the last pre-crisis month for each: June 1997 and June 2008, respectively. Foreign exchange reserves are computed as indices equaling 100 at each period 0.

Source: Bank of Korea, ECOS.

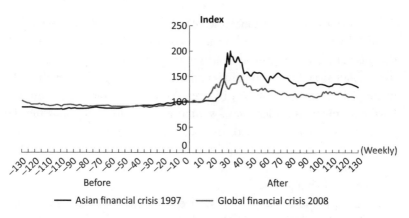

Figure 4.10. Foreign Exchange Rates, Won versus U.S. Dollar

Periods covered range from the week of 7 March 1994 (−130) to 29 November 1999 (+130) for the Asian financial crisis; 7 March 2005 (−130) to 8 November 2010 (+127) for the global financial crisis. Period 0 corresponds to the first week of June 1997 and the first week of June 2008, respectively.

Source: Bank of Korea, ECOS.

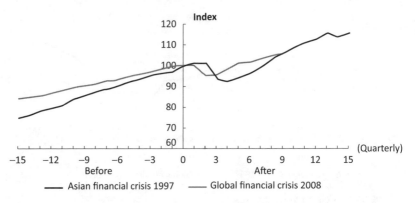

Figure 4.11. Gross Domestic Product
Periods covered range from the third quarter of 1994 to the first quarter of 2001 for the Asian financial crisis, and from the third quarter of 2004 to the third quarter of 2010 for the global financial crisis. Period 0 corresponds to February 1997 and February 2008, respectively. GDP is computed as indices equaling 100 in each period 0.
Source: Bank of Korea, ECOS.

We can see that proportional reserve losses in the two crises were roughly equal.[40] In 2008, Korea relied primarily on its own reserves to cope with the speculative attack instead of asking the IMF to come to the rescue. It spent about $50 billion, compared with the $57 billion pledged by the IMF in 1997. The stock of reserves recovered quickly in 1998 following the IMF agreement, and there was a similar recovery in 2009 following the currency swap agreement with the U.S. Federal Reserve. Both the IMF program in 1997 and the swap in 2008 succeed in turning the tide of capital outflows, whereas the use of reserves by themselves did not seem capable of achieving this.

Figures 4.11 and 4.12 show that the decline in GDP was deeper in 2008–2009. However, the economy rebounded sooner in the second crisis, even though exports dropped much further. Taken together these changes indicate that recovery from the second crisis was driven by domestic demand.

The 2011 Collapse of the Mutual Savings Bank Industry

In 1997 Korea had 237 mutual savings banks, which provided financial services for low-income households, self-employed individuals, and

---

40. Note, however, that 100 in 2008 corresponds to a volume 7.7 times larger than 100 in 1997.

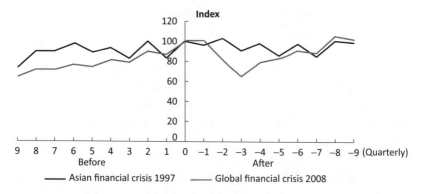

Figure 4.12. Exports

Periods covered range from the first quarter of 1995 to the third quarter of 1999 for the Asian financial crisis; from the first quarter of 2006 to the second quarter of 2010 for the global financial crisis. Period 0 corresponds to February 1997 and February 2008, respectively.
Source: Bank of Korea, ECOS.

small firms with limited access to commercial banks. In the aftermath of the 1997–1998 financial crisis the majority were closed, acquired by other savings banks, or merged, reducing their number to 116 at the end of 2002. Over the next eight years, 18 more savings banks merged or shut down.

The country's 105 savings banks experienced losses of 472.6 billion won in the fiscal year ended 30 June 2010, equal to 5.4 percent of their combined assets of 87 trillion won at the end of 2009. Financial difficulties at many small savings banks had been rumored but did not surface until January 2011 when the Financial Services Commission suspended Samhwa Mutual Savings Bank, the fourth largest in terms of assets, because its Bank for International Settlements (BIS) capital adequacy ratio had fallen below zero. This ignited a run on other savings banks, forcing the suspension of 7 more, including the largest single group of savings banks in Korea, Busan Savings Bank and its affiliates. It appears that the regulators knew that nonperforming loans were reaching alarming proportions but failed to act earlier for fear of precipitating further runs.

Like the credit card crisis in 2003, the savings bank crisis was home-grown. It did not threaten the stability of the financial system because the savings bank industry was small, accounting for about 5 percent of the total assets and capital of the banking system, and because savings banks are not allowed to borrow or lend foreign currency. It was regulatory failure that escalated a relatively minor issue of insolvency at a limited number of savings banks into a crisis.

Savings banks obtain more than 80 percent of their loanable funds from deposits. To compensate for their weaknesses vis-à-vis commercial banks and other depository institutions competing for the same funds, they pay higher interest rates.[41] These higher rates, coupled with the fact that deposits are guaranteed, attracted depositors seeking income. Between 2000 and 2010 savings bank deposits grew, on an annual average, at twice the rate of those of commercial banks.

In the wake of the 1997–1998 financial crisis, commercial banks began moving out of corporate lending, where default risk was now high, in favor of consumer loans. The proportion of total loans (by commercial banks and NBFIs) extended to the household sector more than doubled by 2005. As a result, savings banks lost consumer loan business and were forced to seek new, riskier business by extending a larger share of their loans against real estate. In addition, many savings banks were too small and had too few business lines to achieve economies of scale and scope.

To overcome these disadvantages, some savings banks set out to consolidate their activities by forming, through stock purchases, horizontally integrated alliances with other banks operating in different localities. By mid-2010, 11 groups comprising 31 savings banks had been established. This strategy offered economies of scale and scope by enabling alliance members to jointly develop new services and products and to consolidate data-processing and back-office functions. Consolidation allowed for more efficient risk diversification and larger service areas. Group and alliance members also engaged in cross lending and pooled their funds to make loans to special-purpose companies through which they financed housing and other real estate projects requiring large commitments. When the real estate boom ended following the 2008 liquidity crisis, many savings banks experienced losses as a result of their own lending decisions as well as those of their alliance partners.[42]

In 2006, the FSC exempted savings banks with BIS ratios above 8 percent and substandard loans below 8 percent from the rule prohibiting them

---

41. Depositors could own many guaranteed deposit accounts at many different banks; deposit insurance covers up to 50 million won per person per deposit-taking institution.

42. See Kang and Ma (2007).

from lending a single borrower more than 8 billion won or more than 20 percent of their capital, an initiative designed to expand business to include project finance and make these banks more profitable. Freed from the 8 billion won limit, savings banks began making large loans to special-purpose companies set up to engage in project financing. Since their main funding source was savings deposits, they were effectively borrowing short and lending long, and in the course of doing so incurring maturity mismatches. By 2010 corporate loans accounted for almost 90 percent of saving banks' total lending, and more than 50 percent of their loans were for project finance, mainly to construction and real estate rental firms.

The 2008 liquidity crisis hastened the downfall of the savings bank industry by further depressing a weakened real estate market. As property prices fell, the proportion of unpaid mortgage loans soared and expected cash flow from project financing did not materialize. By the end of 2010, 11 percent of savings bank loans were nonperforming.[43] Loans to property developers in arrears for more than a month rose to more than 24 percent of total loans.[44] By the end of June 2010, two savings banks—Samwha and Daejeon—were declared insolvent. Daejeon Savings Bank was acquired by the Busan Savings Group, and Samwha was suspended in January 2011. In September 2012 the financial regulator suspended operation of seven more savings banks that had failed to meet the capital adequacy ratio set by the Bank for International Settlements. This followed the suspension of nine banks early in the year.

A logical step at this point would have been to close the insolvent savings banks. Instead, regulators adopted a stance of regulatory forbearance; they did not have sufficient funds in the deposit insurance fund to pay off depositors and did not want to admit that they failed to adequately supervise the savings banks in question. It was also found that some regulators had been taking bribes or arranging loans for their acquaintances in return for ignoring accounting irregularities.

Investigations conducted by the prosecutor's office exposed lending irregularities and corruption scandals involving Busan Savings Bank Group and Samhwa Mutual Savings Bank. Shareholders and senior managers of Busan Savings Bank were indicted for financial crimes involving nearly

---

43. This is a conservative official estimate by the FSC; market estimates were higher.

44. These estimates are likely to be lower than actual figures, given the widespread practice among savings banks of "window-dressing" the books.

7.7 trillion won ($7.1 billion). Samhwa Mutual Savings Bank senior executive officers were indicted for lending 200 billion won illegally. Investigators also discovered that these banks had lobbied government officials and politicians to prevent their businesses from being shut down. Samhwa Bank even tipped off its employees' relatives and other customers of its impending suspension, to enable them to withdraw their deposits in advance. When the FSS denied knowledge of all this, it became the subject of mounting public criticism and mistrust.

Ultimately, five FSS employees were detained by prosecutors for suspected collusion with savings banks. A commissioner of the Board of Audit and Inspection (BAI) was arrested on suspicion of having used his influence to help Samhwa Bank avoid having to exit the market and receiving hundreds of millions of won in exchange for overlooking the bank's illegal lending early in 2010, when the BAI was conducting an investigation into Busan Savings Group. A commissioner of the Korea Financial Intelligence Unit attached to the FSC was arrested for taking tens of millions of won in bribes from a troubled savings bank in 2003 in return for promising to use his influence to help the bank escape punishment for its illegal loans.

There is little doubt that weak regulation set the stage for the crisis and that regulatory forbearance worsened it. Instead of closing down insolvent banks, regulators turned a blind eye to accounting irregularities and nonperforming loans. This attitude increased the moral hazard for savings banks. Knowing that the regulators were unwilling to put them out of business, these banks did not have an incentive to restructure; instead, they became even more reckless in their lending and lobbied the regulators and politicians to conceal their problems. The bottom line is that Korea still has a considerable way to go in making its regulatory institutions accountable and independent of politics.

Implications for Growth and Efficiency

In his survey of the literature on finance and growth, Levine (2005) suggests that finance will positively affect growth insofar as it improves the allocation of capital by easing external financing constraints on firms.[45] However, the effects of financial reform on saving are more difficult to

---

45. See also Bekaert, Harvey, and Lundblad (2006) for a positive assessment. Others would disagree with this conclusion, however. See, for example, Stiglitz (2000) and FitzGerald (2006).

determine (Bandiera et al. 2000).[46] Moreover, even if the effect is positive, an increase in domestic savings may or may not lead to a corresponding increase in investment if some of those savings are exported, as was the case in Korea after 1998.

Following the 1997 crisis, gross investment fell below 25 percent of GDP before it recovered around 2000, while progress in financial liberalization was on an upward trend (see Figure 4.1). Deregulating and opening the financial system should increase the availability of funding and reduce its cost. Other things being equal, these changes should stimulate investment. But Galindo, Schiantarelli, and Weiss (2007) show, using cross-country growth regressions, that measures of financial development do not have a significant impact on the quantity of investment, although they positively affect total factor productivity. The most important growth channel is therefore likely to be the effect of financial reform on the efficiency with which investment is allocated across firms and sectors.

J. Park and Y. C. Park (2014) ask whether the same conclusion follows from Korean experience. They examine whether financial liberalization has enhanced the productivity growth of individual firms and industries through improvements in the efficiency of lending operations—better screening and monitoring—at banks and NBFIs and by expanding the scope of capital market financing during the 1990–2007 period. In addition they ask whether there is evidence that banks rationalized their lending to allocate loanable funds more efficiently, whether firms and industries with better access to bank financing did better at raising TFP, and whether reliance on capital market financing had any impact on the productivity growth of firms and industries.

Their findings suggest that a firm's rate of return on assets is important for screening borrowers at banks and NBFIs. But the significance of this result is weakened by another finding: a positive and significant effect of the interaction of a firm's ROA with the liberalization index. These results provide some evidence that financial liberalization has changed the conduct of asset management at banks and NBFIs in ways that attach more weight to potential borrowers' ROA.[47]

---

46. At an early stage of liberalization, consumption smoothing through borrowing may reduce saving as a proportion of GDP.

47. This finding is bolstered further by the increasing importance banks have given to the ROA in their loan allocation decisions over time.

In addition, changes in the structure of finance (changes in a lagged share of direct financing) fail to show any significant effect on firms' TFP growth. Interaction terms between lagged loan growth and financial liberalization are mostly insignificant. These findings suggest that improvements in the availability of capital market financing have had little bearing on productivity growth.

Finally, Park and Park compare industries as well as firms (J. Park and Y. C. Park 2014). Their estimated coefficient on a variable representing lagged value-added growth, which corresponds to the ROA in the firm-level analysis, suggests that this has played little role in the amount of loans extended by banks and NBFIs. Unlike in the firm-level analysis, the interaction between an industry's value-added growth and financial liberalization appears to have been insignificant in influencing bank loan operations. And as in their firm-level analysis, they do not find any evidence of a positive effect of increases in bank loans to various industries on their TFP growth. Improved access to capital markets has evidently done little to upgrade industry's TFP growth. The interactive relations between loan growth and financial liberalization do not show any measurable contribution of financial reform to efficiency improvements at the industry level. The subsample regressions produce qualitatively the same results.

Overall the findings do not support the conclusions of Levine (2005); Bekaert, Harvey, and Lundblad (2006); and Galindo, Schiantarelli, and Weiss (2007). They provide only weak evidence that financial liberalization enhances efficiency, and they suggest that greater reliance on capital market financing had little positive impact on productivity growth. The explanation for this contrast may lie in the banking-sector consolidation that took place in Korea after the 1998 financial reform. Instead of nurturing a competitive banking environment, that reform created an oligopolistic market in which the four largest banks accounted for nearly three-quarters of total bank assets at the end of 2010. Rather than searching for new corporate borrowers, the banks sat on those funds to preserve the status quo.

Implications for the Distribution of Income and Wealth

Following the 1997 crisis, the distribution of income in Korea became more unequal: the Gini coefficient rose from 0.283 in 1997 to 0.310 in 2006.

Some have asked whether financial liberalization was responsible for this change. At the early stages of financial development, relaxing financial repression can bring into the organized financial system a large segment of the population that relies on informal financial markets for financing consumption and investment, but at high cost. Self-employed persons and small and medium-size firms with the ability to seek out and manage profitable businesses with high returns may have been unable to do so because they lacked access to formal financing. Financial liberalization can improve their access to banks and other formal financial intermediaries, assuming that those institutions are prepared to invest in screening borrowers efficiently. New borrowers will then benefit from the reduced cost and greater availability of finance, which in turn can create opportunities for them to move up the income and wealth ladder.

Deregulation post-1997 opened the door for banks and other financial institutions to increase consumer loans. But this did not enhance access to loans for low-income households and self-owned small businesses to any noticeable degree. Banks and other financial institutions tend to shun low-income households and small firms without real-property collateral, and even more so when they are dealing with customers without established credit. Small and medium-size firms and aspiring entrepreneurs therefore continued to enjoy little access to bank credit, whereas well-to-do households with collateral were the main beneficiaries of increased mortgage and consumer lending.

Y. C. Park and J. Park (forthcoming) use the individual household panel data from the Korea Labor and Income Panel Study (KLIPS) for the period 1999 to 2010 to analyze the effects of bank loan allocation among different income groups (quintile and decile brackets) on income distribution. The total number of household observations for the sample period was 52,505, with an average number of annual household observations of 4,773. According to their findings:

- The Gini coefficient for income distribution depicts a trend similar to those from other national household income surveys, but the Gini for the distribution of bank loans is highly skewed toward high income brackets. The two Ginis are not highly correlated to each other and their causal relation is indeterminate.
- The shares of income and bank loans are highly correlated to each other in both the quintile and decile income groups, but a Granger causality test shows that the causality between the two could run either way.

- For 1999–2008 in quintiles 1 and 2, a larger proportion of households with loan-income ratios above the bracket average eventually moved up to a higher income bracket within two years, compared with households with a below-average ratio. In the first quintile the proportion was, on average, 57 percent. The average in the second quintile was 46 percent, and with only 12 percent sliding down into the first bracket. The moving-up probability is lower for the higher income groups and declines over time. This finding suggests that a financial policy directed to allocating more bank loans to low-income households could improve the distribution of income.

The lopsided access to bank loans could have worsened the distribution of wealth, especially in the period of the real estate boom, when increases in property prices allowed already wealthy borrowers to obtain more loans and increase their net worth more than proportionately. Park, Kim, and Park (forthcoming) also examine the impact of the expansion of consumer loans on the distribution of wealth between 2000 and 2006.[48] The 2000–2006 period saw large increases in nominal wealth and income per household. There was a huge difference, however, in the growth of wealth and income. Household wealth grew by 143 percent, whereas household income grew by only 25 percent. This difference was mainly due to the real estate boom that inflated the value of housing and other real property, which was disproportionately owned by the wealthy.[49]

The inequality of wealth distribution can be measured by a comparison of the asset share of the lowest 40 percent with that of the highest 20 percent (known as the decile distribution ratio, or DDR), by the Gini coefficient, and by Theil's L index.[50] In terms of holdings of financial

---

48. Household wealth consists of real and financial assets, where financial assets include bank deposits, stocks, bonds, and net equity in life insurance and pension funds, and real assets include residential housing, commercial real estate, and land. The data are from the National Survey of Household Income and Expenditure for the year 2000 and the Survey on Household Wealth for 2006 of the Korea's National Statistical Office.

49. A growing proportion of households displayed a preference for bank deposits and for the contractual savings instruments issued by insurance companies and pension funds. The proportion of households with a stock portfolio did not change, although the share of stocks in their total financial assets fell from 8.4 percent to 6.0 percent between the two sample years. On the liability side of the household balance sheet, high-income households accumulated more debt, mostly as a result of their acquisition through bank loans of housing and other types of real estate, whereas low-income households reduced their debt.

50. In estimating Theil's L index, also known as the general entropy measure (GE), the parameter is set at zero, that is, $GE(0)$. The sum of the log of the ratio of total wealth

assets, there was a decrease in the share of the top 20 percent (56.8 percent to 53.2 percent) and a small increase in that of the lowest 20 percent (9.1 percent to 9.4 percent). In terms of real assets, however, the opposite was observed: the share of the top 20 percent of households rose (from 63.8 percent to 69.2 percent) while that of the lowest 40 percent fell (from 6.2 percent to 4.8 percent). Thus the data confirm the conclusion that inequality in wealth rose partly as a result of financial liberalization.

On balance, then, there is little indication that financial liberalization has resulted in strong increases in firm and industry efficiency or in enhanced access to external finance for working-class households and small and medium-size enterprises. If anything, it has led to a more unequal distribution of income and wealth. It also has not insulated the economy from financial disturbances, as underscored by the global credit crisis of 2008–2009.

Challenges and the Road Ahead

What to do now depends on what lessons one draws. If the lesson is that the global economy is dangerously unstable, then Korea should fundamentally rethink its strategy of economic engagement. But the idea that the global economy is so unstable as to render engagement with the rest of the world undesirable surely overstates the costs of integration relative to the benefits. The idea that Korea should turn its back on economic integration ignores the past 50 years of history, during which its engagement with the international system has helped to invigorate the economy. Instead, Korea should be prepared to take measures to safeguard itself against future crises, in the event that the global community fails again to adequately reform the international monetary and financial system.

To this end, we suggest four ways in which the country's economic and financial strategy should be rethought. First, Korea should reconsider the advantages, such as they are, of financial conglomeration. As we have observed, since the crisis of the late 1990s the Korean banking sector has come to be dominated by a small handful of relatively large institutions. The Capital Markets Consolidation Act that came into effect in February 2009 allowed these large institutions to branch into new activities with the goal of using synergies to cut costs and enhance competitiveness. It

---

per household to total wealth of the *i*th household is then divided by the household population.

consolidated the country's fourteen separate capital-markets laws into one. Notably, it removed regulations limiting the ability of bank and nonbank financial firms to compete, which in turn augers further consolidation. The authorities believe that Korean financial firms will need the scale and scope offered by conglomeration to compete internationally and provide financial support for Korean consortia seeking to export, inter alia, nuclear-power-related technology and construction services to other countries.[51]

In pursuing this strategy, the authorities are emulating the approach of financially advanced economies like the United States. But recent experience in the United States and Europe suggests that the advantages of financial conglomeration have been oversold. Financial conglomerates are difficult to manage. Cost-reducing synergies may be more mythical than real; the evidence that returns to scale continue to increase after reasonable size has been achieved is ambiguous at best.[52] Allowing financial conglomerates to become large and complex also allows them to become too big and complex to fail, creating moral hazard and encouraging excessive risk taking. This may be a problem everywhere, but it has especially been a problem in small and middle-size economies, from the United Kingdom to Switzerland, where efforts to create national champions with global reach allowed banks to grow so large relative to their economy that they were not only too big to fail but also too big to save. The crisis has breathed new life into the argument that big financial institutions should be broken up into smaller units that can be allowed to fail without threatening financial stability. It has encouraged those who argue that universalism in banking is a mistake and that, instead, deposit-taking functions should be placed in one set of institutions and the tasks of underwriting securities and making risky investments placed in another.

Korean policymakers, in other words, should think twice before traveling further down a road from which other countries have already veered. If Korea intends to remain active in international financial intermediation, policymakers should instead focus on improving the efficiency and stability of a system comprised of smaller entities, and on nurturing

---

51. Thus, in 2010 President Lee bemoaned the inability of Korean banks to provide guarantees to a consortium bidding for a contract to construct nuclear power plants in Dubai.

52. See Wheelock and Wilson (2001).

institutions capable of competing against their foreign counterparts in many of the niche markets where they have a comparative advantage.

Second, regulators should pay closer attention to liquidity management.[53] Banks in Korea rely on wholesale funding even more than banks in other emerging Asian markets.[54] The fact that Korea possesses well-developed financial markets means that households have other investment opportunities in addition to retail deposits. But rather than shrinking their balance sheets in response to the slow growth of the deposit base, Korean banks have turned to more volatile wholesale funding.[55]

Moreover, nearly 10 percent of the wholesale funding of Korean banks on the eve of the 2008 crisis was denominated in foreign currency and sourced offshore.[56] Korean bankers observe, in their defense, that their foreign currency liabilities were matched by foreign currency assets in the form of receivables owed to the country's shipbuilders, against which the banks had extended advances. But this was scant comfort given the maturity mismatch between the banks' foreign assets and liabilities.

This suggests using taxes and regulation to limit recourse to wholesale funding, something that Korea proposed in 2010 when it chaired the Group of 20. It suggests relying less on interbank borrowing. It suggests developing a better-diversified portfolio of foreign funding sources.[57] But while diversification of foreign funding sources cannot hurt, experience suggests that correlations across funding sources are likely to be higher

---

53. The Korean authorities do not oversee the adequacy of the liquidity of foreign bank branches operating in Korean markets. Supervision and regulation of their liquidity is instead the responsibility of their home countries. This is a serious problem, albeit one that is under active discussion by the Basel Committee on Banking Supervision (OECD 2010, 83).

54. See International Monetary Fund (2008).

55. Thus, bonds, borrowing, and certificates of deposit accounted for some 40 percent of Korean banks' funding as of mid-2008. Among Asian countries, only Australia and New Zealand have higher ratios.

56. The total as of mid-2008 may have been only a third of the Bank of Korea's foreign reserves, but combined with other maturing obligations there were worries that if foreign lenders failed to renew their loans the authorities would have to choose between seeing the exchange rate collapse and parting with a substantial fraction of their reserves. Again, there was nothing abnormal about this external financial dependence: countries with relatively well-developed financial systems, of which Korea is one, are in a relatively favorable position to access short-term external debt, as noted above.

57. In fact, in response to volatility in markets for dollar funding Korean banks sought to obtain foreign funding in other currencies.

than posited in conventional stress tests in periods of unusually high volatility. The implication is that banks should be required to match not only the currency composition of their assets and liabilities but also the class of assets for which short-term funding is secured to the maturity of the funding. This could be done by requiring banks to hold only safe and liquid short-term liabilities for short-term funding and to rely more on long-term notes and covered bonds.[58]

Third, the authorities need to tighten the regulation of complex derivative securities. Korea is a leader in the development of securities backed by construction loans, car loans, student loans, and credit-card receivables. Such securities often require enhancement, in the form of guarantees or additional collateral, to attain an investment-grade rating and permit them to be placed.[59] The authorities have encouraged mutual savings banks to issue securities backed by loans for construction projects and then sell the resulting asset-backed securities to institutional investors with restrictive covenants by providing credit enhancements. But in practice the credit guarantees are often provided by the same construction companies that are the recipients of the construction loans.[60] This means that they do not enhance the credit quality of the securities to the intended extent. This is a reminder of how complexity in securities markets can have systemic consequences if it is not overseen by vigorous regulation—regulation that, if vigorously applied, will inevitably slow the development of those markets.

Related to this is the question of how the authorities should manage the development of markets in derivative securities, over-the-counter (OTC) derivatives in particular. The Korea Exchange is the largest derivatives exchange in the world, measured by the number of transactions. Exchange-based trading has the advantage of price transparency and instantaneous clearing. But the CMCA now threatens to jump-start the growth of OTC markets in complex derivatives as financial conglomerates are freed to tailor derivative contracts to their clients' needs. At a time when other countries are seeking to drive OTC transactions onto

---

58. Note that if this regulation were pushed to the limit, banks would no longer be engaged in transforming short-term liabilities into long-term assets—which suggests that there are limits on these kinds of measures. Covered bonds are debt securities backed by the income streams on specific mortgages and other loans.

59. Otherwise, pension funds, insurance companies, and other institutional investors with restrictive covenants will not be able to purchase them.

60. For evidence, see K.-M. Lim (2010).

organized exchanges in order to enhance price transparency and reduce counterparty risk, going too far down this road would be a mistake. This would imply having less instrument diversity and slower market growth as the alternative, but recent experience suggests that this is an acceptable price for stability.

Finally, policymakers need to provide more forceful leadership for regional financial cooperation. In the decade following the 1997–1998 crisis, Korea accumulated nearly a quarter of a trillion dollars of foreign reserves as insurance against financial instability. This response was understandable, given how the inadequacy of reserves relative to the short-term external debt of the banks had played a central role in the earlier crisis. The lesson learned, not inappropriately, was that openness to capital flows, and to short-term offshore bank borrowing in particular, required accumulating reserve cover adequate to replace whatever share of those short-dated obligations might run off.

In 2008 Korea's reserves were more than adequate to cover its maturing debts, but they were not adequate to prevent the exchange rate from moving if foreign investors chose to repatriate their funds and sell their Korean stocks and bonds en masse. Part of the answer would be for Korea to avoid feeling obliged to buy with dollars all the won that foreigners sell. Since 1998 Korea has moved to a more flexible exchange rate, and it should use that flexibility. It is appropriate that the exchange rate should depreciate when capital flows out, just like it is appropriate that it should appreciate when capital flows in. But free floating alone will not be enough to moderate the volatility of capital flows. To reduce that volatility, Korea should consider restrictions on and disincentives for capital flows. The measures adopted in 2010 limiting the ability of banks to hedge their foreign exposures in the forward foreign exchange market, and to thereby discourage them from acquiring foreign exposures, are a step in the right direction.

An additional problem in the 2008 crisis was the belief that $200 billion of reserves did not give the authorities the margin needed to intervene effectively. Letting reserves fall below that threshold was seen as a sign of weakness that, it was feared, would destabilize the markets. And the costs of accumulating even larger reserves were prohibitive.[61] In

---

61. With $250 billion in reserve, Korea's total reserves amounted to some 25 percent of its GDP. In a world where foreigners earned an average of 8 percent on their securities investments in Korea but the Bank of Korea earned only 3 percent on its U.S.

effect the Korean authorities would have been swapping high-yielding Korean securities for low-yielding U.S. treasury bonds, without limit. They would have been using scarce resources to subsidize U.S. public finance rather than underwriting the modernization of the Korean economy. If it is necessary to hold foreign reserves not just against short-term liabilities to foreigners but also against all assets held by foreigners that might be sold, then the costs of opening to foreign investment are too high. Foreign investment in this case provides no net transfer of resources from abroad.

Rather than accumulating more dollars, the obvious way to square this circle is to borrow dollars when you need them. While the IMF is one plausible source, turning to the IMF is political poison for any Korean government. The U.S. Federal Reserve is another source, but swap arrangements with the Federal Reserve are ad hoc and therefore uncertain. Nor is it certain that U.S. political leaders would permit the agency either to provide swaps larger than the $30 billion arranged in November 2008 or to provide them under less extreme circumstances. In 2010, as G20 chair, Korea proposed the creation of "a global financial safety net," essentially a generalization of its bilateral relationship with the Federal Reserve System. Again, however, it is not clear that other countries would agree to the creation of an IMF-like system of global swaps and credits outside the IMF.

This leaves Korea's neighbors China and Japan, with which it negotiated local currency swaps, and the Association of Southeast Asian Nations Plus Three (ASEAN+3), with which Korea has negotiated a network of swaps and proposed creating a regional reserve pool, the Chiang Mai Initiative Multilateralization (or CMIM). Regional reserve pooling makes sense insofar as different East Asian countries require reserves at different times.[62] Unfortunately, the Chiang Mai Initiative has never been activated, not even in 2008 in the gravest global credit crisis in 80 years. Countries putting money on the barrelhead want assurances that their

---

treasury holdings, even abstracting from exchange rate changes this form of insurance cost the country the equivalent of 2 percent of its GDP each year, or more than a third of its economic growth. The definitive analysis of the cost of holding international reserves, on which these calculations are based, is Rodrik (2006).

62. Not even in the global crisis of late 2008 was the impact on Asian currencies, and hence on the need for reserves, symmetrical across countries.

resources not be used frivolously. They want to know that they will be repaid. But regional neighbors find it hard to criticize one another's policies and demand course corrections. These political sensitivities run especially high in Asia. A step forward would be to transform the ASEAN+3 Macroeconomic Research Office, created in conjunction with the CMIM, into a proper surveillance unit with the independence and staff needed to undertake firm surveillance. The Macroeconomic Research Office could issue a financial stability report and recommend policy adjustments as a precondition for disbursing funds. This would give participants in the CMIM the confidence they need to activate their arrangement. Support for this transformation is something in which Korea could usefully take the lead.

These reforms will not guarantee insulation from shocks to global financial markets. Only financial autarky, for which costs exceed the benefits, would guarantee that. Nor will reforms guarantee an absence of homegrown crises. Crises happen. The goal of policy should not be to suppress them entirely, insofar as they are a concomitant of financial development, but to minimize their costs.

CHAPTER 5

Government and Business Groups

A well-functioning economy achieves a balance between the roles of government and the market appropriate to its level of economic, political, and institutional development.[1] In the early stages of growth, the role of government is often pervasive, but in later stages the economy depends increasingly on the effectiveness of the business sector. The effectiveness of that business sector, in turn, hinges on the quality of corporate governance. Good corporate governance allows businesses to run in a way that promotes economic efficiency. Good corporate governance can also refer to the running of a business in the interest of its shareholders, including minority shareholders. But from a national-development point of view, running a business for its shareholders is a means to the end of achieving economic efficiency, particularly in the industrial and large-scale service sectors of the economy. Shareholder value is not an end in itself.

The government-business relationship and corporate-governance issues that have featured so prominently in Korea relate mainly to the country's large family-based business groups, the chaebol. Much of the debate is about the problem of "too big to fail" and the financial crises that have characterized the government-business relationship at key points in the country's history. It reflects how close ties between government and business produced expectations of implicit government guarantees against

---

1. Multiple literatures in economics address this issue, including the extensive literature on rent-seeking, starting with Krueger (1974); the literature on the developmental state, starting with Amsden (1989), Evans (1995), Johnson (1982), and Wade (1990); and the literature on varieties of capitalism, including Hall and Soskice (2001).

large-scale bankruptcies. But the government-business relationship debate has also been about the concentration of power, including political power, in the hands of the chaebol, and about the implications for rent-seeking, capture, and inequality.

In analyzing these issues it is important to understand how the relationship between the government and the large business groups evolved, what efforts have been made to reform that relationship, and why those efforts have failed. One concern we address in this chapter is the idea that once a country starts down a path relying on close ties between government and business groups, those ties become increasingly difficult to loosen.

In Korea's case, ties between government and business grew closer in the 1960s and 1970s as a consequence of the country's distinctive approach to industrial development. In the 1960s the government provided financial and other support to firms primarily on the basis of their export performance. This performance-based mechanism rewarded successful experiments and penalized unsuccessful ones—in the extreme, phasing them out—especially in the labor-intensive manufacturing sector. In the 1970s, when the government launched its ambitious drive to promote heavy and chemical industries (HCIs), the logic of scale economies and catch-up growth called for a more interventionist approach in which the government provided massive support and implicit guarantees against bankruptcy and controlled market entry and investment. Government support and protection went hand in hand with government influence. As a result, government-business ties became stronger, especially for those business groups selected to implement the Heavy and Chemical Industry Drive. Starting in the 1980s, successive governments then attempted to loosen those ties and reshape the behavior of the chaebol in the direction of better corporate governance. Loosening government-business ties proved to be difficult, however, and simply relaxing government control did not guarantee improved corporate governance. Although liberalization and democratization weakened government control, expectations of government protection against bankruptcy, especially of large family-owned business groups, remained strong. Even as entry restrictions and investment controls were lifted, institutional reforms and credible market signals (such as warnings of large-scale corporate failures) designed to replace weakening government control with market-based discipline were only slowly introduced.

This combination of implicit guarantees against failure without explicit restraints on management decisions allowed business groups to discount downside risks and embark on a massive spending spree, setting the stage for the 1997–1998 financial crisis.[2] The crisis forced the government to intervene directly in the affairs of the chaebol and the banking system, reversing the trend of previous years. But it also helped bring competitive pressures, including international competitive pressures, to bear on business group behavior. Efforts to protect minority shareholders from predation by controlling business group families, however, are best described as a work in progress.

Business Group Formation in Korea

A business group is a corporate structure consisting of legally independent firms operating in multiple industries and bound together by formal and informal ties (Khanna and Yafeh 2007). In contrast to multidivision structures under common ownership, a business group can have different shareholders for different firms in the same group. Groups can form through repeated contact, giving rise to long-term relationships, or from the fact that a controlling share of the ownership of each of the constituent firms is in the hands of the same economic coalition, often members of the same family.

With family ties or their equivalent serving as a guarantee of good faith, cash-rich firms can provide finance for not yet profitable but potentially viable affiliates. In many developing countries, the costs of doing business in sectors where capital requirements are high but finance is uncertain can be prohibitive. In business groups these risks can be managed through intragroup transfers, either directly or via a bank that is a member of the group. In addition, when firms are members of the same business group, they can outsource the production of specialized inputs without fear of being held up. Finally, when constituent firms operate in related industries, they can appropriate or internalize the returns from innovation to a greater extent than otherwise would be possible.

Business groups can also be a source of inefficiency, however. Horizontal groups whose members do business mainly with other members are insulated from the chill winds of competition. Groups with captive

---

2. See Hahn (2000), 215–251, and Chapter 4 of this volume.

banks may not have to compete for funds. Groups organized as pyramids, with the firm at the top owning a controlling interest in the next tier of firms, each of which owns a controlling interest in a next level of firms, and so on, may widen the gap between ownership and control and create agency problems. The controlling family may divert resources provided by outside investors or engage in "tunneling"—transferring resources from firms in which it has a smaller stake to others where its stake is larger. Management may become entrenched, frustrating attempts by outside investors to fix problems. The firms at the top of the pyramid may become too big and politically connected to fail and, knowing that, may assume excessive risk and distort policymaking.

The benefits of these extramarket arrangements may outweigh the costs in the early stages of economic growth, when market mechanisms remain underdeveloped and there is a need to jump-start industry to address coordination and innovation externalities. But with growth and modernization come improvements in the information environment and stronger contract enforcement, at which point it is possible to rely more on arms-length transactions for coordination. Multiple suppliers of inputs, domestic and foreign, mean fewer holdup problems. And with growth of the domestic market and penetration of foreign markets, adequate demand is assured. At this point the benefits of using extramarket arrangements for coordination (most of which involve direct actions by government) are overtaken by their higher costs.

The dynamic is different for innovation. Even as a country approaches the technological frontier, the role of government as a risk partner to support R&D remains important owing to the externalities thrown off by basic research.[3] Here too, however, the need to rely disproportionately on government research institutes to perform applied or industrial R&D will recede as the capacity of the private sector improves and intellectual property protections are strengthened. Even in the realm of innovation, then, the value of extramarket arrangements will likely decline in the course of economic development and maturation.

The problem is that business groups that serve as institutional substitutes for missing markets have a tendency to become entrenched. They do not slip quietly into the night. This problem of inheritance, or "institutional overhang," is not peculiar to Korea. However, it has arguably been

---

3. This is especially likely to be the case in fields such as defense and health.

a greater problem in Korea than elsewhere because of the extent to which the economy's early growth relied on extramarket mechanisms and because of the telescoped nature of the country's economic, financial, and institutional development.

The Early Years

Many of Korea's large business groups began as small family businesses, in some cases even before World War II. Of the 22 largest groups in 2000, however, only 7 trace their origins to the period before 1945. The most prominent—Hyundai, Samsung, and LG—were small family-based enterprises until the 1940s. Eleven were founded during the American occupation (1945–1948) and the Syngman Rhee government (1948–1960). Four founded in the 1960s, including Lotte and Daewoo, expanded with sufficient speed to be counted among the largest business groups in 2000 (W. Lim 2003, 37–40).

Under the Rhee government, businesses used government ties to gain access to scarce foreign exchange and valuable government contracts. Government officials generated rents for themselves and their agencies by granting favored access and contracts. Although limited industrial development did take place behind high trade barriers, the government focused on maximizing foreign exchange from aid and United Nations payments.

The situation changed, however, with the coming to power of Park Chung Hee in a military coup in May 1961, barely a year after the student revolution of April 1960. Park established an economic secretariat in the presidential mansion. In July 1961, implementing an idea that had been around for some time, he created the Economic Planning Board, merging the policymaking functions of various ministries. The EPB was charged with formulating and implementing five-year economic development plans. In 1963 it became a bona fide superministry headed by a deputy prime minister (H. Kim 1999).

In addition to these innovations to centralize the formulation of economic policy, the Park government took steps to strengthen the role of the state. Influenced by the fact that businessmen had been criticized by student protesters for having grown rich (for engaging in "illicit wealth accumulation") through political connections with the Rhee government, the Park government accused prominent businessmen of tax evasion and other illegal business practices. In lieu of fines, it demanded and received their equity shares in commercial banks. This allowed the Park government to exert direct control over the commercial banks.[4] It also meant that the government could exercise firm control over the flow of domestic credit, since there did not yet exist securities markets or nonbank financial institutions of any consequence.[5]

The authorities then created a number of quasi-governmental organizations to facilitate communication with business and labor. Business associations were used as channels for government-business interaction and were granted special favors, such as the right to allocate import quotas among member firms. Labor unions were disbanded following the 1961 coup, and the restructured Federation of Korean Trade Unions was forced to abandon its earlier militancy.

The Park government meanwhile adopted and pursued ambitious measures to reduce the investment risks facing the private sector. In particular it provided explicit repayment guarantees to foreign financial institutions on loans to Korean private-sector firms. In effect, the government took it upon itself to solve the problem of asymmetric information for foreign financial institutions, which were unwilling to spend the time and energy to examine the credit worthiness of relatively inconsequential (to them) Korean firms.

State guarantees from a country with a poor credit rating obviously would not carry much weight. Importantly, then, this state guarantee became effective only after Korea established a track record of earning hard currency through exports and paying back foreign loans. It was extended to foreign financial institutions providing loans to Korean firms and *not* to the owner-managers of those firms. Unfortunately subsequent developments starting in the 1970s would blur this distinction.

Although Park Chung Hee initially condemned business leaders as illicit wealth accumulators, eventually he concluded that state monitoring combined with private entrepreneurship offered the most effective means of carrying out his development plans. It is important to note that the government's interlocutors were not yet large business groups

---

4. The country had begun privatizing the banks in 1957, but many ended up in the hands of wealthy families and their companies, feeding disquiet over corruption and setting the stage for Park's subsequent renationalization. In addition to nationalization of the commercial banks, the capital base of the Korea Development Bank, a government-owned and operated entity, was expanded, and the Bank of Korea was placed under the control of the Ministry of Finance.

5. The Korea Stock Exchange had been created in 1956, but there were few listings of economic consequence.

but family-owned firms, often trading companies that had moved into the production of light manufactures. Owner-managers had considerable autonomy in decision making—the private sector still possessed ownership and exercised control—but they were subject to government monitoring. This monitoring could have major consequences for access to capital and thus for a private concern's broader economic prospects.

Through direct monitoring and performance-based support, the government sought to limit the costs of state-backed debt financing. All applications for foreign loans required authorization, and the resulting loans were allocated according to the policy priority of investment projects. Companies seeking foreign loans had to apply for approval from the EPB. The Ministry of Commerce and Industry advised the EPB on the technological merits of projects, and the Ministry of Finance reviewed the financial status of borrowing firms. Through the Deliberation Council for Foreign Capital Mobilization, the EPB then determined the appropriate amount of foreign funding for each application.

At this point the government introduced measures to facilitate export-oriented industrialization. To provide institutional support for foreign marketing and technology imports, in 1962 it established the Korea Trade Promotion Corporation (now the Korea Trade-Investment Promotion Agency, or KOTRA). Financially, the essence of the new system was the automatic approval of loans by commercial banks to those with an export letter of credit, which allowed businesses access to trade financing without posting collateral. The government also gave tax deductions, wastage allowances, tariff exemptions and concessional credits to exporters (Y. J. Cho and Kim 1997, 36–37). Importantly, these subsidies were sector-neutral and based on export performance. The resulting incentives were uniform and available across the board; they were the same for each U.S. dollar of export earnings. In other words, they were based on corporate performance in competitive global markets, regardless of sector.

When exports reached $100 million in 1964, the Minister of Commerce and Industry asked President Park to chair monthly export promotion meetings. Attended by high-ranking government officials and business representatives, the meetings provided a forum for monitoring progress and devising institutional solutions to emerging problems.[6] More generally,

---

6. Export insurance was one of many institutional innovations introduced in these meetings (G. Shin 1994).

regular meetings between the government and the private sector provided opportunities to attract the sustained attention of top leadership, and for leaders to monitor progress with a long-term vision, and to detect and mitigate constraints as they emerged.

That the regime was headed by a former military general with extensive police powers meant that the government's sanctions had teeth. Police power could also be used to monitor the civil service, limiting rent-seeking and corruption. And by making its support contingent on firms' performance in competitive global markets, the government tried to limit self-serving discretion on the part of the civil service. At the same time, the government sought to improve life for public officials by increasing their salaries and introducing retirement pensions.

Although Korea lifted a large number of quantitative restrictions in the mid-1960s, it maintained tariffs at a weighted average of more than 50 percent until the end of the decade. Imported intermediate inputs were made available to exporters at international prices, but tariffs on final goods were set at high levels to protect infant industries and discourage conspicuous consumption. The results turned out favorably insofar as, at this early stage in the country's industrial development and in the wake of the corruption scandals of the 1950s, policymakers had leverage over businesses rather than vice versa. So long as capital was flowing in, more borrowing meant more capacity expansion, more exports, and more foreign borrowing. In 1968 and 1969, investment increased at an annual rate of nearly 50 percent.

At the same time, foreign debt service as a share of exports rose from 6 percent in 1965 to 18 percent in 1968, 22 percent in 1969, and 31 percent in 1970.[7] Domestic loans increased as well. Overall, the debt/equity ratio of manufacturing firms soared from 92.7 percent in 1965 to 328.4 percent in 1970.

As these debts mounted and firms moved down the schedule of available investment projects, officials and others began to ask questions. In 1969 some 30 firms were already unable to meet their foreign loan obligations. As guarantor of their debts, the government assumed control of their financial operations. Concerned with the moral hazard implications of blanket bailouts, it took a principled stance against insolvent firms and held their management accountable for business decisions. Government,

---

7. Krueger (1979), 147.

after all, had guaranteed only the repayment of private-sector foreign debt to foreign lenders; it had never guaranteed the protection of governance rights to the incumbent owner-managers (W. Lim 2000).

As the Korean economy showed signs of overheating at the end of the 1960s, the IMF stepped in with a stabilization package. Monetary expansion slowed from 52 percent in 1968 to 45 percent in 1969 and 11 percent in 1970. Given tight credit controls, the commercial banks could not provide much relief to companies with heavy debt loads. Financially strapped firms were forced to turn to the last available resort, the curb market, where interest rates in 1970 hovered around 50 percent.[8] Currency devaluations by 18 percent in 1971 and an additional 7 percent in 1972 then increased the foreign-currency-denominated debt burden. A worldwide economic slowdown, combined with tight credit control and the devaluation, took a heavy toll on Korean firms.

By 1972, as a result, hundreds of firms could not meet their debt obligations. The most heavily indebted members of the corporate sector were pushed to the brink of collapse. Faced with the prospect of a systemic crisis, the government concluded that it could no longer take a principled stance against financially distressed firms, unlike in 1969. On 3 August 1972 it issued a "Presidential Emergency Decree for Economic Stability and Growth," placing an immediate moratorium on the payment of all corporate debt to curb lenders who had charged rates well above the legally mandated interest ceiling. The moratorium on debt to the curb market lasted for three years, at the end of which the debts were converted into five-year low-interest loans.[9] This was the first crisis in Korea's modern financial history. It would not be the last.

The final tally showed that curb loans had amounted to 345.6 billion won, or 80 percent of the amount of money in circulation in notes, coins, current accounts, and deposit accounts. It turned out that, in addition, more than a few company owners had made "camouflaged" curb loans to their companies as a way of evading taxes. These loans amounted to 113.7 billion won (C. Kim 2011).

Although the government subsequently pushed large companies to go public and to improve their governance and financial structure, this had

---

8. In comparison, the nominal interest rate on general bank loans was around 24 percent (Y. J. Cho and Kim 1997, 82).

9. W. Lim (2003), 45–46.

a limited effect on the chaebol. Founding families hesitated to dilute control; they therefore preferred debt over equity finance. Even when they went ahead with public offerings, the weakness of shareholder rights meant that this only placed additional distance between ownership and control, aggravating agency problems. Despite its success in averting a massive debt crisis, the 1972 moratorium on curb loans remains controversial because it seems to have exacerbated moral hazard and fueled expectations that the government would bail out debt-plagued companies if they again found themselves on the verge of bankruptcy.

The Heavy and Chemical Industry Drive

In promoting upstream industries in the 1970s, Korea faced a choice. It could play it safe and develop heavy and chemical industries for the domestic market but risk the inefficiencies of small scale and entrenched protectionism. Alternatively, it could aim to penetrate global markets but risk chronic capacity underutilization and financial strain. Ultimately, policymakers chose the second alternative, despite its risks, because it promised a dynamically efficient growth trajectory if the country managed to develop technological prowess in these sectors before financial burdens became overwhelming.

To exploit scale economies in establishing capital-intensive industries, the government decided to rely on a select group of state-owned enterprises and chaebol with successful track records, such as the Pohang Iron and Steel Company and Hyundai.[10] Well before the term came into vogue, they adopted a "cluster approach." To provide water, electricity, and transportation and to secure backward and forward linkages, the government enacted an Industrial Complex Development Promotion Law in December 1973 and set up a machinery complex in Changwon, a petrochemical complex in Yeocheon, and an electronics complex in Gumi. National universities located near these industrial complexes were encouraged to specialize in related engineering fields.

To support the Heavy and Chemical Industry Drive, the government drafted a national manpower development plan. The demand for technicians who had graduated from technical high school and obtained at least

---

10. The government felt that scale economies called for regulated monopoly or oligopoly until demand became large enough to support effective competition (O 2009).

three years of job experience was projected to rise from 340,000 in 1969 to 980,000 in 1975 and 1,700,000 in 1981. To meet this need, the government expanded technical and vocational training, strengthened science and engineering education, and established government labs to conduct R&D. In December 1973 the National Technical Certification Law introduced a system of technical training and certification based on the highly successful German model. The government established technical high schools and provided employment guarantees to ensure an adequate supply of graduates. Curricula emphasized practical training, and students were expected to acquire technical certificates before graduating.

The government had already established the Korea Institute of Science and Technology (KIST) in 1966 and the Korea Advanced Institute for Science and Technology (KAIST) in 1971. In 1972 it adopted a Technology Development Promotion Law providing tax and other incentives to encourage private-sector R&D. It established industry-specific government research institutes in the shipbuilding, electronics, machinery, metal, and chemical industries under the provisions of a Specialized Research Institute Promotion Law of December 1973. Through these efforts the government sought to address innovation externalities critical to sustained growth. In many respects this was a successful effort. Between 1973 and 1979 heavy and chemical industries accounted for 36.5 percent of facility investment in the manufacturing sector, in accordance with the government's plans (K.-M. Kim 1988).

Although the Heavy and Chemical Industry Drive was called off two years before the originally planned date of 1981, by then the government had invested $8.3 billion, or 86 percent of the intended amount.[11] Although capacity underutilization was a major problem at the end of the 1970s (not all the capacity built ahead of demand was yet fully utilized), the Heavy and Chemical Industry Drive created the foundation of Korea's defense industry as well as such leading civilian industries as steel, shipbuilding, electronics, petrochemicals, and machinery. It strengthened backward and forward linkages involving these industries as well as related industries, like automobile manufacturing, to increase the local content of exports. The establishment of the HCIs helped Korea take full advantage of the three-low boom (a low dollar, low oil prices, and low interests rates) in the second half of the 1980s and to respond effectively to industrial

11. See K.-M. Kim (1988).

restructuring challenges posed by China from the 1990s onward. Most important, the Heavy and Chemical Industry Drive set the stage for Korea's transition to an innovation-driven economy by expanding technical and engineering education and establishing a nucleus of R&D labs.[12] Thus by the late 1970s Korea had moved up from labor-intensive manufacturing to a wide range of HCIs that subsequently provided it with the internationally competitive industries that sustained growth in GDP and exports for the next two decades.

Debt, Crisis, and Stabilization

But an unintended, or underappreciated, consequence of the Heavy and Chemical Industry Drive was the accumulation by the chaebol of high levels of debt, especially external debt enjoying explicit or implicit government guarantees. The debt/equity ratio in Korean manufacturing rose from an already high 300 percent in 1974 to nearly 400 percent in 1980 and 500 percent in 1982 (Figure 5.1). Such high levels of leverage can be a serious source of financial fragility, as would become apparent soon enough.

Prominent among these debts were those owed to foreign banks. While savings rose with the growth of the Korean economy, investment rose faster. By the early 1970s, domestic savings rates had risen to 15 percent of GDP (in current prices), but investment rates were as high as 25 percent. By 1979 saving and investment rates had reached 28 and 35 percent, respectively. As in the second half of the 1960s, the difference was funded by foreign borrowing. As a result, by 1979 the country's external-debt-to-GDP ratio approached 50 percent.

The dangers of this situation were evident even to officials committed to the prevailing policies. In April 1979 President Park announced a comprehensive stabilization package designed to wind down borrowing for investment in HCIs. At its center were reduced preferences for heavy industry, together with initiatives to direct additional resources to small firms

---

12. Hidalgo et al. (2007, 482) note that high-income countries tend to specialize in "the core," a set of sophisticated industries that require a great deal of knowledge and skill, and low-income countries tend to operate in "the periphery," consisting of labor-intensive and natural resource sectors of industry. They observe that countries tend to develop goods close to those they currently produce, and can reach the core from the periphery "only by traversing empirically infrequent distances," which may explain why poor countries fail to converge with the income levels of rich countries.

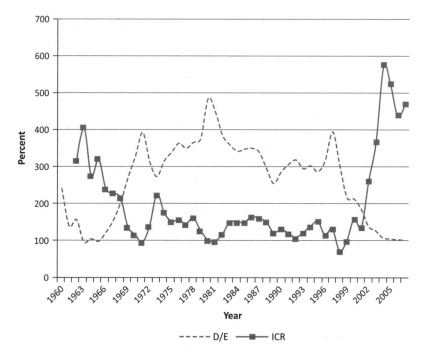

Figure 5.1. Debt/Equity Ratio (D/E) and Interest Coverage Ratio (ICR) in Korea's Manufacturing Sector
The interest coverage ratio is calculated by dividing operating income by interest expenses.
Source: Bank of Korea, Economic Statistics System (ECOS).

and light industry (Stern et al. 1995). This was a major step toward a market footing. These measures were to be backed by macroeconomic stabilization and a reduction in the rate of money and credit growth, in particular, to protect against further overheating.

From the perspective of corporate governance, the nation had also created an economy in which the implementation of industrial development programs was in the hands of the private sector, while the overall design and direction of growth and investment policies was largely handled by the government. Private businesses were beholden to the government for whatever success they achieved. The government, through its control of the banks and its guarantees of foreign loans, provided firms with credit, often at subsidized rates, and with access to foreign exchange and hence to critical imported inputs. Instead of exercising its power in an arbitrary manner, however, the government adopted a performance-based reward policy and allowed all exporters to import needed inputs duty-free and to access export financing on the submission of letters of credit from foreign buyers. It built much of the infrastructure, particularly that used by heavy industry. And it allowed chaebol entering new industries temporary oligopolies in their domestic market. What R&D existed was undertaken largely by government research institutes. The government also used its control of the education system to push educational initiatives that directly supported industrial policy initiatives.

Significant moral hazard was built into this system. When large firms got into financial trouble, as in 1972, the government took steps to bail them out at the expense of curb-market lenders. When the chaebol accumulated heavy debts in the late 1970s, the government again bailed them out, with most of the actual steps to do so being taken after President Park's assassination in October 1979. It was not so much that businesses across the board were seen as too big to fail. Rather, it was that sustaining Korea's rapid economic growth depended on the success of these large business groups. The government was clearly unwilling to jeopardize its overall development program by letting them go under. From time to time, to be sure, it was prepared to step in and discipline chaebol management. But the government's capacity to do even that was weakening, aggravating the moral hazard problem.

By the end of the Park era, the large business groups' dominance over the economy was fully established. Close connections between government and the chaebol were also firmly in place. Changing this system in fundamental ways to promote better corporate governance and less concentrated economic and political power would prove a formidable undertaking.

Partial Reform and Asymmetric Liberalization

With the change in government following Park's assassination and then Chun Doo Hwan's coup against the interim government, Korea entered into a new development phase that placed more emphasis on achieving price stability and less on government-led industrial development. When he came to power in May 1980, Chun did not have close ties to the chaebol nor did he have a particular interest in supporting them. But he inherited a system in which government had traditionally shared investment risks with private-sector firms, in part by effectively guaranteeing them against bankruptcy.

This government protection had encouraged firms to invest aggressively in the 1970s. To maintain economic stability, the government had then found itself forced to intervene in the investment decisions of private-sector firms, and in particular to place caps on the overall level of investment. For years, this combination of government control on investment and government protection against bankruptcy, with government support based primarily on export performance, had delivered remarkable economic growth. However, an abrupt withdrawal of implicit government guarantees now threatened to depress investment and, even worse, to trigger a systemic crisis. The government had to find a way to lift investment controls and remove implicit guarantees without slowing economic growth. This was a tall order when removing guarantees would likely involve corporate bankruptcies and powerful players were invested in the system.

On both economic and political economy grounds, therefore, the case for radical reform was not as clear-cut as suggested by some market-oriented technocrats. There was a shift in focus in the 1980s from industrial policy to competition and corporate governance policy, but this shift was partial, owing to both "institutional overhang" and the residual efficiency advantages of extramarket arrangements. And the resulting liberalization was asymmetric in that expectations of implicit government guarantees remained, even when government controls on investment and market entry were lifted.

Despite the sharp decline in across-the-board industrial targeting in the 1980s, selective targeting of policy, notably toward the electronics industry, continued. Policymakers agreed that the field of electronics and information technology (IT) was an important sector with large spillovers, but they were divided on Korea's prospects in this fast-moving industry.[13] Companies like LG were still producing relatively simple IT products, such as radios and television sets. Telecommunication services were poor, and the innovative capacity that had begun to develop in conjunction with the Heavy and Chemical Industry Drive was still low by the standards of the advanced industrial nations. The Economic Planning Board, not convinced that Korea could become a major player in this knowledge-

---

13. The IT sector covers information and communication instruments ranging from home electronics (e.g., televisions and radios) to electronic parts and components (e.g., semiconductors), and information communication services ranging from instrument rentals to the development, distribution, and provision of all types of software.

and capital-intensive sector, opposed making significant budget allocations to promote it. The Ministry of Commerce and Industry, for its part,
was preoccupied with the HCIs and related industries, such as automobiles. Although the Ministry of Post and Communication could claim
jurisdiction over some IT services, it did not have the stature within the
government to lead industrial policy.

In the end, Kim Jae Ik, senior presidential secretary for economic affairs, restructured the Office of the Presidential Secretary for Science and
Technology. Over the objections of other policymakers, he recruited individuals who believed that Korea had a realistic chance in the IT industry to lead promotion efforts in the early 1980s (Oh and Larson 2011).

For TV sets and telephones, deregulation was the key policy instrument because multiple private-sector firms were ready to step in. Until
1980, to discourage "conspicuous consumption," only black-and-white television broadcasting was allowed, even though Korean manufacturers were
already exporting color TV sets. In addition, consumers had to purchase
their telephones through the Ministry of Post and Communication. Noting that the private sector already possessed the capacity to produce color
TV sets as well as telephones, the Chun government lifted the ban on
color TV broadcasting in 1980 and also allowed consumers to purchase
telephones from private businesses.

With more sophisticated IT products and services, the government
played a more interventionist role. The Blue House separated the communication business from the Ministry of Post and Communication and
corporatized it as the Korea Telecommunication Authority (now known
as KT) to make it more flexible and business-oriented. Three percent of
its revenue was used for R&D and infrastructure improvement. Oh
Myung, presidential secretary for science and technology, subsequently
left the Blue House and took the position of vice minister of the post and
communication to spearhead the effort. Working together with research
institutes and private-sector companies, the government made extensive
investments to develop digital electronic switching systems for telephones
(TDX), semiconductors, and computers. In the case of semiconductors,
companies like Samsung and LG, conscious that they had to "move upstream" to survive in consumer electronics, asked the government to lead
R&D efforts because they lacked the resources to develop sophisticated
products on their own. The government also installed the National Backbone Information System as a way of creating procurement demand for

IT products and services while computerizing essential information on personal identity and property. These programs helped to lay the foundation of Korea's modern IT industry.

In 1986 the government began in a more systematic way to move away from industrial targeting, even of the limited IT variety. It consolidated sector-specific promotion laws into the Industry Development Law and shifted toward a nondiscriminatory (horizontal) industrial policy. Instead of targeting specific sectors, it focused increasingly on supporting R&D and other activities characterized by a high degree of externality. The evolving global trading regime also favored this nondiscriminatory approach.

A New Emphasis on Competition and Corporate Governance

The next step was to introduce more competition. On the last day of 1980, the government enacted the Monopoly Regulation and Fair Trade Act. The MRFTA was passed by the Emergency Committee for National Security, the governing organization set up by General Chun Doo Hwan's new military regime after he declared martial law, disbanded the National Assembly, and banned all political activities.

In the wake of the Heavy and Chemical Industry Drive, there was growing concern in Korea about the dominance of the chaebol, which had benefited enormously from concessionary, policy-oriented loans in the 1970s. As Table 5.1 shows, the share of GDP held by the top chaebol increased greatly during the drive. The Chun government embraced the popular sentiment and presented the MRFTA as a symbol of its commitment to ensuring fairness while at the same time improving economic efficiency and promoting consumer welfare.

The Monopoly Regulation and Fair Trade Act thus had a multidimensional objective, as was stated in Article 1: "to encourage fair and free competition by preventing the abuse of market dominating position and excessive concentration of economic power and by regulating undue collaborative acts and unfair trade practices, thereby stimulating creative business activities, protecting consumers and promoting the balanced development of the national economy." To prevent excessive concentrations of economic power, the newly formed Fair Trade Commission designated the largest business groups by asset size and imposed restrictions on intragroup, interfirm transactions.

Table 5.1. Chaebol's Value Added as Share of GDP (percent)

	1973	1974	1975	1976	1977	1978	1979	1980	1981
Top 5	3.5	3.8	4.7	5.1	8.2	8.1	—	—	—
Top 10	5.1	5.6	7.1	7.2	10.6	10.9	—	—	—
Top 20	7.1	7.8	9.8	9.4	13.3	14.0	—	—	—
Top 46	9.8	10.3	12.3	12.3	16.3	17.1	16.6	19.5	24.0

Source: SaKong (1993).

As Table 5.2 shows, the ownership share of the founding families in the major business groups had fallen by 1987. When ownership and control are separated, it is important to devise an incentive and monitoring scheme to ensure that managers work in the interest of owners. As the gap between ownership and control widened in chaebol-affiliated firms, the effectiveness of the state-led monitoring and incentive system was reduced but few financial institutions or institutional investors were available to step in and provide those functions. The MRFTA was an imperfect substitute.

Although the MRFTA signaled a shift away from industrial policy, the institutional legacies did not disappear overnight. Article 7 of the MRFTA prohibited mergers that would substantially restrain competition in any line of business, but it also provided exemptions for anticompetitive mergers if the Fair Trade Commission wanted to rationalize an industry or strengthen international competitiveness. This gave the commission considerable discretion in merger decisions.

With respect to collusion, the MRFTA required parties to a restrictive agreement to register it with the Fair Trade Commission for prior approval. In contrast to countries with a long tradition of antitrust law, where collusion is illegal except in special cases such as cooperative R&D, the MRFTA adopted a more discretionary approach. For example, it provided exemptions for cartels formed for the purpose of overcoming economic recession and facilitating industrial rationalization.

More import competition would have weakened market power, but the chaebol resisted trade liberalization. Although entry by foreign multinationals was another conceivable source of competition, the chaebol opposed this as well. Where there was a need for corporate restructuring, the authorities engineered mergers and acquisitions, sometimes with the

Table 5.2. In-Group Ownership Share for the Top Chaebol (percent)

	1983	1987	1989	1990	1991	1992	1993	1994	1995	1996	1997	1998	1999	2000
Top 30 chaebol	**57.2**	**56.2**	**46.2**	**45.4**	**46.9**	**46.1**	**43.4**	**42.7**	**43.3**	**44.1**	**43.0**	**44.5**	**49.6**	**43.4**
Family	17.2	15.8	14.7	13.7	13.9	12.6	10.3	9.7	10.5	10.3	8.5	7.9	5.4	4.5
Subsidiaries	40.0	40.4	31.5	31.7	33.0	33.5	33.1	33.0	32.8	33.8	34.5	36.6	45.1	38.9
Top 5 chaebol	—	**60.3**	**49.4**	**49.6**	**51.6**	**51.9**	**49.0**	**47.5**	—	—	**45.2**	**46.6**	**53.5**	—
Family	—	15.6	13.7	13.3	13.2	13.3	11.8	12.5	—	—	8.6	—	—	—
Subsidiaries	—	44.7	35.7	36.3	38.4	38.6	37.2	35.0	—	—	36.6	—	—	—
Hyundai	81.4	79.9	—	60.2	67.8	65.7	57.8	61.3	60.4	61.4	56.2	53.7	—	—
Samsung	59.5	56.5	—	51.4	53.2	58.3	52.9	48.9	49.3	49.0	46.7	44.6	—	—
Daewoo	70.6	56.2	—	49.1	50.4	48.8	46.9	42.4	41.4	41.7	38.3	41.0	—	—
LG	30.2	41.5	—	35.2	38.3	39.7	38.8	37.7	39.7	39.9	40.1	41.9	—	—

Source: Korea Fair Trade Commission, various years; Yoo (1999).

Note: The in-group ownership share for a chaebol is calculated by obtaining the weighted average of the founder's extended family's combined ownership of shares in the original family company and in all subsidiaries.

Table 5.3. Interest Rate Differential between Export Loans and General Loans, 1961–1991

	1961–1965	*1966–1972*	*1973–1981*	*1982–1986*	*1987–1991*
Export loan interest rate	9.3%	6.1%	9.7%	10.0%	10.0–11.0%
General loan interest rate	18.2%	23.2%	17.3%	10.0–11.5%	10.0–11.5%
Differential	8.9%	17.1%	7.6%	0–1.5%	0–0.5%

Source: Y.-J. Cho and Kim (1995), as cited in Park, Kim, and Park (forthcoming).

help of public funds, instead of placing distressed chaebol into bankruptcy and possibly damaging confidence and aggravating unemployment. So much for removing the expectation of too big to fail.

The record of financial reform was similarly mixed. Interest rates on policy loans provided by entities like the Korea Development Bank were brought up to market levels in 1982 (Table 5.3). The major commercial banks were privatized in 1982–1983. However, the fact that the Ministry of Finance retained the right to approve the appointment of bank presidents indicated a reluctance to relinquish the government's long-standing control of the allocation of credit. Officials at this point may have wished to favor SMEs rather than large enterprises, but the problem of inadequate distance between government and finance remained.[14] Outside directors on bank boards, for their part, did not have well-defined roles or display the activism necessary to restrain top management from pursuing their own personal and political agendas.

Officials had fewer qualms about strengthening the firewalls between the banks and chaebol. When it became evident that the chaebol planned to acquire controlling stakes in the banks in order to remain insulated from financial-market discipline and retain their preferential credit access, the authorities imposed an 8 percent ceiling on the share of bank equity that an individual chaebol could purchase. But this did not prevent chaebol from collectively purchasing larger controlling stakes. The chaebol also responded by establishing and purchasing nonbank financial

---

14. In 1980 the authorities mandated that 55 percent of the increase in local bank credit and 35 percent of city banks' credit should go to SMEs. In 1984 it temporarily froze bank credits for the top 5 chaebol and set credit ceilings for the top 30. The Office of Bank Supervision was given authority to limit the share of loans to individual chaebol in individual banks' asset portfolios.

institutions, including merchant banks, securities companies, investment trusts, and insurance companies.[15] Chaebol acquired 19 of the 31 investment finance companies established between the 1980s and early 1990s. Supervision of NBFIs was lax; even basic prudential regulations such as capital adequacy requirements were absent prior to the 1997–1998 financial crisis. Lim and Morck (forthcoming) conclude that the position of the chaebol was in fact strengthened by the reforms of the 1980s and specifically by their greater freedom of access to finance resulting from the process of partial liberalization.

This uneasy tension between inherited extramarket structures and the desire to move the Korean economy to a market footing characterized such matters for the better part of fifteen years. Although all was not well below the surface, the fact that the economy was continuing to grow meant that there was no real commitment to do anything about underlying problems. The interest-coverage ratio (operating income divided by interest expenses) basically hovered around one (or 100 percent) in the pre-crisis period, except in the mid-1970s when Korean firms benefited from artificially low interest rates following the emergency decree of 3 August 1972, and in the second half of the 1980s. No one wanted to mess with apparent success.

Reform after Democratic Transition

Starting in 1987, however, a series of developments heightened the underlying tension. The most obvious of these was democratization. In most respects the transition to democracy was overdue. It gave a voice to homeowners protesting against land grabs by big real estate developers, to retirees, and to other social groups. It provided a check on the arbitrary exercising of concentrated power. It curtailed the state's police power. But in the short run democratization also weakened preexisting restraints on

---

15. From a market-liberalization perspective, the decision in the early 1980s to relax entry barriers affecting nonbank financial institutions can be understood as a response to the danger that commercial banks with Ministry of Finance–approved presidents might still fail to make lending decisions on a purely commercial basis; competition from NBFIs was a limited way of subjecting them to market discipline. The critical mistake was assuming that NBFIs, controlled by the chaebol, would themselves be motivated to allocate resources in a manner consistent with market efficiency, and not simply cater to the needs of the chaebol.

the large business groups. Competitive elections, run without checks on campaign finance, allowed the chaebol to cultivate political connections. These connections left them confident that they would receive official aid in the event of difficulties. And when the government attempted to push back, chaebol owners became formidable political opponents.[16] If there had been an incentive before to engage in aggressive capacity expansion and to become more leveraged, that incentive was even greater now.

A second development was further financial liberalization in the early 1990s that afforded the large business groups even freer access to debt financing. The governments of Roh Tae-woo and Kim Young-sam sought to move away from the cloistered environment dominated by the chaebol and from the old government–big business partnership by placing the banks on a commercial footing and more fully opening the market to international competition. Policy lending was to become the exclusive domain of the few remaining state banks and to be funded directly, via the government budget. Financial opening also promised reciprocal treatment for Korean firms seeking to set up in other countries. It encouraged joint ventures with foreign firms. It offered more diversified sources of finance for banks and firms seeking to fund investments.

However, supervision and regulation were not upgraded at the same speed with which financial markets were liberalized. In principle, regulators subscribed to international best practice. From 1995 they required Korean banks to adhere to the Bank for International Settlements (BIS) capital adequacy ratios of 8 percent and to publish up-to-date information on their balance sheets. Banks also were required to provide detailed information to government authorities along the lines of the capital adequacy, asset quality, management ability, earnings quality, and liquidity level ("CAMEL") system followed in the United States.

But world-class rules did not create world-class practice. Supervisors could waive requirements. They required only partial application of

---

16. In 1991 Hyundai chairman Chung Ju-Yung launched the Unification National Party with the aim of running in the National Assembly elections of 1992. That the government had slapped a $180 million fine on Hyundai for illegal stock transactions had more than a little to do with Chung's political activism. In April of 1992, coincident with the campaign for National Assembly elections, the government arrested more than a dozen Hyundai executives on charges of tax evasion. Chung did run for president in December 1992 but finished third after Kim Young-sam and Kim Dae-jung. We discuss their contest in Chapter 2.

provisioning requirements in order to avoid weakening banks' earnings reports, for example. Rather than requiring financial institutions to value their investments at market price, they allowed them to value securities at their historical cost.[17] Regulators focused on commercial banks' exposures while neglecting those of specialized banks and nonbank intermediaries. The Office of Banking Supervision focused on exposures to the top business groups rather than on concentrated exposures generally. All of these problems became evident well before the crisis of 1997–1998.[18]

A new deposit insurance scheme with a low uniform premium did little to encourage market discipline. In 1996 the OECD observed that a Korean bank had never been allowed to fail and warned that deposit insurance further weakened the incentive to monitor depository institutions. It warned that the disclosure of bad loans was less complete in Korea than elsewhere, and that the level of management risk taking was greater than in other OECD countries.[19]

However bad things were in commercial banking, in merchant banking they were worse. Merchant banking in Korea had been a small backwater until 1994, when entry barriers were reduced as part of the financial liberalization drive. The population of merchant banks then exploded, and many new entrants were chaebol owned (Table 5.4). Because merchant banks did not accept deposits, the authorities maintained that they posed minimal risk to the financial system, thus justifying light regulation. But in fact the retail products offered by the merchant banks— notably, individual investment accounts with a guaranteed rate of return— were close substitutes for deposits and created many of the same liquidity risks. In addition to investing in risky high-yield assets, merchant banks borrowed abroad—short-term, in foreign currency—and then lent those funds on to the chaebol, creating currency and maturity mismatches that

---

17. This practice of "marking investment positions to market" is controversial, since it can increase financial distress and force banks and firms to engage in fire sales of assets when things go wrong. The consensus in the literature would appear to be that marking to market is desirable in normal times (it forces banks and firms to acknowledge capital gains and losses) but that it may be necessary to suspend or delay the practice in exceptional circumstances (during crises when systematic stability is threatened). In practice, the line between the two sets of circumstances is not easy to draw.

18. All this is noted in, inter alia, OECD (1996).

19. OECD (1996), 78–79.

Table 5.4. Number of Financial Institutions, Selected Years

	1983	1997	2000
Banks	23	33	22
Merchant banks	6	30	9
Securities firms	25	36	43
Insurance companies	21	50	40
Investment trust companies	3	31	27
Leasing companies	8	25	18
Mutual savings and financial companies	239	231	164
Total	325	436	323

Source: Shin and Chang (2003), Table 3.8.

posed further risks to the financial system, as would become clear in 1997–1998.

A third new development, related to the second, was capital account liberalization. Opening Korea's capital account was part and parcel of the efforts of the Roh Tae-woo and Kim Young-sam governments (1987–1997) to globalize the economy. It was a policy adopted by other advanced economies with market-based financial systems, and it was an obligation for membership in the OECD.[20]

Unfortunately, the uneven manner in which the capital account was liberalized heightened financial vulnerabilities.[21] The only nonfinancial companies permitted to tap foreign capital markets were companies investing in infrastructure projects, subsidiaries of foreign companies in technology-related industries, companies prepaying existing foreign debts, and SMEs (which were unlikely to be able to access those markets in any case). Other companies, notably chaebol, could obtain foreign credits only by applying to domestic financial institutions. Thus, if capital inflows turned around, the result would be more than just corporate finance distress and isolated bankruptcies. It would be a systemic liquidity crisis, an attack on the lifeblood of the financial system.

---

20. For additional details, see Chapter 4.

21. Here we draw on Park, Kim, and Park (forthcoming), as well as on Chapter 4 of this volume. For further analysis of Korean capital-account policy in this period and its implications, see Cho and Koh (1999); Kim, Kim, and Suh (2009); Kim, Kim, and Wang (2004); and Shin and Wang (1999).

In addition, starting in 1994 the authorities lifted ceilings on short-term foreign currency borrowing by commercial banks while leaving in place the ceiling on medium- and long-term loans. The view in official circles was that these short-term debts posed few risks. Short-term borrowing, it was believed, was mostly trade-related and would be rolled over so long as exports continued to grow, as everyone confidently expected. Short-term foreign liabilities did not add to the stock of effective foreign obligations since they matured and were repaid once the underlying export and import transactions were completed, typically within a year.[22]

The reality, of course, was different. The freeing up of short-term borrowing ahead of long-term borrowing was later seen as a major mistake.[23] If foreign equity investment slowed or, worse, reversed direction, equity prices could simply decline. If foreign finance was long-term—if it flowed into bonds—bond prices would simply fall. If it took the form of inward FDI, its slowing would not jeopardize the financial system. But the reversal of short-term capital flows intermediated by the banks, in contrast, might pose a dire threat to financial stability.

No one had better access to the cheap foreign financing now available as a result of this policy than the chaebol, which could access it via merchant as well as commercial banks. The average debt/equity ratio for Korea's manufacturing sector reached 400 percent in 1997 (see Figure 5.1).[24] The average debt/equity ratio among the top 30 chaebol was even higher, reaching an astonishing 518 percent in 1997. Confident that they were too big to fail, the chaebol used foreign finance both to expand capacity in their existing business lines and to branch into additional activities. That the borrowing in question was mainly intermediated by the banks, which borrowed funds from abroad and lent them to domestic businesses, had

---

22. See the discussion in Park, Kim, and Park (forthcoming).

23. A related problem was letting merchant banks borrow from overseas. The government loosened market entry and business restrictions for merchant bank corporations (MBCs) over the course of a few years, prior to the 1997 crisis. As a result, the number of MBCs jumped from 6 to 30, and they were allowed to engage in overseas borrowing despite their lack of experience with risk management. Faced with increased competition for overseas borrowing from MBCs, commercial banks increased their own overseas borrowing. Foreign bank lending, which had soared from an annual average of $4.0 billion in 1990–1993 to an annual average of $19.9 billion in 1994–1996, abruptly declined to $2.8 billion in 1997 as foreign creditors refused to roll over existing loans.

24. Chopra et al. (2001), 21.

a further advantage in that it did nothing to dilute the control of corporate insiders. Indeed, capital account liberalization had the unintended consequence of widening the gap between ownership and control and aggravating moral hazard problems.

The government's efforts to encourage the chaebol to go public worked in the same direction. There were as yet few independent directors to advocate for outside shareholders. Chaebol corporate boards were still captives of the founding families, and controlling shareholders could still select directors. Investors holding fewer than 5 percent of shares could not remove a director, demand a shareholders' meeting, or scrutinize a company's books. Additionally, it was hard for outsiders to reliably determine what was going on, given auditing and accounting practices that did not approach international standards. Poor share-price performance did not translate into market discipline, since the prevalence of circular ownership and pyramiding prevented hostile takeovers.

These problems had consequences. Notwithstanding the 1994–1995 boom in the important semiconductor industry, chaebol performance continued to disappoint. The return on assets in manufacturing for the top 30 chaebol was just 0.7 percent in 1996, well below the cost of capital, which bode ill for financial stability.[25] Moreover, it trended downward as the period progressed, indicating that problems were mounting. These disappointing returns reflected aggressive expansion, as discussed in Chapter 3, as well as excessive diversification. Indeed, despite the authorities' best efforts, the number of industrial branches in which the top chaebol had operations continued to rise. The result among chaebol was neglect of core competencies and the inability to control far-flung operations. All of this was common knowledge among investors: equity claims on the chaebol, which had traded at a premium relative to claims on other companies in the 1980s, were at this point being traded at a discount.[26]

Seen in this light, the 1997–1998 Asian financial crisis reflected more than just panic on the part of foreign investors.[27] To be sure, the crisis was fed by events beyond Korea's control. It occurred against the backdrop

---

25. See Krueger and Yoo (2002) and Lim, Haggard, and Kim (2003).

26. See Lim and Morck (forthcoming).

27. It is not our purpose to provide a full account of the 1997–1998 crisis here. Fuller accounts and analyses can be found in Park, Kim, and Park (forthcoming) and Eichengreen, Perkins, and Shin (2012).

of Thailand's abrupt currency devaluation and then the contagious crisis of confidence that affected Indonesia, Hong Kong, and other East Asian economies. When the vulnerability of other emerging Asian economies was so visibly revealed, there was no reason to think that South Korea would remain immune. Among other events, there was the tightening of U.S. monetary policy. There was the slowdown in the global electronics industry. There was the rise of Chinese competition. But to attribute Korea's crisis to these foreign factors and to panicked foreign investors is to overlook the importance of domestic factors. In some sense the crisis was only the culmination of ongoing problems stemming from the uneven financial development and weak corporate governance inherited from the earlier era of government-business symbiosis.

Post-Crisis Reform and the Unfinished Agenda

The 1997–1998 financial crisis, which coincided with the election of President Kim Dae-jung, began a process of more fundamental change, but one constrained by the nature of inherited government and corporate systems. President Kim was beholden neither to the chaebol nor to policies of past governments (governments that had tried to marginalize and even kill him). However, he inherited an economy and a set of laws that assumed the existence of that inherited system.

In the wake of the crisis, the president and the country faced three serious challenges. First, problems resulting from mistaken or unlawful decisions of the past had to be addressed. Foremost among these were massive nonperforming loans resulting from unprofitable investments. Public funds had to be injected to rehabilitate the financial sector. Then a measure of accountability had to be imposed on individuals who had engaged in fraud and other unlawful practices that contributed to corporate failures. Finally, to avoid a repeat of this disaster, institutional reforms had to be implemented to enhance prudential regulation, strengthen competition, reduce moral hazard, and improve corporate governance.

The first wave of post-crisis reforms was shaped by the need to staunch the bleeding, stabilize the financial sector, and restructure corporate finances and operations. Prudential supervision was consolidated in the newly created Financial Supervisory Commission. The banking system was reorganized around a core of strong banks, and the FSC formulated a rehabilitation or resolution strategy for each institution. Those strategies were then executed by the Korea Asset Management Corporation, which purchased impaired assets, and by the Korea Deposit Insurance Corporation, which injected capital and reimbursed depositors.[28]

Earlier problems created by the partial and uneven opening of the capital account were then addressed. Firms were permitted to borrow abroad on long as well as short terms, and other restrictions on foreign exchange transactions were relaxed.

The red tape to which foreign direct investment was subject was now simplified, with the goal of attracting rather than restricting FDI. In May 1998 all industries except those related to national security and the environment were thrown open to foreign competition. This included the financial sector: foreign investors were allowed to acquire Korean financial institutions. Foreign owners brought with them their business plans and practices. They trimmed staff and branches. They strengthened internal systems. They demanded representation on the boards of the institutions in which they were invested.

The Fair Trade Commission, meanwhile, became more receptive to structural solutions as the limitations of behavioral restrictions became clear. The February 1999 amendment of the MRFTA changed the provision on mergers and scrapped industrial policy exemptions. For an anti-competitive merger to receive an exemption, merger-specific efficiencies now had to clearly outweigh the harmful effects of reduced competition.[29] This change was in line with the competition-advocacy role of the Fair Trade Commission. The Omnibus Cartel Repeal Act enacted in January 1999 meanwhile removed legal exemptions for 20 cartels under 18 statutes.

Corporate restructuring, while more limited, was nonetheless extensive. By the end of 1999, 14 of the 30 largest chaebol had entered bankruptcy or a restructuring program worked out between their creditors and debtors. In some survivors, such as Samsung, management still remained

---

28. KAMCO bonds were given to banks in exchange for NPLs. KAMCO financed its operations by issuing its own bonds, guaranteed by the government, and by borrowing from the Korea Development Bank. KAMCO was to purchase nonperforming assets at their fair market value. It presented the price on a take-it-or-leave-it basis, given that there were few other buyers, in the event that a financial institution resisted the terms.

29. Otherwise the merger had to involve a failing company whose assets would be underutilized or result in anticompetitive mergers, as in the so-called failing firm defense invoked in antitrust litigation.

in the hands of descendants of the founding family, but this was not the case with others. Large corporations desperate for cash sold off important subsidiaries, such as Samsung Motor and Hyundai Construction.[30]

While some top chaebol were devastated, others seized the opportunity afforded by the failure of their competitors in the immediate wake of the 1997 crisis. They resisted downsizing. They resisted becoming more transparent. They resisted efforts to open their sheltered markets to foreign competition. The large chaebol were still able to access external finance by issuing bonds, some of which were still purchased by their captive investment-trust insurance companies. They used these resources to scoop up distressed companies and restructure their operations.

The government sought to force the business groups to focus on their core competencies by engineering a series of so-called Big Deals. They encouraged Hyundai Electronics to acquire LG Semiconductor and, in the refinery industry, urged Hyundai to take over Hanwha. Korea Heavy Industries was encouraged to buy up the power-generation facilities of Hyundai Heavy Industries and Samsung Heavy Industries. However, simply encouraging a firm to concentrate on a specific industry did not guarantee technological progress or prevent investment in excess capacity. In a sense, the approach was another legacy of the authorities' long-standing preference for scale and top-down planning, with the government proposing which affiliates should merge and which chaebol should sell or acquire specific units.

In a market economy, Big Deals of this sort, with the government directly dictating terms, are not a normal component of corporate restructuring. Bankruptcies in advanced market economies are handled by courts that bring together the various stakeholders to work out either a restructuring or a liquidation; they are not directed by the executive office of the president.[31] But Korea did not have a judicial system with experience or competence in bankruptcies, corporate restructuring, or corporate governance issues. Consequently the executive branch of the government had to step in.

Many Big Deals were never consummated. While Samsung, Hyundai, and Lotte took steps to reduce the cross-industry dispersion of their

---

30. See Lim and Morck (forthcoming).

31. There are exceptions, such as in the United States, where the White House played a major role in the restructuring of General Motors and Chrysler in 2009.

activities, there was little evidence of this for other groups, such as LG and SK Group.

The decision in August 1999 to allow Daewoo, the second largest chaebol, to declare bankruptcy was intended to signal the passing, once and for all, of the concept of too big to fail. But the action had unintended consequences. Daewoo had 85 trillion won of debt, the equivalent of 15 percent of Korea's GDP. Allowing this debt to lapse into default threatened to destabilize the investment trust companies (ITCs) that held some four-fifths of Daewoo's speculative securities. The ITCs were forced to liquidate their assets, including the bonds and commercial paper of other big corporations. This was a blow to firms already in a weakened financial state. The government was consequently forced to organize a 20 trillion won capital-market stabilization fund to bail out medium-size chaebol with commercial paper coming due. As Lim and Morck put it, these new explicit partial government guarantees replaced earlier implicit full guarantees.[32] This experience indicated that it would be more difficult than expected for the government to distance itself from the corporate and financial sectors.

The most fundamental of the reforms, those directly affecting corporate governance, were similarly incomplete. Corporate governance reform had been part of Korea's agreement with the IMF, and Kim Dae-jung, as a political outsider elected in the wake of the crisis, saw it as a route to a more transparent and equitable society. The government opted for the Anglo-Saxon approach, in which shareholders, seeking to maximize the value of their investments, are the source of discipline on insiders. Some observers questioned whether the Anglo-Saxon model was suited to Korea, given the continuing dominance of the chaebol, which make it relatively hard to obtain information on individual firms. In such an economy, they argued, the monitoring of corporate insiders is better undertaken by banks. But the banks in Korea reflected the directions of government more than any independent assessment of company loan applications (and to some degree they still do). Be that as it may, the government was committed to developing capital markets and reducing the role of the banks in the economy, thus precluding a much larger role for banks in monitoring the business groups.

---

32. Again, see Lim and Morck (forthcoming).

Efforts therefore focused on strengthening the role of directors with the goal of empowering outside shareholders. Directors were given a fiduciary responsibility. Those appointed by controlling shareholders were subjected to the same legal obligations as elected directors. Starting in 1998, all listed companies were required to appoint at least one outside director. In the case of companies listed with the Korea Stock Exchange, outside directors had to account for at least a quarter of the board. In 2001, this requirement was raised to at least half of directors in the case of listed corporations with total assets of more than two trillion won. By the end of 2006 some 1,200 outside directors had been appointed by 725 listed companies.

To protect minority shareholders, the numbers of voting shares needed to initiate the removal of a director, file a derivative suit, or inspect the corporate accounts were all lowered. In June 1999 a cumulative voting system was introduced to enable minority shareholders to elect a director to represent their interests. This permitted shareholders with less than 3 percent of the outstanding stock to appoint a director, placing an additional check on the ability of controlling interests to exploit minority shareholders. However, this system is not mandatory and most of the listed firms affiliated with chaebol have amended their charters to prevent cumulative voting.

Of course the presence of outside directors does not ensure the representation of minority investors when those filling the seats were previously associated with the company or the controlling family, as has not infrequently been the case. Similarly, simply mandating the publication of accurate financial statements does not make it happen. There remained significant gaps between the principle and practice.

That said, there was improvement in corporate management and performance in the first post-crisis decade. Reflecting in part the pressure to deliver shareholder value, there was a tendency for chaebol groups to consolidate their smaller affiliates into larger, more efficient entities, as described by Choe and Roehl (2007). Chaebol groups were most inclined to divest themselves of loosely coupled units outside their core competencies. Choe and Roehl concluded that the majority of business groups that survived the crisis transformed themselves into more focused organizations. Empirical studies have found a clear acceleration of productivity growth in the manufacturing sector after the turn of the century.[33]

---

33. Chun, Pyo, and Rhee (2008) put TFP growth at 0.7 percent per annum in 1999–2005, up from 0.3 percent in 1991–1997. See also Chapter 3.

This acceleration was most pronounced in chaebol-dominated sectors: industries producing motor vehicles, chemicals, telecommunications equipment, and miscellaneous electronics.

Improvement in corporate management and performance set the stage for the adoption of "business-friendly" policies by the Lee Myung-bak government, which saw deregulation as key to raising economic growth from 4 to 7 percent. Being business-friendly is not the same as being market-friendly, but this distinction was often lost in policymaking. The Lee government pushed ahead with a clear agenda on competition and regulatory reform, liberalizing entry restrictions in government-sanctioned monopolies. This provided new opportunities for private-sector companies. At the same time, the Lee government suspended the application of fuel-cost adjustment clauses in electricity and gas pricing rules and forced state-owned enterprises such as the Korea Electric Power Corporation and Kogas to absorb losses when crude oil and gas import prices soared. This kept electricity and gas prices artificially low for businesses and consumers but, unsurprisingly, induced inefficient and excessive fuel consumption.

The Lee government also argued that while restructuring and reform efforts in the post-crisis decade had helped to make Korean companies more efficient than transparent, those efforts had gone too far and created obstacles to international competitiveness in an age of accelerating globalization. Chaebol leaders, for their part, appealed to the government to protect them from hostile takeovers so they could focus on business and investment, which would create jobs for the national economy. In particular, the restriction on interfirm equity investments, capped at a certain percentage of net assets, became a target for deregulation. Even though this regulation had helped to contain the separation of control rights from cash-flow rights (and hence pyramiding), it had few if any international parallels, with most countries choosing to provide protections and remedies to minority shareholders instead of a blanket regulation. In 2009 the Lee government abolished the restriction, but it did not introduce enhanced protections and remedies for minority shareholders. It apparently felt that post-crisis reform should be more than enough to improve Korean firms' corporate governance.

Reality was different. Even though Korean firms improved their management and efficiency, corporate malfeasance and expropriation of minority shareholders persisted. It is one thing to increase the size of a pie, but quite another to split the pie differently between controlling and noncontrolling shareholders. A firm can improve its overall performance and still fail to ensure a fair distribution of investment returns for its shareholders if minority shareholders are not sufficiently protected. Despite the introduction of outside directors in the post-crisis period, their independence has remained weak. According to a recent study, among outside directors for listed companies affiliated with large-scale business groups, the proportion with a connection to controlling shareholders and management, and thus a potential conflict of interest, hovered around 30 percent from 2006 through 2012 (S. Lee 2013). Also, according to the World Bank, Korea was ranked 49th among 185 countries in protecting investors, owing to its weak disclosure and director liability rules (World Bank 2013). The combination of limited director independence and ineffective disclosure and liability rules provided the background for a number of corporate malfeasance cases, including charges of embezzlement and breach of fiduciary duty. The most prominent cases involved the chairmen of the largest business groups, such as Samsung, Hyundai, SK, and Hanwha.

The corporate malfeasance cases convinced politicians and voters that corporate governance reform was still a work in progress. Growing economic disparities between large and small businesses provided further support for chaebol reform. All presidential candidates during the 2012 campaign called for "economic democratization." The eventual winner, Park Geun-hye, proposed the most moderate reform package among the candidates, but even her position marked a clear departure from Lee Myung-bak's business-friendly policy. She pledged to establish "a fair and transparent market regime" and create an economic system in which SMEs, microbusinesses, and consumers could share the benefits of prosperity through equal opportunity and fair compensation. In particular, she pledged to eradicate the illegal pursuit of private interests on the part of controlling families of large business groups, to improve corporate governance, and to strengthen the separation of banking and commerce.

Each of these three tasks has a specific policy agenda. First, the Park government has pledged to introduce legislation to preclude suspended sentences for embezzlement, strictly limit the exercise of amnesty for serious corporate malfeasance, and strengthen regulations on undue intra-group interfirm transactions (tunneling) that benefit controlling families at the expense of minority shareholders. Second, the government proposed to outlaw new circular shareholdings for large-scale business groups, allow noncontrolling shareholders to appoint outside directors in an independent manner, strengthen the exercise of voting rights for the National Pension Fund and other public funds, and introduce in stages cumulative voting, electronic voting, and multiple derivative action suits.[34] Third, the Park government has said it will restrict the voting rights of financial affiliates in nonfinancial affiliates to 5 percent over the next five years and lower the ceiling on bank shares owned by industrial capital. It remains to be seen how much of this reform agenda the Park government will be able implement against the backdrop of a weak global economy and fierce resistance from business groups.

Korea has come a long way in terms of institutional development. Looking at the strength of legal institutions and the efficiency of regulatory processes in 185 countries, the World Bank report *Doing Business 2013* placed Korea in 8th place overall.[35] Although Korea performed poorly in protecting investors (49th) and registering property (75th), it scored well in enforcing contracts (2nd), trading across borders (3rd), getting electricity (3rd), getting credit (12th), and resolving insolvency (14th). This means that market-based transactions are more viable now than during the early years of development and Korea could afford to rely less on extramarket arrangements. The task of updating institutional arrangements to better serve the needs of an advanced economy remains incomplete, however, as evidenced by Korea's ranking in investor protection. Korea still faces the challenge of dealing with the legacies of earlier government interventions, including large business groups and idiosyncratic financial development. Realistically, the solution is not to get the government out

---

34. In a circular shareholding scheme, A owns shares in B, B owns shares in C, and C owns shares in A, thus completing the loop (A-B-C-A). The net effect is the same as a mutual or cross-shareholding scheme (A-B-A). Other presidential candidates in 2012 wanted to phase out existing circular shareholdings in addition to outlawing new circular shareholding arrangements.

35. World Bank (2013). Based on quantitative indicators, the World Bank's *Doing Business* reports assess the strength of legal institutions and the efficiency of regulatory processes by looking at ten items: starting a business, dealing with construction permits, getting electricity, registering property, getting credit, protecting investors, paying taxes, trading across borders, enforcing contracts, and resolving insolvency. The international competitiveness reports by the International Institute for Management Development (IMD) and World Economic Forum, in contrast, rely much more heavily on opinion surveys that are subject to respondents' preferences and sentiments. Korea ranked 22nd and 25th in 2013, respectively, according to IMD and the World Economic Forum.

of the economy or to break up the chaebol. These inherited structures are not going away. The challenge, rather, is to reform and update the structures so that they are better positioned to help the country meet the challenges of the twenty-first century. We provide some recommendations in the concluding chapter.

CHAPTER 6

Population, Employment, Education,

and Welfare

At the start of the Industrial Revolution and through the development of modern manufacturing, it used to be that individuals could count on being in the same occupation throughout their adult life, and in many cases their children and grandchildren followed them into similar lines of work. While changes did occur—the share of the population involved in farming in Europe and North America gradually dwindled to less than 5 percent of the workforce, and service jobs began replacing manufacturing employment in the latter part of the twentieth century—they occurred gradually, taking decades if not longer to affect employment patterns.

In Korea, the transition was more abrupt. Whereas in the early 1960s there were seven times as many adults employed in farming as in factories, just two decades later, in the mid-1980s, industry surpassed agriculture as a source of employment. Then, only two decades after that, three-quarters of all employment was in service jobs. Additionally, during the initial decades of Korea's rapid economic growth educated urban women remained in the workforce for only a short time. Today, in contrast, women make up 42 percent of the employed labor force.

In the past half century Korea has also experienced not one demographic transition but two: a first transition to a younger population and a lower dependency ratio resulting from declining mortality and fertility rates, and then a second, more recent transition to a rapidly aging population. By 2030, if demographic projections are correct, Korea will experience a third transition, from being a country with a growing total population to one with a declining total population. This shift to negative population growth will further exacerbate the problems of an aging population. A decline in the size of Korea's working-age population (ages 15 to 64) will begin even earlier, in 2016.[1]

Rapid change creates strains. Whereas in traditional Korean society families were responsible for the welfare of the elderly, many families today are no longer willing or able to care for elderly parents. Meanwhile, the need of elder care will continue to increase as life expectancy improves and the population ages while the birthrate begins to decline. On the other hand, child care needs have also grown as more women have engaged in work outside the home.

This chapter opens with a discussion of changes in the age structure of the population during the demographic transitions. We then turn to changes in the structure of employment in Korea as it moved from a primarily agrarian society to one in which first manufacturing and then services came to dominate the economy. Accompanying the changing structure of employment, there have been educational developments as the country has gone from having just a handful of high school and university graduates to one in which the great majority of the population has a tertiary-level education.[2]

Demographic Transitions

Korea's first demographic transition took place following World War II and the Korean War. After the wars, improved nutrition and the control of infectious diseases brought death rates down sharply, while family planning programs, combined with higher incomes, urbanization, and the education of women, led to a decline in the fertility rate (following the brief rise in births in the immediate aftermath of the Korean War that gave rise to Korea's baby boomers). Distinctive features of the decline in the birth rate were its unusual rapidity and a female total fertility rate well

---

1. The implications of a declining population for the growth of Korean GDP are discussed in Chapter 3.

2. The rapid growth in the quantity of education Koreans received, however, was not always accompanied by a comparable growth in quality, something that created further strains on society as college graduates sought what they considered to be appropriate employment.

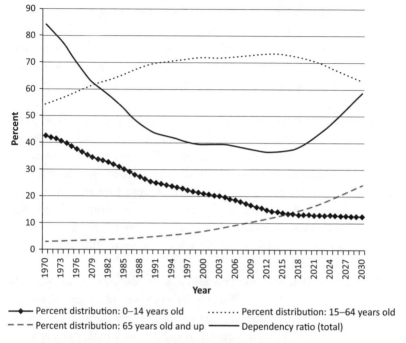

Figure 6.1. Youth and Aged Dependency Ratios, 1970–2030
Source: Korean Statistical Information Service (KOSIS), http://kosis.kr/eng/.

below that of most other OECD countries.[3] Whereas in the 1960s the share of the population that was too young or too old to participate in the workforce was almost as large as the number of people in the labor force (the dependency ratio was higher than 80 percent), by the mid-1980s, a decade and a half later, the population outside the labor force was only half the size of the working population (Figure 6.1).

This declining dependency ratio was a major factor in the growth of the economy. Without having to care for elderly parents or large numbers of children, households were better able to save and invest.[4] Where Korea in the early 1960s had a very low savings rate (less than 5 percent

---

3. The fertility rate declined from 4.53 in 1970 to 1.23 in 2010. Korea's fertility rate was the lowest among 34 OECD member countries in 2010, when the OECD average was 1.74.

4. The theoretical basis for the connection between the dependency ratio and the savings rate is known as the "life cycle hypothesis" for which Franco Modigliani won the Nobel Prize in Economics. For a fuller discussion of the impact of these demographic

of national income), by the 1970s its domestic saving rate was among the highest in the world (averaging 31 percent of national income in 1975–1979).[5] A declining dependency ratio also meant that the government did not have to devote significant resources to pensions, and the need to increase spending on schools was less than it otherwise would have been.

Korea now has ten more years before the dependency ratio is projected to rise with a vengeance. The proximate cause of the continued decline in the dependency rate is that the number of children born as a share of the total population is continuing to fall. The share of the elderly in total population, in contrast, is rising rapidly.[6] Going forward, the pace of aging will be unprecedented among high-income countries (Table 6.1). In most OECD countries it took nearly a century for the aged population to rise from 7 percent to 20 percent of the total. This will occur in Korea in just a quarter century.[7]

This second demographic transition will substantially increase the government's welfare burden. There is little prospect of increasing the size of the workforce in the next 20 years except possibly through changes in the retirement age, a major increase in the rate of female participation, or large-scale and probably politically infeasible changes in the country's immigration policies.[8] Savings and investment rates will come

---

changes on savings and investment in Korea and elsewhere in East Asia, see Higgins and Williamson (1996).

5. Economic Planning Board (1980), 20, 32.

6. Raising the retirement age could help ameliorate the impact of aging on the dependency ratio. We return to this later in the chapter.

7. The aged population is considered to be those 65 years of age and older. Even in Japan, it took 24 years for the share of the elderly to rise first from 7 percent to 14 percent and then another 12 years for it to reach 20 percent of the total population. According to Table 6.1, it will take 18 years for the share of the aged in Korea's population to rise from 7 percent to 14 percent and then just 8 years for it to reach 20 percent.

8. An and Bosworth (2013) call for an increase in immigration into Korea, but it would take a very large increase to reverse the trend toward a sharply higher share for the aged population within the next 10 to 20 years—a rate of immigration perhaps comparable to that found in countries such as the United States that, unlike Korea, were founded by immigrant populations. At its peak in the United States in 1901–1910, for example, the annual immigration rate was 1 percent of the total U.S. population, but in the second half of the twentieth century it averaged only 0.15 to 0.36 percent. For Korea, an annual immigrant flow of 0.3 percent would involve 150,000 new immigrants a year, or 1.5 million over a decade. The population over age 65 in the decade 2015–2025 in

Table 6.1. Speed of Population Aging in the World

| | Year | | | Time to next level (years) | |
Country	Aged at 7% of population	Aged at 14% of population	Aged at 20% of population	From 7% to 14%	From 14% to 20%
Japan	1970	1994	2006	24	12
France	1864	1979	2020	115	41
Germany	1932	1972	2012	40	40
United Kingdom	1929	1976	2021	47	45
Italy	1927	1988	2007	61	19
United States	1942	2013	2028	71	15
Korea	2000	2018	2026	18	8

Source: An and Bosworth (2013).
Note: The aged population is defined as those 65 years of age and older.

down, leading to a lower rate of growth in GDP and in household incomes as well, making the increase in welfare payments that much more difficult.

The Changing Structure of Employment

The rate of growth of the employed labor force declined steadily from 3.9 percent per annum in the 1970s to 2.6 percent in the 1980s and 1.5 in the 1990s, before rising slightly to 1.7 percent in the first nine years of the twenty-first century. From the 1960s through the 1980s, however, the impact of the slowing growth of the labor force was to a substantial degree offset by the shift of low-productivity labor out of agriculture and into higher-productivity industries and services (Figure 6.2). That shift of labor out of agriculture may have raised the overall GDP growth rate by as much as 1 percent per annum.[9] By the 1990s, however, this process

---

Korea, in contrast, is projected to increase by nearly 7 million (Korea National Statistical Office 2006, 125).

9. The shift in labor out of agriculture probably accounts for roughly 0.6 percent of the growth of GDP in the boom years of the 1970s and 1980s. The shift involved 1.6 percent of the labor force per year, and the share of labor income in national income at that time was roughly 0.7 percent. Assuming that productivity in urban employment

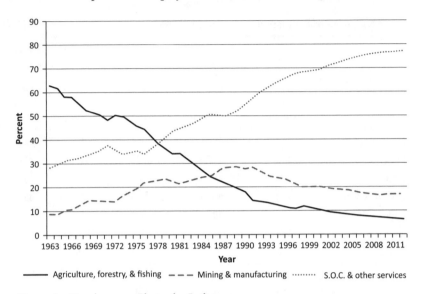

Figure 6.2. Employment Shares by Industry
Source: KOSIS data for employed workers by industry, based on the Survey of the Economically Active Population.

had largely run its course. In 1991 less than 15 percent of the labor force was still in agriculture, and in 2012 the figure was 6 percent.[10] In the future, the percent of workers moving out of agriculture will be even smaller. Eventually the flow will come to a halt altogether.

In contrast, the changing role of women in the workforce is ongoing. In 2012, women constituted 42 percent of workers, up from 35 percent in 1965 (Figure 6.3). Most women working outside the home in the 1960s were in agriculture or in low-productivity service occupations. As the economy's rapid growth proceeded, the increase in women in the labor force was mainly in manufacturing (for young low-skilled women) and service jobs (including increasing numbers of high-income jobs in recent years). The role of women in the labor force still lags behind that in other high-income OECD countries, however, leaving room for further increases in the share of women in the workforce in general, and in higher-income positions in particular. These changes are likely to be gradual, however.

---

was double that in agriculture, using growth accounting the contribution of the shift to overall GDP growth would be 0.7×1.6×0.5=0.56.

10. This meant a shift in the share of labor at a rate of only 0.4 percent per year (in contrast to a shift rate of 1.6 percent a year between 1972 and 1991).

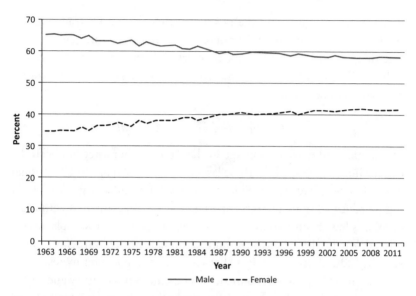

Figure 6.3. Gender Shares in Employment
Source: KOSIS.

Societal views of the role of women are shaped by cultural norms that are slow to change, and Korea's cultural norms are no exception. It is useful to observe, however, that Korea now lags behind Japan in terms of female labor force participation, despite the fact that cultural norms discouraging such participation traditionally prevailed there as well. This is a caution not to place too much emphasis on cultural arguments as opposed to economic and social policies in this regard.

Other major workforce changes include the rapid rise of the share of labor in manufacturing, followed by an equally rapid decline in manufacturing jobs beginning in the early 1990s. This decline, often referred to as "deindustrialization," is common to all high-income countries. Deindustrialization refers mainly to the declining share of industrial employment in total employment and, to a lesser extent, to the declining share of manufacturing in GDP.[11] In Korea this decline in the labor force in manufacturing occurred somewhat earlier than in other high-income countries (in terms of per capita GDP). Explanations include increasingly vigorous international competition in labor-intensive manufacturing, par-

---

11. In most high-income countries (except during major recessions, such as in 2008–2009), the real value of manufacturing output continues to increase.

ticularly from China, and the possibility that the greater tradability of services has led to an earlier shift of labor from manufacturing to services. But there is no reason to think that deindustrialization reflects major policy failures on the part of the government or unusual behavior by Korean manufacturers.[12]

Education and Human Capital

The single most dramatic change in the Korean labor force has been the extraordinary pace at which those laborers have moved up the educational ladder.[13] Korea had relatively high literacy rates and a large number of highly educated individuals before the modern era, compared with most of today's low-income countries in that earlier period.[14] The explanations offered for the difference have ranged from Korea's Confucian values, stressing education, to the fact that Korea had a more commercial society than most low-income countries in the nineteenth century and a government that chose officials partly on the basis of their education in Confucian classics.

Whatever the reason, this gave Korea a foundation on which to build a greatly expanded education system. The Japanese colonial occupation furthered the creation of this education base, although the degree to which this was the case remains controversial. Education was for the most part conducted in the Japanese language during the colonial period. A large proportion of the teaching staff in Korea was Japanese, which posed a problem when Japanese teachers left Korea after the defeat of Japan in World War II and the restoration of Korean independence. The Korean War was then a further setback, with education disrupted and many schools destroyed.

Korea thus started its modern development from a low base by modern high-income-country standards and then proceeded to expand its ed-

---

12. The deindustrialization phenomenon is discussed at greater length in Eichengreen, Perkins, and Shin (2012).

13. This section of the chapter draws on the work of Freeman, Choi, and Kim (forthcoming).

14. In this respect Korea is like other East Asian societies. There is no formal estimate for the level of literacy in Korea in the nineteenth century or earlier, but visitors to Korea, such as Elizabeth Bird Bishop, mentioned that in most of the villages they saw, a significant number of people could read simple materials written in Hangul, the Korean phonetic writing system. At the higher end of society, formal academies trained scholars and officials in the Confucian classics.

ucation system at an unprecedented rate. At the end of the Korean War, 60 percent of children in the relevant age cohort were in primary school, but only 21 percent were in middle school and 12 percent in high school (Table 6.2).[15] Enrollment in higher education was even lower, at 3 percent, although that was a much higher figure than during the Japanese colonial period.[16]

Today some 85 percent of young people in Korea attend university or junior college. This is an unprecedented level of university enrollment for any country. Figure 6.4 shows that there is a close correlation between a country's per capita income and the percentage of the relevant age cohort enrolled in universities. Korea, however, is an outlier on the high side. While the United States, Sweden, Norway, and Australia come close in terms of enrollment rates, their per capita GDP is much higher.

The rapid development of Korea's education system, especially at the tertiary level, is attributable more to the actions of the Korean people and the response of the private sector than to the efforts of the Korean government. The Park Chung Hee government did not believe that industrialization required rapid increases in university enrollment. It is likely that political considerations influenced the government's position, since large numbers of idle university graduates would have aggravated the problem of student demonstrations. In 1978 there were only 76,000 university slots available to the 320,000 high school graduates taking college entrance exams. The Chun Doo Hwan government increased the number of places substantially during the 1980s, however, and in the mid-1990s the Kim Young-sam government eliminated enrollment quotas for universities outside the Seoul metropolitan area.

Enrollment restrictions created a large unmet demand for education at all levels, eliciting a private-sector response. Privately run school enrollments accounted for 78 percent of students in kindergarten, 1 percent in primary schools, 18 percent in middle schools, 46 percent in aca-

---

15. Korea has a "6-3-3" education system, referring to the number of grades at the primary, middle, and high school levels.

16. The precise number of Korean university attendees in the colonial period is difficult to calculate because some Koreans went to universities in Japan. Keijo Imperial University (now Seoul National University), the main university in Korea at the time, did enroll Koreans, but many of the students were Japanese. Yonsei University was also founded early, with its medical school program set up by Dr. H. N. Allen in 1886 and its college established by Christian missionaries in 1915, but most of the private and public universities in Korea were founded after the restoration of independence.

Table 6.2. School Enrollment Rates (ER) and Advancement Rates (AR), 1953–2012

	Kindergarten	Primary school		Middle school			High school			Higher education
	ER	ER	AR	ER	AR	ER	AR-academic	AR-vocational		ER
1953	—	59.6	—	21.1	—	12.4	—	—		3.1
1955	—	77.4	44.8[a]	30.9[a]	64.6[a]	17.8	—	—		5.0
1960	—	86.2	39.7[b]	33.3[b]	73.3[b]	19.9	—	—		6.4
1965	—	91.6	45.4[c]	39.4[c]	75.1[c]	27.0	—	—		6.9
1970	1.3	92.0	66.1	36.6	70.1	20.3	40.2	9.6		5.4
1975	1.7	97.8	77.2	56.2	74.7	41.0	41.5	8.8		4.3
1980	4.1	97.7	95.8	73.3	84.5	48.8	39.2	11.4		6.6
1985	18.9	—	99.2	82.0	90.7	64.2	53.8	13.3		16.2
1990	31.6	100.5	99.8	91.6	95.7	79.4	47.2	8.3		19.1
1995	26.0	98.2	99.9	93.5	98.5	82.9	72.8	19.2		31.7
2000	26.2	97.2	99.9	95.0	99.6	89.4	83.9	42.0		47.8
2005	31.4	98.8	99.9	94.3	99.7	92.7	88.8	67.6		62.2
2010	40.2	99.2	99.90	97.0	99.7	91.5	81.5	76.2		70.1
2012	44.0	98.6	99.9	96.1	99.7	92.6	71.1	54.9		68.4

Source: Freeman, Choi, and Kim (forthcoming). Data for years before 1970 are from McGinn et al. (1980); data since 1970 are from KEDI, Education Statistics Database, Brief Statistics on Korean Education 2–4; Enrollment, Advancement, Employment and Discontinuation Rate by Year, http://cesi.kedi.re.kr/.

Note: ER is the percentage of students enrolled out of corresponding school-age children (kindergarten, ages 3–5; primary school, ages 3–5; primary school, 6–11; middle school, 12–14; high school, 15–17; and higher education, 18–21). AR is the percentage of students who advance to the next level of schooling. High school AR includes advancement to all types of higher-education institutions.

[a] 1956–57.
[b] 1959–60.
[c] 1964–65.

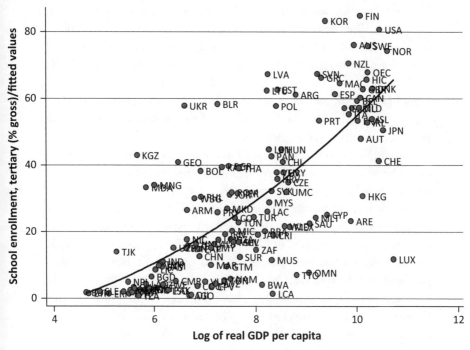

Figure 6.4. Proportion of Age Group Enrolled in College or University versus Income Per Capita
Source: T. Kim (2009) as reported in Freeman, Choi, and Kim (forthcoming).

demic high schools, 45 percent in technical high schools, 97 percent in junior colleges, and 79 percent in four-year universities. In 2012, 376 of Korea's 432 institutions of higher education were privately owned, although most relied on government support for a significant share of their budgets.

The role of private expenditure is also highlighted by the fact that government spends 3.6 percent of GDP on primary and secondary education, basically the same as the OECD average (3.7 percent).[17] But families spend an additional 1.1 percent of GDP on school tuition, textbooks, and other teaching materials, more than triple the OECD average (0.3 percent). On top of that, Korean families spend 2.0 percent of GDP on primary and secondary education outside formal institutions, for example for private *hagwon* ("cram school") tuition, private tutoring, and paid

---

17. Data for 2009 are from OECD (2012), 246, Table B2.3.

Internet lectures (excluding public Education Broadcasting Service programs). The combined total of 6.7 percent of GDP is significantly in excess of the OECD average (4.0 percent).[18] This combination of substantial government and private expenditures is a major reason why Korea has succeeded in lowering the student-teacher ratio in elementary school from 62 in 1965 to 25 in 2005 while also raising enrollment rates. However, the high private-sector share of the spending means that the burden on families is considerable.

Expenditures on tertiary education are dominated to an even greater extent by private payments. While Korea in 2009 spent 2.6 percent of GDP on tertiary education, an exceptionally large share (1.9 percent of GDP) was in the form of private tuition payments. The OECD averages for total and private expenditures on tertiary education in the same year were 1.6 percent and 0.5 percent of GDP, respectively. The comparable figures for the United States were 2.6 percent and 1.0 percent. But these tuition payments, while high even by OECD standards in the absence of other large sources of financial support, have not been enough to make most Korean universities competitive with better universities in other OECD countries. Universities still receive only modest sums for research (Table 6.3). In contrast to the situation in primary and secondary schools, student-teacher ratios in junior colleges and universities have not improved substantially. Rapidly rising enrollment has not been matched by equally rapid expansion in the number of teachers, especially at the tertiary level.[19]

Private ownership does not necessarily mean private control. Up through secondary school, the government has set curricula for all schools, although private schools have been allowed to choose whom to hire. Korea's former military governments played an active role in the selection of high-level public university leaders, but with democratization that approach gave way to a system in which university presidents and deans are elected

---

18. For the OECD data, see OECD (2012); the Korean data are from Statistics Korea (2009). The Korean survey has been conducted annually since 2007 to address concerns about the burden of private education expenditures on households. Comparable surveys on private education expenditures outside formal primary and secondary educational institutions are not available, but except for in Korea and Japan, such private education is not prevalent in OECD countries.

19. The student-to-teacher ratio in universities peaked around 35 in the mid-1980s, and subsequently improved to 25 just before the 1997 economic crisis. It then rose once again to reach 40 in 2002 and has come down slightly since.

Table 6.3. Expenditures on Higher Education per Student, Korea versus
OECD Average and Selected Other Countries, 2009

	All tertiary education spending per student relative to GDP (%)	*All tertiary education spending excluding R&D (%)*
Korea	35	30
OECD average	42	30
United States	65	58
Japan	49	—
Germany	44	27
Sweden	54	25
Switzerland	48	21
	Total expenditures per student in US$ at PPP	*Expenditures less R&D in US$ at PPP*
Korea	9,513	8,095
OECD average	13,728	9,526
United States	29,201	26,313
Japan	15,957	—
Germany	15,711	9,594
Sweden	19,961	9,464
Switzerland	21,577	9,464

Source: Data from OECD (2012), Table B1.2, Table B1.4, 229, 231.
Note: PPP = purchasing power parity.

by faculty for short terms (typically two years). But the government still plays an active role by the shaping of rules governing education.

Government investment and control, combined with large private expenditure and a major role for private educational institutions, have produced impressive quantitative results, but the qualitative picture remains mixed. Korean students consistently score near the top on internationally standardized tests, but the question is whether those scores reflect high-quality education or teaching to the test.[20] Private tutoring and much

---

20. In *2011 Trends in International Math and Science Study*, Korea ranked second in math and third in science among 42 countries. In the 2009 Programme for International

regular classroom teaching are geared toward doing well on tests, particularly university entrance examinations.

A distinguishing feature of Korea's education system is its emphasis on rank-ordering at the entrance point of higher education. High school graduates are ranked based on their performance in school, on standardized national tests, and in interviews. Implicitly, universities are also rank-ordered based on their reputation and the strength of their alumni networks. High school graduates typically give greater weight to perceived university ranking than any other factor when making application decisions, since the rigid hierarchy of Korean universities has a powerful influence on social status and career success. Perceived university rankings are based primarily on opportunities available after graduation because of school ties; what goes on in universities between entrance and graduation tends to receive less attention. Universities' teaching and research functions are therefore secondary to their rank-ordering and network-enhancing roles. This preoccupation with rankings and network enhancing has shaped Korea's education system and led to a rat race that demands great sacrifices from parents and students as they seek to gain access to high-status institutions.

The massive expansion of higher education has thus created quality problems, due in part to the way this expansion has taken place. The number of universities and junior colleges rose from a little more than 200 in 1980 to more than 300 in 2010 without much consideration for quality control or scale economies. The student-teacher ratio in universities meanwhile deteriorated (rose), going from 27:1 in 1980 to 36:1 in 2006, compared with the OECD average of 17:1.

These quality issues are why Korean universities do not do better when ranked against their peers in other high-income countries. The Jiaotung University 2008 rating of the top 500 research universities in the world included only 8 Korean universities, and none in the top 150. The Times Higher Education World University Rankings for 2012 placed only 6

Student Assessment (PISA) tests, within a 95-percent confidence interval fifteen-year-old Korean students' ranks ranged from second to fourth in reading, third to sixth in math, and fourth to seventh in science among students in 65 countries taking the tests. Among the 34 OECD countries, Korean students ranked from first to second in reading, first to second in math, and second to fourth in science. These data come from the testing organizations.

Korean universities among the top 400 in the world: 3 in the top 100—Pohang University of Science and Technology, Seoul National University, and the Korea Advanced Institute of Science and Technology—and 1 in the second 100, the highest ranking private Korean institution, Yonsei University; the remaining 2, Korea University and Sunkyungkwan University, were ranked in the 200–250 range. Given that 71 of the top 200 universities are in the United States and 20 are in the United Kingdom, this is a respectable outcome.[21] But beyond the top 10 to 15 Korean universities, quality falls off sharply.

The number of high school students (15–17 years of age) in the population began to decline starting in 2010, and the number of university and junior college students (18–21 years of age) will begin to decline after 2014. This demographic transition has added urgency to restructuring, as many universities on the fringe in terms of scale and quality are expected to suffer declining enrollments. However, university merger and consolidation experience to date suggests that restructuring will produce the desired effects only when partner institutions (separate campuses of a merged university) are sufficiently close geographically to facilitate specialization by campus and when the prospective partners share a strong interest in consolidation.

In addition, there is growing acknowledgment that the proliferation of universities offering general curricula has run its course. The government has acknowledged the need for greater specialization and differentiation among universities, including the establishment of truly research-oriented universities with a sufficient number of full-time graduate students and good R&D facilities alongside other, more teaching-focused campuses.

The massive expansion of higher education, combined with perceived university rankings primarily based on the strength of alumni networks, has led to a growing mismatch between supply and demand in the labor market. Too many young Koreans with bachelor's degrees are ill equipped to deal with real-world challenges, while there are too few technical specialists and people with postgraduate qualifications in high-technology fields. Those who might have gone to technical high schools or specialized engineering schools in the 1970s now mostly go to universities to

---

21. Japan has 5 universities in the top 100, Germany has 4, and France has 2, by way of comparison.

reccive a general education. Because the ranking of universities is based on their general reputation rather than the performance of individual departments in terms of teaching, research, and postgraduation employment, universities are shielded from the pressure to adapt to changing realities in the labor market. Different universities generally offer the same broad profile of academic curricula instead of differentiated and specialized programs designed to respond to industry needs or strong liberal arts programs that seek to develop students' creative and critical faculties. Korea ranked 42nd among 59 countries in 2012 in the International Institute for Management Development's competitiveness ranking for university education, based on surveys of business executives.

The government has been encouraging universities to specialize, preferably in fields in which graduates are likely to find employment. Under pressure from students and businesses, universities are increasingly working with firms and local governments to redesign their curricula and make courses responsive to the skill needs of society and business.

To ensure that competition among universities is based on reliable information about their performance, the government introduced a University Information Disclosure System in 2008 to provide information on graduate employment rates, enrollment rates, full-time faculty ratios, scholarship provision, research achievements, curricular operations, and school management. However, it has yet to develop assessments that center on individual departments or faculties so as to encourage specialization and move away from the current perceived university ranking system based on general reputation. The government should also use periodic assessments of faculty and departmental research performance to reinforce the link between research and graduate education (OECD 2009b, 25). Given that the installed base effect of alumni networks is so strong and has little connection to the value added provided by a university education, the government could also promote better education (and better rank-ordering) by making financial support for universities contingent on measured improvement in students' skills between entrance and graduation.

Koreans complain about the inefficiently long hours students spend studying, particularly at the secondary level. The typical Korean secondary school student spends 50 hours a week in class or in a classroom-like setting, not counting homework, 40 percent above the OECD average (Table 6.4). From 8:00 a.m. to 4:00 p.m. and again after dinner until 9:00 p.m., students study in school. They then go to cram schools for

Table 6.4. Weekly Hours Secondary Students Spent Studying: Korea, OECD Average, and Selected Other Countries

	Total study hours per week	School instructional time, remedial and enrichment classes	Homework	Outside classes, tutoring, other study
Korea	**49.9**	**37.1**	**3.5**	**9.3**
OECD average	**33.8**	**25.9**	**5.9**	**3.0**
United States	33.1	25.2	5.7	2.2
Japan	32.1	25.7	3.8	2.6
Switzerland	29.8	24.6	4.6	1.6
Sweden	28.0	22.9	3.9	1.2
Finland	29.7	24.7	3.7	1.3
Turkey	45.6	28.0	5.9	11.7
Mexico	46.2	31.3	5.8	9.1
Greece	44.9	26.6	8.3	10.0

Source: OECD data from T. Kim (2009), as reported in Freeman, Choi, and Kim (forthcoming).

private tutoring, often until midnight. This enormous effort is aimed at the college entrance exam, because the highest scorers gain entrance to the best universities and, given Korean employment practices, the best jobs. For government occupations and the private sector alike, gaining entrance to Seoul National University and a handful of other elite universities is seen as a signal that a person is destined for elite employment.

The long hours of private tutoring are widely seen as why many Korean students lack interest in classroom work, since much of what is presented in school has already been covered in the tutoring sessions, a phenomenon referred to by the media and others as "classroom collapse" or "public school collapse." In addition, the reliance on *hagwon* places such a heavy financial burden on families that surveys suggest it is a factor in the country's low birth rate.

Private spending on education rose from 3.4 percent of household spending in 1990 to 7.2 percent in 2007. Not surprisingly, spending was relatively low among low-income households. Between 2000 and 2007 the public sector's share of spending on tertiary education declined from 27 percent to 21 percent, well below the OECD average of 69 percent. Consequently, postsecondary education in Korea is mainly financed by tuition fees paid by students' families. College tuition fees in Korea are the fourth highest among OECD countries, reflecting high charges at both public and private universities. Nevertheless, government-funded scholarships and grants to students (4.4 percent of public spending on education) and student loans (5.7 percent) are well below the OECD averages of 11.4 percent and 8.8 percent, respectively. As a consequence, socioeconomic background is significantly correlated with the type of higher-education institutions students attend: the lower their income level, the more likely they are to attend junior colleges, which focus more on vocational education. This makes it important to expand student loans in order to improve low-income students' access to more expensive and prestigious universities. Repayment could be made contingent on income after graduation to help reduce the risk of extending such loans.

The government has sought to improve the quality of public education and the diversity of schools as a way of reducing reliance on *hagwon*. In addition, the role of the College Scholastic Ability Test (CSAT) in the university admission process has been deemphasized as part of a new "admission officers" system now used to determine which students are admitted. Even with such reforms, however, costly *hagwon* are likely to continue to play an important role, making it necessary to improve access to extra help for low-income students as well. This could be accomplished by expanding after-school programs in schools and further developing Internet-based educational programs.

Equity issues can also be addressed by establishing and funding the kind of high-quality preprimary (preschool and kindergarten) programs that enhance later school achievement. Spending on preprimary education in Korea was less than $2,000 per student in 2010, far below the OECD average of $3,000. In addition, less than half of the outlay was made by the public sector, compared with an OECD average of 80 percent, reflecting the fact that kindergartens in Korea are mostly private. The low level of spending and the high private share suggest that preprimary education for children from low-income families is relatively weak, with negative implications for equity.

Finally, the top-down control of educational policy by the central government is criticized as inefficient. Government efforts to reduce the emphasis on examinations and private tutoring have largely failed. The Chun Doo Hwan government outlawed private tutoring in 1980, but the Roh

Tae-woo government allowed private tutoring by university students in 1989, and the Constitutional Court ruled broad restrictions on private tutoring were unconstitutional in 2000. The Lee Myung-bak government tried to outlaw tutoring after 10:00 or 11:00 p.m., with results not yet apparent. Efforts by the government to introduce merit pay in the hope of improving classroom instruction have been thwarted by the teachers' unions.

During her campaign for the presidency, Park Guen-hye, elected in 2012, vied with her opponent Moon Jae-in over who would do the most to relieve the burden of education costs on household income. Park advocated improving public education to reduce the need for households to spend so much of their income on education, and called for schools to provide all-day care for students, with sports, arts, and other similar activities offered until 5:00 p.m. and after-school classes extended to 10:00 p.m. She also called for free universal high school education, lower university tuition payments, tuition burdens geared to specific family income levels, and zero-interest college loans (net of increases in the consumer price index). This list of reforms, involving a substantial reduction in private household expenditures for high school and university education as well as an expansion of the role of public education, imply a commitment to a major expansion of government expenditures on education. Whether these reforms will in fact occur remains to be seen.

The Changing Structure of Income and Wages

How have these changes in demographic structure and access to education affected the distribution of income, structure of wages, and incidence of poverty?[22] Standard logic suggests that wage differentials should have narrowed with increases in the percentage of the population with higher levels of education, while poverty among those out of the labor force because of age should have increased absent a major welfare program for retirees.[23] Skill-biased technological change and the globalization of the

---

22. This section is based in part on An and Bosworth (2013).

23. In contrast, there are no easy a priori expectations for what should have happened to property income and undistributed corporate profits, especially since undistributed corporate profits would show up in the increased wealth of shareholders, particularly controlling shareholder families, rather than as recorded family income. Given the

Table 6.5. Alternative Estimates of Gini Coefficient of
Inequality, 1965–1993

	Choo	Social Statistics Survey	Ahn
1965	0.344	—	0.337
1970	0.332	—	0.313
1976	0.391	—	0.390
1980	—	0.389	0.357
1982	0.357	—	0.377
1985	—	0.345	0.380
1986	0.337	—	0.377
1988	—	0.336	0.384
1990	0.323	—	0.402
1993	—	0.310	0.380

Source: Data are from Ahn (1997), Choo (1993), and National Statistical
Office (1988, 1997), as reported in An and Bosworth (2013).

skilled-labor market, on the other hand, would have tended to increase income inequality.

Data on inequality are presented in Tables 6.5–6.7 and Figure 6.5. Figures for the early high-growth years are not entirely reliable insofar as household surveys did not cover high-income families. But there is little doubt that inequality was low. Land reform had eliminated rural landlords, and war had destroyed concentrations of urban property.[24]

It would appear that the Gini coefficient has not changed significantly since the 1960s. Most estimates suggest that inequality rose during the 1970s and then held steady until the late 1980s, when it began a steady decline until the financial crisis of 1997–1998. Korea's Gini is higher than Taiwan's but substantially below that of the United States. In comparison with all members of the OECD, the Korean Gini coefficient before

---

way in which families that controlled minority shares in the large chaebol nevertheless exercised control of those corporations, it is likely that there was considerable diversion of corporate income to family uses in one way or another, a phenomenon that is known as "tunneling."

24. While much of this property was rebuilt in the 1950s, there were still very few high-income individuals in the 1960s.

Table 6.6. Income Shares by Income Deciles, 1979–2012

	1st decile	2nd decile	3rd decile	4th decile	5th decile	6th decile	7th decile	8th decile	9th decile	10th decile	1st/10th decile
1979	3.11	4.82	5.90	6.96	7.99	9.16	10.45	12.27	15.09	24.25	7.80
1980	3.05	4.76	5.97	7.00	8.02	9.10	10.45	12.21	15.13	24.31	7.97
1981	3.12	4.87	5.99	6.97	7.97	9.03	10.30	12.12	15.13	24.49	7.86
1982	2.95	4.86	6.00	6.95	7.95	9.02	10.35	12.18	15.09	24.66	8.35
1983	3.08	4.89	5.93	6.95	7.85	8.91	10.29	12.14	15.11	24.84	8.06
1984	2.98	4.82	5.90	6.92	7.86	9.03	10.38	12.28	15.14	24.68	8.29
1985	2.94	4.87	6.01	6.92	7.81	8.94	10.30	12.18	15.18	24.85	8.46
1986	2.98	4.89	6.05	6.97	7.91	8.99	10.38	12.28	15.21	24.33	8.17
1987	2.98	4.92	6.01	6.97	7.93	9.03	10.39	12.25	15.24	24.28	8.14
1988	3.13	5.01	6.07	6.98	7.95	9.03	10.36	12.14	15.10	24.23	7.74
1989	3.14	5.01	6.04	6.97	7.93	8.98	10.30	12.06	14.97	24.59	7.83
1990	3.21	5.15	6.16	7.08	8.04	9.11	10.40	12.09	14.85	23.90	7.44
1991	3.33	5.20	6.26	7.18	8.15	9.21	10.50	12.15	14.68	23.35	7.01
1992	3.27	5.24	6.31	7.26	8.21	9.28	10.58	12.23	14.71	22.90	7.00
1993	3.34	5.26	6.32	7.28	8.24	9.29	10.57	12.27	14.74	22.69	6.80
1994	3.34	5.19	6.24	7.21	8.19	9.28	10.61	12.30	14.79	22.86	6.85
1995	3.31	5.19	6.24	7.22	8.22	9.33	10.62	12.34	14.90	22.64	6.84

(continued)

Table 6.6. (Continued)

	1st decile	2nd decile	3rd decile	4th decile	5th decile	6th decile	7th decile	8th decile	9th decile	10th decile	1st/10th decile
1996	3.17	5.01	6.13	7.13	8.19	9.33	10.67	12.44	15.06	22.85	7.20
1997	3.19	5.09	6.28	7.29	8.31	9.43	10.76	12.45	14.95	22.25	6.98
1998	2.64	4.71	5.89	6.95	7.99	9.15	10.56	12.32	14.97	24.83	9.41
1999	2.71	4.63	5.81	6.81	7.86	9.09	10.53	12.33	14.96	25.28	9.34
2000	2.86	4.67	5.82	6.86	7.90	9.10	10.49	12.18	14.75	25.36	8.86
2001	2.89	4.63	5.75	6.76	7.84	9.08	10.49	12.25	14.96	25.35	8.78
2002	2.98	4.68	5.84	6.87	7.94	9.15	10.51	12.35	15.07	24.60	8.25
2003	3.25	5.12	6.40	7.44	8.51	9.59	10.84	12.53	14.87	21.44	6.59
2004	3.13	4.92	6.13	7.25	8.41	9.62	10.98	12.69	15.04	21.83	6.98
2005	3.09	4.85	6.14	7.36	8.47	9.65	10.91	12.55	15.02	21.94	7.11
2006	3.14	4.94	6.09	7.25	8.43	9.68	11.06	12.70	14.95	21.75	6.93
2007	2.96	4.76	6.00	7.22	8.41	9.63	11.05	12.70	15.18	22.08	7.45
2008	3.02	4.82	6.03	7.19	8.39	9.62	11.00	12.67	15.25	22.01	7.29
2009	3.01	4.84	6.13	7.24	8.41	9.65	11.03	12.68	15.09	21.91	7.28
2010	3.15	4.99	6.33	7.44	8.50	9.71	10.99	12.58	14.93	21.37	6.79
2011	3.13	5.02	6.36	7.43	8.50	9.65	10.95	12.55	15.01	21.40	6.83
2012	3.16	5.05	6.32	7.39	8.45	9.61	10.92	12.51	14.97	21.62	6.84

Source: Korean Statistical Information Service, http://kosis.kr/gen_etl/start.jsp?orgId=101&tblId=DT_1L6o002&conn_path=I3&path= for 1963–2002; http://kosis.kr/gen_etl/start.jsp?orgId=101&tblId=DT_1L9H008&conn_path=I3&path= for 2003–2012.

Note: Shaded rows correspond to periods of contraction of business activities, based on business cycle data provided by Statistics Korea.

Table 6.7. Comparisons of Inequality and Relative Poverty: Korea, Taiwan, and the United States

	1996	2000	2006
Korea[a]			
Gini coefficient	0.326	0.393	0.375
90-10 ratio	4.90	7.05	8.05
90-50 ratio	1.94	2.15	2.17
50-10 ratio	2.52	3.27	3.72
Relative poverty			
All	8.4	11.5	12.6
Elderly member	17.1	20.9	26.7
Nonelderly, with children	6.3	8.9	8.4
Taiwan[b]			
Gini coefficient	0.313	0.326	0.345
90-10 ratio	4.63	5.11	5.62
90-50 ratio	1.97	2.03	2.12
50-10 ratio	2.35	2.52	2.65
Relative poverty			
All	4.8	5.0	6.0
Elderly member	7.8	8.4	10.4
Nonelderly, with children	3.0	3.1	3.0
United States			
Gini coefficient	0.454	0.460	0.468
90-10 ratio	10.38	10.65	11.27
90-50 ratio	2.63	2.68	2.76
50-10 ratio	3.95	3.98	4.09
Relative poverty			
All	21.2	20.5	21.1
Elderly member	15.0	15.5	19.3
Nonelderly, with children	21.9	20.9	21.8

Source: Korea: 1996 and 2000 National Survey of Household Income and Expenditure, 2006 Household Income and Expenditure Survey (HIES); Taiwan: Family Income and Expenditure Survey (FIES); United States: Current Population Survey, as reported in An and Bosworth (2013).

Note: Elderly is defined as 60 years of age and older; children are defined as those 19 years old and younger.

[a] HIES 2006 values for Korea are annual averages of monthly observations.

[b] 2006 values are 2005 values for Taiwan.

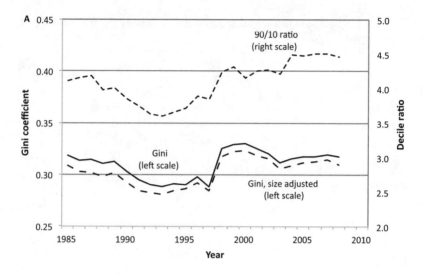

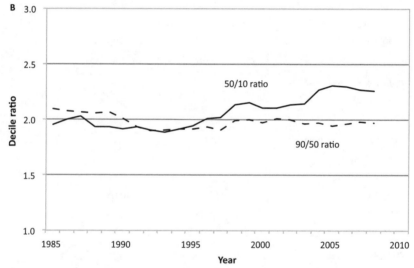

Figure 6.5. Alternative Measures of Income Inequality: Total Household
Income, 1985–2008

Estimates are based on data from the microdata files of the Household Income and Expenditure
Survey. (*A*) Gini coefficient is computed using percentiles. (*B*) Ratio of earnings in 90th decile to
10th, and earnings in the 50th decile to the 10th. The adjustment for family size is number of members raised to the 0.5 power.

Source: An and Bosworth (2013), 37.

taxes, at 0.34, is well below the OECD average of 0.45. After taxes and transfers it is identical to the OECD average.[25]

While the Gini coefficient attempts to summarize inequality in a single figure, analyzing separately the high, middle, and low ends of the distribution paints a richer picture. The share of the top 10 percent of income earners held steady at between 24 and 25 percent of total income throughout the 1980s and then fell beginning in 1990, before rising again from 1998 through 2000, and then falling yet again and stabilizing between 21 and 22 percent. At the other end of the spectrum, the income share of the bottom two deciles rose from just under 8 percent in 1987 to 8.5 percent in 1995 before falling to below 7.5 percent in 1998. It then climbed above the 8 percent mark again in 2003.[26] The middle-income deciles, in contrast, have seen almost no change in their share of total income in the past three decades.

Gini coefficients and shares of population deciles in total income may not be the best measure of the inequalities that create social tensions. An alternative is an index of bipolarization, which is designed to capture inequality between groups or classes in a society where within-group inequality is low. In Korea this index has been used to analyze "the disappearing middle class." This refers to the tendency for low-income groups to have trouble moving up into the middle-income classes, while many in the middle-income groups climb more easily into the upper-income strata.[27] The bipolarization index captures the distance between these two groups.

Between 1997, on the eve of the financial crisis, and 2004, after full recovery was achieved, the bipolarization index for Korea increased by 59 percent. In the United States between 1974 and 1997, it rose by a much smaller 16 percent. Among the countries considered by Shin (2008, 79), the largest rise in bipolarization after Korea was seen in the United Kingdom in 1986–1891, where the increase was 22 percent, less than half of Korea's. While overall inequality has been low by the standards of

---

25. OECD.Stat Extracts, http://stats.oecd.org/Index.aspx.

26. These differences may seem small, but if the average level of income had remained constant, the bottom two deciles would have first experienced an increase in income of 8 percent and then a fall of 12 percent. The full picture is more complicated because average income was rising rapidly until the 1997–1998 crisis, when it fell sharply before rising again after 1999; the point is, there was a marked rise in inequality after 1997, as the Gini coefficient also indicates.

27. The discussion in this paragraph is based on D. Shin (2008).

other middle- and high-income countries, it would appear that something was happening that was leaving the bottom fifth of the Korean population behind.

Explanations for these changes include (1) aging of the population and the workforce, (2) greater education of the workforce, (3) government tax and minimum-wage policies, (4) the nature and effectiveness of the change in the role of trade unions after 1987, and (5) skill-biased technological change. As pointed out earlier, the share of those older than 65 in the total population passed 10 percent in 2008. Most individuals over age 65 depend for income on their savings, their pensions, their children, and government programs (which in Korea are still limited). Since corporate pensions are modest for most workers, and children of the elderly are mostly urban residents with a limited capacity to incorporate parents into their household, personal savings determine where a retired person ends up on the income scale.[28]

The impact of aging on income distribution is more complex. As An and Bosworth (2013) show, an increase in the share of the population over age 65 initially may be associated with a decline in inequality, but inequality rises as that share rises above 6 percent of the total population.[29] Korea's over-65 population first exceeded 6 percent in 1996, before the onset of the financial crisis. This makes it hard to say how much of the rise in inequality is due to aging and how much is attributable to the crisis. But as the following discussion of poverty documents, there is no doubt that the current high and rising share of people over age 65 is an important contributor. Overall, however, aging has a mixed impact because earnings in Korea are to a large degree based on experience and seniority, and thus typically rise rapidly as workers increase in age between 25 and 50, before declining when their age exceeds 50.

---

28. As we will discuss further, much of the problem of absolute and relative poverty in Korea rests with the elderly.

29. An and Bosworth (2013) run two regressions that include the over-65 share of the population. The first is an inverse logistic function with current income distribution as the dependent variable and an increase in the proportion of those over age 65 as one of the independent variables. In this calculation, an increase in the over-65 population raises inequality. Their second method, and the one referred to in the text, uses a nonparametric Kernel fit that yields a U-shaped relationship, where the share of the over-65 population first has a positive impact on the distribution, but after it goes above 6 percent it has a negative impact, raising inequality.

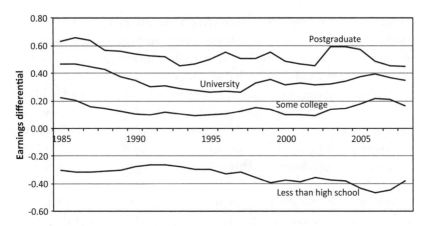

Figure 6.6. Earnings Differentials by Level of Educational Attainment
Earnings differentials are measured relative to the earnings of high school graduates.
Source: Household Income and Expenditure Survey, Male Household Head Earnings (Wage-Earners Only), as reported in An and Bosworth (2013), 83.

The huge increase in education at the tertiary level has also led to some narrowing of the income gap between university graduates and those with less education (Figure 6.6). The relative wages of 25- to 34-year-old university graduates compared with high school graduates of the same age fell from 155 percent in 1980 to 115 percent in 1993. The ratio of junior college graduates to high school graduates in this age group declined meanwhile, from 119 to 90 percent; in other words, there was no premium at all for junior college graduates.[30]

Age has such a large impact on Korean wages for all levels of education that one cannot easily generalize from the experience of a younger cohort about the overall impact on inequality. The relative wages of university graduates age 45 to 54 relative to high school graduates, for example, remained stable at 1.9 before falling in the early 1990s to 1.75 and then rising again after 1997–1998.[31] When An and Bosworth (2013) regress the log of income on five educational categories and ten five-year age categories, they find that education had an equalizing effect before the financial

---

30. After 1993, however, the wage premium for university graduates began to rise again, reaching 135 percent in 2005. These data are from Freeman, Choi, and Kim (forthcoming).

31. Freeman, Choi, and Kim (forthcoming).

crisis but the opposite effect thereafter. One interpretation is that the shift in employment from manufacturing to services led to a widening of the wage gap between university graduates at the high-paying end of the service sector and those with only a high school education at the low-skill, traditional end of that sector. More generally there is a trend in high-income countries toward employment requiring high skill levels (technological change is particularly skill biased in services), while those without the requisite skills and education are finding it increasingly difficult to find well-paid employment. This may explain the rise in the bipolarization index.

Although the Korean tax system is somewhat progressive, it has had only a modest impact on inequality. The same can be said of the country's minimum-wage laws. A large share of Korea's nonfarm labor force, roughly 20 percent, is in the informal sector, where pay is relatively low and minimum-wage laws are difficult to enforce (and where family workers in small family businesses are exempted from the law). While industrial policy designed to promote exports of manufactures, labor-intensive manufactures in particular, may have had some impact on the level of inequality in the early years of high growth, labor-intensive manufactures have been on the decline for a long time as unskilled-labor-intensive industry has moved offshore to China and elsewhere.

Poverty

The commonly used metric for absolute poverty in Korea is all households falling below the minimum standard of the National Basic Livelihood Security (NBLS) scheme, while the standard international measure of relative poverty is income less than 50 percent of national median household income. Although Korea does not have an official absolute poverty line, the NBLS scheme's estimated minimum cost of living needed for subsistence is often used by scholars as a substitute.[32] From this perspective there are two things to note about poverty in Korea. On the positive side, only 10 percent of children live in families with income below the relative poverty line, compared with the OECD average of 12 percent and

---

32. This is a much higher standard than the $1- and $2-a-day standards used by the World Bank for developing countries. The bottom 10 percent of Korean households in 2008 earned, on average, about 7 million won per year, or 19,180 won per day; with 2.52 persons per household, that becomes 7,610 won per person per day. At an exchange rate of 1,200 won=US$1, that would be roughly $6 per person per day.

Table 6.8. Incidence of Absolute and Relative Poverty by Household Type: 1996, 2000, and 2006

	1996 (%)	2000 (%)	2006 (%)
Absolute poverty[a]			
All persons	2.7	8.7	8.8
Persons in households with:			
No elderly member	1.1	4.8	4.8
Elderly member:	8.6	20.2	20.7
Elderly household head	9.1	18.9	18.8
Elderly household head living alone	26.0	45.7	33.5
Household with aged dependent	1.4	7.1	9.3
Nonelderly, without children	1.3	4.1	7.4
Nonelderly, with children	1.0	5.6	4.2
Relative poverty[b]			
All persons	8.4	11.5	12.6
Persons in households with:			
No elderly member	6.1	8.5	7.8
Elderly member:	17.1	20.9	27.4
Elderly household head	25.9	25.6	30.6
Elderly household head living alone	71.6	74.7	56.3
Household with aged dependent	7.6	9.4	10.5
Nonelderly, without children	6.4	7.7	10.4
Nonelderly, with children	6.3	8.9	7.7

Source: An and Bosworth (2013), calculations from 1996 and 2000 National Survey of Household Income and Expenditure, and 2006 Household Income and Expenditure Survey. The 2006 data are computed from the averages of the monthly values for each household. Excludes farm and fishery households.
[a] The absolute poverty rate is the percentage of persons in households with income below the minimum standard of the National Basic Livelihood Security scheme.
[b] Relative poverty is defined as the percentage of persons in households with less than 50 percent of the median equivalized household income (income divided by square root of household size).

the U.S. average of 21 percent (Table 6.8). The impact of these low levels of poverty among children in Korea can be seen from data on infant and child mortality, where Korea's rate of 4.1 and 4.8 per 1,000 for infant and child mortality makes it one of the ten best countries in the world on these important measures of the health of children.

In the early decades of high growth, in contrast, poverty among children and the population at large was considerably higher and concentrated in rural areas. Average rural household income in the mid-1970s was only $1,000 for a family of 5.72 people (just over US$170 per capita, or around US$1,200 per capita in 2009 prices). This is roughly $3 per day, but many rural families, despite extensive land reform, were under the World Bank poverty standard of $2 per day.[33] Rural poverty is now largely a thing of the past, since farm households are only 7 percent of the total population and many of those in farming receive substantial public support.

Poverty today is heavily concentrated among the elderly. Of those of retirement age, 45 percent live in relative poverty as compared with the OECD average of 13 percent.[34] Older Koreans in low-paying jobs, mostly without private pensions, cannot save enough for a comfortable retirement. Public pensions are in their infancy, and most workers have not been in the system long enough to be eligible for more than a minimal pension.[35] Because wages are based on seniority, companies also have an incentive to get rid of elderly workers, and there are no age-discrimination laws to protect them.

Labor Satisfaction and Strife

Given the relatively low level of income inequality and the fact that less than 10 percent of the population lives in absolute poverty, one might expect Koreans to be reasonably satisfied with their standard of living. Real wages rose during the high-growth period at a rate not far below the rate of increase in GDP.[36] In retail and wholesale services, restaurants, hotels, and businesses employing large numbers of low-skilled workers, real wages grew at an annual average rate of 6 percent per annum both in the twelve years through democratization (that is, between 1976 and 1988) and in the nine years leading up to the financial crisis (1988–1997). Manufacturing wages, where the skill level of workers was higher and rising more rapidly, grew by nearly 8 percent a year in both periods.[37] Workers in

---

33. These estimates were derived from data in Mason et al. (1980), 418.

34. An and Bosworth (2013).

35. We will return to the public pension system and its reform later in the chapter.

36. GDP grew at 8.5 percent per year in the 21 years from 1977 through 1997.

37. These data are from National Statistical Office (1999), 155. These data are not for a single skill category and thus do not reflect what was happening to wages in specific skill categories.

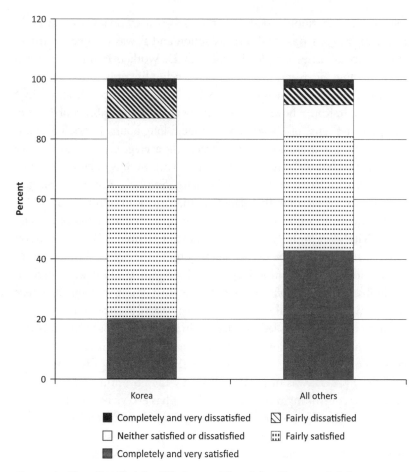

Figure 6.7. How Satisfied Are Workers in Their Jobs? Korea and Other Countries in the International Social Science Programme
Source: Freeman, Choi, and Kim (forthcoming).

large parts of the economy saw their real wages double every ten to twelve years, something that would be the envy of most workers around the world.

But Korean workers were evidently not especially satisfied with their jobs. As Figure 6.7 shows, more than a third expressed no satisfaction or some degree of dissatisfaction, compared with less than a fifth of workers in other countries surveyed by the International Social Science Programme. Whereas more than 80 percent of workers in other countries were at least somewhat satisfied with their jobs, only 64 percent in Korea felt some satisfaction. Koreans put themselves at 5.7 on an 11-point ranking scale, where 1 was total dissatisfaction and 11 was complete satisfaction, in 30 countries sampled by the OECD. Workers in other countries in the sample, on average, ranked their level of life satisfaction at 6.7.[38]

At the most general level, the problem is the rise in polarization since 1997–1998. In Korea, however, two additional factors plausibly contribute to this pervasive sense of dissatisfaction. One is long hours. In 2008 Koreans work nearly 900 more hours per year than the average German worker, for example (Table 6.9).[39] The average Korean work week is roughly 48 hours, compared with barely 30 hours in Germany. Similarly, Koreans spend 500 more hours at work than their Japanese and American counterparts.

Prior to democratization, Korean governments regularly suppressed labor activity, allowing only one officially sanctioned union. The unionization rate fell steadily over the decade leading up to the political transition in 1987. With democratization it began rising again, peaking at 20 percent of eligible workers in 1989. Since then, the shift in employment structure (the changing industrial mix and the shift toward service-sector employment, in particular) has led to a decline in unionization: as of 2011, barely 10 percent of 17.1 million eligible workers were unionized.[40] There are two major unions in Korea today. One, the Federation of Korean Trade Unions (FKTU), was originally set up by the government in 1961 as a vehicle for controlling union activity, but it has evolved into an independent union that focuses on increased wages and benefits for its members. The other, the Korean Confederation of Trade Unions (KCTU), uses more aggressive tactics to pursue fundamental changes in Korean society.

Labor relations in Korea are mostly confrontational. In one international ranking based on the level of cooperation in labor-management relations, Korea ranked 55th out of 55 countries, and in another it ranked 95th out of 134.[41] Strikes are numerous and prolonged. Korean workers lost 90 days of work per 1,000 total employees (including nonunion

---

38. Korea also scored below the regression line in this sample when controlling for per capita income. OECD (2009b), 121, as reported in Freeman, Choi, and Kim (forthcoming).

39. Earlier, in 1980, the difference was more than 1,200 hours.

40. Figures are from Ministry of Employment and Labor (2012).This latter figure rose from 8.2 percent in 2004 after the government in 2006 recognized the right of government workers to organize and accepted the Korean Government Employees Union as a legal entity.

41. See again Freeman, Choi, and Kim (forthcoming).

Table 6.9. Average Annual Hours Worked, All Employed Persons, 1980–2008, and Average Annual Hours Worked per 15- to 64-year-old, 2008

	Hours per employee				Hours per 15- to 64-yr-old
	1980	*1990*	*2000*	*2008*	*2008*
Korea	2,876	2,688	2,394	2,316[a]	1,478
Japan	2,121	2,031	1,821	1,772	1,253
Spain	2,003	1,824	1,815	1,627	1,062
France	1,842	1,702	1,591	1,542	996
United States	1,819	1,836	1,841	1,792	1,271
Canada	1,802	1,788	1,768	1,727	1,273
Belgium	1,801[b]	1,754	1,554	1,568	972
United Kingdom	1,773	1,771	1,711	1,653	1,201
Germany	1,751	1,578	1,473	1,432	1,005
Denmark	1,646	1,518	1,554	1,610	1,262
Norway	1,580	1,503	1,455	1,422	1,111
Sweden	1,517	1,561	1,625	1,625	1,230
Netherlands	—	1,504	1,372	1,389	1,057
Unweighted average×Korea	1,787	1,698	1,632	1,597	1,141
Ratio, Korea to average	1.61	1.58	1.47	1.45	1.3

Source: Susan Fleck "International Comparisons of Hours Worked: An Assessment of the Statistics," *Monthly Labor Review,* May 2009, Table A-1; figures are OECD based. Hours for 2008 are from OECD, *Employment Outlook 2009,* Table F. They differ modestly from those in the *Monthly Labor Review* time series and from the figures in the OECD productivity database, www.oecd.org/statistics/productivity/compendium.

Note: Hours per 15- to 64-year-old estimated by multiplying average annual hours by the employment-population rate of 15- to 64 year-olds from OECD, *Employment Outlook 2009,* Table B.

[a] 2007.

[b] Belgium estimated from Bureau of Labor Statistics (BLS) series in OECD, *Employment Outlook 2009,* Table F, using the overlap year 1983 when the BLS series showed 6.57 percent more hours than the OECD series.

members) in 1995–2004, compared with an OECD average of 45 days per 1,000 employees and 225 days per 1,000 union members.[42]

The militancy of the unions has been matched by the government response. Authoritarian governments often put union leaders in jail, and

---

42. Korea came in last in the sample of 24 countries.

the first democratic government of President Roh Tae-woo incarcerated nearly 2,000 union leaders. More surprising is that left-of-center governments elected with union support also put union leaders in jail during their time in office (722 of them, in the case of the presidency of Kim Dae-jung, and 921 through 2006 during the presidency of Roh Moo-hyun).

Analyses of Korean labor-management relations after the transition to democracy suggested that Korea might follow the path of Japan's unions after World War II, which started out militant and confrontational but quickly evolved to the point that strikes were rare and short.[43] That hope has not materialized. Militancy and confrontation remain the rule, and the government regularly intervenes in labor-management disputes. Unions represent only a small fraction of the workforce, mainly workers in large companies. The tripartite commission of representatives of management, labor, and government thus actually represents mainly the large firms and only a small minority of the labor force.[44] The unions frequently make excessive demands because they know that large firms can pass on the increase in costs to their customers and squeeze their suppliers.[45]

The 1997–1998 law designed to enhance the ability of firms to shed redundant workers has instead made it difficult to fire workers because of a stipulation that layoffs can be activated only when firms are faced with insolvency or its equivalent. This has encouraged employers to finesse the rule. By 2009 fully 33 percent of wage earners were contract workers who could be let go without contravening the law. In 2007 the National Assembly did pass a law requiring that contract workers who had been on the job for more than two years be given permanent positions, but the law's immediate effect in the context of the 2008–2009 global recession was to encourage firms to shed those contract workers in cost cutting efforts. The jobless rate among contract workers thus rose to double the 4 percent national average unemployment rate in early 2009.

Also affecting the prospects for labor is the worry that Korea's low fertility rate and rapidly aging population will give rise to labor shortages. But the immediate problem is not so much the slowed growth and future decline in the size of the workforce as it is limits on the ability and

---

43. Lindauer et al. (1997) provide details.
44. The history of this problem is laid out in Chapter 2.
45. Most of those suppliers are small and medium-size firms staffed by nonunion workers.

willingness of companies to employ the workers that are available now. Korea still has a substantial pool of reserve labor, given that female participation was only 55 percent in 2008, contrasted with the 62 percent average of OECD countries as a whole, 63 percent for women in Japan, and more than 70 percent in such high-income countries as the United Kingdom (OECD 2013, 244).

Social Welfare Programs

Central government budgets in OECD countries typically devote 50 percent or more of expenditures to social welfare programs and only 10 percent to programs designed to promote economic growth. In Korea, the priorities have been reversed. Korean social welfare expenditures in the 1990s amounted to only one-sixth of the OECD average (Table 6.10). Up to that point Korea relied mainly on growth to eliminate poverty. That approach began to change under the governments of Presidents Kim Dae-jung and Roh Moo-hyun. By 2005, total welfare expenditures were a third of the OECD average. By 2009 they were a little less than half of the OECD average.

The National Pension Service was introduced in 1988 to provide old-age security, reflecting changes in the intergenerational compact from Korea's traditional family safety net to a social safety net. The national pension was designed as a social insurance system, with subscribers making contributions based on their income and deriving benefits proportional to a combination of their own income for the duration of their subscription and the last three years' average income of all subscribers before retirement.[46] The scheme thus had a built-in redistributive function. It also offered generous benefits relative to contributions. Present and future taxpayers would have to make up the difference between benefits and contributions. The average income replacement rate was set initially at 70 percent in 1988 and lowered to 60 percent in 1998.[47]

---

46. Monthly pension benefit $= m \times (A + B) \times [1 + 0.05 \times n]/12$, where m is 2.4 for 1988–1998, 1.8 for 1999–2007, $1.5 - 0.015 \times (t - 2008)$ for each passing year t for 2008–2027, and 1.2 for 2028 and beyond; A is the average monthly income of all subscribers for the last three years before retirement; B is the average monthly income of the individual subscriber for the duration of subscription; and n is the duration of subscription in years minus 20.

47. Suppose a subscriber joined the national pension in 1988 and contributed for 30 years, and then received pension benefits from 65 years of age to the average life

Table 6.10. Public Social Expenditures as Percent of GDP: Korea and OECD Average, 1990–2009

	1990	1995	2000	2005	2009
Total					
Korea	2.8	3.2	4.8	6.5	9.6
OECD	17.6	19.5	18.9	19.7	22.1
Old age					
Korea	0.6	1.1	1.3	1.5	2.1
OECD	6.0	6.4	6.4	6.6	7.3
Health					
Korea	1.5	1.4	2.2	3.0	4.0
OECD	4.7	5.0	5.3	5.8	6.6
Family					
Korea	0.0	0.1	0.1	0.3	0.8
OECD	1.6	1.8	1.9	1.9	2.3
Labor market					
Korea	0.0	0.0	0.4	0.1	0.6
OECD	0.5	0.6	0.6	0.5	0.5
Other					
Korea	0.2	0.1	0.3	0.7	0.8
OECD	0.4	0.5	0.5	0.7	0.8

Source: OECD Social Expenditure Statistics, www.oecd-ilibrary.org/social-issues-migration-health /data/oecd-social-expenditure-statistics_socx-data-en.

By 1999 the NPS was supposed to provide coverage to all workers, including the self-employed.[48] In practice, however, some 15 percent of workers still lacked coverage. In addition, 25 to 30 percent of those nominally

---

expectancy. If his or her average monthly income for the duration of subscription was 500,000 won (approximately US$450), then his or her benefits would equal 4.4 times the contributions, all in present value terms. If the subscriber's income was in the top bracket and averaged 3,600,000 won per month, his or her benefits would be 2.0 times the contributions. Before the 1998 reform, which lowered the income replacement rate from 70 to 60 percent, the return on contributions was even higher.

48. This takes into account the fact that government employees and private school teachers had separate pension systems.

covered did not pay into the system because they were low-paid, self-employed, part-time workers who had to pay the full 9 percent of their wages into the system, whereas for regular employees of companies, that burden was shared equally with the company. Participants in the National Pension Service had to contribute for 10 years to be eligible for partial benefits and for 20 years to be eligible for full benefits.

In 2007 the government undertook a significant reform of the National Pension Service, proposing to gradually reduce the average income-replacement rate from 60 percent to 40 percent by 2028. Faced with the rapid aging of the population and a very high rate of poverty among the elderly, however, in 2009 it introduced a basic old-age pension as a sup-plementary measure, based on public support (i.e., tax revenue) rather than on social insurance principles, and separate from the National Pension Service and National Basic Livelihood Security programs. This basic old-age pension is provided to the 70 percent of those 65 and older with the lowest incomes (whether they are enrolled in the National Pension Service or not). It adds about five percentage points to the average income replacement rate. The basic old-age pension is similar to the NBLS enti-tlement program in that both programs are designed to alleviate poverty and both are means-tested. For means testing, however, the basic old-age pension looks at the income of the elderly only; it does not take into ac-count the income of their children. In contrast, the NBLS program looks at imputed household income, including the income of those who are ex-pected to support their elderly parents, whether or not they live with them. Introduced in 2000, the National Basic Livelihood Security program in-cludes this means-testing provision to address concerns about the spread of "welfare disease" but is clearly inconsistent with the approach taken in designing the basic old-age pension.

In her 2012 election campaign, President Park Geun-hye called for the consolidation of the tax-supported and contributory pension systems and an end to means testing. All those over 65 would receive a substantially increased pension of 200,000 won a month. Whatever the merits of this particular plan and the various other proposals, Korea clearly needs to sort out the alternative benefit programs in a systematic way that pro-vides affordability, limits poverty among the elderly, and serves as a source of retirement income that has some relationship to the amount of money individuals have paid into the system. This could best be achieved by des-ignating a nonpartisan commission to come up with a realistic plan. Even for a nonpartisan commission, however, the challenge will be daunting, given the pace at which Korea's population is growing older.

The pension system has not yet had a major impact on poverty. Only in recent years have any workers become eligible for full benefits as defined by the law, and only for a dozen years have retirees been eligible for any benefits whatsoever. One can argue that this problem of limited pension coverage will be solved as future retirees come to make up a steadily growing share of the workforce. But this hopeful view flies in the face of a rapidly aging population. The ratio of pension recipients to contributors to the pension fund will rise from 0.13 in 2008 to 1.5 in 2065. The cost of pensions will thus rise from the current 3 percent of the tax base to 23 percent in 2065.[49] The balance currently being accumulated in the pension fund will be exhausted once the full impact of this rising ratio of recipients to contributors is realized. For pensions set up on a pay-as-you-go basis, the contribution rate would have to jump from 9 percent to 23 percent of wages, and on a fully funded basis the rate would rise to 18 percent. The political will to raise rates to these levels is notably absent. If employers, alternatively, are asked to pick up a larger share of the cost, there will be an impact on their international competitiveness and their willingness to hire. Korea may want to consider raising the statutory retirement age, which is how a growing number of OECD countries have responded to similar problems.

Mandatory health insurance was introduced in 1977 and became universal in 1989. In 2000, the different categories within this system were merged into a single mechanism. The contribution rate was 5.9 percent of wages in 2012, with half paid by the employer in companies with regular employees. However, some 15 million workers had to pay the full amount because they were self-employed or in some other way were not regular employees of traditional companies.[50] Unlike the case with pensions, most of the population does pay into the health insurance system.

Health care delivery is largely carried out by the private sector; only 10 percent of hospitals are publicly owned. National insurance also covers only a portion of health care expenditures, although that share has been rising and now constitutes 55 percent. Public expenditure on health

---

49. An and Bosworth (2013), 143–144.

50. The amount of this payment was based on income, gender, age, and motor vehicle ownership.

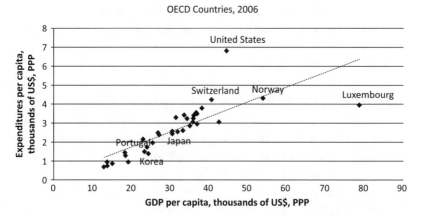

Figure 6.8. International Comparison of Health Care Expenditures, 2006
Figure shows total health expenditure per capita versus GDP per capita for OECD countries.
Source: OECD Health Data, 2008.

in Korea was 4.1 percent of GDP in 2011, a much lower percentage of total health expenditures than in other countries, with the notable exception of the United States and developing economies like Mexico. Overall, Koreans spent about 6 percent of GDP on health care, a considerably
smaller share than in other OECD countries and well below the average
relationship between health expenditures per capita and per capita GDP
(Figure 6.8).

While the health care system is criticized for such things as its excessive reliance on pharmaceuticals, none of the criticisms rises to the level
of calling for fundamental changes. Low levels of infant and child mortality and a long life expectancy relative to many other OECD countries
indicate that health care is probably the strongest component of the Korean
welfare system.

Two other aspects of the social welfare system, unemployment benefits and the National Basic Livelihood Security system, involve minimal
expenditures (whether stated as a percentage of GDP or in comparison
to the level of expenditure in other OECD countries). In 1995 Korea introduced the Employment Insurance System, having relied up to that point
on economic growth to provide ample job opportunities and on laws that
made it difficult for companies to discharge employees. In 2012, 84 percent of wage and salary workers were eligible for the employment insurance, but only 61 percent were actually enrolled in the program. To be

eligible for benefits a worker must have been employed for 180 days in the preceding 18 months and have been involuntarily discharged, and must be actively seeking employment. Benefits are provided for 180 to 240 days, depending on the worker's age and how long he or she has paid into the system. Compensation is typically about 50 percent of the previous basic wage. In practice, only a minority of the unemployed appear to receive these benefits.[51]

Finally there is the National Basic Livelihood Security program, established in 2000 as an expanded and reformed version of earlier welfare programs. For individuals and families meeting the means test, it provides cash benefits for housing, living expenses, education, and health care. In principle, the amounts are enough to raise recipients up to a "basic standard of living." In addition to having an income below a certain threshold, eligible individuals and families must not have children or parents capable of providing support. Recipients must also participate in public works projects. In 2011, 2.9 percent of the population was enrolled in the NLBS system. Expenditures on the program rose from 0.29 percent of GDP in 2002 to 0.36 percent in 2008 before declining slightly in 2011.

Overall, Korea's spending on income support for the working-age population, at 1.3 percent of GDP, remains far below the OECD average of 4.8 percent. Only five other OECD countries devote a lower share of their social expenditure budget to income support for individuals of working age.[52] Clearly Korea has a long way to go before it has a welfare system for poor families that meets even the low end of what is achieved elsewhere among OECD countries.

Fiscal Policy and Infrastructure Development

Over the past fifty years, fiscal policy played a critical role in generating rapid, resilient, and inclusive growth in Korea. Established in 1961 and shielded from particularistic interests, the Economic Planning Board was put in charge of formulating five-year economic development plans and bestowed with powers to draft the budget and coordinate policy. In the mid-1960s, Korea launched a tax policy reform and strengthened its tax

---

51. The 0.3 percent of GDP spent for this purpose is small by average OECD standards.

52. This income support covers incapacity benefits, family cash benefits, and unemployment and other social policy areas (OECD 2013, 74).

collection efforts to secure fiscal independence. As a result, tax revenue as a percentage of GDP increased from 7.3 percent in 1964 to 14.7 percent in 1969, even as GDP rose rapidly. In response to the oil price shock in 1973, instead of subsidizing consumption Korea raised energy prices, instituted various energy conservation measures, and made a decisive shift away from oil to coal and nuclear power. When another oil shock, combined with macroeconomic imbalances and political upheavals, buffeted the economy at the end of the 1970s, Korea reduced monetary growth, adjusted the exchange rate to reflect previous inflation, and evaluated budget expenditure items from a zero base. Korea's fiscal discipline provided a countercyclical buffer to mitigate downturns in the wake of the 1997–1998 Asian economic crisis and the 2008 global financial crisis (Figure 6.9).

In terms of central-government budget allocations, Korea has traditionally placed much greater emphasis on national defense, human capital, and infrastructure, and much less on social protection. In fact even

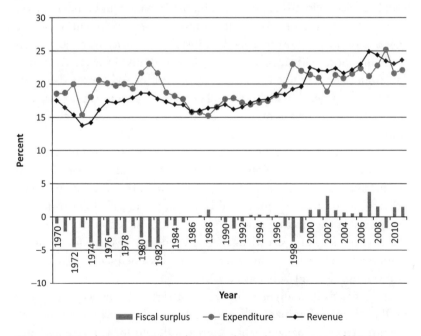

Figure 6.9. Fiscal Revenue, Expenditure, and Surplus as Percent of GDP
Source: Statistics Korea (1995), *Korean Historical Statistics* for 1970–1979, and Korea Institute of Public Finance, www.kipf.re.kr/TaxFiscalPubInfo/TaxFiscalFinances/B01/1#not, for 1980–2011.

as late as 2011, compared with the OECD averages in 2011 Korea spent much more of the central government budget on defense (8.6 percent versus the OECD average of 3.6 percent) and economic affairs (20.1 percent versus 10.5 percent), slightly more on education (15.8 percent versus 12.5 percent) and health (15.2 percent versus 14.5 percent), and much less on social protection (13.1 percent versus 35.6 percent); see Table 6.11. Korea mainly relied on investment and growth to create jobs and reduce poverty. However, the differences between Korea and the OECD averages have been narrowing, with Korea placing greater emphasis on social protection and less on economic programs between 2001 and 2011 (Table 6.12). Figures 6.10 and 6.11 provide long-term time series data on Korea's central government budget allocations by function.

The most important element of Korea's economic affairs budget has been infrastructure development. Korea has invested in power, transport, communications, and water infrastructure to facilitate economic growth and human development. One the most critical challenges for Korea in the early stages of its development was to secure an adequate and stable supply of electricity to support rapid industrialization and modernize rural areas (C. Kim 2011). By making infrastructure investment in electric power a priority, Korea increased its installed capacity from 367 megawatts in 1961 to 9,835 megawatts in 1981, and it raised the electrification rate from 12 percent to 98 percent over the same period. Korea also made massive investments in highways and ports to support its export-oriented industrialization, and in multipurpose dams and other water-delivery infrastructure to promote agricultural and social development. In the 1970s, as a part of its Heavy and Chemical Industry Drive, Korea enacted the Industrial Complex Development Promotion Law and provided essential infrastructure, such as water, electricity, and transportation. National universities located near industrial complexes were called on to specialize in related engineering fields (O 2009). In more recent decades, with the development of a knowledge-based economy, investments in information and communications infrastructure became increasingly important (Hong, Ko, and Volynets 2007).

In Korea, as in many developing countries, state-owned enterprises (SOEs) played a dominant role in the infrastructure sector, and improving infrastructure management required SOE reform. Through trial and error, Korea learned that neither general neglect nor multilayered central control provided appropriate incentives to SOE management. In 1983,

Table 6.11. General Government Expenditures by Function as Percent of Central Government Budget, 2011

	General public services	Defense	Public order and safety	Economic affairs	Environmental protection	Housing and community amenities	Health	Recreation, culture, and religion	Education	Social protection
Germany	13.6	2.4	3.5	7.8	1.5	1.2	15.5	1.8	9.4	43.3
Japan	11.0	2.2	3.1	9.8	2.9	1.8	17.3	0.8	8.4	42.7
Korea	**15.2**	**8.6**	**4.2**	**20.1**	**2.4**	**3.3**	**15.2**	**2.2**	**15.8**	**13.1**
Sweden	14.4	2.9	2.7	8.2	0.7	1.5	13.7	2.2	13.3	40.5
United States	12.4	11.7	5.5	9.4	0.0	2.1	21.4	0.7	15.5	21.3
OECD	**13.6**	**3.6**	**3.9**	**10.5**	**1.6**	**1.6**	**14.5**	**2.7**	**12.5**	**35.6**

Source: OECD (2013); Government at a Glance 2013, OECD Publishing, http://dx.doi.org/10.1787/gov_glance-2013-en, p. 77.

Table 6.12. Change in General Government Expenditures by Function as Percent of Central Government Budget, 2001 to 2011

	General public services	Defense	Public order and safety	Economic affairs	Environmental protection	Housing and community amenities	Health	Recreation, culture, and religion	Education	Social protection
Germany	1.0	0.0	0.1	-1.4	0.0	-0.9	1.4	0.0	0.7	-0.8
Korea	**1.8**	**-1.9**	**-0.9**	**-3.2**	**-0.3**	**-0.6**	**4.2**	**-0.1**	**-2.2**	**3.2**
Sweden	-0.5	-0.5	0.2	1.0	0.1	-0.3	1.8	0.2	0.1	-1.6
United States	-2.5	-2.5	-0.4	-1.7	0.0	0.5	2.2	-0.2	-0.2	1.7
OECD	**-1.1**	**-0.5**	**-0.1**	**-0.6**	**-0.1**	**-0.5**	**1.2**	**0.0**	**-0.3**	**2.0**

Source: OECD (2013); Government at a Glance 2013, OECD Publishing, http://dx.doi.org/10.1787/gov_glance-2013-en.

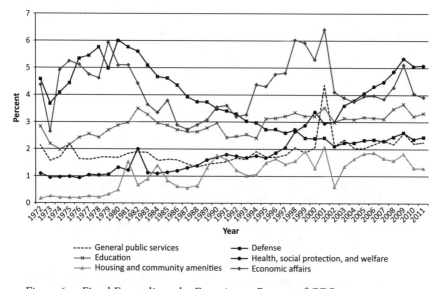

Figure 6.10. Fiscal Expenditure by Function as Percent of GDP
Source: Statistics Korea (1995), *Korean Historical Statistics* for 1972–1994, and Korea Institute of Public Finance, www.kipf.re.kr/TaxFiscalPubInfo/TaxFiscalFinances/B01/1#not, for 1995–2011.

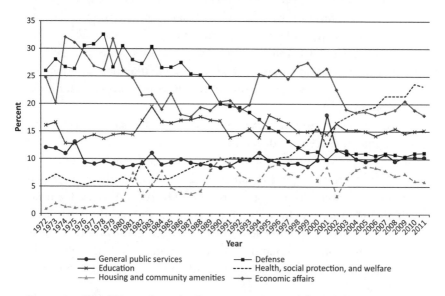

Figure 6.11. Fiscal Expenditure by Function as Percent of Central Government Budget
Source: Statistics Korea (1995), *Korean Historical Statistics* for 1972–1994, and Korea Institute of Public Finance, www.kipf.re.kr/TaxFiscalPubInfo/TaxFiscalFinances/B01/1#not, for 1995–2011.

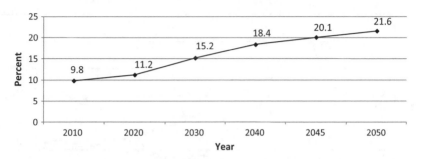

Figure 6.12. Trajectory for Public Social Spending as Percent of GDP
Public social spending as percent of GDP in 2010 for Korea was 9.8 percent. For the United States, Japan, and the OECD average, it was 15.2 percent, 18.4 percent, and 20.1 percent, respectively. This graph thus shows one possible trajectory for public social spending for Korea, in which Korea reaches the 2010 U.S., Japan, and OECD average levels in 2030, 2040, and 2045.
Source: Korea Institute of Public Finance.

Korea sharply reduced political appointments at SOEs, streamlined various controls, and established an interministerial council to evaluate SOE performance on an annual basis. Civilian experts worked with government officials and SOE mangers to develop both general and enterprise-specific performance indicators that could clarify managerial objectives. The payment of special annual bonuses was linked to performance. This reform was widely regarded as a success. In subsequent years, Korea made efforts to improve regulation and to push ahead with market liberalization and privatization (in the steel, telecommunications, and power generation sectors, for example).

Although infrastructure investment has helped to facilitate economic development, there is evidence that some infrastructure is reaching a saturation point. For instance, despite continued construction, daily traffic on expressways and national roads in 2012 is only 95 to 98 percent of 2003 levels, according to a recent KDI study. At the same time, demand for social welfare programs is increasing as the traditional investment-growth-employment nexus is breaking down. It remains to be seen how Korea will maintain fiscal sustainability as it responds to increasing demands for social welfare and adjusts its budget priorities (Figure 6.12).

Environmental Sustainability

Korea has also made efforts to ensure environmental sustainability since the early stages of development. The best known example in this regard is reforestation. By the end of the Korean War, Korea was totally deforested, owing to a combination of heavy logging during the Japanese occupation and Korea's reliance on wood for fuel. The government enacted a series of laws promoting nationwide reforestation efforts; legislation included the Forest Law (1961), Forest Products Regulation (1961), Erosion Control (1962), Voluntary Forest Guard Dispatchment (1963), and the Temporary Law to Promote Reforestation (1963). National reforestation was reinforced by Saemaul Undong (the New Village Movement) in the early 1970s. The First Ten-Year Forest Rehabilitation Plan was embarked on in 1973, implemented as a part of Saemaul Undong in conjunction with other village projects, including the construction of village entrance roads and bridges, sanitary water supply systems, and electrification. The plan called for a massive reforestation effort to be carried out by encouraging all people and organizations to participate in the village fuel-wood plantation project, thus creating the source of income for villagers. The reforestation target of 1 million *ha*, which was originally projected to be reached in 1982, was achieved in 1978 (Figures 6.13 and 6.14).

The success of the national reforestation project was possible because of the powerful influence of the Ministry of Home Affairs and its well-established local network. While people participated in the village project for reforestation on the local level, administrative structural reform was also undertaken, placing the Korea Forest Service (KFS) under the Ministry of Home Affairs in 1972 to further strengthen the implementation of laws related to reforestation. Once KFS was moved to the Ministry of Home Affairs, many synergies between KFS's reforestation policies and the ministry's promotion of Saemaul Undong were created. Such a centralized system, led by the KFS with a local network of government officers, greatly enhanced government cooperation in implementing reforestation policies (C. Kim 2011).

Korea's achievement in reforestation is indeed extraordinary. As of 2010, the average stock volume of timber per hectare was 109 cubic meters, which is a remarkable twentyfold increase over the 5.6 cubic meters per hectare in 1959 (Lee and Kim 2011). Korea's success is exceptional in that its rapid reforestation came about after the lengthy desolation of mountains and forests nationwide, and it took less than 20 years to accomplish. The UN's Food and Agriculture Organization lauded Korea as "the only developing country that succeeded in reforestation after World War II," in comparison with efforts made by advanced nations such as West Germany, the United Kingdom, and New Zealand (K. J. Lee n.d., 1–2).

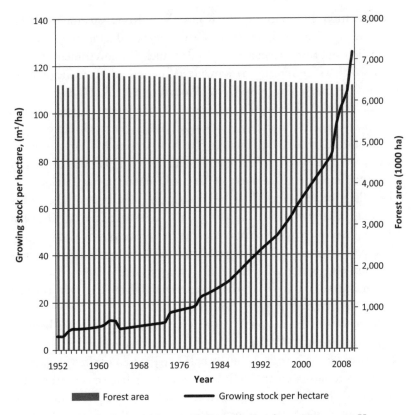

Figure 6.13. Trends in Forest Area and Growing Stock per Hectare in Korea, 1952–2010
Source: Korea Forest Service and Korean Statistical Information Service.

In 2008, "low-carbon green growth" was presented as Korea's new development vision: "Green growth seeks sustainable growth by reducing GHGs [greenhouse gases] and environmental pollution. It is a new paradigm for national development which creates a new growth engine and new jobs with green technologies and clean energies."[53]

Conclusion

The Korean people enjoyed rapidly rising standards of living during the high-growth period, and this rising income was widely shared. Today, as

---

53. Presidential Committee on Green Growth (2012), citing remarks by President Lee Myung-bak on the 60th anniversary of the republic, 15 August 2008.

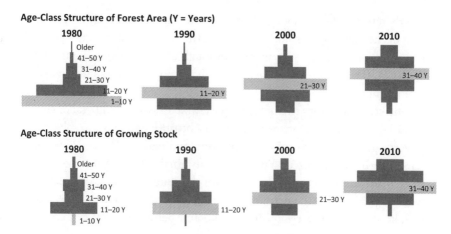

Figure 6.14. Age-Class Structure of Korea's Forest Area and Growing Stock, 1980–2010
Source: Korea Forest Service and Korean Statistical Information Service.

a result, inequality is low by international standards. The number of children living in poverty is also low by OECD standards. Rapid income growth has been accompanied by effective health care that, together with higher incomes, has produced low infant mortality and long life expectancy. The education system has also expanded rapidly, and Korea today has an unprecedented share of its population in tertiary-level educational institutions.

Notwithstanding these achievements, discontent among Korean workers is pervasive. One reason is the growing polarization between those with good educations and job prospects and those with lower levels of education and poorer prospects. Additional contributing factors are long work hours and confrontational labor-management relations. While legislation could reduce the number of hours worked, and other government policies might help improve labor-management relations, major changes in this area will probably have to come primarily from the actions of management and labor unions themselves.

The rapid rate at which the population is aging is a major social welfare and human resource problem. In the past, the care of aging parents fell to their children, but this traditional approach no longer works in Korea's modern urban society. Solving the problems of the aged is also central to alleviating poverty, since a high proportion of those in poverty are elderly retirees. Public-policy efforts to address these issues rely on expansion of the National Pension Service, but the current system is not politically and economically sustainable. Although this challenge is not unique to Korea, the extraordinary pace at which the population is aging makes action imperative.

The key policy initiative of future governments, whether liberal or conservative, should therefore be to institute a broad-based effort to solve the poverty problems of Korea's rapidly aging population. The pension system must be restructured to put it on a sustainable footing. Efforts need to be made to increase the size of the workforce and hence the number of workers paying into the pension system, to raise the retirement age, and to take steps, such as establishing more and better day care centers, to increase the share of women in the workforce.

Legislation limiting the number of hours worked and extending unemployment benefits to a larger number of the unemployed would be useful steps toward lowering labor dissatisfaction and reducing labor strife. As pointed out in Chapter 3 and in the discussion of education in this chapter, Korea also needs to improve the quality of its tertiary education. The results will hinge on private efforts to gradually upgrade the quality of faculty and university facilities, but government can play a role by increasing research funding available to universities. In all, social welfare initiatives for the aging population, measures to deal with labor dissatisfaction, and efforts to improve tertiary education should be the Korean government's priorities today and going forward.

CHAPTER 7

Developing and Maintaining
Export Competitiveness

Growth in Korea has always been bound up with the growth in the world economy. Korea is energy and natural-resource poor. Manufacturing requires importing energy and raw materials, which implies the need to export something else. Even more than in other countries, therefore, Korean growth is shaped by export competitiveness.

The economy's export performance remained quite positive right up to the eve of the 2008 crisis, as we detail in this chapter. But past performance is no guarantee of future success. Korean firms, like firms elsewhere in the OECD, feel pressure from China and other developing-country competitors. As Korean companies respond by moving upmarket, they come into competition with leading-edge firms in advanced economies such as Japan and the United States. Some argue that, in seeking to meet these challenges, Korea should focus on further developing its long-standing comparative advantage in heavy industry. Others argue, to the contrary, that it is in high tech, where the country has been gaining market share, that the future of its exports lies. Still others suggest that the future of Korean exports is in tradable services—both traditional service industries such as construction, where the country already has a foothold, and modern services such as software—since the share of employment accounted for by the service sector, in Korea as in any advanced economy, will continue to rise over time.

There will be no single solution to the problem of developing and maintaining Korea's export competitiveness. It will be necessary for firms and policymakers to pursue all of the avenues available. Korea will have to continue building on its existing strength in heavy industry, it will have to invest in the capacity to develop leading-edge high-tech products, and it will have to expand its capacity to export tradable services. Specializing exclusively in heavy industry, high tech, or tradable services will not provide the broad-based employment growth and diversification required of an internationally competitive advanced economy.

Nor can the processes by which these outcomes are achieved be directed by government to the same extent as before. In an economy far from the technological frontier, officials can emulate the example of more technologically advanced economies. They can use direct and indicative planning to channel resources in the requisite directions. But once an economy approaches the technological frontier, the direction of progress and productivity growth is less clear. This implies a greater role for markets and entrepreneurs and a more limited one for politicians and bureaucrats, as argued in Chapter 5. In these circumstances, the role for government in enhancing Korea's international competitiveness, like its role in fostering economic growth more generally, is to enhance the capacity of markets to identify the most promising activities and respond more effectively to the opportunities they afford. Public policy interventions should focus on internalizing specific externalities—on capturing the spillovers from innovation, for example—and on addressing concrete, well-specified coordination problems that cannot be adequately solved by market forces alone.

The Challenge

The Park Chung Hee government understood by 1964 the importance of exporting. It understood that exporting meant exporting manufactures, given that Korea possessed a limited amount of fertile agricultural land and that virtually all of the peninsula's exportable natural resources, other than tungsten, were in the north. Korea's focus on exporting mineral and agricultural products in the 1950s had delivered only limited results. As described in earlier chapters, the Park government and its successors therefore provided tax breaks and other subsidies and incentives to encourage exports of labor-intensive light manufactures in the 1960s; the products of the more capital-intensive steel, chemical, shipbuilding, and machine-building industries in the 1970s; and semiconductors, telecommunications equipment, and consumer electronics in the 1980s.

A striking feature of Korea's export profile is the extent to which electronics, automobiles, chemicals, steel, machinery, and shipbuilding—the product lines promoted by these early policies—still loom large in the country's export portfolio today, fully a quarter of a century later. However, these same industries also feel intense competition from countries that are equally export oriented, have cheaper labor, and can access standardized technology. Shipbuilding, where Korea is a world leader, illustrates the point. In 2012 China was the world's second largest shipbuilder, with a global market share of 33 percent, just behind Korea at 35 percent. Prior to the global financial crisis, which disrupted trade and the demand for shipping, shipbuilding in China had been growing at an average annual rate of more than 40 percent. In the production of standardized vessels, where labor costs matter as much as technical sophistication, it is not clear that Korea will be able to meet the Chinese competition. Maintaining market share will require it to continue moving upmarket into even more technologically sophisticated vessels, such as luxury cruise ships and high-tech natural gas tankers that supercool their cargo and regasify methane before piping it offshore.

In addition, with the global tendency toward production fragmentation, Korean firms will have to unbundle product design and fabrication. As a relatively high-wage economy with an abundance of skilled labor, Korea has a comparative advantage in product design. But with the elaboration of global supply chains, the merchandise designed in Korea can be fabricated and assembled at lower cost in less developed economies. In this scenario, Korea exports and earns the revenues associated with the design while its low-cost partner earns the revenues associated with the assembly. Everyone's favorite example of this is the iPad. Apple does the design work in Cupertino, California, but fabrication and assembly are carried out almost entirely in Shenzhen, China.[1] The components and assembly account for only half of the sale price of the final product, design for the other half. Thus, when an iPad is sold in Korea, half of the export revenue accrues to the U.S.-based company, Apple, and half to its China-based, Taiwanese-owned assembler, Foxconn, and Foxconn's suppliers.

Some Korean exporters have already moved in this direction. Samsung, for example, does the bulk of its mobile-phone design at home but much

---

1. In 2013 Apple announced plans to bring a limited amount of iPad production work back to the United States.

of its production in places like Tianjin, China, where it has built a 65,000-square-meter mobile phone production facility. It has cooperated with the Chinese computer maker TCL to build an eight-million-unit liquid crystal display factory in Huizhou and a second two-million-unit LCD-module plant in Suzhou.[2]

Outsourcing the assembly of tradable goods to other lower-labor-cost countries is a way for Korean firms to maintain their profitability and market share, but the practice raises troubling questions about the growth of employment in Korea itself. It provides remunerative employment for limited numbers of highly skilled designers but not for large numbers of manufacturing workers. This causes concern that the linkages from exports to employment may be growing weaker. These worries are not unique to Korea, of course; they are also present in other advanced economies. But given the important role that exports have historically played in the growth of the Korean economy, special importance attaches to how Korea addresses them.

An Aggregate Overview

Figure 7.1 shows the evolution of the export/GDP ratio since the start of the "economic miracle." The role of trade in the economy's takeoff is clear. But behind these aggregates lurk sharp changes in the composition of exports. Table 7.1 shows the top ten Korean exports for each of five different years. In the 1960s the country exported mainly relatively unsophisticated manufactures and, to a lesser degree, agricultural products and raw materials. Starting in the 1970s it moved into more sophisticated industrial exports, and in the 1980s high-tech products started to dominate.

Accompanying this shift in product composition was a shift from labor- to capital- and skill-intensive exports of manufactures. Over time South Korea has accumulated both skills and capital, reflecting its investments in education, equipment, and physical infrastructure. According to the predictions of the Heckscher-Ohlin model, exports should have become more skill- and capital-intensive. The evidence in Table 7.1 is consistent with this view.

---

2. LCD modules are the most expensive component in flat-screen televisions and account for the majority of their parts-and-components cost. Samsung already had another facility in Suzhou for the production of displays for notebook computers.

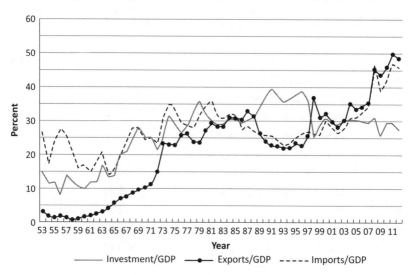

Figure 7.1. Korea's Exports, Imports, and Investment
Source: Bank of Korea, Economic Statistics System (ECOS), http://ecos.bok.or.kr/.

Another perspective is gained by distinguishing low-, medium-, and high-tech exports. Figure 7.2, from Eichengreen, Perkins, and Shin (2012), documents the shift toward more technology-intensive exports. Two decades ago South Korea was a net exporter of low-tech products, had balanced trade in medium-tech products, and was a net importer of high-tech products. Now, in contrast, the medium- and high-tech segments constitute the majority of Korea's exports. Eichengreen, Perkins, and Shin ask whether the technological sophistication of exports is exceptional for a country at Korea's stage of economic development. Their findings suggest that once upon a time—in the late 1960s, when the country initially moved into export activities like the assembly of consumer electronics, and especially in the 1970s when it started exporting capital goods— Korea's exports were more sophisticated technologically than its per capita income and other observable characteristics would have led one to predict. Over time, however, Korea has reverted to the mean. While the unit value and technological sophistication of its exports have continued to rise, they have risen more slowly, and the sophistication of Korea's export basket is now in line with what one would expect for a country with its per capita income.

Table 7.1. Top Ten Korean Exports, Various Years

	Series name	Amount	Ratio
	1967		
1	Prepared text. fibres; fabrics	59.96	18.73%
2	Wearing apparel, except fur	51.72	16.16%
3	Plywood, particle board & oth.	35.87	11.20%
4	Preserved fish & fish products	25.91	8.09%
5	Other miscell. manuf. articles	25.52	7.97%
6	Nonferrous metal ores, exc. nucl.	15.99	4.99%
7	Vegetables, horticult. spec.	9.89	3.09%
8	Cereals and other crops n.e.c.	9.84	3.07%
9	Footwear	8.52	2.66%
10	Iron ores	5.61	1.75%
	Total	**320.13**	
	1977		
1	Wearing apparel, except fur	1,664.26	16.67%
2	Prepared text. fibres; fabrics	828.71	8.30%
3	Preserved fish & fish products	648.73	6.50%
4	Footwear	544.91	5.46%
5	Building & repairing of ships	536.77	5.38%
6	TV & radio receivers, record.	453.87	4.55%
7	Electronic valves and tubes	405.02	4.06%
8	Manuf. basic iron and steel	374.55	3.75%
9	Plywood, particle board & oth.	372.87	3.73%
10	Knitted fabrics & articles	314.92	3.15%
	Total	**9,985.84**	
	1987		
1	Wearing apparel, except fur	5,582.42	11.83%
2	TV & radio receivers, record.	4,438.03	9.40%
3	Prepared text. fibres; fabrics	3,316.68	7.03%
4	Motor vehicles	3,120.87	6.61%
5	Footwear	2,850.89	6.04%
6	Electronic valves and tubes	2,393.39	5.07%
7	Manuf. basic iron and steel	2,316.73	4.91%
8	Office and computing machinery	1,704.45	3.61%
9	Knitted fabrics & articles	1,614.79	3.42%

(continued)

Table 7.1. (*Continued*)

Series name		Amount	Ratio
	1987		
10	Preserved fish & fish products	1,397.56	2.96%
	Total	**47,206.59**	
	1997		
1	Electronic valves and tubes	19,731.08	14.49%
2	Motor vehicles	11,561.76	8.49%
3	Manuf. basic non-ferr. metals	7,753.17	5.69%
4	Prepared text. fibres; fabrics	7,564.41	5.56%
5	Office and computing machinery	7,544.70	5.54%
6	Manuf. basic iron and steel	5,859.49	4.30%
7	Building & repairing of ships	5,839.01	4.29%
8	TV & radio receivers, record.	5,668.27	4.16%
9	Refined petroleum products	5,196.75	3.82%
10	Plastics and synthetic rubber	4,241.33	3.12%
	Total	**136,151.02**	
	2009		
1	Building & repairing of ships	38,180.71	10.50%
2	Electronic valves and tubes	32,101.99	8.83%
3	Motor vehicles	29,589.04	8.14%
4	TV & radio transmitters & tel.	26,927.80	7.41%
5	Optical instr. & photo equip.	26,172.11	7.20%
6	Refined petroleum products	22,840.41	6.28%
7	Manuf. basic iron and steel	17,878.37	4.92%
8	Basic chemicals, exc. fertil.	15,738.41	4.33%
9	Plastics and synthetic rubber	15,318.54	4.21%
10	TV & radio receivers, record.	12,285.75	3.38%
	Total	**363,470.55**	

Source: CHELEM (International Industrial Standard Classification [ISIC] 4 code); selected series from 1967 to 2009 (ISIC classifications).

Note: Amounts are in millions of U.S. dollars; ratio is the percentage of total exports. Export zone: South Korea; import zone: Worldwide.

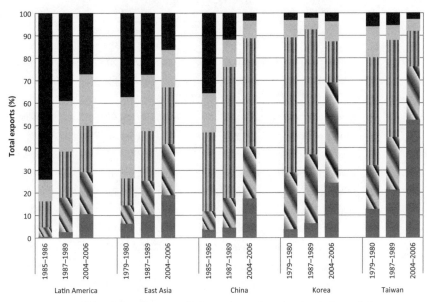

Figure 7.2. Export Composition by Technology Content, Various Periods
Countries included in the regions vary over time depending on data availability.
Source: Eichengreen, Perkins, and Shin (2012), 180.

If the commodity composition, factor content, and technological so-phistication of its exports are not unusual for a country with Korea's re-source endowment and at its stage of economic development, two aspects of its exports stand out nonetheless. First, an unusually large share of ex-ports is accounted for by large firms, and by the chaebol in particular. Firms with more than 300 employees or a capitalization of more than eight billion won account for more than two-thirds of Korean exports.[3] The second distinctive aspect of Korea's exports, also evident in Table 7.1, is the extent to which the industries that became exporters in the course of the Heavy and Chemical Industry Drive of the 1970s continue to loom large. These are sectors that have been largely abandoned by higher-wage economies like those of Europe and the United States, with the composition

---

3. Many small and medium-size companies have subcontracting arrangements with these same large enterprises, however, and the parts and components they produce ac-count for a significant fraction of the export values of the latter. Again, see Eichen-green, Perkins, and Shin (2012), ch. 4.

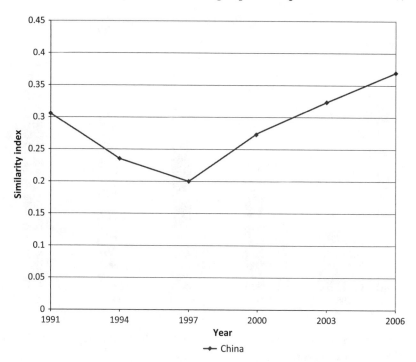

Figure 7.3. Similarity Index for Chinese Exports Compared with Korean Exports, Based on 1991 Weights

The export similarity index is constructed by following Hennessy and Lapan (2007) to measure how similar export shares of destination countries and commodities are for competitor countries. *Source:* Based on Eichengreen, Perkins, and Shin (2012), 171.

of U.S. exports shifting toward services and European countries like Germany focusing on more specialized machinery produced by small and medium-size firms.[4] The question is whether Korea will follow suit.

Figures 7.3 and 7.4 consider the overlap of Korean and Chinese exports, since many argue that the rise of Chinese competition has had powerful effects on Korea's exports. Figure 7.3 documents the increase in overlap in the export baskets of Korea and China in the past ten years.[5] Figure 7.4 compares China and Korea's market shares in the principal markets to

---

4. Competition in these medium- and high-tech sectors from lower-wage countries has not been overwhelming, reflecting the need for relatively rigorous quality and production standards.

5. There was a decline in overlap in the preceding decade, presumably reflecting Korea's exit from old labor-intensive export sectors like textiles, apparel, and footwear.

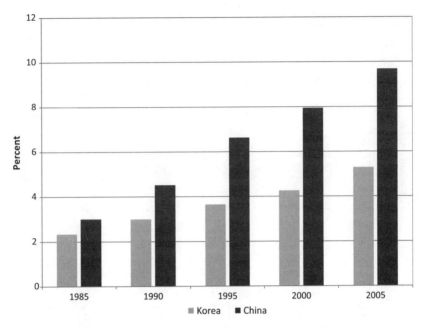

Figure 7.4. Shares of Korea and China in the Total Imports of Countries to Which Korea Exports

Korea's share is defined as the average share of imports from Korea in the total imports of countries to which Korea exports. China's share is defined similarly for the same countries to which Korea exports. Korean exports are used as weights in calculating both averages.

Source: Eichengreen, Perkins, and Shin (2012), 174.

which Korea exports. China being a larger economy, its exports already slightly exceeded Korea's in the mid-1980s. But one then sees the bars denoting Chinese penetration of those markets rising dramatically starting in the mid-1990s. In 1990 China was a consequential competitor with Korea only in the case of the declining labor-intensive products like footwear and children's toys (Figure 7.5A), but by 1995 it had emerged as a consequential competitor in cargo vessels, iron and steel, and telecommunications equipment (transmitters, televisions, and cellular handsets) (Figure 7.5B). By 2005, Chinese competition was evident across the board, although China has attained significant market shares relative to Korea only in optical instruments, electronic components, and, to a lesser extent, ocean-going vessels (Figure 7.5C).

China's other role in Korea's trade, in addition to that of competitor, is as assembly platform, as we have noted. Table 7.2 provides one way of

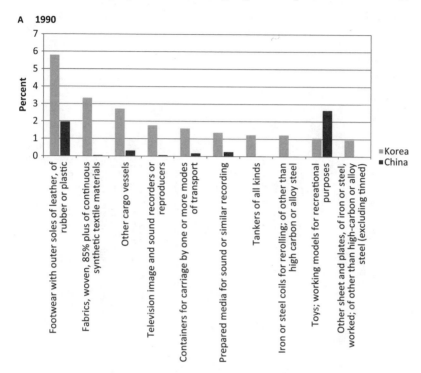

Figure 7.5. Korean and Chinese Market Shares in World Exports for Korea's Ten Most Important Export Products, Selected Years: 1990, 1995, 2005 *(Continued)*
Source: Calculations based on UN Comtrade data, rev. 2. Eichengreen, Perkins, and Shin (2012), 176, 177, 179.

characterizing the phenomenon. It follows Greenaway, Hine, and Milner (1994) and Wakasugi (2007) in categorizing two-way trade between Korea and other countries in the products of the same industry as either horizontal (if the unit values of what they ship back and forth are very similar) or vertical (if they are very different). Vertical intraindustry trade is associated with assembly operations (with, for example, Korea shipping the most sophisticated components used in consumer electronics to China, and China shipping back the assembled product). The table shows that vertical two-way trade with China rose in two steps, first in the mid-1990s and then again more recently, after the turn of the century. There is a similar rise in vertical two-way trade between Korea and East Asia as a whole, although the timing is different; that rise occurred almost entirely before the turn of the century.

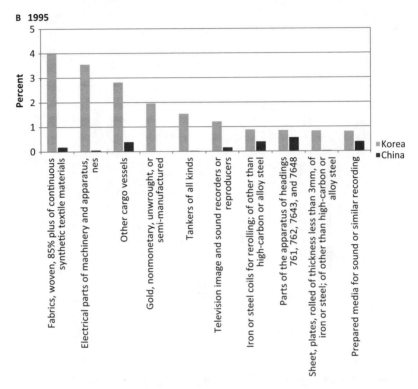

Figure 7.5. Korean and Chinese Market Shares in World Exports for Korea's Ten Most Important Export Products, Selected Years: 1990, 1995, 2005 *(Continued)*

Eichengreen, Perkins, and Shin (2012) explore the possibility that, owing to growing foreign content, a given increase in exports is having a smaller impact on the growth of Korean employment. They analyze this possibility using input/output tables that are available for every five years, starting in 1973. The data make it possible to compute the worker-requirement coefficient of exports—in effect, how many additional employees are required, by sector, as a result of a given change in exports. They find that worker-requirement coefficients have declined across the board—this is the flip side of the increase in labor productivity documented in Chapter 3 of this volume. This is true of exports just as it is of other sources of final demand. But in the case of exports, unlike other sectors, the decline in worker-requirement coefficients has accelerated over time: between 1973 and 1990 the worker-requirement coefficient

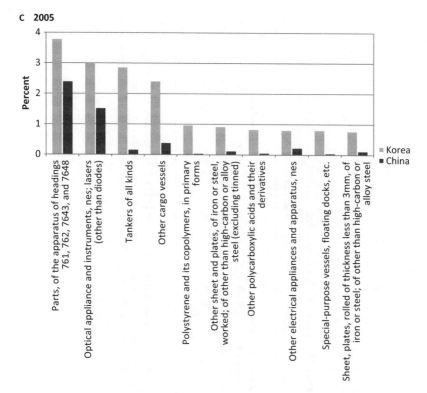

Figure 7.5. Korean and Chinese Market Shares in World Exports for Korea's Ten Most Important Export Products, Selected Years: 1990, 1995, 2005

associated with exports declined by 44 percent; between 1990 and 2003 it declined by fully 61 percent.[6] This confirms that the worry that Korean exports are doing less to directly create employment is not entirely unfounded.

Aggregate statistics take one only so far in terms of understanding the prospects and challenges facing Korean exporters. We will now look more closely at what Korean producers need to do to maintain their competitiveness in heavy industry, to become competitive in a wider range of

---

6. At the time of writing, the last year for which an input/output table is available is 2003. In contrast to exports, the decline in worker-requirement coefficients for other components of final demand decelerated between the two periods (from 55 to 51 percent for consumption and from 50 to 34 percent for investment).

Table 7.2. Horizontal and Vertical Intraindustry Trade between Korea and Other Countries

Year	China		Japan		East Asia		European Union		United States	
	HIT	VIT	HIT	VIT	HIT	VIT	HIT	VIT	HIT	VIT
1992	0.0247	0.0467	0.0534	0.1679	0.0248	0.1209	0.0089	0.0659	0.0326	0.1789
1996	0.0490	0.1455	0.0496	0.2249	0.0536	0.1291	0.0190	0.0753	0.0173	0.2411
2000	0.0587	0.1686	0.0378	0.2853	0.0739	0.2009	0.0120	0.0934	0.0240	0.3035
2006	0.0980	0.2372	0.0763	0.2404	0.0575	0.2196	0.0317	0.0668	0.0425	0.1837

Source: Authors' calculations, based on the UN Comtrade database.

Notes: For each country, we construct the bilateral measure of horizontal and vertical intraindustry trade (HIT and VIT). The definition of HIT and VIT follows Greenaway, Hine, and Milner (1994). The HIT and VIT measures for East Asia and the European Union are simple averages of the bilateral measures. East Asia includes eleven countries: China, Hong Kong, Indonesia, Japan, Korea, Malaysia, Taiwan, Philippines, Singapore, Vietnam, and Thailand. The European Union includes fifteen countries.

high-tech industries, and to solve the problems that have made Korea uncompetitive as an exporter of services.

Competitiveness in Heavy Industry

Korea still relies heavily on the exports of the industries fostered by the Heavy and Chemical Industry Drive, as we have seen. In early days these sectors thrived on high investment, low labor costs, and the availability of foreign technology with a relatively limited tacit component, which was transferred in the embodied form of imported capital goods. The problem now is that other countries, such as China, invest more, have even lower labor costs, and can similarly access foreign technology.

To some extent Korea's competitiveness in these industries continues to be supported by its early start compared with other emerging markets. Where the minimum efficient scale is high, as in shipbuilding, the fact that Korea has already sunk the investment needed to build a competitive shipyard is a deterrent to foreign entry. (We choose shipbuilding here as an example of broader trends in heavy industry because it remains Korea's number one four-digit category of exports, in terms of value, and also because it illustrates the enduring legacy of the Heavy and Chemical Industry Drive.) Korean shipbuilders have the advantage of scale: their shipyards are among the largest in the world. They benefit from proximity to complementary industries: iron and steel, electrical equipment, and electronics. They have been able to streamline and boost labor productivity: labor hours to construct one cubic gross ton of capacity fell from 23.3 in 1990 to 9.2 in 2005.[7] Increasingly, Korean shipbuilders have specialized in high-value-added ships, including sophisticated drillships, floating production and offloading platforms, liquefied natural gas carriers, and mega-container ships with capacities exceeding 8,000 twenty-foot-equivalent units.[8] Employment in shipbuilding more than doubled from just over 50,000 to some 120,000 between 1996 and 2011. Orders in cubic gross tons rose from 16 million at the turn of the century to more than 45 million in 2006, just prior to the global financial crisis. The order book is well diversified, with about half of the orders accounted for by tankers, a quarter by container ships, and a sixth by liquid natural gas carriers.

---

7. Figures are for the three largest producers; Korea Times (2007).

8. Twenty-foot-equivalent units (TEUs) are the standard used for measuring container length.

But shipbuilding also provides a caution. Demand for the products of the Korean shipbuilding industry has been unusually buoyant as a result of the rapid growth of world trade (which has increased the demand for container ships), high energy prices (which boost the demand for oil and natural gas tankers), and China's economic growth (which has raised the demand for ore ships). What would happen if China, and the world economy more generally, slowed down? A natural experiment along those lines was conducted in 2007–2010 as a result of the global financial crisis. Orders for new vessels plummeted from 9,350 ten thousands of cubic gross tons globally in 2007 to 1,532 in 2009 before recovering to 3,800 in 2010. Korean production fell from 3,251 ten thousands of cubic gross tons in 2007 to 439 in 2009 and then rose to 1,265 in 2010. While the dip was sharp, Korean shipbuilders survived the crisis because they had diversified into other product lines. One example is Hyundai Heavy Industries; previously very dependent on shipbuilding, by 2009 ships accounted for only 42 percent of sales as the company branched out into the production and export of other machinery. This suggests that activity in shipbuilding is indeed sensitive to market cycles but that shipbuilders can pursue diversification strategies to buffer the effects.

What is true of shipbuilding and repair, Korea's top export category, is true of other Korean heavy-industry exports such as motor vehicles, chemicals, and iron and steel, all of which feature prominently in Table 7.1. These products, associated with the Heavy and Chemical Industry Drive, remain disproportionately important to the country's export portfolio. They have benefited from the rapid growth of global trade and from China's voracious demand. But the growth of global trade has slowed since the financial crisis, and there are indications that China's economic growth is slowing as well. The chaebol and other Korean firms that dominate the country's heavy industries will have to continue to diversify and move up market to maintain their competitiveness, in the same manner as the country's shipbuilding firms. A less favorable external environment will not make this easier.

Competitiveness in High Tech

Korea is an increasingly prominent supplier of electronics, office machinery, computer parts, and other electronic components. Yet there is evidence, as we have shown, that its profile as a producer of high-tech products is not exceptional; it is in line with what one would expect given

Korea's per capita income, resource endowment, and stage of economic development. Once upon a time, it is true, the country's exports were more sophisticated technologically than one would have expected given the economy's stage of development. But that is no longer the case.

One way of reconciling these observations is by considering that Korea's status as a leader in high tech is limited to certain product lines, mainly consumer electronics, computers, and office machinery. The challenge, therefore, is to broaden the country's competitiveness in high tech and to foster the innovation on which such competitiveness rests. Strengths of the Korean system of innovation include a skilled workforce with high levels of science and engineering education, extensive R&D spending by government and firms, and large firms with the capacity to undertake a portfolio of research projects. Strengths also include Korea's experience with quality production, and its proximity to China as a low-cost assembly platform. Weaknesses include the still heavy concentration of those R&D resources in the chaebol, which are not always the fastest-moving firms, an underdeveloped venture-firm sector, and slow development of the interorganizational links and open-network culture that characterize high-tech sectors in, inter alia, the United States.[9]

High tech runs on R&D. Table 7.3 shows data on R&D spending and numbers of researchers. At 4.0 percent of GDP in 2011 and 3.7 percent of GDP in 2010, Korea's R&D/GDP ratio is higher than that of the United States (2.9 percent), Germany (2.8 percent), and Japan (3.3 percent), and is second only to Israel (4.4 percent). In absolute terms Korea ranks sixth in the world, but of course it lags far behind a number of its larger and richer competitors. Compared with those other countries, moreover, R&D spending in Korea is heavily concentrated in the business sector, and is predominantly for applied research. This points to weaknesses in the Korean system: the contribution of universities to R&D is relatively limited, and basic research is underdeveloped.

Table 7.4 breaks down R&D spending by industry, distinguishing among electronic components and equipment, motor vehicles, and manufacturing, and between manufacturing and nonmanufacturing. In 2011, 47 percent of all R&D spending was done by the electronic components and equipment industry and another 12 percent was by the motor vehicle industry, while only 12 percent was accounted for by all nonmanufacturing industries together. Also in 2011, 74 percent of all industrial R&D

---

9. We return to these points later in the chapter.

Table 73. R&D Spending and Number of Researchers Each Year, 2001–2011

Year	Variables	Large firms		SMEs		Venture firms		Total	
		Amount	%	Amount	%	Amount	%	Amount	%
2001	R&D spending	87,370	71.2	19,588	16.0	5,778	12.9	122,736	100
	Researchers	57,019	51.2	29,520	26.5	24,760	22.2	111,299	100
2002	R&D spending	93,371	72.0	18,133	14.0	18,249	14.1	129,753	100
	Researchers	62,459	52.9	28,470	24.1	27,231	23.0	118,160	100
2003	R&D spending	110,842	76.4	18,260	12.6	15,994	11.0	145,096	100
	Researchers	71,698	57.8	27,390	22.1	24,942	20.1	124,030	100
2004	R&D spending	134,641	79.1	18,902	11.1	16,655	9.8	170,198	100
	Researchers	79,910	59.5	28,683	21.4	25,707	19.1	134,300	100
2005	R&D spending	146,429	78.9	19,911	10.7	19,302	10.4	185,642	100
	Researchers	91,514	59.3	30,619	20.9	32,173	19.8	154,306	100
2006	R&D spending	160,217	75.8	25,031	11.8	26,019	12.3	211,267	100
	Researchers	99,029	56.9	36,055	22.3	38,820	20.7	173,904	100
2007	R&D spending	175,119	73.4	32,710	13.7	30,820	12.9	238,649	100
	Researchers	102,473	55.2	41,566	22.4	41,594	22.4	185,633	100
2008	R&D spending	187,139	72.0	38,250	14.7	34,611	13.3	260,000	100
	Researchers	106,007	53.8	47,905	24.3	43,111	21.9	197,023	100
2009	R&D spending	199,699	70.9	44,873	15.9	37,086	13.2	281,658	100
	Researchers	108,136	51.4	55,179	26.2	46,988	22.3	210,303	100
2010	R&D spending	242,129	73.8	48,503	14.8	37,401	11.4	328,032	100
	Researchers	120,105	53.1	59,338	26.2	46,725	20.7	226,168	100
2011	R&D spending	283,462	74.2	52,192	13.7	46,179	12.1	381,833	100
	Researchers	132,004	52.7	63,623	25.4	54,999	21.9	250,626	100

Source: National Science and Technology Commission and Korea Institute of Science and Technology Evaluation and Planning (KISTEP) (2011).

Note: Amounts shown are in 0.1 billion won for R&D spending, number of persons for researchers.

Table 7.4. R&D Spending by Industry (100 million won)

Industry	2005	2006	2007	2008	2009	2010	2011
Manufacturing	164,524	190,110	213,351	229,984	243,345	287,373	334,254
Electronic equipment	91,311	104,528	108,534	120,807	128,279	158,315	179,747
Motor vehicles	27,903	31,987	38,318	34,427	35,325	39,997	45,373
Other manufacturing	45,310	53,595	66,499	74,750	79,741	89,061	109,134
Nonmanufacturing	21,119	21,157	25,298	30,016	38,283	40,659	47,579
Total	185,642	211,268	238,649	260,001	281,659	328,032	381,833

Source: National Science and Technology Commission and KISTEP (2011).

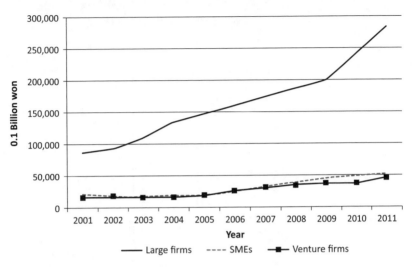

Figure 7.6. Increase in Korea's R&D Spending over Time
Source: National Science and Technology Commission and Korea Institute of Science and Technology Evaluation and Planning (2011).

was undertaken by large firms; SMEs accounted for 14 percent and start-ups (so-called venture firms) only 12 percent.[10] (Figure 7.6 shows the development of their spending over time.) In this respect, Korea is more like Sweden and Finland, where a handful of "dancing elephants" are leaders in innovation, than it is like the United States and Israel, where innovation is driven by a vibrant ecosystem of start-ups and small firms. While international experience suggests that both structures can work, the former is prone to being thrown off course by poor decisions made by

___

10. According to the Law on Special Measures on the Promotion of Venture Companies, enacted in 1997, a venture company is defined as an SME (1) in which a venture capital firm has invested 10 percent or more of the company's capital and 50 million won or more in amount (a "venture capital invested company"); (2) that has its own research lab and an annual R&D expenditure of 50 million won or more, equal to at least 5 to 10 percent of its sales (an "R&D company"); (3) that has obtained a guarantee from Korea Technology Finance Corporation (Kibo) or a loan from the Small and Medium Business Corporation (SBC) in the amount of 80 million won or more and equivalent to 5 percent or more of total assets. Note that the United States, which has a vibrant venture capital sector, basically uses 1, above, for its definition of venture companies. Many countries whose venture capital sector is not so strong use 1 and 2 for their definition. Using definition 3 as well as 1 and 2 to define venture companies, as Korea does, can be problematic if guarantees and loans are influenced by something other than the applicant's technology, such as policy support for SMEs in general.

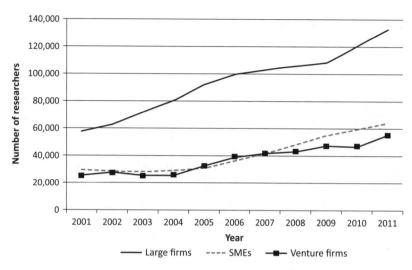

Figure 7.7. Increase in Number of Korean R&D Researchers over Time
Source: National Science and Technology Commission and Korea Institute of Science and Technology Evaluation and Planning (2011).

a handful of producers, while the latter may have more effective self-correcting tendencies. This suggests that broadening Korea's profile as a producer and exporter of high-tech products will require further developing venture capital and strengthening the weak intellectual-property protections that pose barriers to entry for start-ups and venture firms. In turn, this will make possible a more diverse portfolio of R&D projects.

The Korean government has sought to address these problems by enhancing the coherence and effectiveness of technology policy. In 2008, the Lee Myung-bak government merged the Ministry of Science and Technology with the Ministry of Education, and the Ministry of Commerce, Industry, and Energy with the Ministry of Information and Communication. It launched an R&D Council to improve coordination. Time will tell whether this new integrated strategy can deliver the desired results, or whether the larger and more bureaucratic entity in each new ministry (e.g., education) will dominate the smaller and more innovative one (e.g., science and technology).

Success in high tech of course requires adequate supplies of scientists and engineers. Science and engineering training in Korea is extensive by international standards (Figure 7.7). In particular, Korea invests heavily in foreign training for its scholars, scientists, and engineers. But this heavy emphasis on foreign training reflects the limitations of Korea's domestic

Table 7.5. Allocation of Researchers and R&D Expenditures among Sectors of Performance, 2011

	Universities	GRIs	Industries	Total
Researchers (no. persons)	95,750	28,800	250,626	375,176
	25.50%	7.70%	66.80%	100%
Researchers holding PhDs (no. persons)	54,287	13,743	16,644	84,674
	64.10%	16.20%	19.70%	100%
R&D expenditure (KRW 100 million)	50,338	66,733	381,833	498,904
	10.10%	13.40%	76.50%	100%
R&D financed by government only (KRW million)	5,536,742	3,554,627	1,750,995	10,842,364
	51.07%	32.78%	16.15%	100%
R&D financed by government, govt.-invested institute, and national public university (KRW million)	6,083,371	4,160,160	2,322,205	12,565,736
	48.41%	33.11%	18.48%	100%
R&D expenditure per researcher (KRW million)	52.6	231.7	152.4	133.0

Source: National Science and Technology Commission and KISTEP (2011).
Note: GRI denotes government research institute.

higher education, as manifested in large class sizes, limited involvement of students in research, and a failure to encourage out-of-the-box thinking. Korean universities have traditionally been charged with teaching rather than research, as discussed in more detail in Chapter 6. Thus, research infrastructure is inadequate. The underdevelopment of university-business linkages also makes it difficult for universities to increase their research productivity and to tailor that research to the needs of industry.

Universities employ around 70 percent of all Korea's PhDs yet account for only about 10 percent of spending on research (Table 7.5). Many Korean universities are not equipped with good R&D facilities and do not have full-time doctoral students. The high status and light workload afforded to university staff, in turn, have resulted in an internal brain drain from government research institutes (GRIs) to universities, even though GRIs have better R&D facilities and research support.

The government has acknowledged that mobilizing latent research capacity will be essential if Korea is to achieve technological parity with the leading economies. Accordingly, it has offered funding to universities to establish research centers and to attract foreign scientists capable of helping to establish research groups. Universities, for their part, have increased their patenting activities and established technology licensing offices. It will take time for these efforts to produce results. Meanwhile, a useful supplemental strategy would be to solidify relationships between universities and GRIs, where efforts at solidification might range from loose cooperation to mergers.[11]

The authorities have also taken steps to promote the development of venture capital.[12] Unlike the situation in the United States, however, venture capital remains heavily governmental rather than commercial. Public funds spent to support the establishment of new SMEs, mainly venture businesses, rose by a factor of 36 between 1997 and 1999.[13] As of 2000 Korea ranked third among OECD countries in venture capital investment as a share of GDP, with two-thirds of that funding going to information technology.[14] By 2012, cumulative venture funding amounted to 9.4 trillion won (approximately US$8 billion), or some 0.8 percent of GDP. The amount invested continued to grow strongly right through the global financial crisis (Table 7.6).

Korea has seen the establishment of thousands of venture businesses by university professors, scientists, and other researchers, as well as by entrepreneurs. These firms have not had a high survival rate, however. While venture firms rarely do, Korean start-ups appear to experience particularly high mortality, reflecting the relatively undiscriminating approach of the public sector to venture funding.[15] In some cases the government has

---

11. At the same time, the government should ensure that research-spending increases in the universities do not create ivory towers (OECD 2009a, 20).

12. The discussion in this chapter focuses mainly on the growth of venture firms; Chapter 4 focuses on the obstacles to the growth of the venture capital industry.

13. Shin and Chang (2003), 109.

14. OECD (2003), 164.

15. Prior to 2005 there are no systematic data on the establishment date of disqualified venture companies. Due to this data problem, Song et al. (2010, 67) focus on the survival rate of 760 venture companies disqualified between March 2006 and December 2009. The average survival period for these firms was 81.8 months; the five-year survival rate was 57.9 percent, and the ten-year survival rate was 20.1 percent. The authors used the Kaplan-Meier product-limit method to estimate the survival function and the hazard function; see Song et al. (2010). Based on Census of Mining and Manufacturing data, J.-H. Kim (2005, 63–64) reports that, with an SME is defined as a company with employees numbering between 5 and 300, out of 56,472 SMEs in 1993, only 14,315 still survived in 2003, for a survival rate of 25.3 percent. (Note that the SMEs with fewer than 5 employees by 2003 are not counted as surviving.) Moreover, only 75 companies (0.13 percent) and 8 companies (0.01 percent) had grown to 300 or more employees and 500 or more employees, respectively, in 2003.

Table 7.6. Number and Status of Venture Companies, 1998–July 2011

| Year | Increase | | | Decrease | | | | | Difference | Year end (month end) |
	New	Reaffirmed	Total	Expiration	Closure	Other (cancel, etc.)	Total			
1998	2,049	—	2,049	—	3	4	7		2,042	2,042
1999	3,676	33	3,709	729	63	25	817		2,892	4,934
2000	5,532	1,055	6,587	2,601	62	60	2,723		3,864	8,798
2001	3,914	2,479	6,393	3,489	221	89	3,799		2,594	11,392
2002	1,672	4,781	6,453	8,419	261	387	9,067		−2,614	8,778
2003	1,272	2,945	4,217	5,113	145	35	5,293		−1,076	7,702
2004	1,886	2,718	4,604	4,221	100	18	4,339		265	7,967
2005	2,823	2,957	5,780	3,935	62	18	4,015		1,765	9,732
2006	4,127	2,955	7,082	4,467	59	70	4,596		2,486	12,218
2007	5,286	3,952	9,238	7,274	163	4	7,441		1,797	14,015
2008	6,276	8,243	14,519	13,123	2	8	13,133		1,386	15,401
2009	7,762	10,184	17,946	14,351	0	103	14,454		3,492	18,893
2010	6,899	6,647	13,546	7,556	0	238	7,794		5,752	24,645
July 2011	3,808	3,310	7,118	5,219	0	57	5,276		1,842	26,487
Total	56,982	52,259	109,241	80,497	1,141	1,116	82,754		26,487	173,004

Source: Small and Medium Business Administration (2011).

been too prescriptive, throwing large amounts of venture funding at specific activities. This has led firms to go into business whether or not they have a viable business plan and has encouraged existing companies to masquerade as venture firms. Solving these problems will entail further privatizing venture funding and putting it on a firmer commercial basis.

Korea continues to make good progress in expanding its exports of high-technology products, in line with what would be expected of a country with its per capita income and at its stage of economic development. Electronics, optical instruments, and photographic equipment are all among its top-ten export categories. Further progress will require developing a more vibrant ecosystem of high-tech producers that extends beyond the large business groups that currently dominate these activities. That in turn will require developing a more active venture capital industry. It will require more effective business-university collaboration, increased research activity at the university level, and higher education that is better tailored to the needs of industry. Here, clearly, there will be roles for both business and the public sector.

Competitiveness in Services

Exports of services are Korea's future, and exports of services are also currently Korea's problem. Globally, the share of services in trade is 21 percent; in Korea it is only 17 percent. Eichengreen, Perkins, and Shin (2012) show that the country exports significantly fewer services than its per capita income, proximity to foreign markets, and other characteristics would lead one to expect. This is true of travel services, transport services, medical services, and miscellaneous commercial services alike.

Medical services illustrate the problem. Despite a reputation for providing high-quality care at affordable prices, Korea's health-services industry has only begun to establish itself as an international player. While some patients from the Russian Far East have begun coming to Korea for medical services, the industry has a long way to go. In 2012, Korean hospitals attracted 155,000 patients from overseas, for an estimated revenue of 240 billion won (approximately US$200 million). This pales in comparison with the much smaller Singapore, which attracted 1 million patients, for a revenue of US$3 billion. Linguistic and cultural barriers limit Korea's attractiveness as a provider of medical services. Korean doctors' reluctance to live overseas also handicaps the country in its attempt to become a major player in the field, given the value of overseas experience in learning to deal with foreign patients.

Korea's underperformance is greatest, however, in miscellaneous commercial services, a category that includes finance and insurance. In 2003 President Roh Moo-hyun announced a plan for developing Seoul into a Northeast Asian financial hub. In 2004 a Financial Hub Planning Division was established within the Ministry of Finance and Economy. In July 2005 the authorities published an action plan. In June 2007 the National Assembly adopted the Capital Market Consolidation Act, which came into force in February 2009. This was an attempt to enhance the competitiveness of financial firms by liberalizing the market and streamlining regulation. Barriers to competition were removed by allowing brokerages to provide retail payment and settlement services, traditionally the exclusive preserve of banks. The new law eased impediments to product development and innovation by allowing firms to market all financial service products not explicitly proscribed. This approach was intended to encourage proprietary trading, a profit center for investment banks in the United States and other advanced countries, by encouraging the establishment of financial investment companies and placing departments active in securities trading, asset management, merchant banking, trust business, and futures trading all under one roof.

Attempts at streamlining focused on shifting from institutional to functional regulation. Previously, different financial institutions were overseen by different regulators; they were subject to different regulatory frameworks, despite offering similar products and services. Under the new regime, different regulators focus instead on different market functions: dealing, intermediation, asset management, investment advising, and custodial management.[16] This system is designed to address the problem of fragmented regulation, which creates uncertainty and inflates costs.

In the event, the effort to transform Korea into an exporter of financial services has encountered multiple obstacles. First, the production of financial services is subject to increasing returns; this is why so much international activity is concentrated in a handful of financial centers.[17]

---

16. Securities firms engaged in any of these six business areas were required to secure a new license or undergo a registration process.

17. Indeed, this is why financial *centers* exist in the first place.

Here, Korea faces a problem: other financial centers are already active in Northeast Asia. Japanese financial firms dominate their domestic market, and Hong Kong is an established financial center with strong links to China.[18]

Second, to the extent that scale is important for achieving first-class financial center status, it is a problem that Korea is only a midsize economy. Iceland and Ireland serve as cautionary tales of the problems that can arise when a country attempts to grow a banking and financial system out of proportion to its economy. Tokyo and Hong Kong have the Japanese and Chinese governments standing behind them. Those governments have the capacity to recapitalize even international megabanks, if things go wrong. Doing so would be more difficult for a smaller economy like Korea's.

Third, the financial services industry descended into a severe crisis in 2008, auguring a period of slow growth. The share of financial services in value added had risen strongly across the advanced countries, reflecting the combined effects of deregulation and accommodating monetary policy. Subsequent evidence suggests that some of that apparent growth was in fact a mirage. The period of strong growth has now given way to retrenchment as financial institutions deleverage and consolidate. This suggests that financial services may not be as dynamic a growth engine as previously expected, in Northeast Asia or globally.

Fourth, the idea that light-touch regulation of the sort once embraced by the Korean authorities is suitable for the financial services industry has been replaced by recognition of the need for rigorous supervision. The global credit crisis raised questions about the originate-and-distribute model of securitization. It cast doubt on the future of over-the-counter markets in complex, opaque derivative securities. The fact that Korea has relatively well-developed derivatives markets emerges as something of a mixed blessing in this connection.[19]

---

18. These links are mainly to Southern China, but with entry into Southern China come links to Northern China. There is also competition from Singapore, but that country has positioned itself mainly as an exporter of financial services to Southeast Asia as opposed to Northeast Asia.

19. All these markets and activities are now likely to expand more slowly insofar as they will be subject to vigorous regulation. Similarly, making Korea an attractive base for the regional operations of global financial firms requires eliminating most if not all

Questions were also raised about functional regulation. When diverse functions like dealing, intermediation, asset management, investment advising, and custodial management all take place within a single financial conglomerate, it makes no sense for them to be overseen by separate regulators, since no one is then responsible for the viability of the entity as a whole. Here "twin peaks regulation" (two regulators, one responsible for financial stability and the other for consumer protection) may be more effective. Similarly, the crisis raised questions about the wisdom of placing supervision in the hands of a Financial Services Commission separate from the central bank, given the importance of coordinating supervision with the lender-of-last-resort function.

Finally, the global credit crisis raised questions about the wisdom of following the investment-banking model as the template for Korea's initiatives, and about the growth of trade in financial services generally. The fact that the Korea Development Bank contemplated taking over Lehman Brothers just prior to its failure in September 2008 is a caution. More generally, the idea that profitability should be based on proprietary trading by investment banks using wholesale funding has been dealt a blow by the crisis. With the disappearance of large investment banks in the United States, culminating in the conversion of the two principal survivors, Goldman Sachs and Morgan Stanley, into bank holding companies, it is no longer clear that the authorities' vision of developing one or more Korean investment banks to function as regional and global players remains viable.[20]

If not in financial services, then in what other tradable services might Korea develop a comparative advantage? One possibility is logistics. Korea has a revealed comparative advantage in transport services, reflecting its status as a leading trading nation.[21] And yet its share of global logistics

---

restrictions on foreign exchange and capital transactions. This is a less appetizing prospect as a result of the recent crisis.

20. On the other hand, insofar as financial institutions in the United States and other countries appear to be evolving into universal banks—as is evident in Goldman Sachs and Morgan Stanley's attempts to obtain a base of deposits as a more secure form of funding and to branch into activities less dependent on leverage—Korea may have an advantage. The conglomerate form is not unfamiliar to the country. Large entities like Samsung Securities might well follow Goldman, Morgan Stanley, and other global institutions in the universal-bank direction.

21. Using a trade specialization index, a revealed comparative advantage index, and a contribution to the trade balance index, Hur, Seo, and Lee (2007) analyze the performance of tradable services in twelve OECD countries. They classify these countries

is quite low, and no Korean company is a world-class player. In 2009, Korea's share of the $3.3 trillion global logistics market was only 2.6 percent.[22]

A successful international logistics company must provide a global network and integrated services (i.e., intermodal transport, storage, and processing services). Korean companies have typically provided only a limited range of geographical and functional services. Business groups often rely on in-house logistics companies, in part motivated by corporate governance considerations (e.g., problems of tunneling). Glovis, which handles logistics for Hyundai and Kia automobiles, is the best-known example. In-house companies tend to be shielded from competition, and reliance on them tends to stifle the development of third-party logistics providers.[23] Moreover, the loosening of entry restrictions and lack of consolidation since the 1980s has led to a fragmented market structure. In 2007–2008, the average number of employees at any one logistics company was 6 in Korea, compared with 23 in Japan, 13 in Germany, and 14 in Britain. There were 21,000 logistics companies in Korea, 8,300 in Japan, 15,000 in Germany, and 10,000 in Britain.[24]

Clearly the scope of geographical and functional services must be expanded if Korean logistics companies are to become competitive worldwide.[25] If industry rationalization and stand-alone expansion are too difficult, then interested parties should join forces to establish a global net-

---

into four groups: (1) Britain, Ireland, and Switzerland, which are strong in finance, information, and communications; (2) the United States, whose revealed comparative advantage extends over knowledge-based services ranging from intellectual property to entertainment; (3) Australia, France, and Italy, whose strength is mainly in travel services; and (4) Germany, Japan, and Korea, which have revealed comparative advantage in transport services. Based on their analysis of changes over time, the authors find that transport and financial services have become increasingly important exports for Korea.

22. By 2020, the global logistics market is projected to increase to $8.1 trillion.

23. It is not impossible for an in-house logistics provider to branch out and offer services to other companies. In 2006 CJ GLS Company bought Singapore's Accord and took over its Southeast Asian logistics network. In 2011 it then acquired Korea Express as a way of moving into port services. This was more the exception than the rule. It should also be noted that rivalry among business groups tends to make third-party logistics a difficult proposition in Korea. In 2009 Samsung Electronics made quite a stir by using Hyundai's advertising agency (Innocean) instead of its own (Cheil Worldwide).

24. See Lee, Kim, and Song (2010).

25. See Lee, Kim, and Song (2010) for details.

work and provide integrated services. Another option would be to use an existing state-owned enterprise, such as Korea Post, as the basis for a global logistics company a la Deutsche Post, although other countries have had mixed success in attempting to transform such state-owned enterprises into true competitors in the commercial market.

More broadly, Korea's underperformance as an exporter of services reflects the problem of relatively low service-sector productivity. It will become more urgent to fix this as a larger share of the labor force is employed in the production of services, something that is a natural corollary of economic maturity. It will become even more urgent as other emerging markets, not least China, become competitive with Korea in the production of heavy manufactures and high-tech products.

Conclusion

For more than four decades the external sector has been one of the strengths of the Korean economy. Export growth has held up well despite the slowing that comes with economic maturity and the difficulties of the 1997–1998 financial crisis. Korea's export performance compares not unfavorably with that of other countries at similar levels of economic development, whether that performance is gauged by the growth of export volumes or the technological sophistication of those export products. The firms that rose to prominence during the Heavy and Chemical Industry Drive of the 1970s remain the leaders in world markets for steel, petrochemicals, electrical equipment and electronics, ocean-going tankers, and automobiles.

At the same time, there is disquiet in Korea about external-sector performance. Some observers are disconcerted by the slowing of export growth from the 20 to 30 percent annual rates of the 1970s and 1980s. Others are alarmed by the tendency toward outsourcing, multinational production, and foreign investment by Korean firms, which has weakened the linkage from exports to employment creation. They fear that Korea will lose market share to China as the latter moves up the technological ladder into the production of more technologically sophisticated goods. They worry about Korea's capacity to shift its export specialization from goods to services.

Sometimes-exaggerated worries notwithstanding, the strength of the external sector will depend on how successfully these challenges are met. Success will require capitalizing on the presence of a large, low-cost as-

sembly and production platform next door. In turn, this will require negotiating a free trade agreement with China and navigating a global trading system characterized by bilateral agreements and regional blocs. Success
will also mean redeploying domestic resources from the assembly line to
the design center. It will require providing incentives and resources to invest in the new generation of technologies. It will mean supplementing
Korea's traditional strength in the export of manufactures with exports
of services, a sector in which productivity growth continues to lag. These
changes are an important part of the larger policy agenda, to which we
turn in our concluding chapter.

CHAPTER 8

Challenges of Reunification

East Asia has witnessed a great deal of conflict and tension since the mid-nineteenth century, when the traditional Sino-centric "world order" in the region came under attack. In a fifty-year period, China and Japan fought two major wars, as did Japan and Russia. China's defeat in the Sino-Japanese War of 1894–1895 accelerated the demise of the Qing dynasty, and the destruction of the Russian fleet by the Japanese navy in 1905 dealt a devastating blow to the Russian Empire. China and Russia returned the favor in World War II with help from the United States. Although many hoped that the end of World War II would open a new era of reconciliation and cooperation in East Asia, the Cold War made it all but impossible for countries to work together toward a common future. Instead, the intense U.S.-Soviet rivalry led to the partition of the region along ideological lines and greatly increased the risks of conflict. Nowhere was this more evident than in Korea. The nation was divided along the 38th parallel in 1945 and became a battleground for an internationalized civil war in 1950–1953, pitting South Korea and the United States against North Korea and China, with the Soviet Union in the background. The Cold War may have now ended, but the Korean question remains unresolved.[1]

Will a reunified nation-state become a reality for the Korean people? This question has internal, inter-Korean, and international dimensions: What kind of political and economic system should reunified Korea have?

---

1. For historical and international relations perspectives on the Korean question, see Cumings (1997), Harrison (2002), Oberdorfer (2001), and Pollack (2004).

How should Koreans overcome national division and move toward reunification? How should the Korean nation position itself as an international player? There is a broad consensus in South Korea that a democratic market economy should be the system of choice for reunified
Korea, but North Korea's political and economic system, a communist
regime based on dynastic succession, is far removed from that destination. The second dimension of the question has to do with political and
economic integration between South and North Korea. On this front there
is an ongoing policy debate about how best to set the pace of integration
and the degree of linkage between political and economic issues. The third
dimension has to do with international relations, including alliance and
regional cooperation issues. Placing Korean reunification within the
broader context of inclusive regional integration may be an effective geopolitical strategy for the Korean nation, but the architecture of inclusive regional integration remains an unfinished design.[2]

Two Divergent Paths

Table 8.1 shows how far apart the two sides are economically. South
Korea's population is about twice as large as North Korea's, but its economy is 36 times bigger in purchasing power parity terms. Even if South
Korea's economy grows at only 3 percent per year, it is expanding annually by an amount equivalent to the size of North Korea's economy. The
volume of South Korea's international trade is 171 times as large as North
Korea's, reflecting its far greater integration with the global economy.[3]

Inter-Korean economic disparities were not always this extreme, nor
even of this form. In 1960, North Korea's exports ($146.9 million) were
more than four times South Korea's ($32.8 million). Some estimates even
put North Korea's per capita income in the early 1960s at twice South
Korea's. Having successfully carried out economic reconstruction from
the ashes of the Korean War, with help from the Soviet Union and China,

---

2. A good introduction to the scholarly literature on this subject is Green and Gill
(2009).

3. For a more detailed discussion on population, income, international trade, and
food production trends for South and North Korea since 1945, see Lee and Kim (2011).
For a comparative discussion of the two economic systems before North Korea's economic crisis, see L.-J. Cho and Kim (1995). For a comparative perspective after North
Korea's crisis, see Noland (2000).

Table 8.1. Major Economic Indicators for South Korea and North Korea, 2011

	South Korea	North Korea	South-North ratio
GDP (PPP)	$1,459 billion	$40 billion	36
GDP per capita (PPP)	$30,000	$1,800	17
Population	50.0 million	24.5 million	2
International trade	$1,079.6 billion	$6.3 billion	171

Source: The World Factbook 2013–14 (Washington, DC: Central Intelligence Agency, 2013); www.cia.gov/library/publications/the-world-factbook/index.html.
Note: PPP = purchasing power parity. International trade in this table does not include inter-Korean transactions ($0.9 billion from the North to the South and $0.8 billion from the South to the North in 2011).

Kim Il Sung boasted of North Korea's achievements and in 1960 proposed a confederation scheme, in a speech on the occasion of the fifteenth anniversary of Korea's liberation from Japan. He confidently declared: "The most urgent problem today is to rebuild the South Korean economy and to improve the living conditions of the people who have fallen into great misery . . . This problem cannot be solved without economic exchanges between the South and the North. It is a simple truism of economics that no country can develop light industries and agriculture and improve people's lives without the support of heavy industries. In our country, only the northern half has such industries . . . We also have a plenty of experience with economic development." When Joan Robinson, the renowned British economist, wrote "Korea, 1964: Economic Miracle," she was talking about North Korea. After her visit there in October 1964, she proclaimed that North Korea's achievements eclipsed "all the economic miracles of the post-war world," and she gave the credit to a "well-conceived economic strategy" and "patriotic rage and devotion expressing itself in enthusiasm for hard work."[4] Park Chung Hee thus confronted the cold reality that South Korea faced a formidable adversary that was winning "the economic war which comes ahead of military or political battle."[5]

---

4. Robinson (1965), quotations on 208–209.
5. C. Park (1963), 172–173. Deploring the fact that South Korea depended on U.S. assistance for 52 percent of its government budget, Park summarized South Korea's economic conditions as follows: "From 1956 to 1962, economic assistance averaged about $280 million per year, and military assistance, about $220 million per year. Add

Table 8.2. Two Divergent Paths: South Korea and North Korea, 1960–2010

Year		Population (thousand persons)	Current GDP (US$ billion)	Total trade (US$ million)
1960	South Korea	24,989	2.0	376
	North Korea	10,789	1.2	304
	South-North ratio	2.3	1.7	1.2
1970	South Korea	31,435	8.1	2,819
	North Korea	14,619	4.9	796
	South-North ratio	2.2	1.7	3.5
1980	South Korea	37,407	64.3	39,797
	North Korea	17,298	9.9	3,451
	South-North ratio	2.2	6.5	11.5
1990	South Korea	43,390	270.3	134,859
	North Korea	20,000	16.7	4180
	South-North ratio	2.2	16.2	32.3
2000	South Korea	45,985	533.5	333,174
	North Korea	22,963	10.6	2,394
	South-North ratio	2.0	50.3	139.2
2010	South Korea	47,991	1,014.3	893,508
	North Korea	24,387	12.3	6,086
	South-North ratio	2.0	82.5	146.5

Source: Population figures are from Lee and Kim (2011); GDP figures come from the UN Comtrade database; and total trade figures, covering both international and inter-Korean trade, are from Korea Trade-Investment Promotion Agency, "North Korea's External Trade," for 1990–2010, and S.-Y. Choi (1991).

As Park made clear in his Revolutionary Pledges of 16 May 1961, he was determined to "channel all energy into developing real capability to confront communism, in order that the people's long-standing wish for national unification may be achieved."

Over the following decades, South Korea and North Korea took divergent paths. As Table 8.2 shows, South Korea's population remained roughly twice as large as North Korea's over the entire period from 1960 to 2010. Over the same period, however, the South-North ratio went

---

to this total an average trade deficit of $50 million per year, and the conclusion is that we must earn anew an average of $550 million per year. And, what are we going to do with the additional pressure from a population growth rate of 2.88 percent, namely 720,000 newborns per year?" Ibid.

up from 1.7 to 82.5 for current GDP at official exchange rates and from 1.2 to 146.5 for total trade (which includes both international and inter-Korean trade).

As we have seen, South Korea employed a development strategy focused on export-oriented industrialization and human resource development, encapsulated in the slogans "exportization of all industries" and "scientification of all people." In the 1960s, it was able to exploit its latent comparative advantage in labor-intensive manufacturing by relying on prior investments in education and by correcting the government and market failures of the past. From the 1970s onward, South Korea upgraded its comparative advantage, focusing relentlessly on increasing domestic value added and the local content of its exports. South Korea progressively developed its own capacity to produce and export, even as it actively engaged in external interaction to learn from, and trade with, the outside world. Through the joint efforts of the government and the private sector, it was able to discover and upgrade its comparative advantage, and to reinforce successful experiments through rewards based on performance in competitive global markets.[6]

North Korea took a different path. Extensive resource mobilization in the early stages of development yielded tangible results and rewarded people for their "patriotic rage" with improved living standards. However, the initial spurt of rapid growth through extensive resource mobilization then gave way to diminishing returns, owing to the limits of autarkic policy and a command economy. In the 1970s, Pyongyang tried to take advantage of détente by expanding economic cooperation with Western countries, but when it defaulted on its loan payments it basically shut itself off from further opportunities to access advanced technology and capital. Economic stagnation led to, and was in turn fed by, the loss of workers' enthusiasm. The collapse of the socialist bloc in the late 1980s then dealt a devastating blow to North Korea's command economy.[7]

North Korea's Crisis and Response

In the 1980s and 1990s, a series of further external and internal shocks rocked the North Korean economy, forcing Pyongyang to explore

---

6. W. Lim (2011).
7. Chun and Park (1997). See also Eberstadt (1999).

nontraditional measures to ensure regime survival. The breakdown of the Soviet trading bloc made it difficult for North Korea to import essential food and energy inputs, which had serious repercussions for the economy as a whole. In 1993–1994, North Korea's nuclear standoff with the United States greatly raised tension on the Korean Peninsula, aggravating existing economic difficulties. In July 1994, the death of Kim Il Sung, who had ruled North Korea since its establishment in 1948, fueled speculation about its impending collapse from political as well as economic instability. The regime dealt with the nuclear crisis by signing the Geneva Agreed Framework with the United States in November 1994, but, despite the breakthrough its external relations did not improve significantly. The economy suffered further setbacks in 1995–1996, when heavy floods devastated an agricultural sector already weakened by unsustainable farming methods. Although North Korea managed to cope with these shocks through what it called "an arduous march," they left an indelible imprint on the economy.[8]

As Figure 8.1 shows, North Korea's trade suffered a catastrophic decline after the collapse of the socialist bloc. The former Soviet Union not only accounted for 60 percent of North Korea's total trade in the late 1980s but also provided de facto aid worth hundreds of million dollars by running a chronic trade surplus with North Korea. With the disintegration of the Soviet Union, that trade all but vanished. As a consequence, North Korea's trade volume declined by more than 50 percent, from $4.2 billion in 1990 to $1.7 billion in 1998. In addition, North Korea no longer could conduct trade on "friendly terms" with China, which began insisting on commercial terms.

As a result, North Korea's crude oil imports plummeted from 18.5 million barrels in 1990 to 2.9 million barrels in 2000, a whopping 84 percent decline. Although North Korea tried to maximize the use of domestic energy resources, such as coal, its primary energy supply declined from 24.0 million tons of oil equivalent in 1990 to 15.7 million tons in 2000. Food imports, which accounted for as much as 20 percent of total food consumption in 1990, also plummeted, and domestic food production suffered a significant decline as well, owing to the lack of critical inputs such as fertilizers. According to the estimates of the Food and Agriculture

---

8. What follows is an updated and revised version of the analysis presented in W. Lim (2004), 171–195.

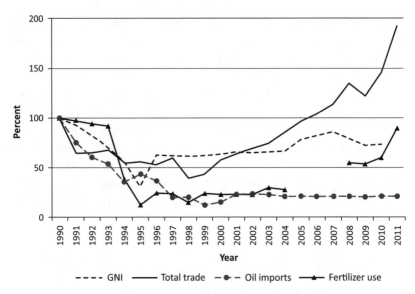

Figure 8.1. Economic Trends in North Korea, 1990–2011
GNI = gross national income. Trade-level values are converted to index numbers and normalized at 100 in base year 1990. Base-year values are as follows: GNI, $16.7 billion; total trade, $4.2 billion; oil imports, 18.5 million barrels; and fertilizer use, 832,400 tons. Total trade and oil import figures are deduced from mirror statistics, and fertilizer-use figures are checked by Food and Agriculture Organization/World Food Program missions to North Korea, but GNI estimates are of questionable reliability; see Lee and Kim (2011).
Source: Korean Statistical Information Service (KOSIS).

Organization (FAO), North Korea's fertilizer use declined from 832,000 tons in 1990 to 104,000 tons in 1995.

Unable to generate the hard currency needed to finance the imports of raw materials and critical inputs, the North Korean economy broke down. Kim Il Sung's last policy speech, on July 6, 1994, was filled with references to the country's economic troubles, especially in the area of infrastructure and basic industries. He set three policy directions: (1) expanding trade with any country that would be willing to engage in economic exchanges with North Korea; (2) devising ways to sell manufactured goods overseas instead of exporting labor; and (3) eradicating bureaucratism and learning from the people.

However bold the ambitions, actual policy measures in the first half of the 1990s were halting and tentative. In fact, lengthy articles in North Korea's official propaganda channels argued that the reforms undertaken by former socialist countries had led to their demise and that North

Korea, with its "unique characteristics," had no need for fundamental reform. Even when Pyongyang opted for economic opening, as with the establishment of the Rajin-Sonbong Free Economic and Trade Zone in December 1991, the emphasis was on limiting foreign influence rather than ensuring commercial viability. Far removed from major cities, in the northeastern corner of North Korea where there was inadequate infrastructure for an industrial complex, the Rajin-Sonbong Free Trade Zone indicated that Pyongyang was more interested in isolating the effects of its economic experiments than ensuring their success.

By the late 1990s it had become clear that half-hearted measures would not end North Korea's economic troubles. The public distribution system, the very symbol of the socialist economy, could no longer provide people with food on a consistent basis, and many citizens had to engage in "illegal" activities in order to survive.[9] These activities included cultivating private plots and crossing the border to China to obtain food. Economic activities outside the plan increased, and these unsystematic improvisations on the part of individuals served as both a complement and a threat to the dysfunctional command economy.[10] Although the growth of the informal sector helped to alleviate economic difficulties for ordinary citizens, it created financial problems for the state because of the increasing gap between informal and formal prices. Although rice was supposed to be procured at 0.80 won and sold at 0.08 won per kilogram in the formal sector in 2002, for example, the price of rice was around 40 to 50 won per kilogram in the informal sector. If farmers siphoned off rice from the formal sector to the informal sector, they could profit handsomely. The result was a financial hollowing out of the state.[11]

---

9. For an early discussion of North Korea's emerging food crisis, based on available statistics and refugee accounts, see W. Lim (1997), 568–585. The Korea Buddhist Sharing Movement (later renamed Good Friends) conducted interviews with nearly two thousand North Korean food refugees in China in 1997–1998. For later assessments, see Haggard and Noland (2007), S. Lee (2003), Natsios (2001), and H. Smith (2005).

10. On the growth of the informal sector in North Korea in the 1990s, see H.-T. Chun (1999).

11. According to an internal document circulated in October 2001 titled "On Improving and Perfecting Socialist Economic Management in Line with Requirements for Building a Strong and Prosperous Nation," Kim Jong Il described these problems as follows: "Because official prices set by the state are lower than farmers' market prices, there aren't enough goods in the formal sector, but individuals have stocked up goods ranging from rice to automotive parts . . . The state is producing goods, but most

In seeking new directions for economic policy, Pyongyang faced three interrelated challenges. First, it had to provide ideological and political justifications for any major departure from "the one and only system." Second, it had to strike a balance between the formal sector and the informal sector; it had no choice but to condone informal economic activities to a certain extent, to compensate for the woeful performance of the formal sector, but at the same time it had to limit arbitrage opportunities between the formal and informal sectors. Third, faced with limited domestic resources, Pyongyang had to create an investor-friendly environment, at least in special zones, to attract capital and technology from the outside world while at the same time managing the risks associated with "foreign infiltration" and economic inequality.

The regime used a number of ideological and institutional innovations to justify changes in its economic policy. When Kim Jong Il, Kim Il Sung's son, officially assumed leadership in 1998, he presented the vision of "a strong and prosperous nation" as his blueprint for the twenty-first century and backed it with several innovations. One was to stretch the definition of socialism. Another was to implement substantive changes without explicitly repudiating what the Kim family had done in the past, simply declaring instead that times had changed. Major economic reforms were introduced as measures to "improve and perfect socialism" rather than to dismantle it. Performance-based rewards were declared the essence of the socialist distribution principle, while rampant "average-ism," according to which everyone was paid equally regardless of the quantity and quality of their work, was condemned as an antisocialist principle.

These ideological innovations were accompanied by institutional changes designed to facilitate economic reform. For instance, Pyongyang introduced or amended major economic laws to allow more flexibility in the drafting of the central economic plan, promote small work teams in agriculture, and recognize the inheritance of personal property such as houses, automobiles, and savings.

---

goods and money end up in the hands of individuals . . . Frankly, the state has no money, but individuals have two years' budget worth . . . There was too much average-ism in distribution. Socially there were too many freebies. In providing food to residents, billions of won were spent annually at the expense of the state . . . Because the socialist distribution principle was not properly observed and because there was socially an excess of freebies and average-ism, it had the effect of promoting hoodlums and discouraging workers' efforts."

After undertaking the ideological and institutional groundwork, Pyongyang turned to striking a balance between the formal and informal sectors. Instead of cracking down on underground market activities or throwing in the towel, Pyongyang chose to transform *and* rehabilitate the formal sector by accommodating the changes that had taken place in the informal sector.[12] The 1 July 2002 reform package consisted of three components: reducing double distortions in prices, increasing and differentiating wages based on performance, and decentralizing enterprise management.

To recover costs of production and prevent further financial hollowing out of the state, Pyongyang adopted far-reaching price reforms. It reduced distortions in relative prices between goods in the formal sector by raising the prices of "basic necessities," which had been heavily subsidized. For example, the sales price of rice per kilogram in the formal sector was raised from 0.08 won to 44 won, and the procurement price was increased from 0.80 won to 40 won, so that the state would no longer incur losses on rice transactions. Moreover, the new procurement price was to be set close to the market price.

To give workers sufficient purchasing power to buy goods at new prices in the formal sector, wages were raised 18 times, to 2,000 won per month. Perhaps more significant than the wage rise was the increase in income differentiation based on skill and performance. The wage differential between highly skilled and unskilled labor was doubled, while performance-based incentives were strengthened.

Finally, Pyongyang gave local plant managers greater autonomy. The scope of central planning was reduced to major indicators such as total industrial output, construction investment, electricity, and steel production; authority to formulate detailed production plans (including labor management) was decentralized. Pyongyang sought to strike a balance between plan and market reminiscent of the "dual-track" strategy adopted by China in its early reform years.[13] Before the reform, enterprises could not freely procure inputs and dispose of their products outside the plan,

---

12. In assessing the significance of the July 2002 reforms, some have tended to focus on the "transformation" aspect, while others have emphasized the "rehabilitation" aspect of the policy package. For an example of the former, see Y.-C. Kim (2002). For a more conservative interpretation emphasizing the rehabilitation of the formal sector, see Jo (2003).

13. For details on China's dual-track strategy, see Lau, Qian, and Roland (1997) and Lin, Cai, and Li (2003).

but now they could legally engage in market transactions so long as they met general production targets. Some enterprises even took loans from merchants and other moneyed individuals to expand their business. In addition, Pyongyang also allowed local enterprises to engage in external trade under the guidance of the Ministry of Trade.[14]

Although the July 2002 reform package was hailed as groundbreaking at the time of its introduction, it did not deliver good results. Price and wage increases stoked inflation; even more disappointing was the limited supply response. While the July 2002 reform package provided incentives, its effectiveness was limited because of the shortage of raw materials and critical inputs. There was only so much North Korea could achieve in the absence of resource flows from outside.

Inter-Korean Relations and Economic Cooperation

One obvious place to get those resource flows was South Korea. Inter-Korean relations have experienced a number of ups and downs over the past quarter century, to put an understated gloss on the point. In the late 1980s South and North Korea seemed to follow the same steps taken by West and East Germany in the early 1970s. Establishing diplomatic relations with North Korea's traditional allies through *nordpolitik*, Seoul applied pressure on Pyongyang to engage in inter-Korean talks. Concerned about regime survival in the aftermath of the collapse of the Soviet bloc, Pyongyang came to the negotiating table. High-level inter-Korean talks ultimately led to the signing of the Basic Agreement. Formally titled the Agreement on Reconciliation, Nonaggression, and Exchanges and Cooperation between the South and the North, the Basic Agreement characterizes the inter-Korean relationship as "a special interim relationship" to be creatively dissolved through reunification.[15] The two sides also

14. See Yang (2005). The author provides an update in Yang (2013). He notes that North Korea's marketization is constrained by the logic of dynastic succession and by the lack of improvement in external relations, especially with the United States, which limits the infusion of external resources.

15. For reunification, South Korea at the time envisaged a three-stage process through which the present regime, with no unified central government, two separate regional governments, and two different systems (0-2-2 formula), would evolve first into a commonwealth (0.5-2-2) and eventually into a single unified state (1-0-1); whereas North Korea proposed to create a confederation of one central government, two separate regional governments, and two *different* systems (a 1-2-2 formula). Note that a

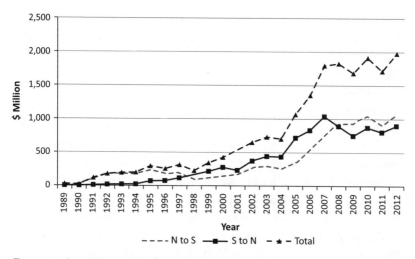

Figure 8.2. Inter-Korean Trade, 1989–2012

The inter-Korean trade figures for 1995 do not include 150,000 tons of rice shipped from the South to the North valued at $237 million. South Korea's food aid to North Korea since 2000 (valued at international rather than domestic prices) is reflected in trade statistics.

Source: Korean Statistical Information Service (KOSIS).

signed the Joint Declaration on the Denuclearization of the Korean Peninsula in December 1991.

Figure 8.2 shows trends in inter-Korean trade since 1989, the year after South Korea made its unilateral 7 July declaration to promote economic exchanges with North Korea.[16] The Inter-Korean Basic Agreement of 1991 provided for the first time an institutional framework for inter-Korean economic cooperation. The total volume of inter-Korean trade reached $100 million in 1991 and nearly $200 million in 1992 as processing-on-commission (POC) trade expanded rapidly. But then the nuclear crisis of 1993–1994 put the brakes on this trend, as South Korea pursued a strategy of linking inter-Korean economic cooperation with the resolution of the nuclear crisis. Although the Geneva Agreed Framework of November 1994 provided renewed impetus, the next four years saw fluctuations

---

commonwealth, based as it is on the free association of separate political entities, does not include a formal structure of central government with binding powers but only a joint consultative conference between the two sides, meeting on a regular basis.

16. What follows is an updated and revised version of the analysis presented in W. Lim (2007).

in the volume of inter-Korean trade as North Korea's food crisis and South Korea's financial crisis buffeted the two economies. In addition, Kim Young-sam's tendency to link political and economic issues and to speculate openly about North Korea's impending collapse were not conducive to cooperation.

Around this time, unification by absorption began to surface as an alternative to the gradual approach that had been the official policy of the South Korean government. North Korea's mounting economic problems, combined with Pyongyang's hostile attitude toward Seoul, encouraged speculation that the inflexible North Korean regime would collapse and that South Korea should be prepared to cope with transitional problems and move ahead with unification by absorption. Some proponents of unification by absorption went further and advocated that South Korea should withhold economic assistance to North Korea and place heavy restrictions on inter-Korean economic exchange; they argued that economic assistance would only prop up a corrupt, oppressive, and ungrateful regime.

Although this policy was supposed to be based on lessons from German unification, it represented a serious misreading of the German experience: West Germany did *not* use sanctions and other pressure tactics to bring the East German government to heel and achieve unification by absorption. Instead, West Germany extended generous assistance to the East. To some critics, this policy only seemed to help prolong the oppressive rule by the socialist regime in East Germany, and in fact, even after unification, some maintained that while the West German government had sought "stabilization with liberalization" in East Germany by providing economic assistance, what it actually achieved was "stabilization without liberalization," as the East German government shrewdly used West German assistance and held its ground until the very end.[17]

West Germany's generous policy certainly failed to soften the Honecker regime; at the same time, however, it is not true that the East German government was able to achieve "stabilization without liberalization" with West Germany's economic support. What transpired in East Germany is best characterized as "destabilization without liberalization." Provided in return for the inter-German exchange of visits and correspondence, West German assistance drove a wedge between the government and the population of East Germany. Although the Honecker regime continued

---

17. See Ash (1993).

to drum up hatred of "imperialistic capitalists," West Germany's humane and generous policy convinced the East German people that such propaganda was groundless. As the prospects for liberalizing reforms then worsened, a sense of alienation and hopelessness began to spread throughout the society. Both the East German exodus and the democratic revolution of 1989 had roots in this discontent; Mikhail Gorbachev's new international policy only provided the spark. Even the East German People's Army for the most part seems to have shared in this feeling and did not intervene when citizens held massive demonstrations. When the East German regime collapsed, it was thus relatively easy for West Germany to push ahead with unification by absorption.

Applied to the North Korean situation, this German experience implies that at least the following two conditions must be satisfied for unification by absorption to succeed. First, the North Korean people must so much envy, and expect generosity from, their southern brethren that they want to be absorbed by the South instead of reforming their own system. And, second, those who have the most to lose by absorption (e.g., the military) must be contained. Neither an active policy of strangling the North nor the passive, wait-and-see variety of unification-by-absorption policy satisfies these conditions.

South Korea's adoption of the Sunshine Policy in 1998 and its recovery from the financial crisis in 1999 began to clear away these obstacles.[18] The Kim Dae-jung government made clear that it would neither condone North Korea's armed aggression nor seek unification by absorption, but would instead focus on promoting inter-Korean reconciliation and cooperation to change facts on the ground in North Korea. The South also gave a green light to companies like Hyundai to undertake investment projects in the North and began to provide a significant amount of humanitarian aid. The inter-Korean summit of June 2000 marked a watershed, as the two sides agreed to push ahead with cooperation projects at a governmental level.

Pyongyang became more proactive in improving external relations around this time. In 2000, North Korea held summits with China, South

---

18. For a comprehensive discussion of Sunshine Policy, see Moon (2012). The name Sunshine Policy is derived from *Aesop's Fables*. In the fable of the North Wind and the Sun, Aesop told how the warmth of sunshine was more effective than the force of a heavy gust of wind in getting a traveler to take off his cloak.

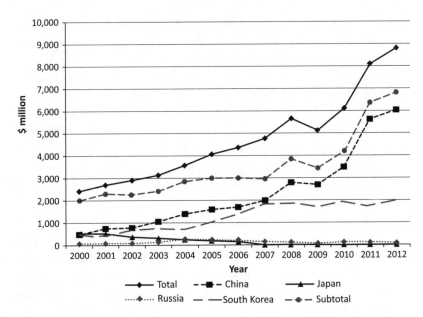

Figure 8.3. North Korea's International and Inter-Korean Trade, 2000–2012
The subtotal line represents the sum of all North Korea's external trade except its trade with South Korea.
Source: Korean Statistical Information Service (KOSIS).

Korea, and Russia in May, June, and July. It also sent a special envoy, General Jo Myong Rok, to the United States in October to meet with President Bill Clinton, and invited U.S. Secretary of State Madeleine Albright to Pyongyang to meet with Chairman Kim Jong Il. As Figure 8.3 shows, North Korea's improved bilateral relations, especially with China and South Korea, helped to raise its trade from $2.4 billion in 2000 to $4.4 billion in 2006, finally surpassing 1990 (pre-Soviet-collapse) levels. Inter-Korean trade alone increased from $0.4 billion in 2000 to $1.3 billion in 2006.

More important, North Korea sought to create an investor-friendly environment in special zones, as China had done earlier, to attract capital and technology from the outside world. In September 2002, it announced the establishment of the Sinuiju Special Administration Zone, and two months later it promulgated the Kaesong Industrial Zone Law and the Mount Kumgang Tourist Zone Law. Among North Korea's economic opening measures, the Kaesong Industrial Zone, located just north of the

Table 8.3. Comparative Factor Prices in Kaesong, China, and South Korea, 2002

	Kaesong (A)	China (B)	South Korea (C)	A/B	A/C
(Minimum) monthly wage[a]	$57.5	$100–200	$423	0.29–0.58	0.14
Working hours per week	48	44	44	1.1	1.1
Corporate income tax rate	10–14%	15%	23–28%	—	—
Land price per *pyong* (36 sq. ft.)[b]	150,000	50,000	407,550	3	0.37

Source: Bank of Korea.
[a] In U.S. dollars.
[b] In South Korean won.

demilitarized zone (DMZ), generated the greatest interest. As shown in Table 8.3, wage and tax rates in Kaesong were set at competitive levels with China at the time. South Korea's state-owned enterprises helped to develop infrastructure and provide electricity for the industrial complex.

Attracted by the availability of well-educated workers at low wages, as well as good infrastructure, South Korean companies set up operations, mostly labor-intensive manufacturing, at Kaesong.[19] The South sent raw materials, parts, components, machinery, and equipment to the North, and the North, in turn, sent back finished goods after processing and assembly. As Table 8.4 shows, the value of inter-Korean transactions at Kaesong increased from $177 million in 2005 to $1,961 million in 2012, and the number of North Korean workers employed at the industrial complex increased from 6,000 to 53,000 over the same period. However, this was well short of the original plan to hire 350,000 workers by 2012.

In practice, the geopolitical risks associated with North Korea limited the infusion of external resources needed for its economic revival. After a long standoff with the George W. Bush administration, Pyongyang tried to force the issue by conducting a nuclear test in October 2006. This shook the political foundations of economic cooperation and led to the adoption of United Nations sanctions against North Korea. Although a new agreement between North Korea and the United States on 13 February 2007 provided another opportunity to deal with the nuclear crisis, the two sides failed to make progress on the phased, reciprocal exchange of

---

19. Details on the development of the Kaesong Industrial Complex are in E. Lim (2005), especially 1–67.

Table 8.4. Inter-Korean Transactions at the Kaesong Industrial Complex, 2004–2012

	Value of transactions (US$ thousand)		North Korean workers employed (no. persons)
	North to South	*South to North*	
2004	50	41,630	—
2005	19,790	156,940	6,013
2006	75,940	222,850	11,160
2007	101,180	339,500	22,538
2008	290,100	518,340	38,931
2009	417,940	522,620	42,561
2010	705,270	737,590	46,284
2011	908,940	788,700	49,866
2012	1,073,110	888,090	53,448

Source: Ministry of Unification and Korean Statistical Information Service (KOSIS).

denuclearization and full normalization of relations. Although the Barack Obama administration reached out to North Korea shortly after taking office in 2009, North Korea conducted its second nuclear test in May of that year. After that experience, the Obama administration became more cautious in dealing with North Korea. As the United States pursued a strategy of "strategic patience," North Korea conducted additional nuclear and missile tests and satellite launches to improve its nuclear missile capability and tried to negotiate with the United States from a position of strength.

Cooling inter-Korean relations after 2007 further limited North-South economic cooperation. The Lee Myung-bak government took a hard line against North Korea, and North Korea in turn responded by escalating tension. After a North Korean security guard shot to death a South Korean tourist who had gone out for an early morning walk at Mount Kumgang in August 2008, Seoul suspended the tourism project. After the sinking of a South Korean naval vessel, the *Cheonan*, in March 2010, Seoul suspended all inter-Korean exchanges as of 24 May 2010, with only a few exceptions (such as, transactions involving the Kaesong Industrial Complex).

Table 8.5 shows inter-Korean trade by transaction type in 2012, including both commercial and noncommercial transactions. Commercial

Table 8.5. Inter-Korean Trade by Transaction Type, 2012 (US$ thousand and percent)

			South to North	North to South	Total
Commercial transactions	Trade	General trade	0	843	843
			—	[273.5]	[273.5]
		POC trade	0	0	0
			—	[–100.0]	[–100.0]
		Subtotal	0	843	843
			—	[–78.5]	[–78.5]
	Economic cooperation projects	Kaesong Industrial Complex	888,086	1,073,109	1,961,195
			[12.6]	[18.1]	[15.5]
		Mt. Kumgang tourism	0	0	0
			[–100.0]	[–100.0]	[–100.0]
		Others	4	0	4
			—	—	—
		Subtotal	888,089	1,073,109	1,961,198
			[12.5]	[18.1]	[15.5]
	Light industry cooperation projects		0	0	0
			—	—	—
	Total commercial transactions		888,089	1,073,952	1,962,042
			[12.5]	[17.6]	[15.3]
Noncommercial Transactions	Aid	Nongovernmental aid	9,064	0	9,064
			[–14.8]	—	[–14.8]
		Governmental aid	0	0	0
			—	[–100.0]	[–100.0]
		Subtotal	9,064	0	9,064
			[–14.8]	[–100.0]	[–20.5]
	Sociocultural cooperation projects		0	0	0
			[–100.0]	[–100.0]	[–100.0]
	Energy aid		0	0	0
			—	—	—
	Total noncommercial transactions		9,064	0	9,064
			[–15.6]	[–100.0]	[–21.4]
Grand total			897,153	1,073,952	1,976,208
			[12.1]	[17.5]	[15.3]

Source: Korea International Trade Association Institute for International Trade (KITA IIT), "Trends in 2012 South-North and North-China Trade," *Trade Focus* 13 (8) (in Korean).

Note: Figures in brackets represent the percentage increase from end of 2011 to end of 2012.

transactions include general trade and POC trade as well as the flows of goods associated with economic cooperation projects such as the Kaesong Industrial Complex and Mount Kumgang tourism. Noncommercial transactions consist of aid to North Korea (e.g., food and fertilizers) and flows of goods associated with sociocultural cooperation projects and the now-defunct Korea Energy Development Organization (KEDO) light-water reactor project.[20] Owing to the suspension of nearly all inter-Korean exchanges since 24 May 2010, inter-Korean trade consists mostly of transactions at Kaesong. However, the future of the Kaesong Industrial Complex itself is in question after North Korea's third nuclear test, in February 2013. In response to North Korea's attempt to escalate tension, South Korea's defense minister spoke about a contingency plan to rescue South Korean managers from Kaesong. North Korea regarded his statement as a hostile act and pulled its workers from the industrial complex in April. South Korea, in turn, pulled its managers, and for more than three months Kaesong was effectively shut down. Although the two sides agreed to reopen it after multiple rounds of tough negotiation, they will have to rebuild trust if they are to achieve the goal of expanding and internationalizing the industrial complex.

As Table 8.6 shows, the share of commercial transactions in inter-Korean trade rose from 62.6 percent in 2004 to 99.5 percent in 2012, mainly due to the termination of the KEDO light-water reactor project in November 2005 and the reduction of humanitarian aid from the South to the North.

Tables 8.7 and 8.8 show trends in South Korea's humanitarian aid to North Korea through both bilateral and multilateral channels. Humanitarian aid provided through multilateral channels has consisted of food, medical supplies, and other aid goods from the South delivered to the North via international bodies such as the United Nations Children's Fund (UNICEF), the World Food Program (WFP), the World Health

---

20. In 1994, to support the implementation of the Geneva Agreed Framework, South Korea agreed to pay 70 percent of the estimated cost of $4.60 billion for two light-water reactors (LWRs) to be supplied to North Korea. In return for freezing and then dismantling North Korea's graphite-moderated reactor, North Korea was to receive the LWRs, which were less susceptible to nuclear proliferation. By the time the KEDO project was terminated in November 2005, South Korea had incurred a total cost of $1.14 billion, most of which was paid to South Korean contractors. See Ministry of Unification (2006).

Table 8.6. Inter-Korean Commercial and Noncommercial Transactions, 2004–2012 (US$ million and percent)

	2004	2005	2006	2007	2008	2009	2010	2011	2012
Commercial	436	689	928	1,431	1,712	1,642	1,889	1,702	1,962
	[62.6]	[65.3]	[68.7]	[79.6]	[94.1]	[97.8]	[98.8]	[99.3]	[99.5]
Noncommercial	261	366	422	367	108	37	23	12	9
	[37.4]	[34.7]	[31.3]	[20.4]	[5.9]	[2.2]	[1.2]	[0.7]	[0.5]
Total	697	1,055	1,350	1,798	1,820	1,679	1,912	1,714	1,971

Source: KOSIS.

Note: Figures in brackets represent percentage shares in total inter-Korean trade.

Table 8.7. South Korea's Bilateral Food and Fertilizer Aid to North Korea, Selected Years 1995–2010 (thousand tons)

	1995	1999	2000	2001	2002	2003	2004	2005	2006	2007	2010
Food	150	—	300	—	400	400	400	500	100	400	5
Fertilizers	—	155	300	200	300	300	300	350	350	300	—

Source: Ministry of Unification.

Table 8.8. South Korea's Multilateral Aid to North Korea, 1996–2012 (US$ thousand)

	WFP	UNICEF	WHO	Others	Total
1996	2,000	1,000	0	50	3,050
1997	20,530	3,940	700	1,500	26,670
1998	11,000	0	0	0	11,000
1999	0	0	0	0	0
2000	0	0	0	0	0
2001	17,250	0	460	0	17,710
2002	17,390	0	590	0	17,980
2003	16,190	500	660	0	17,350
2004	23,340	1,000	870	0	25,210
2005	0	1,000	810	0	1,810
2006	0	2,300	11,670	0	13,970
2007	20,000	3,150	11,810	500	35,460
2008	0	4,080	11,470	190	15,740
2009	0	3,980	14,090	300	18,370
2010	0	0	0	0	0
2011	0	5,650	0	0	5,650
2012	0	0	0	2,100	2,100

Source: Ministry of Unification.
Note: WFP = World Food Program; UNICEF = United Nations Children's Fund; WHO = World Health Organization.

Organization (WHO), and the World Meteorological Organization (WMO). South Korea's bilateral aid to North Korea has been negligible since 2008; likewise for multilateral aid since 2010.

Within the commercial transactions category, Table 8.9 shows that the share of longer-term, investment-oriented economic cooperation projects

Table 8.9. Composition of Commercial Transactions, 2004–2012 (US$ million and percent)

	2004	2005	2006	2007	2008	2009	2010	2011	2012
General trade	176	210	253	330	408	410	318	4	0
	[40.4]	[30.4]	[27.3]	[23.1]	[23.8]	[25.0]	[16.8]	[0.2]	[0.0]
POC trade	171	210	304	461	399	256	117	0	1
	[39.2]	[30.5]	[32.8]	[32.2]	[23.3]	[15.6]	[6.2]	[0.0]	[0.1]
Kaesong Industrial	42	177	299	441	808	941	1,443	1,698	1,961
Complex	[9.6]	[25.6]	[32.2]	[30.8]	[47.2]	[57.3]	[76.4]	[99.8]	[99.9]
Other economic	47	93	72	199	96	35	11	0	0
cooperation projects	[10.9]	[13.5]	[7.8]	[13.9]	[5.6]	[2.2]	[0.6]	[0.0]	[0.0]
Total	436	690	928	1,431	1,712	1,642	1,889	1,702	1,962

Source: Ministry of Unification.

Note: Figures in brackets represent percentage shares in inter-Korean commercial transactions.

Table 8.10. Inter-Korean Trade by Product Category, 2012

Product category (HS codes)	South to North			North to South		
	Amount (US$ thousand)	YOY increase (%)	Share (%)	Amount (US$ thousand)	YOY increase (%)	Share (%)
Textiles (50–63)	318,157	6.4	35.3	442,208	13.7	41.2
Electric and electronic products (85)	258,273	15.4	28.6	355,634	29.1	33.1
Machinery (84)	44,416	16.3	4.9	39,869	–11.4	3.7
Iron and metal products (72–83)	31,187	37.6	3.5	9,662	5.4	0.9
Minerals (25–27)	37,106	20.2	4.1	7	–99.1	0.0
Plastic products (39–40)	26,522	–0.6	2.9	24,710	59.8	2.3
Fats and oils products and delicatessen (15–24)	23,162	25.5	2.6	1,102	86.1	0.1
Agricultural products (06–14)	6,817	–11.9	0.8	5,179	3.3	0.5
Chemical products (28–38)	15,982	–12.4	1.8	11,627	21.7	1.1
Vehicles (87)	16,865	46.2	1.9	14,909	17.1	1.4
Marine and livestock products (01–05)	600	153.2	0.1	722	—	0.5
Miscellaneous products	123,030	19.8	13.6	168,462	11.5	15.7
Total	802,117	12.7	100	1,074,091	17.6	100

Source: Korea International Trade Association Institute for International Trade (KITA IIT), "Trends in 2012 South-North and North-China Trade," *Trade Focus* 13 (8), 2–3 (in Korean).

Note: Product categories include the standardized Harmonized System (HS) codes. YOY = year-on-year.

was rising even before the May 2010 suspension of inter-Korean economic exchanges.[21] Table 8.10 then shows the composition of inter-Korean trade by product category in 2012. Of goods transported from the South to the North, textiles are the largest share, closely followed by electric and electronic products. These basically represent raw materials and intermediate goods, including parts and components. Of goods transported from the North to the South, textiles also represent the largest share, at 41.2

---

21. The Kaesong Industrial Complex's share in total commercial transactions increased from 9.6 percent in 2004 to 57.3 percent in 2009 and then to 99.9 percent in 2012.

percent. These are finished products (e.g., track suits, jackets, shirts, pants, and skirts) shipped back to the South after being assembled in the North. Next in line are electric and electronic products, at 33.1 percent, likewise finished or semi-finished products after processing and assembly in North Korea. This pattern clearly demonstrates the potential for mutual gain between South and North Korea. By comparison, of North Korea's export items to China in 2012, minerals are the largest share at 65.9 percent. The next in line is textiles, at 16.9 percent.[22]

Inter-Korean trade, at slightly less than $2 billion in 2012, amounts to a miniscule 0.2 percent of South Korea's external trade with the rest of the world (valued at $1,068 billion dollars, excluding inter-Korean trade). However, this metric does not do justice to its significance. Credit-rating agencies like Moody's typically downgrade South Korea's rating by a notch (e.g., from A to A–) owing to "North Korea risks" associated with the potential for a military conflict or an economic catastrophe. To the extent that inter-Korean trade improves inter-Korean relations and economic conditions in the North, it is perceived as reducing those risks. Moreover, inter-Korean economic cooperation has great significance for the integration and reunification of the Korean Peninsula in the longer term.

In fact, there are three major rationales for inter-Korean economic cooperation, each of which is important for reunification. First, inter-Korean economic cooperation could help North Korea see a way out of its current predicament as a "rogue state." Through economic exchanges, North Korea would be able to earn money the old-fashioned way rather than through questionable transactions involving counterfeiting, narcotics, and weapons.[23] In fact, blocking legitimate economic transactions runs the

---

22. For a more detailed analysis of trade between North Korea and China, see S.-J. Kim (2013).

23. Although some analysts estimate that North Korea annually derives as much as $500 million from its illicit activities to finance its current account deficit, the very idea of focusing on the current account without taking a serious look at the capital account is fundamentally flawed. Congressional testimony by responsible U.S. government officials also suggests that these estimates may be greatly inflated. For instance, at a U.S. Senate hearing on 25 April 2006 on North Korea's illicit activities, a Secret Service official noted that the total amount of high-quality counterfeit bills (known as "the Supernote") seized since 1989 was $50.0 million, or approximately $2.8 million per year. In comparison, lower-quality counterfeit notes seized in Colombia since 1989 amounted to $380.0 million, and U.S. currency in circulation worldwide is $750 billion (see http://hsgac.senate.gov/_files/042506Merritt.pdf). At the same hearing, another official from

risk of making Pyongyang *more* dependent on illicit activities and arms sales, with negative implications for regional and global security. By helping North Korea to get accustomed to market principles, inter-Korean economic cooperation would also have the effect of facilitating and consolidating North Korea's economic reform. It is a critical component of South Korea's engagement policy, which is based on the principle of "change through rapprochement."

Second, inter-Korean trade could help South Korea undertake its own industrial restructuring less painfully. South Korean firms engaged in labor-intensive manufacturing face increasing competition from China and other late-developing countries, and the "hollowing out" of the economy caused by outward foreign direct investment is increasingly becoming a concern. As Figure 8.4 shows, the increase in outward FDI by small and medium-size Korean enterprises since 2001 is unmistakable, with negative consequences for facility investment and employment in South Korea. Given North Korea's willingness to experiment with special economic zones, these companies may find investment in North Korea a viable alternative, with positive linkage effects in South Korea.

Third, inter-Korean economic cooperation would have the geopolitical significance of counterbalancing China's increasing influence in North Korea. As Table 8.11 shows, China continued to expand its trade with North Korea even after North Korea's second nuclear test in 2009, running a large bilateral current account surplus.[24] China is also expanding its investment in North Korea. In fact, in South Korea, there is a growing concern that North Korea might become "China's fourth Northeastern province" if China's economic and geopolitical influence continues

---

the Bureau of Narcotics and Law Enforcement Affairs in the State Department indicated that the extent of opium production and North Korea's direct involvement in cigarette counterfeiting might be quite limited (see http://hsgac.senate.gov/_files/042506 Prahar.pdf).

24. Of course, China rapidly expanded its trade with other developing countries in Asia as well. From 2007 to 2011, China's trade with Vietnam increased from $15.1 billion to $40.2 billion; Myanmar, from $2.1 billion to $6.5 billion; Mongolia, from $2.0 billion to $6.4 billion; Cambodia, from $0.9 billion to $2.5 billion. Over the same period, China's trade with North Korea increased from $2.0 billion to $5.6 billion. Note that the rate of expansion of China's trade with North Korea was actually lower than with the other countries. A similar pattern is evident for China's outward investment in neighboring countries. See S.-J. Kim (2013), 98.

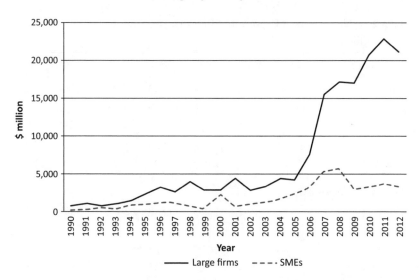

Figure 8.4. Outward Foreign Direct Investment by South Korea's Large Firms and SMEs, 1990–2012

FDI = foreign direct investment; SMEs = small and medium-size enterprises.
Source: Export-Import Bank of Korea.

to rise. Inter-Korean trade is increasingly regarded as a means of preventing North Korea from becoming a Chinese satellite.[25]

Notwithstanding these rationales, inter-Korean economic cooperation has been controversial in South Korea. In fact, there is an ongoing policy debate on two issues: the pace of cooperation and the degree of linkage between political and economic issues.

In pursuing engagement policy, one of the earliest policy questions South Korea faced was how best to promote inter-Korean economic cooperation. There were basically two schools of thought on this issue. One urged gradualism. People advocating gradualism feared that inter-Korean economic cooperation ran the risk of substituting nationalist sentiment and political ambition for commercial logic. They believed that a series of economically sound projects in labor-intensive sectors, undertaken primarily by SMEs, would educate North Korea about market principles and ensure the long-term sustainability of inter-Korean economic cooperation.

---

25. This rationale for inter-Korean trade is somewhat reminiscent of West Germany's effort to keep East Germany from slipping further into the arms of the Soviet Union.

Table 8.11. North Korea's Exports and Imports, 2007–2012 (US$ million)

North Korea's exports, to:	2007	2008	2009	2010	2011	2012
China	582	754	793	1,188	2,464	2,485
Japan	0	0	0	0	0	0
Russia	34	14	21	27	13	11
South Korea	765	932	934	1,044	914	1,074
Total	1,685	2,062	1,994	2,554	3,704	3,954
North Korea's imports, from:						
China	1,392	2,033	1,888	2,278	3,165	3,528
Japan	9	8	3	0	0	0
Russia	126	97	41	84	100	65
South Korea	1,033	888	745	868	800	897
Total	3,053	3,578	3,095	3,528	4,330	4,827

Source: KOSIS.

The other school of thought called for a big bang approach. Members of this group believed that inter-Korean economic cooperation would go nowhere without a clear endorsement from North Korea's top leadership. They argued that it was critical to kick-start inter-Korean economic cooperation on a scale grand enough to draw Pyongyang's attention. They also noted that, because of the poor physical infrastructure in North Korea, SMEs would have limited success unless the South Korean government or large companies led the way by providing electricity, water, communication links, and other essential business supports.

Both approaches proved wanting. SMEs that ventured into North Korea on their own were exposed to a great deal of idiosyncratic risk, and most failed to undertake significant and viable investment projects. Large companies that paid inadequate attention to the commercial side of business also fared poorly. Hyundai may be the most notorious example. In 1998, the company secured Kim Jong Il's endorsement for inter-Korean economic cooperation by launching its ambitious Mount Kumgang tourism project, promising to pay out $942 million over 75 months ($25 million each for the first 6 months, $8 million each for the next 9 months, and $12 million each for the remaining 60 months, from November 1998 to January 2005). Hyundai also secured exclusive long-term rights for seven major investment projects by providing $500 million to Pyongyang at the time of the inter-Korean summit in June 2000. However, Hyundai's big bang approach could not be sustained when the cash flow from its projects in North Korea failed to meet expectations.[26]

Subsequently, it became clear that successful inter-Korean economic cooperation would have to combine the desirable features of both the gradual and big bang approaches. While securing the endorsement of North Korea's top leadership and providing for necessary infrastructure, business projects also had to be commercially viable.

The evolution of Mount Kumgang tourism shows how this new principle was applied. When Hyundai could not meet the payment schedule for $942 million, Pyongyang initially balked at renegotiating the terms of the contract. As a result, tourist services were interrupted. However, Pyongyang came to realize that brinkmanship with a company on the verge of bankruptcy would not work and subsequently agreed to make the tourism project more viable. In place of the fixed monthly payment schedule, the two sides agreed on a flexible scheme by which North Korea would charge a park entrance fee per tourist, starting in September 2001. A tourist staying for one, two, or three days would pay $15, $35, or $70, respectively.[27] North Korea would then have an incentive to improve tourist services, as its revenue from the project was directly linked to the number of tourists coming to Mount Kumgang. Also, to make the tourism project commercially profitable, North Korea agreed to open a ground route to Mount Kumgang. Hyundai no longer needed to lease expensive cruise ships and could offer inexpensive tour packages, starting in October 2003. As a result, the number of tourists visiting Mount Kumgang from South Korea increased from 57,879 in 2001 to 298,247 in 2005. The Mount Kumgang tourism project turned in an operating profit of 5 billion won in 2005. However, the shooting death of a South Korean tourist in 2008 suspended the Mount Kumgang project, as we have noted. Table 8.12 shows trends in North Korea's revenue from the Mount Kumgang tourism project.

---

26. For a critical yet sympathetic look at the development of Hyundai's projects in North Korea, from its late chairman Chung Ju Young's lifelong aspirations to Hyundai's subsequent business and political troubles, see Solomon and Choi (2003).

27. These entrance fees were raised to $30, $48, and $80 in 2006.

Table 8.12. North Korea's Revenue from the Mount Kumgang Tourism Project

	1999	2000	2001	2002	2003	2004	2005	2006	2007	2008
Revenue (US$ million)	206.0	136.0	37.2	21.5	13.1	15.3	13.5	12.3	20.4	11.4
Number tourists (thousand persons)	148	213	58	85	74	268	298	234	345	200

Source: Ministry of Unification and KOSIS.

In short, as demonstrated by the examples of the Mount Kumgang project and the Kaesong Industrial Complex, inter-Korean economic cooperation became more systematic and market-oriented. Drawing lessons from the failure of exclusively gradual or big bang approaches, North and South Korea made inter-Korean economic cooperation more commercially viable and sustainable.

Yet this progress on the commercial front could not overcome political and security problems. The question of whether to link inter-Korean economic cooperation to political and security issues has haunted South Korean policymakers since the nuclear crisis of 1993–1994. Many argued that continuing to engage in inter-Korean economic cooperation in the face of North Korean provocation would send the wrong signal: North Korea would think it could get away with such behavior, and the United States and other countries would conclude that South Korea does not take North's threat seriously. Others argued that while economic cooperation could not be completely unlinked from political and security issues, a tight linkage would shut down important channels of communication with North Korea and run the risk of making South Korea a helpless bystander. Cutting off inter-Korean exchanges would also adversely affect the lives of ordinary people in North Korea and make Pyongyang more dependent on China.

The first nuclear crisis of 1993–1994 showed that these concerns were not unfounded. The Kim Young-sam government tightly linked inter-Korean economic cooperation to the resolution of the nuclear crisis. It banned visits by South Korean entrepreneurs to North Korea and postponed economic cooperation projects. Kim Young-sam made it clear that there would be no inter-Korean summit before the resolution of the nuclear crisis. He apparently did not think that a bilateral summit could help create conditions conducive to progress in nuclear negotiations. As a result, South Korea was reduced to the status of a bystander, and when North Korea and the United States signed the Agreed Framework, South Korea could do little but agree to provide 70 percent of the construction cost for the light-water reactors.

The Kim Dae-jung government took a different approach, attempting to "separate politics from commerce." This new approach was eclectic, combining realist and liberal ideas. It tried to contain North Korea's threat through deterrence and arms control, under the principle of mutual threat reduction, while also promoting internal changes in North Korea through broad economic engagement. Although the idea that economic exchanges can contribute to peace has been around for a long time, there is a limit to how much economic exchanges—or the banning of economic exchanges, for that matter—can do to resolve security issues when vital interests are at stake.[28] When two sides can realize gains by trading, they are likely to try to work out contentious issues and develop the mutually beneficial relationship further, but so long as security risks are perceived to exist, economic interaction alone will not lead to peace. In particular, it is unrealistic to expect one side to disarm unilaterally just because it receives external economic assistance, if it continues to believe it is faced with a security threat. At the same time, however, it would be counter-productive to do away with economic engagement altogether, for that would tend to reduce the chance of internal change. A parallel-track strategy of concurrently pursuing political reconciliation and economic engagement would be more effective than using economic levers to force unilateral disarmament, or broadening economic engagement regardless of its security implications.

Following this line of thought, the Kim Dae-jung government pushed for within-issue rather than cross-issue linkage. In other words, it linked humanitarian issues with humanitarian issues, economic issues with economic issues, and security with security issues, but not economic issues with security issues. Although there was little progress in official inter-Korean dialogue for the first two years of the Kim Dae-jung government, companies like Hyundai and various nongovernmental organizations were able to make headway in economic cooperation and humanitarian assistance. Inter-Korean confidence building through people-to-people

---

28. See Carr (1939).

interaction helped to create an environment conducive to political reconciliation at the governmental level. Hyundai, in particular, came to believe it was in the long-term interest of the company as well as the Korean nation to have an inter-Korean summit. The company thought it could benefit by securing support from the leaders of both sides for its development projects in North Korea and made every effort to facilitate such a historic meeting in 2000. Under the parallel-track strategy, inter-Korean economic cooperation had outpaced political reconciliation, giving economic actors an incentive to serve as political mediators. The summit, in turn, helped to usher in a new era in inter-Korean economic cooperation.

The parallel-track strategy was effective so long as the United States was willing to engage in serious negotiations with North Korea regarding its nuclear and missile programs. The nature of North Korea's weapons programs, with significant implications for regional and global security, made it impractical for South Korea to play more than a facilitating role. It would have been unwise for South Korea to link inter-Korean economic cooperation to progress in these negotiations over which it had little control. At the same time, South Korea would have found economic engagement a difficult position to defend if the United States had refused to negotiate with North Korea on security matters and North Korea had responded by escalating tension.

Under the Agreed Framework of 1994, North Korea agreed to the phased dismantling of its nuclear program in exchange for multilateral energy assistance and a U.S. promise to move toward normalization. When the North Koreans failed to secure the kind of political relationship they had expected from the United States, they complained bitterly even as they maintained the freeze on their plutonium program. In 1998, however, North Korea launched a long-range test missile and procured from Pakistan some equipment that could be used for enriching uranium.[29] Although the Clinton administration learned of this transaction between North Korea and Pakistan, it decided against scrapping the Agreed Framework and instead opted for a "more-for-more" approach. In 1998–1999, through what was known as the Perry process (named for William Perry,

---

29. The onset of the second nuclear crisis on the Korean Peninsula involving North Korea's uranium enrichment program is described by Funabashi (2007). Siegfried S. Hecker (2010), former director of the Los Alamos Nuclear Laboratory, provides an account of his visit to a uranium enrichment facility in North Korea.

U.S. North Korean policy coordinator and former defense secretary), the United States worked with South Korea and Japan to develop a coherent policy toward North Korea. The United States and South Korea essentially agreed on a division of labor by which the United States would address security issues through direct negotiations with North Korea, while South Korea would promote internal changes in North Korea through economic engagement. Recognizing the danger of letting the Agreed Framework unravel, the United States made a more decisive move toward normalization with North Korea in exchange for more comprehensive restrictions on North Korea's missile and nuclear programs. As encapsulated in the October 2000 joint communiqué, the United States reached an understanding with North Korea to secure better access to suspicious facilities in North Korea (such as the large hole in the ground at Kumchangri) as bilateral relations improved.

Through this more-for-more approach, the United States sought to resolve suspicions about North Korea's incipient uranium enrichment program.[30] At the end of 2000, the United States and North Korea appeared very close to concluding a missile deal and moving toward full normalization, but the new Bush administration adopted a completely different approach in March 2001.[31] Its attitude was encapsulated by the words of Vice President Dick Cheney, who reportedly declared in 2003: "We don't negotiate with evil; we defeat it."[32] In October 2002 the Bush administration pressed North Korea to come clean on its uranium enrichment and subsequently stopped heavy fuel oil deliveries, essentially scrapping the Geneva Agreed Framework. Predictably, North Korea responded by restarting its plutonium program.

As the Bush administration put more emphasis on regime change than arms control, the division of labor between the United States and South Korea began to break down. When the second nuclear crisis erupted in October 2002, South Korea made serious efforts to contribute to the resolution of the crisis instead of severely reducing economic exchanges with North Korea. Unlike in 1993–1994, Seoul sent special envoys to Pyongyang

---

30. On this point, see Carlin (2006).

31. See Gordon (2001) and Sherman (2001).

32. Quoted in Leslie Gelb, "In the End, Every President Talks to the Bad Guys, *Washington Post*, 27 April 2008, www.washingtonpost.com/wp-dyn/content/article /2008/04/24/AR2008042401459.html.

to try to persuade North Korea to come to the negotiating table and to secure Kim Jong Il's commitment to denuclearization in exchange for improved relations with the outside world. In fact, a visit by South Korea's special envoy to Pyongyang in June 2005 helped to lay the groundwork for the 19 September joint statement of principles.

For a parallel-track strategy to work, it is imperative that comparable progress be made on both tracks. In 1998–2000 South Korea was able to make a great deal of progress in inter-Korean relations by taking advantage of the synergy between economic cooperation and political reconciliation. During the same period, the United States and South Korea also developed their effective division of labor in dealing with North Korea: the U.S. would work to contain North Korea's nuclear and missile programs through arms control negotiations while South Korea promoted internal changes in North Korea through economic engagement. But this division of labor broke down when the Bush administration dropped arms control negotiations with North Korea. With the United States and North Korea making little progress in security areas, it became increasingly difficult to defend inter-Korean economic cooperation.

Nuclear Conundrum

North Korea's nuclear program seems to serve two major policy goals: as a deterrent against security threats, and as a bargaining chip in diplomatic negotiations. Although North Korea's long-range artillery serves as an effective deterrent against South Korea, North Korea seems to regard nuclear weapons as a possible deterrent against the United States, especially in light of the Iraq War in 2003. Unless the United States credibly abandons what North Korea believes is "hostile policy" toward it, there is little chance that North Korea will give up its nuclear program. North Korea may even try to improve relations with the outside world without completely dismantling the program, instead offering to safeguard nuclear materials within its borders and cease further production of nuclear weapons or fissile material. North Korea could point to India and Pakistan and even China as countries that managed to develop nuclear weapons and then improve relations with the outside world, including the United States. North Korea could also cite the case of Libya, which gave up its nuclear weapons in exchange for the normalization of relations with the United States and Europe but subsequently lacked the military capacity to deter foreign intervention in the wake of a popular uprising. Of course, nuclear weapons cannot safeguard a regime from internal threats. All the nuclear weapons it possessed did not save the Soviet Union from implosion. However, North Korea may still see nuclear weapons as a useful deterrent against external threats.[33]

Other players in Northeast Asia have different perspectives, depending on their perceived national interests. China's priority is to continue its rapid economic growth and "peaceful rise" as a global power and to prevent nuclear proliferation, especially nuclear armament of Japan. China does not want an escalation of hostilities on the Korean Peninsula that could disrupt its economic growth and threaten its position in Northeast Asia. While China is willing to support North Korea as a buffer state and expand its own influence on the peninsula, it does not want North Korea to trigger a nuclear arms race in the region, which would weaken China's position as a nuclear state. China's expression of displeasure toward North Korea in 2012 and 2013, or at least toward the Kim Jong Un regime, can be understood in this context.

Japan is interested in becoming a more "normal country" by freeing itself from the legacies of World War II. However, there is some debate about the best means of achieving that objective. Many Japanese politicians seem to be content to go along as "junior partners" of the United States for the foreseeable future and use the North Korean threat as a justification for remilitarizing Japan. In contrast, others call for a tighter integration with East Asia based on historical reconciliation with Japan's neighbors, including North Korea.

Russia's priority in Northeast Asia is to reestablish its influence and develop the Russian Far East. Russia believes that multilateral diplomacy on the North Korean nuclear issue will enable Moscow to take a more proactive role in Northeast Asia. A comprehensive solution to the North Korea problem, for Russia, is likely to involve energy assistance to North Korea, supporting Russia's plans to develop energy resources and promote economic development in the Russian Far East.

---

33. For a comparative study on how countries such as South Africa, Argentina, Brazil, and Ukraine decided to give up their nuclear weapons, see Reiss (1995). The author analyzed North Korea in one of the chapters as a case of high uncertainty going forward. For U.S. nuclear negotiators' account, see Wit, Poneman, and Gallucci (2004). For two contrasting approaches to dealing with North Korea, see Cha and Kang (2003).

As a divided land bridge in Northeast Asia, South Korea has much to gain from ending North Korea's isolation and building energy and transportation networks to connect the Korean Peninsula with China's northeastern provinces and the Russian Far East. Such projects would create business opportunities and allow South Korean firms to fully reap the benefits of regional integration. In addition, to achieve reunification South Korea must maintain good relations with all its neighbors, as well as the United States, so that a reunified Korea would not be viewed as a threat.

While North Korea's neighbors have different policy priorities, they also share common interests. One is to prevent the outbreak of war on the peninsula. The other is to prevent any one of North Korea's neighbors from dominating it in such a way as to cause a significant change in the regional balance.

North Korea's strategic location enables it to play off its neighbors against one another. South Korea cannot afford to allow North Korea to become overly dependent on China. Russia, seeking to correct its disengagement from the Korean Peninsula during the Yeltsin era, has sought to improve relations with North Korea. Japan has also made diplomatic overtures to North Korea, influenced by traditional geopolitical thinking that sees the Korean Peninsula as a dagger aimed at Japan and a bridge connecting to the Asian heartland.[34] As a result of these competing interests, imposing effective multilateral sanctions on North Korea is a difficult proposition.

Against this background, the outline of a solution to the nuclear problem is reasonably clear. The United States and North Korea should address each other's security concerns. The United States should end what North Korea regards as its "hostile policy" toward it. Under inspection, North Korea should freeze and dismantle its nuclear program. Through various programs to assist North Korea's economic development, the

---

34. At the North Korea–Japan summit in September 2002, Kim Jong Il tried "confessional diplomacy" with regard to the prior abductions of Japanese citizens (issuing a formal apology as North Korea's leader but taking no direct responsibility), but this did not quite work the way he had hoped. Although Japanese prime minister Junichiro Koizumi was serious about normalizing relations between Japan and North Korea and he did receive Kim's apology in exchange for his own expression of regret regarding Japan's brutal colonial rule, his position was overshadowed by the outrage expressed by Japanese politicians, NGOs, and the media, and the further questions raised about other missing Japanese nationals and the possible link to North Korean abductions.

international community should convince North Korea that a nonnuclear future for Pyongyang would be best. Top leaders from both sides, joined by other concerned parties, should make personal commitments to support the agreement and take a series of steps to show that they are implementing the agreement in good faith. Whether the resumed Six Party Talks or some other meeting could reach such a settlement remains to be seen.[35]

Toward Reunification

South Korea and North Korea are so far apart politically and economically that it may seem preposterous to think about reunification. However, because reunification is a process as much as an outcome, thinking about it can clarify the nature of challenges involved. Three interrelated challenges are critical: system transformation, integration, and international positioning.

SYSTEM TRANSFORMATION

Politically, South Korea is now a full-fledged democracy, whereas North Korea is essentially a dynasty supported by a tightly knit group of "revolutionary families." After the transition of socialist regimes in the late 1980s and early 1990s, a large body of work was done that sought to place North Korea's potential transition in comparative context, looking at cases as diverse as Romania, Vietnam, and East Germany.[36] But more than 20 years later, North Korea remains a socialist dynasty. The preamble of North Korea's constitution, as amended in 2009, stipulates that Kim Il Sung was "the founder of the Democratic People's Republic of Korea and the progenitor of Socialist Korea." When Kim Il Sung died in July 1994, Kim Jong Il, his first son, succeeded him. When Kim Jong Il died in December 2011, Kim Jong Un, his third son, repeated the dynastic succession. In 2000, when Kim Jong Il met with Madeleine Albright, then U.S. secretary of state, he expressed interest in a Thailand-style constitutional monarchy,

---

35. A recent discussion of negotiation strategies in the wake of North Korea's nuclear tests is in Revere (2012). For a comprehensive historical perspective, see D. Lim (2012). For a recent assessment of North Korea's nuclear and missile capabilities, see Pifer (2013).

36. See, for instance, Korea Institute of National Unification (1993).

where the king has real power. It remains to be seen whether the Kim family will maintain control indefinitely or whether a palace coup, popular revolt, or outside intervention will precipitate an abrupt political transition.

Economically, North Korea has to cope with essentially the same set of system transformation challenges as the former socialist countries.[37] The fundamental structural problem of the socialist system is that there is a separation between information and decision authority, with little incentive to connect these two critical elements. As the state retains rights to economic output and little material reward is given for increased production, it is natural for each individual production unit to underreport its productive capacity and exaggerate its need for labor and raw materials. In the end, what forms the basis of the central plan is the highly inaccurate and disjointed information provided by production units. Under such a system, the economic necessity of incorporating continually changing information becomes secondary to the political necessity of stable control, and the central plan becomes a reflection of the existing production relationship. The plan in effect "freezes" the existing structure of production and impedes technological innovation, blocking the exit of inefficient plants and the entry of new firms. Much like the production structure itself, prices are frozen to minimize variability within the system and facilitate central planning. When prices bear little or no relation to costs, the profitability of an individual production unit will not be connected to its productive efficiency.[38] If, for instance, the underpricing of a factory's output leads to heavy losses, then it should be the responsibility of the state to provide subsidies to prop up this innocent victim of the system. As such practices become common, however, the budget constraint will lose its binding power, and will become "soft."[39]

The efficient assignment of property rights and liberalization of prices is a critical element in the establishment of a market economy. The assignment of property rights makes it possible for the holder of local information to make decisions on his or her own, and to assume responsibility

---

37. See World Bank (1996).

38. Ahn (1992), 89. As examples, a camera cost 5.3 times as much in East Germany as it did in West Germany. Chocolate cost 3.1 times as much. In contrast, bread in East Germany cost only 16 percent of what it cost in West Germany.

39. For a detailed discussion of soft budget constraints, see Kornai (1990).

for the consequences. By thus decentralizing the authority to make deci-sions, it lays the groundwork for system transformation. Although North Korea has experimented with economic reform measures at least since 1 July 2002, it has yet to tackle the problem of system transforma-tion in a comprehensive manner.

This does not mean that North Korea, or any other socialist economy, must take on the whole reform task in one swoop. Alternatively, it is con-ceivable to go sector by sector—notably freeing up agriculture and going back to household farming for its incentive effect, even though there may be some sacrifice of scale economies. One can also create a dual econ-omy, with a dynamic private sector alongside a subsidized state sector, as was done in China and Vietnam. In any case, the point is that one can-not reform the economy with a few isolated free-trade zones; more fun-damental and interconnected changes are required that eventually will lead to a full market economy.

ECONOMICS AND POLITICS OF INTEGRATION

To examine the economic consequences of increasing integration between South and North Korea, it is instructive to compare the initial state (i.e., the present division of the Korean Peninsula) with the final state (com-plete economic union) and use this "integrated equilibrium" as a refer-ence point—the set of resource allocations and prices that Korea would have if goods and factors were both perfectly mobile. Presently, South Korea's per capita income is nearly 20 times North Korea's in purchasing power parity terms, and other prices, both in the absolute and relative sense, are drastically different between the two sides.

Now, suppose that inter-Korean mobility in goods and factors gradu-ally increases over time. In the Korean context, the South's relatively scarce factor is low-skilled workers, and thus, according to trade theory, increased inter-Korean trade would tend to hurt South Korean workers in labor-intensive industries. However, low-skilled workers in the South have already been largely dislocated by their competitors in China and South-east Asia, and the *marginal* impact on them from increased inter-Korean trade in the future would seem to be minimal. Moreover, although the South's capital investment in the North will reduce investment in the South, its adverse impact on South Korean wages is also likely to be small. In the German case, Hans-Werner Sinn (1990) estimated that the overall decline in West German wages caused by capital flow into East Germany would be only about 5.2 percent.[40] In the Korean case, the two economies complement each other to a much greater extent. Given these factors, it seems likely that the distributional consequences of trade and capital investment in the Korean context are not as serious as they were in the German case.

Unfortunately, trade, even combined with capital mobility, is unlikely to produce a significant reduction in the income gap between South and North Korea. Although inter-Korean trade and investment may well expand much more rapidly in the future, without labor migration and social transfers a significant inter-Korean income gap will unquestionably remain for a considerable period.[41] This means that there will be a strong incentive for migration.

Now suppose there is labor mobility between South and North Korea. As mostly young, potentially productive workers leave a low-wage region, however, the interregional wage gap may nonetheless persist for a long time. Empirical evidence broadly confirms this.[42] For the continental United States between 1880 and 1990, the growth rate of per capita personal income for each state did exhibit a negative relationship with the log of per capita initial income, but the average speed of convergence was only 1.74 percent per annum. Among the subperiods, 1940–1950, encompassing World War II, recorded the highest rate of convergence, at 4.31 percent per annum, followed by the 1960–1970 period, at 2.46 percent per annum. Japanese prefectures and European regions similarly exhibited a slow rate of convergence of 2 to 3 percent per annum. This slow speed of convergence implies that it would take 25 to 35 years to eliminate one-half of the given initial income gap. To sum up, labor mobility seems to have a limited marginal effect on convergence, in the short run.

---

40. See Sinn (1990). Sinn used a simple Kemp-MacDougall diagram to arrive at this result; if capital investment in the East created direct low-wage competition for the West, the relative loss suffered by West German workers would be increased.

41. More generally, the wage equalization condition can be represented by the equation $(r_N - r_S)\, t = ln\,(cw_S / w_N)$, with r_N, r_S = annual growth rate of wages in the North and the South; w_N, w_S = initial wages in the North and the South; c = target convergence ratio ($c = 1$ for 100% convergence); t = amount of time required for convergence.

42. See Barro and Sala-i-Martin (1995), 382–413. Their earlier findings are reported in Barro and Sala-i-Martin (1991).

Migration can also create serious political and social problems. If North Korean workers are allowed to move into the South and are seen as exerting downward pressure on wages, it is highly likely that South Korean workers will take action to protect their jobs and wages. In Germany, West German unions strongly supported the policy of driving East German wages up faster than productivity to reduce the incentive for East-to-West migration and also to dispose of potential low-wage competition. While this high-wage policy was expected to produce high unemployment, East German workers themselves were not necessarily opposed to the policy, for their unemployment benefits, to be paid for two years at most, were set at 68 percent of the average wage of the previous three months—the higher the negotiated wage, the higher the unemployment benefits.[43] In the absence of an agent negotiating for the future management of East German firms, there was no one to exert a moderating influence on wage increases. In an indictment of the high-wage policy, Sinn and Sinn (1994, 167–168) note that there was also a coordination failure and a Prisoner's Dilemma problem: "The high-wage strategy permitted the negotiators to dispose of unwelcome competition from the East within their own respective industry sectors. This was the advantage. The disadvantage was the resulting tax increase, which was necessary to finance the unemployment they themselves had created—but this disadvantage would be shared out among all the West German taxpayers and would thus primarily be borne by individuals who earned their incomes in other industry sectors." Thus, the high-wage policy created massive unemployment in the East, which in turn resulted in a high unemployment insurance bill for the West. When unemployment benefits ran out, former East German workers once again had to consider moving to the West—owing not so much to the wage gap as to the lack of employment opportunities in the East.[44]

The German experience with labor market integration seems to call for active government engagement in the process. The South Korean government should point out that the high-wage policy, though individually rational for labor unions, is a socially expensive Band-Aid. It should provide incentives for North Korean workers by limiting unemployment benefits and linking ownership claims (privatization vouchers, housing,

---

43. Sinn and Sinn (1994), 167–168, 191, 201.

44. For the relative importance of employment opportunities as opposed to higher wages as a migration motive, see Akerlof et al. (1991).

and so on) to their continued residence in the North. The government could also take preemptive measures to ensure that North-to-South migration proceeds on a controlled, orderly basis. As it already does with regard to importing foreign workers, the government could survey labor needs of firms in the low-skilled sector and recruit North Korean workers based on that labor demand. Candidates for work permits could be screened, and those finally selected could then be allocated to firms. The point is to reduce the likelihood of North Korean workers flocking to the South for a limited number of job openings by filling such openings according to a well-defined scheme.

However, unless the government continues to maintain the demilitarized zone, millions of North Korean workers could simply come down to South Korea to get a taste of freedom, and then not go back. That said, the problem of North-to-South migration after reunification might not be as serious as it is feared. High housing and living costs in the South would act as a deterrent against migration. Without extensive reeducation and training, North Korean workers, even at low wages, would be unlikely to displace skilled South Korean workers; setting up low-wage competition in the North in technologically advanced sectors would require massive "greenfield" investment as well. South Korean workers should also keep in mind that even if they managed to raise wages in the North, they could not exert much influence on labor costs in China and Southeast Asia; North Korea is not the only potential destination for direct investment. In low-skilled positions, North Korean workers would be certainly competitive, but again, their *marginal* impact on South Korean workers would be minimal. In fact, since South Korea is already importing foreign workers in labor-intensive industries, North Korean workers seeking employment in this sector should be considered as a complement to rather than a substitute for South Korean workers.

In short, although North-to-South migration after unification would be a problem, its potential consequences should not be exaggerated. Historical data suggest that the inter-Korean wage gap is likely to remain substantial even if economic exchange between the South and the North were greatly expanded prior to unification. Moreover, there are policy measures that might be effective in limiting migration, such as granting property rights contingent on continued residence in the North and establishing a well-defined worker recruiting scheme. It should also be noted that North Korean workers would be less likely to migrate if they found jobs in the

North and their economic prospects continued to improve. In this regard, creating employment opportunities in the North should be a top priority. In dealing with potential North-to-South migration, it should always be kept in mind that the danger actually is *overreaction* on the part of South Korean workers, who may be misled, like West German workers, to push for a high-wage policy and pay North Korean workers to stay unemployed.

Estimates of the cost of unification typically run on the order of hundreds of billion dollars according to the income target method, by which the North Korean per capita income is usually set to reach a certain percentage (e.g., 60 percent) of the South Korean level within a certain period (e.g., ten years).[45] Given such large estimates, concern about unification costs is understandable. But those who question the desirability of unification on these grounds miss some crucial points. First, most of the large "unification cost" represents—and *should* be structured to represent—a long-term investment in the future rather than a one-time cost that cannot be recovered. Second, it is unreasonable to presume that the South will have to pay these costs alone. If the North commits itself to economic reform and the South is willing to help, it will not be difficult for North Korea to secure investment funds from other sources, in an era of global capital mobility. South Korea, one of the world's poorest countries with bleak economic prospects in the early 1960s, was itself able to secure foreign loans in the initial phase of its own economic development, borrowing most heavily from the United States. Third, those who oppose unification on the basis of economic costs do not seem to know what they intend to do should the North Korean regime actually collapse. Their position seems to be based on the fundamentally false premise that the South can reduce unification costs by continuing to ignore the North's economic troubles; however, if the South waits until the North collapses to engage in economic exchange, the eventual bill unification will have become *larger*, not smaller.[46]

---

45. See, for instance, Hwang (1993); Noland, Robinson, and Scatasta (1997); and Yeon (1993). Of course, to be more realistic, North Korea's absorptive capacity and social welfare expenditure must be considered. On this point, see Lee and Kim (2011), 46–67.

46. Noland, Robinson, and Scatasta (1997) show that the total unification bill will more than double with each delay of five years.

Finally, in their preoccupation with unification costs, critics seem to overlook the potentially disastrous cost of national division. In June 1994, South and North Korea nearly went to war. In this regard it is worth noting what German chancellor Helmut Kohl stated in his memoir, that he would still have pushed for the unification of Germany even had he known that it would cost more than ten times the initial estimates. He asserted that a continued division of Germany was too risky a prospect and that unification, though costly, provided the basis for a secure and prosperous Germany.

To prepare for reunification and consolidate public support, the South Korean government should tell the Korean people that national unification is a challenge that will demand patience and sacrifice but also provide a solid foundation for the building of a secure and prosperous nation. With regard to the North Korean regime itself, Seoul should support the North's economic reform efforts.[47] Pyongyang, for its part, should realize that while Seoul would not hesitate to reward its move toward a market economy, support would be withdrawn if it moved in the opposite direction. So far as political reform is concerned, however, the political leadership in the North has shown no inclination to promote a democratic transition, and any attempt to do so by outsiders could lead to a backlash from the North. Under the circumstances, separating politics from other forms of interaction may be the best strategy.

INTERNATIONAL POSITIONING

Just as Germans and their neighbors agreed to make reunified Germany an integral part of Europe rather than risk the emergence of an unhinged revisionist power, Koreans and their neighbors will have to come up with an inclusive regional-cooperation architecture if the solution to the Korean question is to be found. As a divided land bridge, Korea has much to gain from regional integration. In contrast, a maritime-continental

---

47. Certainly some confusion in inter-Korean relations may be inevitable, given the peculiarly dual nature of the Korean situation: South and North Korea fought a war against each other, and their heavily armed troops face each other across the DMZ; at the same time, they have to be the eventual partners for unification. Even under such circumstances, however, it is still quite feasible to have a consistent policy with a clearly defined objective.

confrontation is not in the interest of the Korean people, as it would perpetuate national division and increase the risk of military conflict on the peninsula.

Although there is a general consensus in South Korea that regional integration can bring security and economic benefits, not everyone agrees that it should be a priority, especially in relation to South Korea's bilateral alliance with the United States. Some tend to attach overriding importance to the alliance with the United States. Others take an "Asia-centric" approach and give priority to building a regional community. Still others try to combine the benefits of the bilateral alliance with regional multilateralism and support multilateral cooperation that would include the United States. This is sometimes characterized as a "U.S.-in-Asia" approach.

Those who attach overriding importance to South Korea's alliance with the United States argue that South Korea risks weakening the cornerstone of its security by giving priority to regional multilateralism. In their alliance-centric view, placing too much emphasis on regional multilateralism could be interpreted by the United States as a thinly veiled attempt to dismantle the alliance for the benefit of China, especially if the membership of that multilateral arrangement were to exclude the United States. Instead, South Korea's best option is to curb its enthusiasm for regional multilateralism and strengthen its bilateral alliance with Washington, as Japan did after its strained alliance relationship with the United States in the first half of the 1990s.[48] This school of thought tends to project an ominous future for Asia, in which South Korea essentially will be forced to choose between the United States and China. Rising tension between China and the U.S.-Japan alliance, in this view, will make regional multilateralism little more than a pipedream. South Korea should therefore strengthen its alliance with the United States to guard against the rise of China as well as the threat from North Korea.

Those who take an Asia-centric approach, on the other hand, tend to emphasize that Asian nations' collective interests would be best served by building their own community. Some even argue that the partition of the world into three blocs would place Asian nations in a strong position to deal with Europe and the United States.[49] Although they do not

---

48. For a comparative perspective on the U.S. alliances with Japan and South Korea, see Armacost and Okimoto (2004).

49. W.-S. Choi (2004).

necessarily want to terminate South Korea's alliance with the United States, they feel that strengthening that bilateral alliance runs counter to the objective of creating a regional community.

Finally, there are those who seek to combine the benefits of the bilateral and multilateral approaches. According to this U.S.-in-Asia perspective, the exclusively U.S.-centric approach runs the risk of creating a self-fulfilling prophesy by exacerbating tension between the United States and China, whereas the Asia-centric approach is rather unrealistic because it basically assumes Japan will work with China to create a regional community that excludes the United States. Those who support the U.S.-in-Asia view believe that a combination of hedging alliances and inclusive multilateral arrangements would be a stabilizing force in the region.[50]

With the balance of power shifting in Asia since the end of the Cold War and the rise of China, the U.S.-in-Asia approach may provide the best framework for inclusive regional cooperation. If great powers agree to be bound by a multilateral cooperation arrangement, thanks in part to facilitation by middle powers in the region, this can be an effective means of securing lasting peace. China's proactive multilateral diplomacy since the late 1990s has been putting pressure on the United States to reassess its multilateral policy in Asia, and this competitive dynamic may lead to the creation of multilateral arrangements that include the United States as well as China, as evidenced in the case of the East Asia Summit.

From an international relations perspective, Korea's reunification challenges can be best met by adopting a U.S.-in-Asia approach. An exclusively U.S.- or Asia-centric approach runs the risk of creating a situation in which Korea would be forced to take one side against the other. Korea's interest is in strengthening inclusive regional cooperation and reassuring its neighbors that reunification would not harm their vital national interests.[51]

---

50. See Kim and Lim (2007).

51. On the trade front, for example, Korea's geopolitical imperative demands that Korea bring together the Regional Comprehensive Economic Partnership, based on the ASEAN+6 framework, and the Trans-Pacific Partnership led by the United States to build an overarching architecture for cooperation in the Asia-Pacific region. Korea is in a good position to do so, based on its status as a rising middle power and its strong trade network, including its free trade agreement with the United States.

CHAPTER 9

Conclusion

The economic and social transformation of South Korea over the last half century has been nothing short of miraculous. From a starting point as one of the world's poorest nations, the country has raised its average per capita income to more than US$30,000, measured at purchasing power parity. Where in the 1960s it was not uncommon for commentators to compare Korea, sometimes unfavorably, to various newly independent African nations, the relevant economic comparators today are countries like Israel, France, and Japan.

But per capita incomes remain less than half those in the United States at market exchange rates and barely two-thirds of U.S. levels at purchasing power parity. The fact that living standards are significantly below those of the United States means not just that Korean households enjoy less consumption of goods and services; it is invoked as a justification for the country's relatively low levels of social spending.[1] But while growth will make the provision of social services more affordable in time, Koreans whose incomes have not kept up need help now. The fundamental challenge is thus to reconcile progrowth policies with the provision of additional social protections and to avoid sacrificing one on the altar of the other.

---

1. This of course begs the question, at what per capita income level should a country begin to provide significant levels of social protection? As a percent of GDP, Korea's social expenditure lags such countries as the Czech Republic, Portugal, Slovakia, and Poland—all countries with lower per capita income levels than Korea's. It should also be noted that countries in Western Europe built their welfare states when their per capita incomes were lower than in present-day Korea. For details see Alestalo, Hort, and Kuhnle (2009).

Maintaining High Growth

The fact that labor productivity remains significantly lower in Korea than in the leading OECD economies has a silver lining: it means there is still scope for Korea to grow faster than other OECD members. It can do so by maintaining a relatively high investment rate and boosting its capital/labor ratio. It can do so by increasing the quality as well as the quantity of education—by better complementing physical capital formation with human capital formation. And it can boost productivity not just in manufacturing but also in services, a sector that to date has experienced productivity growth well below that in other OECD countries.[2]

Having invested extensively in education, institutions, and infrastructure, there is no intrinsic reason why, in the long run, Korea should not have a standard of living like that of, say, the United States. The question is, how long is the long run? Figures 9.1 and 9.2 illustrate a set of scenarios for the convergence of Korea's per capita income with U.S. levels, where per capita incomes are measured at purchasing power parity exchange rates.[3] Figure 9.1 assumes that U.S. GDP per capita rises by 1.5 percent per annum, the advanced-country average, while Figure 9.2 assumes, more optimistically and in line with U.S. historical experience, that it rises by 2.5 percent. The different trajectories for Korea assume, alternatively, that GDP per capita in Korea rises by rates ranging from 3.5 percent to 6.0 percent per annum. Even under the most favorable scenario, it still takes a decade or longer, starting from 2011, for Korea to approach U.S. income levels, depending on the assumption one makes about U.S. growth. Under the most favorable scenario of a 4.5-point difference in growth rates, full convergence takes approximately a decade. If per capita incomes grow only 2 percentage points faster in Korea than in the United States, then full convergence takes two decades.

Many economists will be inclined toward the lower end of this range of growth projections for Korea. A TFP growth rate of 2.5 percent per annum is not an unreasonable expectation for an economy starting out

---

2. Our concluding observations in this section draw on Chapter 3, where these issues are analyzed in more detail.

3. We have undertaken similar simulations when per capita GDP is valued at market exchange rates. The picture changes relatively little, reflecting the fact that South Korea is now a middle- to high-income economy.

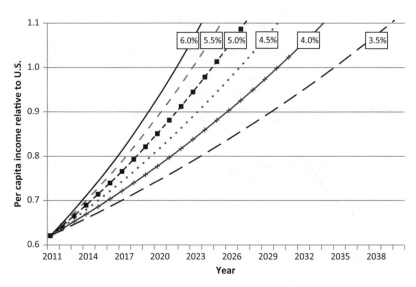

Figure 9.1. Expected Convergence of Per Capita GDP of South Korea and the United States under Alternative Korean Growth Scenarios: U.S. Growth at 1.5 Percent

Per capita incomes are measured at purchasing power parity exchange rates. Projected annual growth rates for Korea range from a high of 6.0 percent to a low of 3.5 percent.

Source: International Monetary Fund, World Economic Outlook Database, September 2013.

behind its OECD partners: it is a full percentage point above the OECD average. Few middle- and high-income countries have persistently displayed a TFP growth rate significantly in excess of this level. Only countries emerging from extended periods of isolation and exceptional economic difficulty, but with high levels of human resource development relative to their income level, such as China after 1978, and countries experiencing exceptional wartime damage as a result of which output and productivity were temporarily depressed, and with scope for exceptionally rapid growth through postwar recovery and reconstruction, such as West Germany and Japan in the 1950s and 1960s, have maintained TFP growth rates of 3 percent for extended periods. Also, TFP growth tends to be slower in services than manufacturing. As incomes rise, the shares of output and employment accounted for by the service sector increase, making the maintenance of rapid TFP growth more difficult, given the intrinsic difficulties of mechanizing service-sector activities. Even assuming a relatively high investment rate, the capital stock is likely to grow by

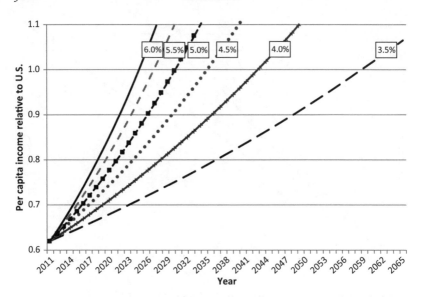

Figure 9.2. Expected Convergence of Per Capita GDP of South Korea and the United States under Alternative Korean Growth Scenarios: U.S. Growth at 2.5 Percent

Per capita incomes are measured at purchasing power parity exchange rates. Projected annual growth rates for Korea range from a high of 6.0 percent to a low of 3.5 percent.

Source: International Monetary Fund, World Economic Outlook Database, September 2013.

only 4 percent per annum, adding perhaps another percentage point to the growth rate.[4] Add a fraction of a percentage point for the contribution of additional human capital formation, and the growth of per capita GDP is still just 4.0 percent per annum.[5] This implies that three to five decades will be required for Korea to converge with U.S. income levels

---

4. Recall that the share of capital in GDP and the elasticity of output with respect to capital are on the order of one-third (or less) and that some of this additional capital stock will be needed to equip a growing labor force in order to keep per capita incomes stable. Similar calculations pointing to a 4 percent rate of growth of the capital stock are in International Monetary Fund (2006).

5. If it recorded a growth rate of 4 percent per annum, Korea would be an outlier compared with the historical performance of advanced economies after they had reached Korea's current income levels. Among the G7 countries, Japan had a growth rate of 3.5 percent when its per capita income level was around $20,000 at PPP exchange rates in 2000 U.S. dollars. Other members of the G7 had 2.5 percent or lower growth rates at similar income levels.

(depending on whether one assumes 1.5 or 2.5 percent annual growth in U.S. per capita income).

Few Koreans will be satisfied by this conclusion, given the importance the society attaches to growth and convergence. For Koreans, the question is: what can the country do to grow faster and at the same time successfully balance growth with social cohesion?

The dominant approach to answering this question has been to attempt to draw lessons from the experience of other successful countries. Korean observers concerned to smooth the country's adversarial labor-management relations in the hope that more harmonious relations might produce faster productivity growth and more investment have looked to European countries, like the Netherlands, with corporatist traditions and good experience with tripartite cooperation. They have looked to the model of "flexicurity" in Denmark, where social protections are combined with an active labor market policy, to enhance labor market flexibility and aid rather than impede productivity growth. They have looked to the United Kingdom to draw lessons from the Blair government's effort to chart a "third way" between laissez-faire and state planning that would embrace free and open competition but also address the needs for state support for technological development and education as well as social justice and security.[6]

Drawing lessons from the experience of other countries is constructive. But assuming that institutions and arrangements that work well in other countries will deliver comparable results when transplanted to Korean soil ignores that country's distinctive history and inheritance. Relying on the experience of other countries to guide the design of progrowth policy is like relying on imported technology to raise total factor productivity. A country in the early stages of economic development can focus on importing technology, but at some point it must start growing its own. Just as it must move from emulation to innovation when acquiring productive technology, at some stage it also must move from emulation to innovation when developing policies and institutions for fostering and sustaining growth. And the policy initiatives it innovates should complement

---

6. Prime Minister Tony Blair's attempt to identify a third way between the conservative policies of Thatcher and Beveridge's welfare state built on the influential writings of Anthony Giddens, as in Giddens (1998), a volume that has been widely cited in Korea.

the economic, social, and political structures and constraints that it has inherited from the past.

Korea has now arrived at this stage. Correspondingly, the weakness of the policy debate is that it is organized around foreign models: Danish flexicurity, Dutch corporatism, the British third way. Korea needs to move from emulation to innovation in the effort to design a set of policy and institutional arrangements tailored to the country's unique inheritance and circumstances.

A distinctive aspect of that inheritance is Korea's unusually large productivity gap between manufacturing and services. Together with the fact that services account for a large and growing share of output and employment, as in other advanced economies, this makes the scope for raising living standards by boosting service-sector productivity greater than virtually anywhere in the developed world.

Korea's low service-sector productivity is partly a result of entry barriers and restrictions on competition designed to protect small family enterprises from competition. These protections for the proverbial mom-and-pop store in turn reflect conventions dictating early retirement, at or soon after age 55, for workers in large firms, and their subsequent employment (or, in many cases, underemployment) in the service sector—in effect, in the family store. Reflecting these practices, self-employment accounted for 30 percent of civilian employment in 2009, nearly double the OECD average of 16 percent. Reforming personnel-management practices so that large firms retained more of their still-productive older workers would reduce the pressure for restrictions on competition in the service sector. Reforming the seniority-based wage system to allow salaries to decline for older, less productive workers would be a useful step in this direction. Some companies have adopted a "peak salary system" that allows salaries to begin to decline five or so years before retirement. Better still would be a salary system that links pay not to age but directly to productivity.[7] This would go a long way toward reducing the labor-market duality—

---

7. This also would help to address problems associated with rapid population aging, including old-age poverty. Korea, which currently has the fourth-youngest population (as measured by the elderly-dependency ratio) among the 34 OECD countries, will be the second oldest by 2050 if current fertility and mortality trends persist. Measured as the share of people who live on less than half the median income, the poverty rate among the elderly is 45 percent, three times the national poverty rate of 14.4 percent. Among older people, the poverty rate increases to 70 percent when there is no income

segmenting workers into regular and nonregular employment (including self-employment)—that is a significant source of inefficiency.[8]

In addition, there is evidence that the productivity-growth gap between manufacturing and services can be closed through the application of information technology, as in the retail, wholesale, and financial-services sectors in the United States. Promoting the application of information technologies to the service sector is an important part of the Korean government's "creative economy" initiative. Samsung's move into the production of IT-enabled medical equipment is an example of how firms are positioning themselves to supply the hardware, but companies need to marry this with the relevant software and delivery systems to raise productivity in the health-care sector and ultimately become exporters of health services.

Harnessing the Chaebol

Another distinctive aspect of Korea's inheritance is the chaebol, which dominate the industrial sector.[9] In the wake of the Asian financial crisis, these large business groups were widely seen as a drag on the economy. Time has shown, however, that their growth and development were no mere happenstance. Suitably exposed to competition, they are among the most technologically and commercially progressive agents in the economy. But their dominance of the industrial high ground has a downside. The chaebol wield considerable economic and political power. They can use their market power to extract rents, most visibly from the small firms that are their suppliers. And they can use their political power in ways that favor the large-firm sector at the expense of the economy as a whole.

History provides three examples of how policymakers elsewhere have dealt with this problem. Latin American countries allowed dominant business groups to continue to expand, choosing to live with the resulting concentration of economic and political power. In Sweden, the Social

---

from work, the highest level recorded in the OECD. Overall, the OECD average is 13 percent for old-age poverty. For more details, see Chapter 6.

8. Complementary initiatives would include improving the social safety net to ensure more equal participation in and access to those programs for workers in nonregular employment, and expanding job training and retraining programs to improve the employability of older workers, as discussed by An and Bosworth (2013).

9. For details, the reader is referred to Chapter 5.

Democrats and family-controlled business groups agreed to a grand bargain: the government imposed strict regulation and high income taxes but in return it also provided subsidies and protection from takeover threats. The third approach is that taken by the United States in the 1930s and the United Kingdom in the 1960s, when they each pursued vigorous anti-pyramiding strategies. They used intercorporate dividend taxes, strict takeover rules, and other measures to make pyramiding less attractive.

The Latin model is essentially a rent-seeking equilibrium in which business groups enrich and finance politicians, who in turn keep institutions weak so business groups' advantages remain valuable. Not only does this approach to dealing with large business groups breed corruption, but it also stifles growth outside the large-firm sector and discourages entrepreneurship and initiative. The Swedish model, though it may have worked in Sweden, owing to an exceptionally strong civil society capable of providing checks and balances, similarly has a tendency to blunt incentives for entry and entrepreneurship. And the Anglo-American approach of attempting to scrap business groups is conducive to innovation but may run the risk of prematurely sacrificing their residual coordination advantages.

Rather than blindly adopting one or another foreign model, the best solution for Korea would be for the government to strengthen investor protections and make it easier for shareholders to seek private remedies against tunneling and other breaches of fiduciary duty. At the same time, the authorities should enhance intellectual property protections, strengthen competition policy, and expand access to finance to promote the kind of entrepreneurship and entry that are vital to innovation but, absent proactive policies, at risk of being stifled by the presence of large groups.

In an example of how this can be done, in 2011 Korea's National Assembly amended the Fair Subcontract Transactions Act to prohibit contractors from demanding, without reason, that their subcontractors provide information on their technology. Significantly, this amendment shifted the burden of proof to the contractor. For the first time, this legislation introduced a provision for treble damages when a contractor's unpermitted use of a subcontractor's technology resulted in the loss of business opportunities by the subcontractor. While the Fair Subcontract Transactions Act was a good start, more must be done to provide better intellectual property protection to innovative firms. Also useful would be better law enforcement against unreasonable restraints of trade, especially in vertical transactions, to ensure access to distribution networks for SMEs, start-ups, and other innovative firms.

Finance for Growth

The authorities should take steps to better develop the venture capital industry, as well, to ensure ready access to funding for start-ups and other SMEs. Students of other countries point to some obvious things that can be done to foster venture capital: encouraging patenting and entrepreneurship, creating a stable financial environment, providing a supportive legal framework. Limited changes in the legal code, notably the 1997 Act on Special Measure for Promotion of Venture Business, have already been adopted to encourage start-ups. Public institutions such as the Korea Technology Finance Corporation and the Small and Medium Business Corporation should focus on supporting innovative companies with growth potential rather than indiscriminately propping up small and medium-size enterprises. Studies also point to labor market rigidities as a deterrent to start-ups and an obstacle to venture-capital-related activities.[10] Enhancing the flexibility of labor markets, an effort that is similarly being undertaken by other countries seeking to encourage start-ups, such as Japan, could therefore have high returns. Finally, creating an environment more welcoming to funds from foreign venture capital firms, which complain about the unevenness of the playing field, would further help to ease this bottleneck.

Korea's large financial sector is another part of its inheritance, the underdevelopment of venture capital notwithstanding. Korean finance remains heavily bank based, although the country also possesses relatively large and well-capitalized equity and derivatives markets. But the approach to financial reform taken after 1998, which might be characterized as concerted liberalization, appears in hindsight to have delivered at least as many costs, in terms of continuing volatility, in particular, as it has benefits in the form of enhanced allocative efficiency.[11] Given this experience, Korea should instead pursue an alternative approach to financial development and management, on two dimensions. First, regulators should put in place strict macro- and microprudential supervision in order to dampen the strongly procyclical behavior of bank lending and limit reliance on offshore foreign currency funding. Korea's experience shows that the strongly procyclical behavior of bank lending accentuates

---

10. See Romain and van Pottelsberghe de la Potterie (2004) for details.

11. This argument is elaborated in Chapter 4 and in Park, Kim, and Park (forthcoming), a companion volume in this series.

business-cycle volatility and that offshore foreign currency funding is an important source of financial fragility. Here the country's innovative taxes on foreign noncore liabilities, imposed in the wake of the 2008–2009 global crisis, point a way forward.

Second, the country should take steps to enhance its access to the kind of short-term foreign-currency liquidity that is so valuable in crises. This can be done through the formalization of bilateral swap lines with, inter alia, the U.S. Federal Reserve System; through further elaboration of the Chiang Mai Initiative Multilateralization; and by taking out an IMF Flexible Credit Line. These steps are not so much alternatives to accumulating foreign exchange reserves as useful supplements. The different avenues should be seen as complements rather than substitutes, in other words. Pursuing them all would be a prudent form of diversification. It is time for Korea to get over its IMF phobia, in particular, and continue to support the governance reform of international financial institutions through channels like the Group of Twenty.

Enhancing Social Cohesion and Reducing Poverty

Economists accustomed to thinking of tradeoffs between equity and efficiency are sometimes inclined to argue that there is an unavoidable conflict between the pursuit of economic growth and social policy reform. We would argue, in contrast, that there are a number of important areas relevant to Korea where social policy reforms can contribute to a higher rate of growth. Foremost among these is the gender wage gap. Eliminating practices that have resulted in Korea's unusually large gender wage gap and actively enforcing the associated prohibitions will require expanding existing measures providing for paid maternity and infant-care leave.[12] It will mean encouraging employers to adopt more flexible hours. It will mean relying less on seniority-based wages.[13]

---

12. Korea currently has a legally mandated paid maternity leave of three months at the normal monthly salary and childcare leave of one year at 40 percent of the normal monthly salary plus a lump-sum payment of 15 percent of the normal monthly salary after the employee returns to work. Large employers pay for the first two months of maternity leave; everything else is paid for by the employment insurance fund.

13. In other words, wages should depend more on hours worked (the variable component) than on years in employment (the fixed component). In most OECD countries the female labor participation rate remains high but hours worked drop for women in their thirties as they have to take care of their young children; in Korea, in contrast, the

Eliminating the gender wage gap will also require removing the glass ceiling that has prevented women from rising to top positions, Park Guen-hye's presidency notwithstanding. Public spending on full-day education and day care that would free more women to participate in the labor force will have a particularly high payoff insofar as Korean women are exceptionally well educated. The country has made progress in raising the glass ceiling for female professionals and younger cohorts, but it needs to make more.[14]

The observation that Korea has achieved an unusually high level of tertiary education, especially among women, is not to say that all is well in higher education.[15] The government spends significantly less on tertiary education as a share of GDP than the OECD average. High levels of enrollment and graduation together with low levels of government spending mean that the financial burden falls on students and their parents. Although government spending on tertiary education as a percentage of GDP is below the OECD average, private spending on tertiary education is much higher than the OECD average. The cost of increasing aid and loans across the board would be prohibitive for a country with a per capita GDP still below the OECD average and a relatively low government-revenue share of GDP. One solution would be to provide additional aid while conditioning it more strongly on family income. Another would be a system of tuition loans, repayment of which would be linked to subsequent income, as suggested in the companion volume in this series by Freeman, Choi, and Kim (forthcoming).[16]

Given constraints on expanding spending on higher education, it is equally important to pursue reforms that enable universities and colleges to deliver their services more efficiently. This means providing

---

female labor participation rate itself declines, reflecting the dominance of the fixed component.

14. Removing the barriers that prevent women from reaching their full potential in the labor force is the supply side of the problem. On the demand side, many jobs for the expanding female workforce will be in the service sector; this reinforces the importance of turning services into a dynamic sector comparable to manufacturing.

15. We elaborate these points in Chapter 6.

16. Students would repay more or less than the amount of the loan, depending on subsequent income or, conceivably, on whether they went subsequently into public service or private employment. Yale University has experimented with this kind of system (although not without problems).

more information on institutions and specialized programs so that students can assess program quality not on the basis of prestige and networking opportunities but on the quality of the education and skills delivered. It means strengthening the incentive for faculty to engage in research. It means more effectively exploiting the complementarities between research and training.[17] It means promoting distance learning and using the Internet to bring classes to the student rather than requiring the student to physically go to class. In the United States, private companies and consortia of private and public universities have moved to develop, commercialize, and export the relevant technologies and expertise for online learning at the university level. Internet-based lectures are already widely viewed in Korea by high school students preparing for university exams. The challenge is for providers to further develop and commercialize their products so that they can be more widely and successfully used.

While strengthening the quality of teaching and research is critical for all universities and colleges, it is especially critical for schools at the low end of the university and junior college ranking. Such schools are often little more than diploma mills. The fact that many of their alumni receive wages similar to those of high school graduates reflects the poor quality of the education, and also helps to explain how it is that Korea has seen a rise in income inequality over the past decade despite the continued increase in the number of students attending tertiary institutions.

Finally, the social protection system is inadequate for a country at South Korea's level of development and income. While the health system is strong and the share of children living in poverty is not high by OECD standards, unemployment insurance remains inadequate. This creates pressure for government policies that make it difficult to lay off workers, something that does little for social welfare, because better-off workers get most of the protection, and reduces labor-market flexibility.

Going forward, perhaps the greatest challenge will be to provide adequate support for Korea's rapidly growing elderly population. Although raising the retirement age will help (to the extent that growth provides sufficient jobs), most poverty among the aged affects those who are no longer capable of labor-force participation. The current system, as it begins to provide substantial benefits to the retired, will become unacceptably

---

17. On this, see also Chapter 7.

expensive. The entire system needs to be restructured to provide a meaningful floor of support under the aging poor at a cost that is acceptable to taxpayers.

Toward the end of her 2012 presidential election campaign, Park Geun-hye pledged to transform the old-age pension into a basic pension by eliminating means testing and doubling benefits to 200,000 won a month (around US$180) regardless of income. She also pledged to consolidate the basic pension with the National Pension Service. Although the basic-pension proposal helped her win overwhelming support among elderly voters, it was criticized after the election for eliminating means testing and conflating a tax-based program (the basic pension) with a social insurance scheme (the National Pension Service).

According to the OECD's *Pension Outlook 2012*, the share of the elderly (65 years of age and older) in Korea's population will be 38.2 percent in 2050, second only to the percentage in Japan among OECD members, while pension expenditures (NPS and basic old-age pension) under the current formulas will be 10 percent of Korea's GDP. Although this is below the projected OECD average of 11.7 percent of GDP, given the high incidence of poverty among the elderly, Korea's politicians will undoubtedly feel pressure to raise the insurance rate between now and then.

The first best solution, in our view, would be to merge the National Basic Livelihood Security program with the basic old-age pension. Means testing should take into account the income of children who live with their elderly parents. A larger tax deduction could be offered to such children as recompense for their contribution to reducing the burden on the welfare state.

An obstacle to dealing with these issues is Korea's unusually low level of total tax revenue (including social security contributions) and social expenditure. Those figures amount to 27 percent and 10 percent of GDP, respectively, compared with OECD averages of 34 percent and 19 percent. The country's tax-and-benefit system does too little to reduce inequality and poverty. Korea also has a low share of quasi-public social services in areas of employment. These observations point to the availability of one quick fix: use increased tax revenue and social expenditure to both create jobs in social services and address problems of inequality and poverty.

On the revenue side, the government needs to restructure the income tax system to increase progressivity and broaden the tax base. Incomplete indexation for inflation has compressed tax brackets, something that should be corrected, and the system also suffers from extensive tax avoidance by the self-employed. The country could usefully increase environmental taxes as part of its response to climate change and green growth challenges, and raise property holding taxes. More controversial is the idea of raising value-added and corporate income tax rates. On the expenditure side, the government should focus on supporting consumer choice through vouchers and public supervision of private providers, instead of adding public employees to offer social services directly.

Korea's challenge in coming decades will be to maintain a growth rate that allows it to catch up to the high-income countries while at the same time providing equality of opportunity and more extensive protection for the vulnerable. The country's enormous economic and political success over the past half century makes these goals attainable. But achieving them will require the best efforts of Korean society.

APPENDIX

On the Romanization of Korean

Basic Principles for Transcription

1. Romanization is based on standard Korean pronunciation.
2. No symbols except Roman letters are used, so far as possible.

Summary of the Transcription System

1. Vowels are transcribed as follows:

- simple vowels

ㅏ	ㅓ	ㅗ	ㅜ	ㅡ	ㅣ	ㅐ	ㅔ	ㅚ	ㅟ
a	eo	o	u	eu	i	ae	e	oe	wi

- diphthongs

ㅑ	ㅕ	ㅛ	ㅠ	ㅒ	ㅖ	ㅘ	ㅙ	ㅝ	ㅞ	ㅢ
ya	yeo	yo	yu	yae	ye	wa	wae	wo	we	ui

2. Consonants are transcribed as follows:

- plosives (stops)

ㄱ	ㄲ	ㅋ	ㄷ	ㄸ	ㅌ	ㅂ	ㅃ	ㅍ
g, k	kk	k	d, t	tt	t	b, p	pp	p

- affricates

ㅈ	ㅉ	ㅊ
j	jj	ch

- fricatives

ㅅ	ㅆ	ㅎ
s	ss	h

- nasals

ㄴ	ㅁ	ㅇ
n	m	ng

- liquids

ㄹ
r, l

Note: The sounds ㄱ, ㄷ, and ㅂ are transcribed, respectively, as *g, d,* and *b* before a vowel; they are transcribed as *k, t,* and *p* when they appear before another consonant or as the last sound of a word. (They are transcribed as pronounced in brackets [ ].)

구미 Gumi	영동 Yeongdong	백암 Baegam
옥천 Okcheon	합덕 Hapdeok	호법 Hobeop
월곶[월곧] Wolgot	벚꽃[벋꼳] beotkkot	

Note: ㄹ is transcribed as *r* before a vowel and as *l* before a consonant or at the end of a word; ㄹㄹ is transcribed as *ll.*

구리 Guri	설악 Seorak	칠곡 Chilgok
임실 Imsil	울릉 Ulleung	
대관령[대괄령] Daegwallyeong		

Special Provisions for Transcription

1. When Korean sound values change as in the following cases, the results of those changes are transcribed as shown below.

- The case of assimilation of adjacent consonants:

백마[뱅마] Baengma	신문로[신문노] Sinmunno
종로[종노] Jongno	왕십리[왕심니] Wangsimni
별내[별래] Byeollae	신라[실라] Silla

- The case of the epenthetic ㄴ and ㄹ:

  학여울[항녀울] Hangnyeoul   알약[알략] allyak

- The case of palatalization:

  해돋이[해도지] haedoji   같이[가치] gachi

- The case when ㄱ, ㄷ, ㅂ, and ㅈ are adjacent to ㅎ:

  | 좋고[조코] joko | 놓다[노타] nota |
  | 잡혀[자펴] japyeo | 낳지[나치] nachi |

Note: However, aspirated sounds are not transcribed in case of nouns where ㅎ follows ㄱ, ㄷ, and ㅂ, as in the examples below:
　　묵호 Mukho　　　집현전 Jiphyeonjeon

Note: Tense (or glottalized) sounds are not transcribed in cases where the morphemes are compounded, as in the examples below:
　　압구정 Apgujeong　　　낙동강 Nakdonggang
　　죽변 Jukbyeon　　　팔당 Paldang

2. When there is the possibility of confusion in pronunciation, a hyphen (-) may be used:
　　중앙 Jung-ang　　　반구대 Ban-gudae
　　세운 Se-un　　　해운대 Hae-undae

3. The first letter is capitalized in proper names:
　　부산 Busan　　　세종 Sejong

4. Personal names are written with the family name first, followed by a space and the given name. Generally, syllables in given names are not separated by a hyphen, although a hyphen may be used. (Transcriptions given in parenthesis are also permitted.)
　　민용하 Min Yongha　　　송나리 Song Nari
　　(Min Yong-ha)　　　(Song Na-ri)

• Assimilated sound changes between syllables in given names are not transcribed:
　　한복남 Han Boknam (Han Bok-nam)

• Additional transcriptions of family names may be established.

5. Administrative units such as 도, 시, 군, 구, 읍, 면, 리, 동, and 가 are transcribed, respectively, as *do, si, gun, gu, eup, myeon, ri, dong,* and *ga,* and are preceded by a hyphen. Assimilated sound changes before and after the hyphen are not transcribed.
　　충청북도 Chungcheongbuk-do　　　제주도 Jeju-do
　　의정부시 Uijeongbu-si　　　양주군 Yangju-gun
　　도봉구 Dobong-gu　　　신창읍 Sinchang-eup
　　삼죽면 Samjuk-myeon　　　인왕리 Inwang-ri
　　당산동 Dangsan-dong　　　봉천1동 Bongcheon 1(il)-dong
　　종로 2가 Jongno 2(i)-ga　　　퇴계로 3가 Toegyero 3(sam)-ga

Note: Terms for administrative units, such as 시, 군, 읍, may be omitted:
　　청주시 Cheongju　　　함평군 Hampyeong

6. Names of geographic features, cultural properties, and man-made
structures may be written without hyphens:

남산 Namsan	금강 Geumgang
독도 Dokdo	불국사 Bulguksa
경복궁 Gyeongbokgung	무량수전 Muryangsujeon
연화교 Yeonhwagyo	독립문 Dongnimmun
안압지 Anapji	남한산성 Namhansanseong
종묘 Jongmyo	다보탑 Dabotap

References

Abiad, A., E. Detragiache, and T. Tressel. 2008. "A New Database of Financial Reforms." IMF Working Paper WP/08/266, International Monetary Fund, Washington, DC (December).

Agenor, Pierre-Richard, Otaviano Canuto, and Michael Jelenic. 2012. "Avoiding Middle-Income Growth Traps." *Economic Premise* 98 (November), World Bank, www.worldbank.org/economicpremise.

Ahn, Dusun. 1992. *Unification of the Korean Peninsula and Economic Integration.* Seoul: Korea Economic Daily Press (in Korean).

Ahn, Kookshin. 1997. "Trends in and Determinants of Income Distribution in Korea." *Journal of Economic Development* 22, 27–56.

Akerlof, George A., A. K. Rose, J. L. Yellen, and H. Hessenius. 1991. "East Germany in from the Cold: The Economic Aftermath of Currency Union." *Brookings Papers on Economic Activity 1991*, 1–87.

Alestalo, Matti, Sven E. O. Hort, and Stein Kuhnle. 2009. "The Nordic Model: Conditions, Origins, Outcomes, Lessons." Hertie School of Governance Working Paper 41, Berlin (June).

Allen, Franklin, and Douglas Gale. 2007. *Understanding Financial Crises.* New York: Oxford University Press.

Amsden, Alice H. 1989. *Asia's Next Giant: South Korea and Late Industrialization.* New York: Oxford University Press.

An, Chong-Bum, and Barry Bosworth. 2013. *Income Inequality in Korea: An Analysis of Trends, Causes, and Answers.* Cambridge, MA: Harvard University Asia Center.

Armacost, Michael H., and Daniel I. Okimoto. 2004. *The Future of America's Alliances in Northeast Asia.* Stanford: Shorenstein Asia-Pacific Research Center, Stanford University.

Ash, Timothy Garton. 1993. *In Europe's Name: Germany and the Divided Continent.* New York: Random House.

Asia Pulse. 2005. "China-ASEAN FTA Feared to Hurt South Korea's Exports: KITA," www.bilaterals.org (19 July).

Asian Development Bank. 2006. *Asian Development Outlook 2006.* Manila: Asian Development Bank.

———. 2008. *Asian Bond Market Monitor.* Manila: Asian Development Bank.

Baldwin, Richard. 1988. "Hysteresis in Import Prices: The Beachhead Effect." NBER Working Paper 2545, National Bureau of Economic Research, Cambridge, MA (March).

———. 2003. "The Spoke Trap: Hub and Spoke Bilateralism in East Asia." Unpublished manuscript, Graduate Institute of International Studies, Geneva.

Baldwin, Richard, and Paul Krugman. 1986. "Persistent Trade Effect of Large Exchange Rate Shocks." NBER Working Paper 2017, National Bureau of Economic Research, Cambridge, MA (August).

Bandiera, Oriana, Gerard Caprio Jr., Patrick Honohan, and Fabio Schiantarelli. 2000. "Does Financial Reform Raise or Reduce Savings?" *Review of Economics and Statistics* 82 (2), 239–263.

Bank of Korea, Economics Statistics System (ECOS), http.//ecos.bok.or.kr/.

Bank of Korea. Various years. *Financial Stability Report.* Seoul: Bank of Korea.

Banker, Rajiv D., Hsihui Chang, and Seok-Young Lee. 2010. "Differential Impact of Korean Banking System Reforms on Bank Productivity." *Journal of Banking and Finance* 34, 1450–1460.

Barro, Robert, and Xavier Sala-i-Martin. 1991. "Convergence across States and Regions." *Brookings Papers on Economic Activity* 1, 107–182.

———. 1995. *Economic Growth.* New York: McGraw-Hill.

Bekaert, Geert, Campbell R. Harvey, and Christian Lundblad. 2006. "Growth Volatility and Financial Liberalization." *Journal of International Money and Finance* 25 (3), 370–403.

Bertola, Guiseppe, and Andrea Ichino. 1995. "Wage Inequality and Unemployment: US vs. Europe." In Ben Bernanke and Julio Rothemberg, eds., *NBER Macroeconomics Annual 1995*, 13–66. Cambridge, MA: MIT Press.

Blanchard, Oliver. 2009. "Emerging Market Countries and the Crisis: Synchronization and Heterogeneity." Presented at the Annual Bank Conference on Development Economics 2009, Seoul (22–24 June).

Blundell-Wignall, Adrian, and Paul Atkinson. 2010. "Thinking beyond Basel III: Necessary Solutions for Capital and Liquidity." *OECD Journal: Financial Market Trends* 1, 1–23.

Bosworth, Barry, and Gabriel Chodorow-Reich. 2007. "Saving and Demographic Change." Working Paper 2007-2, Center for Retirement Research, Boston College (February).

Campbell, Duncan. 1999. "Globalization and Change: Social Dialogue and Labor Market Adjustment in the Crisis-Affected Countries of East Asia." Bangkok: International Labor Organization/EASMAT.

Carlin, Robert. 2006. "Wabbit in Free Fall." Nautilus Policy Forum Online 06-78A, www.nautilus.org/fora/security/0678carlin.html (21 September).

Carr, Edward Hallett. 1939. *The Twenty Years' Crisis, 1919–1939.* New York: St. Martin's Press.

Cecchetti, Stephen G., and Enisse Kharroubi. 2012. "Reassessing the Impact of Finance on Growth." BIS Working Paper 381, Bank for International Settlements, Basel (July).

Cha, Victor D., and David C. Kang. 2003. *Nuclear North Korea: A Debate on Engagement Strategies.* New York: Columbia University Press.

Chandler, Alfred D. 1977. *The Visible Hand: The Managerial Revolution in American Business.* Cambridge, MA: Belknap Press of Harvard University Press.

Chang, Ha-Joon. 2010. *23 Things They Don't Tell You about Capitalism.* London: Allen Lane.

Cheong, Wa Dae. 2011. "Address by President Lee Myung-bak on the 66th Anniversary of Liberation," speech broadcast on 15 August, Seoul.

Chi-Seung, Song, et al. 2010. "An Empirical Analysis of Venture Firms' Growth Trajectories and Policy Recommendations for the Improvement of the Venture Firm Supporting System." Seoul: Korea Small Business Institute.

Cho, Dongchul, and Youngsun Koh. 1999. "Liberalization of Capital Flows in Korea: Big Bang or Gradualism?" In *Changes in Exchange Rates in Rapidly Developing Countries: Theory, Practice, and Policy Issue,* 285–310. Chicago: University of Chicago Press.

Cho, Lee-Jay, and Yoon Hyung Kim, eds. 1995. *Economic Systems in South and North Korea: The Agenda for Economic Integration.* Seoul: Korea Development Institute.

Cho, Yoon Je, and Joon Kyung Kim. 1997. "Credit Policies and the Industrialization of Korea." Seoul: Korea Development Institute.

Choe, Soonkyoo, and Thomas W. Roehl. 2007. "What to Shed and What to Keep: Corporate Transformation in Korean Business Groups." *Long Range Planning* 40 (4–5), 465–487.

Choi, Lee. 2006. "FTA, KORUS FTA, and Challenges of the Labor Movement," www.bilaterals.org (31 August).

Choi, Soo-Young. 1991. "Foreign Trade of North Korea 1946–1988: Structure and Performance." PhD diss., Northeastern University.

Choi, Won-Sik. 2004. "East Asian Initiative as a Scheme to Partition the World into Three Blocs." In *Korean Solidarity for Northeast Asian Intellectuals, ed., Toward a Northeast Asian Community.* Seoul: Dong-A Ilbo (in Korean).

Choo, Hakchung. 1993. "Income Distribution and Distributive Equity in Korea." In Lawrence B. Krause and Fun-Koo Park, eds., *Social Issues in Korea: Korean and American Perspectives*, 335–360. Seoul: Korea Development Institute.

Chopra, Ajai, Kenneth Kang, Meral Karasulu, Hong Liang, Henry Ma, and Anthony Richards. 2001. "From Crisis to Recovery in Korea: Strategy, Achievements, and Lessons." IMF Working Paper 01/154, International Monetary Fund, Washington, DC (October).

Chun, B. K., and H. S. Kwon. 2008. "Assessment of the Degree of Competition in the Banking Industry." *Bank of Korea Monthly Bulletin*, 16 September (in Korean).

Chun, Hong-Tack. 1999. "The Second Economy in North Korea." *Seoul Journal of Economics*, Summer, 173–194.

Chun, Hong-Tack, and Jin Park. 1997. "North Korean Economy: A Historical Assessment." In Dong-Se Cha, Kwang Suk Kim, and Dwight H. Perkins, eds., *The Korean Economy 1945–1995: Performance and Vision for the 21st Century*, 733–755. Seoul: Korea Development Institute.

Chun, Hyunbae, Hak K. Pyo, and Keun Hee Rhee. 2008. "Multifactor Productivity in Korea and an International Comparison: Data and Productivity Estimates of the Korea Industrial Productivity Database." *Seoul Journal of Economics* 21 (4), 551–577.

Chung, Kyuil. 2007. "Decrease in Household Savings Rate and Effectiveness of Monetary Policy." *Economic Papers* 10, Bank of Korea, Seoul.

Clerides, Sofronis, Saul Lach, and James Tybout. 1998. "Is Learning by Exporting Important? Micro-Dynamic Evidence from Colombia, Mexico and Morocco." *Quarterly Journal of Economics* 113 (3), 903–947.

Credit Suisse AG. 2012. "Currency Matters." *Swiss Global Investment Returns Yearbook 2012*. Credit Suisse Research Institute, Zurich.

Crespi, Gustavo, Chiara Criscuolo, and Jonathan Haskel. 2008. "Productivity, Exporting and the Learning-by-Exporting Hypothesis: Direct Evidence from UK Firms." *Canadian Journal of Economics* 41(2), 619–638.

Cumings, Bruce. 1997. *Korea's Place in the Sun*. New York: W. W. Norton.

Dahlman, Carl J., Bruce Ross-Larson, and Larry E. Westphal. 1985. "Managing Technological Development: Lessons from the Newly Industrializing Countries." World Bank Staff Working Paper 717, World Bank, Washington, DC (January). Also published under same title in *World Development* 15 (6), 759–775 (1987).

Dalla, Ismail, and Deena Khatkhate. 1995. "Regulated Deregulation of the Financial System in Korea." World Bank Discussion Paper 292, World Bank, Washington, DC.

Driessen, Joost, and Luc Laeven. 2005. "International Portfolio Diversification Benefits: Cross-Country Evidence from a Local Perspective." Unpublished manuscript, University of Amsterdam and World Bank.

Eberstadt, Nicholas. 1999. *The End of North Korea*. Washington, DC: AEI Press.

Economic Planning Board. 1980. *Handbook of the Korean Economy*. Seoul: Economic Planning Board.

———. 1988. *Economic Statistics of the Korean Economy 1988*. Seoul: Economic Planning Board.

Eichengreen, Barry, Donghyun Park, and Kwanho Shin. 2012. "When Fast Growing Economies Slow Down: International Evidence and Implications for China." *Asian Economic Papers* 11, 42–87.

———. 2013. "Growth Slowdowns Redux: New Evidence on the Middle-Income Trap." NBER Working Paper 18673, National Bureau of Economic Research, Cambridge, MA (January).

Eichengreen, Barry, and Yung Chul Park. 2005. "Why Has There Been Less Financial Integration in Asia Than in Europe?" In Yung Chul Park, Takatoshi Ito, and Yunjong Wang, eds., *A New Financial Market Structure for East Asia*, 84–103. Cheltenham, UK: Edward Elgar.

Eichengreen, Barry, Dwight Perkins, and Kwanho Shin. 2012. *From Miracle to Maturity: The Growth of the Korean Economy*. Cambridge, MA: Harvard University Asia Center.

Evans, Peter B. 1995. *Embedded Autonomy: States and Industrial Transformation*. Princeton: Princeton University Press.

Fair Trade Commission. Various years. "Large-Scale Business Groups." Fair Trade Commission, Seoul.

Feenstra, Robert, and Gordon Hanson. 1999. "The Impact of Outsourcing and High-Technology Capital on Wages: Estimates for the United States, 1979–1990." *Quarterly Journal of Economics* 114 (3), 907–940.

FitzGerald, Valpy. 2006. "Financial Development and Economic Growth: A Critical View." Unpublished manuscript, Oxford University (March).

Fleck, Susan. 2009. "International Comparisons of Hours Worked: An Assessment of the Statistics." *Monthly Labor Review*, May, 1–31.

Frank, Charles, Kwang Suk Kim, and Larry Westphal. 1975. *Foreign Trade Regimes and Economic Development: South Korea*. New York: Columbia University Press for the National Bureau of Economic Research.

Freedom House. 2011. *Freedom in the World: Comparative and Historical Data*. New York: Freedom House.

Freeman, Richard, Kyungsoo Choi, and Sunwoong Kim. Forthcoming. *Hard Work and Human Capital: Korea in the New Global Economy*. Cambridge, MA: Harvard University Asia Center.

Funabashi, Yoichi. 2007. *The Peninsula Question: A Chronicle of the Second Korean Nuclear Crisis*. Washington, DC: Brookings Institution Press.

Galindo, Arturo, Fabio Schiantarelli, and Andrew Weiss. 2007. "Does Financial Liberalization Improve the Allocation of Investment? Micro-evidence from Developing Countries." *Journal of Development Economics* 83 (2), 562–587.

Giddens, Anthony. 1998. *The Third Way: The Renewal of Social Democracy.* Cambridge: Polity Press in association with Blackwell Publishers.

Goldstein, Morris, and Philip Turner. 2004. *Currency Mismatches in Emerging Economies.* Washington, DC: Peterson Institute for International Economics.

Gollier, Christian. 2001. "Wealth Inequality and Asset Pricing." *Review of Economic Studies* 68 (1), 181–203.

Gordon, Michael R. 2001. "How Politics Sank Accord on Missiles with North Korea." *New York Times,* 6 March.

Green, Michael J., and Bates Gill, ed. 2009. *Asia's New Multilateralism: Cooperation, Competition, and the Search for Community.* New York: Columbia University Press.

Greenaway, David, Robert Hine, and Chris Milner. 1994. "Country-Specific Factors and the Pattern of Horizontal and Vertical Intra-Industry Trade in the UK." *Review of World Economics* 130 (1), 77–100.

Habermeier, Karl, Annamaria Kokenyne, and Chikako Baba. 2011. "The Effectiveness of Capital Controls and Prudential Policies in Managing Large Inflows." IMF Staff Discussion Note SDN/11/14, International Monetary Fund, Washington, DC (August).

Haggard, Stephan. 1990. *Pathways from the Periphery: The Politics of Growth in Newly Industrializing Countries.* Ithaca: Cornell University Press.

Haggard, Stephan, Susan Collins, Richard Cooper, Choongso Kim, and Sung-Tae Ro. 1994. *Macroeconomic Policy and Adjustment in Korea, 1970–1990.* Cambridge, MA: Harvard University East Asia Center.

Haggard, Stephan, and Marcus Noland. 2007. *Famine in North Korea: Markets, Aid and Reform.* New York: Columbia University Press.

Hahm, Joon-Ho. 2004. "Financial Restructuring." In Duck-Koo Chung and Barry Eichengreen, eds., *The Korean Economy Beyond the Crisis,* 172–193. Cheltenham, UK: Edward Elgar.

Hahn, Chin Hee. 2000. "Implicit Loss-Protection and the Investment Behavior of Korean Chaebol." In Inseok Shin, ed., *The Korean Crisis: Before and After,* 215–251. Seoul: Korea Development Institute.

———. 2004. "Exporting and Performance of Plants: Evidence from Korean Manufacturing." NBER Working Paper 10208, National Bureau of Economic Research, Cambridge, MA (January).

Hall, Maximilian, and Richard Simper. 2012. "Efficiency and Competition in Korean Banking." Nottingham University Business School Research Paper 2012-07, University of Nottingham, United Kingdom.

Hall, Peter A., and David Soskice, eds. 2001. *Varieties of Capitalism: The Institutional Foundations of Comparative Advantage.* Oxford: Oxford University Press.

Han, Jang Sop. 2007. "The Evolution of the Korean Shipbuilding Industry." Unpublished manuscript, Korea Offshore and Shipbuilding Association, Seoul.

Harrison, Selig S. 2002. *Korean Endgame: A Strategy for Reunification and U.S. Disengagement*. Princeton: Princeton University Press.

Hasan, Parvez. 2011. "Korean Development, 1973–84: A World Bank Economist Remembers and Reflects." KDI Working Paper 2011-01, Korea Development Institute, Seoul (March).

Hecker, Siegfried S. 2010. "A Return Trip to North Korea's Yongbyon Nuclear Complex." Center for International Security and Cooperation, Stanford University (November), http://iis-db.stanford.edu/pubs/23035/HeckerYongbyon.pdf.

Hemmert, Martin. 2007. "The Korean Innovation System: From Industrial Catch-up to Technological Leadership?" In Jorg Mahlich and Werner Pascha, eds., *Innovation and Technology in Korea: Challenges of a Newly Advanced Economy*, 11–32. Heidelberg: Physica Verlag.

Henderson, Gregory. 1968. *Korea: The Politics of the Vortex*. Cambridge MA: Harvard University Press.

Hennessy, D. A., and H. Lapan. 2007. "When Different Market Concentration Indices Agree." *Economic Letters* 95, 234–240.

Hidalgo, C. A., B. Klinger, A.-L. Barbasi, and R. Hausmann. 2007. "The Product Space Conditions the Development of Nations." *Science* 317 (27 July), 482–487.

Higgins, Matthew, and Jeffrey Williamson. 1996. "Asian Demography and Foreign Capital Dependence." NBER Working Paper 5560, National Bureau of Economic Research, Cambridge, MA (May).

Hong, Dongpyo, Sangwon Ko, and Alexei Volynets. 2007. "Information and Communications Technologies for a Knowledge-Based Economy." In Joonghae Suh and Derek H. C. Chen, eds., *Korea as a Knowledge Economy*, 79–105. Washington, DC: World Bank.

Hufbauer, Gary Clyde, and Jeffrey Schott. 2009. "Fitting Asia-Pacific Agreements into the WTO System." In Richard Baldwin and Patrick Low, eds., *Multilateralizing Regionalism*, 554–635. Cambridge: Cambridge University Press.

Hur, Jae-Joon, Hwan-Joo Seo, and Young Soo Lee. 2007. "Structural Changes in the Korean Economy and Employment in Services." Korea Labor Institute, Seoul.

Hur, Seok-Kyun. 2005. "Exploration into the Determinants of Household Consumption: Liquidity Constraint and Family Characteristics." *Korea Development Review* 27 (1), 1–37.

Hwang, Eui-Gak. 1993. *The Korean Economies*. Oxford: Clarendon Press.

Hwang, Insang. 1998. "Long-Run Determinants of Korean Economic Growth: Evidence from Manufacturing." *Applied Economics* 30, 391–405.

International Monetary Fund. 2006. *Republic of Korea: Selected Issues*. IMF Country Report 6/381. Washington, DC: International Monetary Fund (October).

———. 2008. *Republic of Korea Article IV: Selected Issues*. Washington, DC: International Monetary Fund.

———. 2011. *World Economic Outlook*. Washington, DC: International Monetary Fund.

Jo, Dongho. 2003. *Prospects for Changes in North Korea's Economic Policy and the Role of Inter-Korean Economic Cooperation*. Seoul: Korea Development Institute (in Korean).

Johnson, Chalmers. 1982. *MITI and the Japanese Miracle: The Growth of Industrial Policy, 1925–1975*. Stanford: Stanford University Press.

Jones, Leroy, and Il SaKong. 1980. *Government, Business and Entrepreneurship in Economic Development: The Korean Case*. Cambridge, MA: Harvard University Asia Center.

Jorgenson, Dale and Barbara Fraumeni. 1989. "The Accumulation of Human and Nonhuman Capital, 1948–1984." In Robert Lipsey and Helen Tice, eds., *The Measurement of Savings, Investment and Wealth*, 227–282. Chicago: University of Chicago Press.

Kang, Tae Soo, and Gounan Ma. 2007. "Recent Episodes of Credit Card Distress in Asia." *BIS Quarterly Review* (June), 55–68.

Kawai, Masahiro, and Ganeshan Wignaraja. 2007. "ASEAN+3 or ASEAN+6: Which Way Forward?" ADBI Discussion Paper 77, Asian Development Bank Institute, Tokyo, www.adbi.org/discussion-paper/2007/09/13/2359.asean.3.asean.6/ (September).

Khanna, Tarun, and Yishay Yafeh. 2007. "Business Groups in Emerging Markets: Paragons or Parasites?" *Journal of Economic Literature* 45 (2), 331–372.

Kihl, Young. 2004. *Transforming Korean Politics: Democracy, Reform and Culture*. Armonk, NY: M. E. Sharpe/East Gate Books.

Kim, Chung-yum. 2011. *From Despair to Hope: Economic Policymaking in Korea, 1945–1979*. Seoul: Korea Development Institute.

Kim, Heung-ki, ed. 1999. *The Korean Economy in Glory and Disgrace: 33 Years of the Economic Planning Board*. Seoul: Maeil Economic Daily.

Kim, Joo-Hoon, ed. 2005. *The Role of SMEs in a Transition to an Innovation-Led Economy*. Seoul: Korea Development Institute.

Kim, Kwang-Mo. 1988. *Korea's Industrial Development and Heavy and Chemical Industrial Promotion Policy*. Seoul: Jigu Munhwasa.

Kim, Kyungsoo, Byoung-Ki Kim, and Young Kyung Suh. 2009. "Opening to Capital Flows and Implications from Korea." BOK Working Paper 363, Institute for Monetary and Economic Research, Bank of Korea, Seoul (February).

Kim, Seok-Jin. 2013. "Factors for the Expansion of North Korea–China Economic Cooperation and Its Impact on the North Korean Economy." In

North Korean Economy Team, ed., *KDI Review of the North Korean Economy, January 2013*, Publication 2444, 93–119. Seoul: Korea Development Institute (in Korean).

Kim, Soyoung, Sunghyun Henry Kim, and Yunjong Wang. 2004. "Macroeconomic Effects of Capital Account Liberalization: The Case of Korea." *Review of Development Economics* 8 (4), 624–639.

Kim, Sunhyuk, and Wonhyuk Lim. 2007. "How to Deal with South Korea," *Washington Quarterly* 30, 71–82.

Kim, Taejong. 2009. "Education and Education Financing in Korea: Past, Present, and Future." Unpublished manuscript (PowerPoint presentation), Korea Development Institute, Seoul (Summer).

Kim, Won-Ho. 2003. "The Korea-Chile FTA: Comparing Approaches to Trans-Pacific Inter-Regionalism." Unpublished manuscript, Korea Institute for International Economic Policy, Seoul (September).

Kim, Yeon-Chul. 2002. "The Nature and Outlook of North Korea's Economic Management Reform." In Yeon-Chul Kim and Sun Song Park, eds., *A Study on North Korea's Economic Reform*. Seoul: Humanitas (in Korean).

Korea Development Institute. 2010. *National Budget Allocation Plan: A Comprehensive Report on Education*. Seoul: Korea Development Institute.

Korea Economic Daily. 2013. "New President Stresses 'Economic Democracy' in Her Inauguration Speech." *Korea Economic Daily*, 25 February, http://english.hankyung.com/news/apps/news.view?c1=&newscate=1&nkey=2013 02251751421.

Korea Fair Trade Commission, "Large-Scale Business Groups," various years.

Korea Financial Investment Association (2012), "Need and Implications for Balanced Growth of Financial Industries (Korean)" *A report of the research department* (www.kofia.or.kr), July.

Korea Institute of National Unification. 1993. *A Comparative Case Study of Reform and Opening in Socialist Regimes*. Seoul: Korea Institute of National Unification.

Korea JoongAng Daily. 2011. "Mired in Populism." *Korea JoongAng Daily*, 27 June, http://koreajoongangdaily.joinsmsn.com/news/article/article.aspx?aid =2938063.

Korea National Statistical Office. 2006. *Korea Statistical Yearbook of 2006*. Seoul: Korea Statistical Information Service.

Korea Times. 2007. "Korea's Shipbuilders Meet China's Challenge." *Korea Times*, 11 May, www.koreatimes.co.kr.

Korean Statistical Information Service (KOSIS), http://kosis.kr/eng/.

Kornai, Janos. 1990. *The Road to a Free Economy*. New York: W. W. Norton.

Kose, M. Ayhan, Eswar S. Prasad, Kenneth Rogoff, and Shang-Jin Wei. 2009. "Financial Globalization: A Reappraisal." *IMF Staff Papers* 56 (1), 8–62.

Krueger, Anne O. 1974. "The Political Economy of the Rent-Seeking Society." *American Economic Review* 64 (3), 291–303.

———. 1979. *The Developmental Role of the Foreign Sector and Aid.* Cambridge, MA: Harvard University Asia Center.

Krueger, Anne O., and Jungho Yoo. 2002. "Chaebol Capitalism and the Currency-Financial Crises in Korea." In Sebastian Edwards and Jeffrey A. Frankel, eds., *Preventing Currency Crisis in Emerging Markets,* 601–662. Chicago: University of Chicago Press.

Kwon, O. Yul. 2010. *The Korean Economy in Transition.* Cheltenham, UK: Edward Elgar.

Lau, Lawrence J., Yingyi Qian, and Gerard Roland. 1997. "Pareto-Improving Economic Reforms through Dual-Track Liberalization." *Economics Letters* 55 (2), 285–292.

Lee, Kyung Joon. N.d. *Saemaul Movement and Forest Rehabilitation in South Korea.* Seoul: Korea Development Institute School of Public Policy and Management, and World Bank Institute.

Lee, Manroo. 1990. *The Odyssey of Korean Democracy.* Westport, CT: Praeger Publishers.

Lee, Min Hwan, and Mamoru Nagano. 2008. "Market Competition before and after Bank Merger Waves: A Comparative Study of Korea and Japan." *Pacific Economic Review* 13, 604–619.

Lee, Sook-Jong. 2005. "Democratization and Polarization in Korean Society." *Asian Perspective* 29 (3), 99–125.

Lee, Su-jeong. 2013. "An Analysis of the Substantive Independence of Outside Directors and Auditors." ERRI Report 2013-3, Economic Reform Research Institute, Seoul (27 February).

Lee, Suk. 2003. "Food Shortages and Economic Institutions in the Democratic People's Republic of Korea." PhD diss., University of Warwick, United Kingdom.

Lee, Suk, and Duol Kim. 2011. *Comparing Long-term Economic Trends between South and North Korea and Implications for North Korea Policy.* Seoul: Korea Development Institute (in Korean).

Lee, Sungwoo, Geunsup Kim, and Jumi Song. 2010. "A Study on the Advancement of Korea's Global Logistics Industry." Seoul: Korea Maritime Institute.

Lee, Youngjae. 2005. "Law, Politics, and Impeachment: The Impeachment of Roh Moo-hyun from a Comparative Constitutional Perspective." *American Journal of Comparative Law* 53, 2 (Spring), 403–432.

Levine, Ross. 2005. "Finance and Growth: Theory and Evidence." In Philippe Aghion and Steven Durlauf, eds., *Handbook of Economic Growth*, volume 1A, 866–926. Amsterdam: Elsevier.

Lie, John. 2000. *Han Unbound: The Political Economy of South Korea.* Stanford: Stanford University Press.

Lim, Dong-won. 2012. *Peacemaker: Twenty Years of Inter-Korean Relations and the North Korean Nuclear Issue: A Memoir.* Stanford: Shorenstein Asia-Pacific Research Center, Stanford University.

Lim, Eul Chul. 2005. *Welcome to the Kaesong Industrial Complex.* Seoul: Haenam (in Korean).

Lim, Kyung-Mook. 2010. "An Evaluation of the Deterioration in Financial Soundness of the Construction Industry." Unpublished manuscript.

Lim, Kyung-Mook, and Wonhyuk Lim. 2007. "Investment Bust in Post-Crisis Korea: Fact or Fiction?" *Asian Economic Papers* 5, 1–18.

Lim, Wonhyuk. 1997. "North Korea's Food Crisis." *Korea and World Affairs* 21, 4 (Winter), 568–585.

———. 2000. *The Origin and Evolution of the Korean Economic System.* Seoul: Korea Development Institute.

———. 2003. "The Emergence of the Chaebol and the Origins of the Chaebol Problem." In Stephan Haggard, Wonhyuk Lim, and Euysung Kim, eds., *Economic Crisis and Corporate Restructuring in Korea: Reforming the Chaebol,* 35–52. Cambridge: Cambridge University Press.

———. 2004. "North Korea's Economic Futures: Internal and External Dimensions." In Jonathan D. Pollack, ed., *Korea: The East Asian Pivot,* 171–195. Newport, RI: Naval War College Press.

———. 2007. "Inter-Korean Economic Cooperation at a Crossroads." In *Dynamic Forces on the Korean Peninsula: Strategic and Economic Implications,* 139–164. Washington, DC: Korea Economic Institute.

———. 2011. "Joint Discovery and Upgrading of Comparative Advantage: Lessons from Korea's Development Experience." In Shahrokh Fardoust, Yongbeom Kim, and Claudia Sepulveda, eds., *Post-Crisis Growth and Development: A Development Agenda for the G-20,* 173–226. Washington, DC: World Bank.

Lim, Wonhyuk, Stephen Haggard, and Euysung Kim. 2003. "Introduction: The Political Economy of Corporate Restructuring." In Stephan Haggard, Wonhyuk Lim, and Euysung Kim, eds., *Economic Crisis and Corporate Restructuring in Korea: Reforming the Chaebol,* 1–31. Cambridge: Cambridge University Press.

Lim, Wonhyuk, and Randall Morck. Forthcoming. *The Long Shadow of "Big-Push" Partnership: Government and Business Groups in Korea's Economic Development.* Cambridge, MA: Harvard University Asia Center.

Lin, Justin Yifu, Fang Cai, and Zhou Li. 2003. *The China Miracle: Development Strategy and Economic Reform.* Revised edition. Hong Kong: Chinese University Press.

Lindauer, David, Joung Woo Lee, Jong-Gie Kim, Hy-Sop Lim, Jae-Young Son, and Ezra F. Vogel. 1997. *The Strains of Economic Growth: Labor Unrest and Social Dissatisfaction in Korea*. Cambridge, MA: Harvard Institute for International Development.

Lucas, Robert E. 2009. "Ideas and Growth." *Economica* 76 (301), 1–19.

Marshall, Monty, and Keith Jaggers. Various years. "Polity IV Project: Political Regime Characteristics and Transitions, 1800–2012." Center for Systemic Peace, www.systemicpeace.org/polity/polity4.htm.

Mason, Edward S., Mahn Je Kim, Dwight H. Perkins, Kwang Suk Kim, and David C. Cole. 1980. *The Economic and Social Modernization of the Republic of Korea*. Cambridge, MA: Harvard University Asia Center.

McGinn, Noel F., Donald Snodgress, Yung Bong Kim, Shin-bok Kim, and Quee-Young Kim. 1980. *Education and Development in Korea*. Cambridge, MA: Harvard University Press for the Council on East Asian Studies, Harvard University.

Mercereau, Benoit. 2006. "Financial Integration in Asia: Estimating the Risk-Sharing Gains for Australia and Other Nations." IMF Working Paper 06/267, International Monetary Fund (December).

Ministry of Employment and Labor. 2012. *A Report on the Organization of National Labor Unions in 2011*. Seoul: Ministry of Employment and Labor (August).

Ministry of Finance and Korea Development Bank. 1993. *Foreign Capital and Korean Economic Development: A Thirty-Year History*. Seoul: Ministry of Finance and Korea Development Bank (in Korean).

Ministry of Unification. 2006. "A Briefing on the Termination and Liquidation of the Light-Water Reactor Project," 10 January. Seoul: Republic of Korea (in Korean).

Mo, Jongryn, and Chung-in Moon. 1998. *Democracy and the Korean Economy*. Stanford: Hoover Institution Press.

Mo, Jongryn, and Barry R. Weingast. 2013. *Korean Political and Economic Development: Crisis, Security, and Economic Rebalancing*. Cambridge, MA: Harvard University Asia Center.

Modigliani, Franco. 1966. "The Life Cycle Hypothesis of Saving, the Demand for Wealth and the Supply of Capital." *Social Research* 33 (2), 160–217.

Moon, Chung-in. 2012. *The Sunshine Policy: In Defense of Engagement as a Path to Peace in Korea*. Seoul: Yonsei University Press.

Murphy, Kevin, Andrei Shleifer, and Robert Vishny. 1989. "Industrialization and the Big Push." *Journal of Political Economy* 97 (5), 1003–1026.

National Center for Education Statistics, Trends in International Math and Science Study (TIMSS), http://nces.ed.gov/TIMSS.

National Election Commission, Election Statistics System, http://info.nec.go.kr/.

National Science and Technology Commission and Korea Institute of Science and Technology Evaluation and Planning (KISTEP). 2011. *Report on the Survey of Research and Development in Science and Technology.* Seoul: National Science and Technology Commission and KISTEP.

National Statistical Office. 1999. *Major Statistics of the Korean Economy.* Seoul: National Statistical Office (March).

———. Various years. *Social Indicators in Korea.* Seoul: Economic Planning Board.

Natsios, Andrew S. 2001. *The Great North Korean Famine.* Washington, DC: United States Institute of Peace Press.

Noland, Marcus. 2000. *Avoiding the Apocalypse: The Future of the Two Koreas.* Washington, DC: Institute of International Economics.

Noland, Marcus, Sherman Robinson, and Monica Scatasta. 1997. "Modeling Economic Reform in North Korea." *Journal of Asian Economics* 8 (1), 15–38.

O, Won-chol. 2009. *The Korea Story: President Park Jung-hee's Leadership and the Korean Industrial Revolution.* Seoul: Wisdom Tree.

Oberdorfer, Don. 2001. *The Two Koreas.* New York: Basic Books.

OECD. 1996. *Korea: Country Survey.* Paris: Organization for Economic Cooperation and Development.

———. 2003. *Korea: Country Survey.* Paris: Organization for Economic Cooperation and Development.

———. 2006. *Education at a Glance.* Paris: Organization for Economic Cooperation and Development.

———. 2009a. *OECD Reviews of Innovation Policy: Korea.* Paris: Organization for Economic Cooperation and Development.

———. 2009b. *Society at a Glance.* Paris: Organization for Economic Cooperation and Development.

———. 2010. *OECD in Figures.* Paris: Organization for Economic Cooperation and Development.

———. 2012. *Education at a Glance.* Paris: Organization for Economic Cooperation and Development.

———. 2013. *OECD Employment Outlook.* Paris: Organization for Economic Cooperation and Development.

———. Various dates. OECD.Stat Extracts, http://stats.oecd.org/Index.aspx.

Oh, Kie-Chiang. 1999. *Korean Politics: The Quest for Democratization and Economic Development.* Ithaca: Cornell University Press.

Oh, Myung, and James F. Larson. 2011. *Digital Development in Korea: Building an Information Society.* London: Routledge.

Ostry, Jonathan, Atish Ghosh, Karl Habermeier, Marcos Chamon, Mahvash Qureshi, and Dennis Reinhardt. 2010. "Capital Inflows: The Role of Controls." IMF Staff Position Note SPN/10/04, International Monetary Fund, Washington, DC (February).

Padoa-Schioppa, Tomasso. 2003. "Central Banks and Financial Stability: Exploring the Land in Between." In Vitor Gaspar et al., eds., *The Transformation of the European Financial System*, 269–310. Frankfurt: European Central Bank.

Palais, James B. 1975. *Politics and Polity in Traditional Korea*. Cambridge, MA: Harvard University Press.

Panzar, John, and James N. Rosse. 1987. "Testing for Monopoly Equilibrium." *Journal of Industrial Economies* 35, 443–456.

Park, Chung Hee. 1963. *The Country, the Revolution and I*. Seoul: Hollym Corporation.

Park, Jungsoo, and Yung Chul Park. 2014. "Has Financial Liberalization Improved Economic Efficiency in the Republic of Korea? Evidence from Firm-Level and Industry-Level Data." ADBI Working Paper 480, Asian Development Bank Institute, Tokyo.

Park, Kang, and William Weber. 2006. "Profitability of Korean Banks: Test of Market Structure versus Efficient Structure." *Journal of Economics and Business* 58, 222–239.

Park, Seung-Rok, and Jene Kwon. 1995. "Rapid Economic Growth with Increasing Returns to Scale and No Productivity Growth." *Review of Economies and Statistics* 77, 332–351.

Park, Yung Chul. 1998. "Financial Crisis and Macroeconomic Adjustments in Korea: 1997–98." In *Financial Liberalization and Opening in East Asia: Issues and Policy Challenges*, 11–69. Seoul: Korea Institute of Finance.

———. 2006. *Economic Liberalization and Integration in East Asia: A Post-Crisis Paradigm*. Oxford: Oxford University Press.

———. 2010. "Global Economic Recession and East Asia: How Has Korea Managed the Crisis and What Has It Learned?" Bank of Korea Working Paper 209, Institute for Monetary and Economic Research, Seoul (November).

———. 2013. "Financial Development and Liberalization in Korea." In Yung Chul Park and Hugh Patrick, eds., *How Finance Is Shaping the Economies in China, Japan and Korea*, 225–301. New York: Columbia University Press.

Park, Yung Chul, Joon-Kyung Kim, and Hail Park. Forthcoming. *Growth and Structural Changes in Korea's Financial Sector, 1985–2012*. Cambridge, MA: Harvard University Asia Center.

Park, Yung Chul, and Jong Wha Lee. 2002. "Financial Crisis and Recovery: Patterns of Adjustment in East Asia, 1996–99." ADBI Research Paper 45, Asian Development Bank Institute, Tokyo (October).

Park, Yung Chul, K. L. Lee, and Y. S. Lee. 2011. "The Role of Foreign Banks in Korea." Unpublished manuscript, Korea University and Seoul National University.

Park, Yung Chul, and Hail Park. 2014. "Stock Market Co-Movement and Exchange Rate Flexibility: Experience of the Republic of Korea." ADBI Working Paper 479, Asian Development Bank Institute, Tokyo.

Park, Yung Chul, and Jungsoo Park. Forthcoming. "Financial Liberalization and Income Distribution in Korea: Evidence from Household Data." In Yung Chul Park, Joon-Kyung Kim, and Hail Park, *Growth and Structural Changes in Korea's Financial Sector, 1985–2012*. Cambridge, MA: Harvard University Asia Center.

Perkins, Dwight. 1997. "Structural Transformation and the Role of the State: Korea, 1945–1995." In Dong-Se Cha, Kwang Suk Kim, and Dwight H. Perkins, eds., *The Korean Economy 1945–1995: Performance and Vision for the 21st Century*, 57–98. Seoul: Korea Development Institute.

Piazolo, Marc. 1995. "Determinants of South Korean Economic Growth, 1955–1990." *International Economic Journal* 9, 109–133.

Pifer, Steven. 2013. "North Korea and Nuclear-Armed Missiles: Calming the Hyperbole." Up Front blog, Brookings Institution (15 April), www.brookings.edu/blogs/up-front/posts/2013/04/15-north-korea-nuclear-missiles-pifer.

Pollack, Jonathan D., ed. 2004. *Korea: The East Asian Pivot*. Newport, RI: Naval War College Press.

Presidential Committee on Green Growth. 2012. "An Update on Korea's Green Growth: Progress and Prospects." Presidential Committee on Green Growth, Seoul (May).

Public Fund Management Committee. 2004. *White Paper on Public Fund Management*. Seoul: Ministry of Economy and Finance.

———. 2009. *White Paper on Public Fund Management*. Seoul: Ministry of Strategy and Finance.

Pyo, Hak K., S. Young Chung, and C. Sam Cho. 2007. "Estimates of Gross Capital Formation, Net Capital Stock and Capital Intensity: II Assets and 72 Industries (1970–2005)." *Korean Economy Analyses* 13, 137–191 [in Korean].

Reiss, Mitchell. 1995. *Bridled Ambition: Why Countries Constrain Their Nuclear Capabilities*. Washington, DC: Woodrow Wilson Center Press.

Revere, Evans J. R. 2012. "Tough Challenges, Hard Choices: Dealing with North Korea after the Collapse of the Leap Day Agreement." *American Foreign Policy Interests* 34 (4), 171–177.

Rhyu, Sang-young, and Dong-No Kim, eds. 2013. *Kim Dae-jung and Mass Economy Theory*. Seoul: Yonsei University.

Robinson, Joan. 1965. "Korea, 1964: Economic Miracle." *Monthly Review* (January). Reprinted in Joan Robinson, *Collected Economic Paper: Volume 3*, 207–215. Oxford: Basil Blackwell, 1974.

Rodrik, Dani. 2004. "Industrial Policy for the Twenty-First Century." CEPR Discussion Paper 4767, Centre for Economic Policy Research, London (November).

———. 2006. "The Social Cost of Foreign Exchange Reserves." *International Economic Journal* 20 (3), 253–266.

Rodrik, Dani, and Andres Velasco. 2000. "Short-Term Capital Flows." *Annual World Bank Conference on Development Economics*. Washington, DC: World Bank.

Romain, Astrid, and Bruno van Pottelsberghe de la Potterie. 2004. "The Determinants of Venture Capital: A Panel Data Analysis of 16 OECD Countries." Working Paper CEB 04-015.RS, Université Libre de Bruxelles, Brussels (April).

Rosenstein-Rodan, Paul. 1943. "Problems of Industrialisation of Eastern and South-Eastern Europe." *Economic Journal* 53 (210/11), 202–211.

SaKong, Il. 1993. *Korea in the World Economy*. Washington, DC: Institute for International Economics.

Sala-i-Martin, Xavier. 1997. "I Just Ran Two Million Regressions." *American Economic Review* 87, 178–183.

Schott, Jeffrey. 2007. "The Korea-U.S. Free Trade Agreement: A Summary Assessment." Policy Briefs in International Economics 07-7, Peterson Institute for International Economics, Washington, DC (August).

Schott, Jeffrey J., Scott C. Bradford, and Thomas Moll. 2006. "Negotiating the Korea–United States Free Trade Agreement." Policy Briefs in International Economics 06-4, Peterson Institute for International Economics, Washington, DC (June).

Sherman, Wendy R. 2001. "Talking to the North Koreans." *New York Times*, 7 March.

Shin, Dong Jin, and Brian Kim. 2011. "Efficiency of the Banking Industry Structure in Korea." *Asian Economic Journal* 25, 355–373.

———. 2013. "Bank Consolidation and Competitiveness: Empirical Evidence from the Korean Banking Industry." *Journal of Asian Economies* 24, 41–50.

Shin, Donggyun. 2008. "Inequality, Polarization, and Social Unrest." In Richard B. Freeman, Sunwoong Kim, and Jaeho Keum, eds., *Beyond Flexibility: Roadmaps for Korean Labor Policy*, 65–97. Seoul: Korea Labor Institute.

Shin, Gukhwan. 1994. *Choices and Challenges for the Korean Economy on the Road to an Advanced Industrial Nation*. Seoul: Wooshinsa.

Shin, Inseok, and Yunjong Wang. 1999. "How to Sequence Capital Market Liberalization: Lessons from the Korean Experience." KIEP Working Paper 99-30, Korea Institute for International Economic Policy, Seoul (December).

Shin, Jang-Sup, and Ha-Joon Chang. 2003. *Restructuring Korea Inc.* London: Routledge.

Sinn, Gerlinde, and Hans-Werner Sinn. 1994. *Jumpstart: The Economic Unification of Germany*. Cambridge, MA: MIT Press.

Sinn, Hans-Werner. 1990. "Macroeconomic Aspects of German Unification." In P. J. J. Welfens, ed., *Economic Aspects of German Unification*. Heidelberg: Springer.

Small and Medium Business Administration. 2011. *Start-up Venture Bureau Statistical Data*. Seoul: Small and Medium Business Administration.

Small and Medium Business Administration and Korea Small Business Institute. 2012. *Programs to Support SMEs: A Summary*. Seoul: Korea Small Business Institute (in Korean).

Smith, Adam. 1977. *An Inquiry into the Nature and Causes of the Wealth of Nations*, Bicentennial Edition. Chicago: University of Chicago Press.

Smith, Hazel. 2005. *Hungry for Peace: International Security, Humanitarian Assistance, and Social Change in North Korea*. Washington, DC: United States Institute of Peace Press.

Solomon, Jay, and Hae Won Choi. 2003. "Southern Exposure: At Huge Korean Conglomerate, Bridge to North Takes Its Toll." *Wall Street Journal*, 4 March.

Song, Chi-Seung, Soo-Hwan Kim, Roh Yong Hwan, and Eun-Joo Choi. 2010. *An Empirical Analysis of Venture Firms' Growth Trajectories and Policy Recommendations for the Improvement of the Venture Firm Supporting System*. Seoul: Korea Small Business Institute.

Song, Tae-Jeong. 2001. "The Long- and Short-Term Impact of Facility Investment Decline on Our Economy." *LG Weekly Economy* (15 August), 4–9 (in Korean).

Statistics Korea. 2009. *2009 Private Education Expenditures Survey*. Seoul: Statistics Korea.

Stern, Joseph J., Ji-hong Kim, Dwight H. Perkins, and Jung-ho Yoo. 1995. *Industrialization and the State: The Korean Heavy and Chemical Industry Drive*. Cambridge, MA: Harvard Institute for International Development.

Stiglitz, Joseph E. 2000. "Capital Market Liberalization, Economic Growth and Instability." *World Development* 28 (6), 1075–1086.

Sufin, Fadzlan. 2011. "Benchmarking the Efficiency of the Korean Banking Sector: A DEA Approach." *Benchmarking: An International Journal* 18, 107–127.

Suh, Sang-Chul. 1978. *Growth and Structural Changes in the Korean Economy 1910–1940*. Cambridge, MA: Harvard University Asia Center.

Transparency International. 2009. Corruption Perceptions Index 2009, www .transparency.org/policy_research/surveys_indices/cpi/2009.

U.S. Department of Commerce. 2009. *International Trade Administration, Potential Exports of U.S. Clean Coal Technology through 2030*. Washington, DC: U.S. Department of Commerce.

Wade, Robert. 1990. *Governing the Market: Economic Theory and the Role of Government in East Asian Industrialization*. Princeton: Princeton University Press.

Wakasugi, R. 2007. "Vertical Intra-Industry Trade and Economic Integration in East Asia." *Asian Economic Papers* 6 (1), 26–39.

Wheelock, David, and Paul Wilson. 2001. "New Evidence on Returns to Scale and Product Mix among U.S. Commercial Banks." *Journal of Monetary Economics* 47 (3), 653–674.

Winters, L. Alan, Wonhyuk Lim, Lucia Hanmer, and Sidney Augustin. 2010. "Economic Growth in Low Income Countries: How the G20 Can Help to Raise and Sustain It." Working Paper 2010-01, Korea Development Institute, Seoul (November).

Wit, Joel S., Daniel B. Poneman, and Robert L. Gallucci. 2005. *Going Critical: The First North Korean Nuclear Crisis.* Washington, DC: Brookings Institution Press.

Woo, Jongseok. 2000. *Security Challenges and Military Politics in East Asia: From State Building to Post-Democratization.* New York: Continuum International Publishing.

Woo, Jung-en. 1991. *Race to the Swift: State and Finance in Korean Industrialization.* New York: Columbia University Press.

Woo-Cumings, Meredith. 1999. "The State, Democracy, and the Reform of the Corporate Sector." In T. J. Pempel, ed., *The Politics of the Asian Financial Crisis*, 116–142. Ithaca: Cornell University Press.

World Bank. 1993. *The East Asian Miracle: Economic Growth and Public Policy.* New York: Oxford University Press.

———. 1996. *From Plan to Market.* Oxford: Oxford University Press.

———. 2013. *Doing Business 2013: Smarter Regulations for Small and Medium-Size Enterprises.* Washington, DC: World Bank and International Finance Corporation, www.doingbusiness.org.

World Trade Organization. 2010. *Measuring Trade in Services.* Geneva: World Trade Organization/OMC (November).

Yang, Moon-Soo. 2005. "North Korea's General Markets: Realities, Repercussions, Character and Significance." *KDI Review of the North Korean Economy*, February, 19–21 (in Korean).

———. 2013. "North Korea's Marketization: Trends and Structural Transformation." *KDI Review of the North Korean Economy*, June, 45–70 (in Korean).

Yeon, Ha-Cheong. 1993. "Economic Consequences of German Unification and Its Policy Implications for Korea." KDI Working Paper 9303, Korea Development Institute, Seoul.

Yoo, Seung Min. 1999. "Corporate Restructuring in Korea: Policy Issues before and during the Crisis." KDI Working Paper 9903, Korea Development Institute, Seoul.

Yue, Chia Siow. 2007. "Challenges and Configurations of a Region-Wide FTA in East Asia." Unpublished manuscript, Singapore Institute of International Affairs (14 August).

Yun, Seong-Hun. 2004. "Impact of Direct Regulations on the Korean Credit Card Market and Consumer Welfare." *Economic Papers* 7 (1), 142–157, Bank of Korea (August).

Index

Harvard East Asian Monographs
(titles now in print)

Harvard East Asian Monographs

Harvard East Asian Monographs

191. Kerry Smith, *A Time of Crisis: Japan, the Great Depression, and Rural Revitalization*
192. Michael Lewis, *Becoming Apart: National Power and Local Politics in Toyama, 1868–1945*
193. William C. Kirby, Man-houng Lin, James Chin Shih, and David A. Pietz, eds., *State and Economy in Republican China: A Handbook for Scholars*
194. Timothy S. George, *Minamata: Pollution and the Struggle for Democracy in Postwar Japan*
195. Billy K. L. So, *Prosperity, Region, and Institutions in Maritime China: The South Fukien Pattern, 946–1368*
196. Yoshihisa Tak Matsusaka, *The Making of Japanese Manchuria, 1904–1932*
197. Maram Epstein, *Competing Discourses: Orthodoxy, Authenticity, and Engendered Meanings in Late Imperial Chinese Fiction*
199. Haruo Iguchi, *Unfinished Business: Ayukawa Yoshisuke and U.S.-Japan Relations, 1937–1952*
200. Scott Pearce, Audrey Spiro, and Patricia Ebrey, *Culture and Power in the Reconstitution of the Chinese Realm, 200–600*
201. Terry Kawashima, *Writing Margins: The Textual Construction of Gender in Heian and Kamakura Japan*
202. Martin W. Huang, *Desire and Fictional Narrative in Late Imperial China*
203. Robert S. Ross and Jiang Changbin, eds., *Re-examining the Cold War: U.S.-China Diplomacy, 1954–1973*
204. Guanhua Wang, *In Search of Justice: The 1905–1906 Chinese Anti-American Boycott*
205. David Schaberg, *A Patterned Past: Form and Thought in Early Chinese Historiography*
206. Christine Yano, *Tears of Longing: Nostalgia and the Nation in Japanese Popular Song*
207. Milena Doleželová-Velingerová and Oldřich Král, with Graham Sanders, eds., *The Appropriation of Cultural Capital: China's May Fourth Project*
208. Robert N. Huey, *The Making of 'Shinkokinshū'*
209. Lee Butler, *Emperor and Aristocracy in Japan, 1467–1680: Resilience and Renewal*
210. Suzanne Ogden, *Inklings of Democracy in China*
211. Kenneth J. Ruoff, *The People's Emperor: Democracy and the Japanese Monarchy, 1945–1995*
212. Haun Saussy, *Great Walls of Discourse and Other Adventures in Cultural China*
213. Aviad E. Raz, *Emotions at Work: Normative Control, Organizations, and Culture in Japan and America*
214. Rebecca E. Karl and Peter Zarrow, eds., *Rethinking the 1898 Reform Period: Political and Cultural Change in Late Qing China*
215. Kevin O'Rourke, *The Book of Korean Shijo*
216. Ezra F. Vogel, ed., *The Golden Age of the U.S.-China-Japan Triangle, 1972–1989*
217. Thomas A. Wilson, ed., *On Sacred Grounds: Culture, Society, Politics, and the Formation of the Cult of Confucius*
218. Donald S. Sutton, *Steps of Perfection: Exorcistic Performers and Chinese Religion in Twentieth-Century Taiwan*

Harvard East Asian Monographs

Harvard East Asian Monographs

Harvard East Asian Monographs

Harvard East Asian Monographs

Harvard East Asian Monographs